THE MORAL AND MARKET ECONOMIES OF BREAD

Food in Modern History: Traditions and Innovations

Series Editors:
Peter Scholliers
Amy Bentley

This new monograph series pays serious attention to food as a focal point in historical events from the late eighteenth century to present day. Employing the lens of technology broadly construed, the series highlights the nutritional, social, political, cultural and economic transformations of food around the globe. It features new scholarship that considers ever-intensifying and accelerating tensions between tradition and innovation that characterize the modern era. The editors are particularly committed to publishing manuscripts featuring geographical areas currently underrepresented in English-language academic publications, including the Global South, particularly Africa and Asia, as well as monographs featuring indigenous and underrepresented groups, and non-western societies.

Published:
Food and Aviation in the Twentieth Century: The Pan American Ideal, Bryce Evans (2021)
Feeding the People in Wartime Britain, Bryce Evans (2022)
Rebellious Cooks and Recipe Writing in Communist Bulgaria, Albena Shkodrova (2022)
Globalization in a Glass: The Rise of Pilsner Beer through Technology, Taste and Empire, Malcolm Purinton (2023)
Apples and Orchards since the Eighteenth Century: Material Innovation and Cultural Tradition, Joanna Crosby (2023)
A History of Bread: Consumers, Bakers and Public Authorities since the 18th Century, Peter Scholliers (2024)

THE MORAL AND MARKET ECONOMIES OF BREAD

Regulation and Reform in Vienna, 1775–1885

Jonas M. Albrecht

BLOOMSBURY ACADEMIC
LONDON • NEW YORK • OXFORD • NEW DELHI • SYDNEY

BLOOMSBURY ACADEMIC

Bloomsbury Publishing Plc, 50 Bedford Square, London, WC1B 3DP, UK
Bloomsbury Publishing Inc, 1359 Broadway, New York, NY 10018, USA
Bloomsbury Publishing Ireland, 29 Earlsfort Terrace, Dublin 2, D02 AY28, Ireland

BLOOMSBURY, BLOOMSBURY ACADEMIC and the Diana logo are
trademarks of Bloomsbury Publishing Plc

First published in Great Britain 2024
This paperback edition published in 2026

Copyright © Jonas M. Albrecht, 2024

Jonas M. Albrecht has asserted his right under the Copyright,
Designs and Patents Act, 1988, to be identified as Author of this work.

For legal purposes the Acknowledgements on pp. xv–xvi constitute an
extension of this copyright page.

Cover image: Alt Jacob - Blick Auf Wien Von Der Spinnerin Am Kreuz -
Austrian School - 19th Century © Artepics / Alamy Stock Photo

All rights reserved. No part of this publication may be: i) reproduced or transmitted in any form, electronic or mechanical, including photocopying, recording or by means of any information storage or retrieval system without prior permission in writing from the publishers; or ii) used or reproduced in any way for the training, development or operation of artificial intelligence (AI) technologies, including generative AI technologies. The rights holders expressly reserve this publication from the text and data mining exception as per Article 4(3) of the Digital Single Market Directive (EU) 2019/790.

Bloomsbury Publishing Plc does not have any control over, or responsibility for, any third-party websites referred to or in this book. All internet addresses given in this book were correct at the time of going to press. The author and publisher regret any inconvenience caused if addresses have changed or sites have ceased to exist, but can accept no responsibility for any such changes.

A catalogue record for this book is available from the British Library.

A catalog record for this book is available from the Library of Congress.

ISBN: HB: 978-1-3503-9847-4
PB: 978-1-3503-9850-4
ePDF: 978-1-3503-9848-1
eBook: 978-1-3503-9849-8

Series: Food in Modern History: Traditions and Innovations

Typeset by Integra Software Services Pvt. Ltd.

For product safety related questions contact productsafety@bloomsbury.com.

To find out more about our authors and books visit www.bloomsbury.com
and sign up for our newsletters.

For Sanni

CONTENTS

List of Images	ix
List of Figures	x
List of Maps	xi
List of Tables	xii
List of Currencies and Measures	xiii
List of Abbreviations	xiv
Acknowledgements	xv
INTRODUCTION	1

Part I
FROM MORAL TO MARKET ECONOMIES

Chapter 1
A GREAT TRANSFORMATION? KARL POLANYI, E.P. THOMPSON AND MICHEL FOUCAULT — 17

Karl Polanyi: The disembedded market and fictitious commodities	17
E.P. Thompson: The moral economy	24
Michel Foucault: Disciplinary and security mechanisms and the birth of biopolitics	25
A great transformation? Moral and market economies, disciplinary and security mechanisms and biopolitics of bread	35

Part II
BETWEEN MORAL AND MARKET ECONOMIES OF BREAD. ECONOMIC AND INSTITUTIONAL CHANGE, 1770s–1860

Chapter 2
INSTITUTIONS OF EMBEDDEDNESS — 43

Regulating people and places	43
Regulating products: The assize	50
Knowing and regulating nature and the market	57
The just price of bread	61

Chapter 3
THE MUNICIPAL LANDSCAPE OF BREAD, 1790s–1859 — 65

Geographies	68
Business structures	73

Wheatification	87
Competing circuits of bread provision	94

Chapter 4
THE CONQUEST OF CORNUCOPIA — 101
  The fruits of cornucopia: Hard reds and the coming of 'good bread' — 112

Chapter 5
REFORMING THE ASSIZE? — 123
  'Free competition is the magic phrase of our time' — 131
  Total liberalization — 139
  Conclusion — 143

Part III
THE BREAD QUESTION, 1861–85

Chapter 6
A FREE MARKET LANDSCAPE OF BREAD, 1860–80s — 151
  Mobilization and continued diversification — 151
  The hawker's question — 156

Chapter 7
THE BREAD QUESTION — 169
  The price of bread — 169
  The bread question — 181
  Standardizing bread – Again — 190
  Marking bread — 200
  Rediscovering the right price of bread — 203
  The end of the bread question? — 211
  Epilogue: The bread question solved — 220
  Conclusion — 222

Conclusion
BIOPOLITICS OF BREAD — 229

Bibliography — 235
Index — 256

IMAGES

1 Wochenmayr's Steam Oven 91
2 *Baunzeln* and *Kreuzersemmeln*, early twentieth century 186
3 Tariff Model for Bread Retail according to Standardized Loaf Weights Provided by Vienna's Magistrate, 27 March 1872 192

FIGURES

1	Hired and Discharged Apprentices by Vienna's Guild Bakers, 1824–58, per annum	82
2	Dispersion of Bakers across Size Categories according to Flour Stocks, 1793 and 1857, in Muth	87
3	Cereal and Bread prices in Vienna, 1750–1890, in gAg per One Kilogram	172
4	Ratio of Silver Prices for One Litre of Grain and One Kilogram Bread in Vienna, 1750–1890	174
5	Ratio of Silver Prices of Various Bakery Products, per Pound 1750–1882	177
6	Real Prices for Various Major Bakery Products, in grams of Silver per Pound, 1750–1885	178
7	Price Index for Various Major Bakery Products and Cereals, 1750–1890, 1750=100	179

MAPS

1	Bakeries in Vienna, 1775–1847	69
2	Bakers' Compulsory Flour Stocks 1793, in Muth	77
3	Composition of Bakers' Flour Stocks, 1793	78
4	Detailed Composition of Flour Stocks, 1793	79
5	Bakers' Compulsory Flour Stocks 1857, in Muth	85
6	Composition of Flour Stocks, 1857	92
7	Detailed Composition of Flour Stocks, 1857	93
8	Country Bakers per Parish, 1815–58	96
9	Grain Trade by Ship on Major Rivers of Austria-Hungary, 1865, in Centners	112
10	Urban Bakers 1847 and 1882 within the *Linienwall* and in Favoriten district	154
11	Country Bakers per Parish, 1815–82	154
12	City Centre Bakers and Registered Retailers, 1857	162

TABLES

1	Compulsory Monthly Flour Stocks, 1793–1857	80
2	Composition of Cereal Supplies, 1780–1870	99
3	Lower Austrian Average Wheat Harvests and Vienna's Average Wheat Supplies 1789–1857, in Tonnes	106
4	Vienna Exchange Wheat Flour Prices, January 1863, per Wiener Centner	119
5	Share of Women Named as Shopkeepers, 1815–82	153

CURRENCIES AND MEASURES

Currencies:

fl. C.M. – *Gulden Conventions-Münze*. Silver currency in circulation between 1753 and 1858. 1 Gulden contained 60 Kreuzer (kr.).

fl. W.W. – *Gulden Wiener Währung*. Silver currency in circulation between 1753 and 1858. 1 Gulden W.W. also contained 60 Kreuzer. From 1820, 2.5 Gulden W.W. corresponded to 1 fl. C.M.

fl. Ö.W. – *Gulden Österreichische Währung*. Silver currency circulating from 1858 to 1892. 1 Gulden contained 100 Kreuzer.

Note: It is not clear in all primary sources used in this book to which currency the authors refer. If no explicit information is given in narrative sources providing simple descriptive information, the respective figures will be indicated by 'fl.' only.

Measures:

1 Muth (wholesale grain and flour volume measure) = 30 Metzen = 1,845 litres
1 Muth of fine wheat flour = 1,147 pounds
1 Muth of wheat flour = 1,116 pounds
1 Muth of coarse wheat flour = 1,054 pounds
1 Muth of rye flour = 992 pounds
1 Metzen (grain volume measure) = 61.5 litres
1 Centner = 56 kilograms
1 Pfund/Pound = 0.56 kilograms

ABBREVIATIONS

C.M. – Conventions-Münze
fl. – Gulden
gAg – Grams of Silver
k.k. – kaiserlich-königlich
kr. – Kreuzer
Ö.W. – Österreichische Währung

ACKNOWLEDGEMENTS

This book initially began as a research seminar on the food provisioning of Vienna by Peter Eigner and Friedrich Hauer at the University of Vienna. Since these first and early inquiries into the topic and the completion of the present book a decade has passed during which I had the privilege to meet a great variety of people who have influenced my research and writing decisively. As a first strand, I am heavily indebted to the faculty of the Department of Economic and Social History at Vienna University. I have especially benefitted from Erich Landsteiner's and Peer Vries's highly stimulating work on theories and histories of global capitalism as well as from Peter Eigner's comprehensive lessons on the history of Vienna.

I am also indebted to the school of environmental history around Verena Winiwarter and Martin Schmid, who raised my attention to the historical consideration of the environment, nature and the relationship between humans and their environments.

Third, the faculties of both the Department of Social and Economic History and the Institute of Modern and Contemporary History at Johannes Kepler University Linz have provided a highly fruitful academic environment to this book's research process. Michael John, Klemens Kaps, Marcus Gräser, Regina Thumser-Whös and Birgit Kirchmayr have either read or commented on parts of this book and decisively improved both its research outline and the text. I am especially indebted to Michael Pammer for his introductions into the methodologies and mechanics of historical geographic information system (GIS).

I am also grateful for the many comments and improvements the participants of various conferences such as the World Economic History Congress 2018 in Boston, the Urban History Conference 2018 in Rome or the Rural History Conference 2019 in Paris have contributed to this book, as well as for the critique of various anonymous reviewers who have highly improved different parts of the following text. Other special thanks goes to late Astrid Faltinger, Hermine Synka, Iris Bäuchler and Werner Höbarth for their administrative work necessary to write this book, and to the staff of the Municipal and Provincial Archives of Vienna for their generous support in identifying and collecting the sources used. I would also like to express my gratitude to Maddie Smith and Megan Harris of Bloomsbury Publishing for their outstanding supervision and guidance throughout the publication process and their decisive impact to making this a real book.

Finally, I am deeply grateful for Ernst Langthaler's guidance during the formation of this book, which has been incredibly enriching in intellectual, theoretical and methodological terms. For his constant engagement to promote me as a historian, which has also resulted in the awarding of my dissertation with the Johannes Kepler University Young Researchers' Award, the Pro Civitate Austriae

Stiftungspreis and the Michael Mitterauer Preis für Gesellschafts-, Kultur- und Wirtschaftsgeschichte (Förderungspreis), I am also deeply grateful.

Besides the academic impacts and inputs I have been privileged to enjoy, friendships have been an invaluable asset not only to secure academic productivity, but to provide community, mutual support and fun; Daniel Hanglberger, Sofie Pfannerer-Mittas, Leonie Kapfer, Klemens Kaps, Nora Lehner and Michael Adelsberger have all contributed to this book one way or the other. For that, too, I am thankful.

Parallel to the academic world, I am grateful for my friends and family for their enduring support outside academia. This book would not exist without the many-faceted support of especially my parents Ingrid and Einar and my godfather Christoph.

Finally, I am most grateful to my partner Sanni for her love and support as well as for sharing our home as an office during the lockdowns of the Covid-19 pandemic. Having written most of the following text under such outstanding circumstances, I could not have done this without her. This book is for her.

INTRODUCTION

'The energy market is broken'; 'wild-west vibes on the energy markets'[1] – thus or similar read the titles of many newspaper contributions by mid-2022, when the economic consequences of Russia's war of aggression against Ukraine came to affect the European energy market and both energy suppliers and consumers faced spectacular price hikes in a commodity of first necessity. In the year and a half that passed since the Russian invasion, politicians across Europe, including President of the European Commission Ursula von der Leyen, debated over and argued for large-scale interventions into the union's energy market as 'those are no real prices anymore'.[2]

Another major factor of economic uncertainty amidst the aftermath of the global Covid-19 pandemic and the accelerating challenges of climate change, the war-induced energy crisis severely questioned the liberalized European energy market as this setting 'is no longer fit for purpose', as von der Leyen and many other politicians of various political colours and in different positions came to believe. 'The skyrocketing electricity prices are now exposing, for different reasons, the limitations of our current electricity market design. … That is why we, the

---

1. Paul Lewis, 'The Energy Market Is Broken – but Only One Thing Needs to Change to Fix It: Our Regulator Has Made a Catalogue of Errors and It Has Cost Consumers Billions', *The Telegraph*, accessed 10 July 2023, https://www.telegraph.co.uk/money/consumer-affairs/energy-market-broken-one-thing-needs-change-fix/; Will Hutton, 'Lost in Space and a Broken Energy Market: Blame It on the Obsession with a Small State', *The Guardian*, 31 July 2022, accessed 10 July 2023, https://www.theguardian.com/commentisfree/2022/jul/31/lost-in-space-and-broken-energy-market-blame-it-on-tories-small-state-stupidity; Bernhard Junginger and Christian Grimm, 'Wildweststimmung auf dem Energiemarkt sorgt für Verzweiflung bei Verbrauchern', *Augsburger Allgemeine*, 24 August 2022, accessed 10 July 2023, https://www.augsburger-allgemeine.de/politik/verbraucherschutz-wildweststimmung-auf-dem-energiemarkt-sorgt-fuer-verzweiflung-bei-verbrauchern-id63718086.html.

2. Thomas Kaiser, 'Die EU plant einen Strompreisdeckel, der nicht so heißen darf', *Welt*, 3 September 2022, accessed 10 July 2023, https://www.welt.de/wirtschaft/article240837405/Energiepreise-EU-Kommission.html.

Commission, are now working on an emergency intervention and a structural reform of the electricity market. We need a new market model for electricity that really functions and brings us back into balance', von der Leyen stated by August 2022.[3]

Facing the dramatic energy price increases induced by the Russian war of aggression against Ukraine, EU communities and leaders turned to introduce certain forms of market intervention aimed to freeze or cap energy and other living costs. After decades of rather market-liberal policies, examples for energy price caps in most European countries abounded; nationalizations of energy providers returned to the political agenda even in Germany, some governments introduced certain caps or even froze food prices, like in France, and many European countries also created some sorts of household subsidies to meet higher consumer prices.

While these developments also need to be analysed in the context of the beginning end of 'cheap nature' (Jason W. Moore) for 'Western' populations and the political and economic failures to accelerate shifts away from the excessive reliance on relatively cheap fossil fuels during the last century and a half, these were debates over how to organize a market for scarce resources in a way it ensures a certain baseline access to items of daily need for all (albeit very high daily 'needs' in global and historic comparison, and certainly not 'all' in a global perspective). At the same time, the calls to finance such intervention by taxing 'Übergewinne' in German-speaking debates and preventing 'greedflation' of energy companies in English-speaking contexts highlight how much these discussions are also loaded with notions of morality regarding 'fair' prices and 'unethical' profits regarding commodities everyone depends upon.

Among the prime popular political issues in 2022 and 2023, such debates over market structures, prices and the provision of basic life necessities can be viewed in the context of a more general and global critique of 'the market' in general as institution and means to ensure common wellbeing and of policies often described by the terms 'privatization', 'deregulation' and 'liberalization', usually perceived as core aims of neoliberal politics. Especially since the financial crisis of 2008 such criticisms of the 'free market' have increased and accelerated notably in popular and learned media, and the Covid-19 pandemic since 2020 with its many-faceted restrictions on global production, trade and mobility has poured even more fuel on the fire. While popular movements like Occupy Wall Street expressed such notions in the streets in the years following 2008, newspapers, magazines and monographies addressed such criticism in letters. Among many other examples,

---

3. Jorge Liboreiro, 'Energy Crisis: Ursula Von Der Leyen Calls for "Emergency Intervention" in Electricity Market', *Euronews*, accessed 10 July 2023, https://www.euronews.com/my-europe/2022/08/29/energy-crisis-ursula-von-der-leyen-calls-for-emergency-intervention-in-electricity-market.

already in December 1997 critical *Le Monde Diplomatique* published an article by Ignacio Ramonet, which called for a 'mitigation of the markets', criticized financial deregulation and eventually contributed to the founding of Attac.[4] At the same time, facing the Asian financial crisis, Joseph Stiglitz started to voice sincere doubts about neoliberal globalization.[5] By April 2021, the German version of Michael J. Sandel's 2012 book *What money can't buy. The Moral Limits of Markets*, in which Sandel centrally addressed the marketization of goods not suited to be subjected to the market, was ranked number 202 on Amazon's bestsellers in Ethics and number 97 in Introductions to Philosophy Books. Already a rich field before 2020, the global Covid-19 pandemic and the Russian war of aggression against Ukraine accelerated such popular scepticism over 'free markets' decisively. Newspaper contributions like Jacobin's 'The Pandemic Has Exposed the Free Market's Fundamental Flaws' in January 2020, the German TAZ's 'Corona-Dämmerung für Neoliberalismus' in March 2020 or *Die Zeit*'s 'Der Markt regelt das nicht' published in April 2020 abounded throughout the year almost everywhere.[6] By October 2020, Pope Francis popularly iterated the '"magic theories" of market capitalism have failed',[7] and criticized 'those who would have had us believe that the freedom of the market was sufficient to keep everything secure' in his encyclical letter Fratelli Tutti.[8] In early 2021, Austrian and German politics were prominently shaken by 'mask scandals' as politicians of the reigning CDU/CSU in Germany and businesspersons close to the reigning ÖVP in Austria were found out to have profited from deals with and the production of FFP2 masks – commodities necessary to tackle the pandemic and publicly considered off-limits for individual

---

4. Ignacio Ramonet, 'Die Märkte entschärfen', *Le Monde diplomatique*, 1997, 12, reprinted in 5/2020, Jubiläumsausgabe.

5. Quinn Slobodian, *Globalisten: Das Ende der Imperien und die Geburt des Neoliberalismus* (Bonn: bpb: Bundeszentrale für politische Bildung, 2020), 9.

6. Jule Govrin, 'Der Markt regelt das nicht', *Zeit Online*, 9 April 2020, accessed 4 May 2021, https://www.zeit.de/kultur/2020-04/pandemie-coronavirus-kapitalismus-wirtschaft-wachstum-deutschland; Hadas Thier, 'The Pandemic Has Exposed the Free Market's Fundamental Flaws. We Need a Democratically Planned Economy', *Jacobin*, 1 November 2020, accessed 4 May 2021, https://www.jacobinmag.com/2020/11/planned-economy-coronavirus-hospitals-ppe-masks; Ulrike Herrmann, 'Corona-Dämmerung für Neoliberalismus', *taz*, 21 March 2020, accessed 4 May 2021, https://taz.de/Corona-Daemmerung-fuer-Neoliberalismus/!5669238/.

7. *Deutsche Welle*, 'Pope Says Capitalism Failed Humanity during Coronavirus Pandemic', 4 October 2020, accessed 4 May 2021, https://p.dw.com/p/3jPoa.

8. Pope Francis, 'Encyclical Letter Fratelli Tutti of the Holy Father Francis on Fraternity and Social Friendship', accessed 4 May 2021, http://www.vatican.va/content/francesco/en/encyclicals/documents/papa-francesco_20201003_enciclica-fratelli-tutti.html.

gain.⁹ By that time, even Klaus Schwab, one of the founders of the World Economic Forum in Davos and by some perceived as a guardian of a neoliberal world order, argued that 'the world must move on from neoliberalism after the pandemic' because 'the covid-19 crisis has shown us that our old systems are not fit anymore for the 21st century'.¹⁰ In April 2021, US President Joe Biden's stimulus packages to meet both the pandemic and climate change as well as his plans to introduce a global minimum corporate tax were heralded as the 'waning of the "neoliberal" era' by some observers as 'Biden is getting ready to bury neoliberalism'.¹¹ By 2023, the market interventions to tackle the 'energy crisis' in Europe might represent another step towards market re-regulation, at least in some markets.

The scope, range and clout of both such policies and claims about the perceived end of 'neoliberal' and 'free market' politics remain subject to the future. However, whereas the popular discourse about neoliberalism is relatively straightforward at least among rather leftist contributors, among academic discourses the characteristics, nature and indeed the existence of neoliberalism are much less clear and much more debated. Scholars involved into those arguments warn of generalizations as well as unclear definitions and call for detailed analysis and fine-grained definitions. In that perspective, it remains quite debated what neoliberalism actually is and what kind of ideas and policies it involves. The term 'neoliberal' has been decisively criticized to 'suffer from either under- or overspecification'. Academic research has pointed to the various and differing branches of a broad 'neoliberal thought collective', whose 'character of transdisciplinary and interdisciplinary efforts' should prevent students from reducing 'neoliberalism

---

9. *Der Spiegel*, 'Maskenaffäre. Alle Unionsabgeordneten unterzeichnen Ehrenerklärung', 12 March 2021, accessed 4 May 2021, https://www.spiegel.de/politik/deutschland/cdu-csu-nach-masken-skandal-alle-unionsabgeordneten-unterzeichnen-ehrenerklaerung-a-f6d1943b-76a6-430c-a690-8f50cfdddf12; Verena Kainrath, Jan M. Marchart, and Aloysius Widman, 'Maskenkrise. Hygiene Austria: Wie aus einem Zufallsfund ein Maskenskandal wurde', *Der Standard*, 13 March 2021, accessed 4 May 2021, https://www.derstandard.at/story/2000125011151/hygiene-austria-wie-aus-einem-zufallsfund-ein-maskenskandal-wurde.

10. World Economic Forum, 'The World Must Move on from Neoliberalism after the Pandemic', accessed 4 May 2021, https://www.weforum.org/videos/20462-the-world-must-move-on-from-neoliberalism-after-the-pandemic-davos-agenda; Ishaan Tharoor, 'World Leaders Pledge a "Great Reset" after the Pandemic', *The Washington Post*, 29 January 2021, accessed 4 May 2021, https://www.washingtonpost.com/world/2021/01/29/davos-merkel-macron-coronavirus/; Marcus Gatzke, Marlies Uken, and Klaus Schwab, '"Der Neoliberalismus hat Ausgedient"', *Zeit Online*, 21 September 2020, accessed 4 May 2021, https://www.zeit.de/wirtschaft/2020-09/corona-kapitalismus-rezession-wef-neoliberalismus-klaus-schwab.

11. Ishaan Tharoor, 'Biden and the Waning of the "Neoliberal" Era', *The Washington Post*, 5 April 2021, accessed 4 May 2021, https://www.washingtonpost.com/world/2021/04/05/biden-infrastructure-plan-neoliberalism/.

to an economic idea'.¹² At the same time, the diversity of policies dubbed 'neoliberal' across the globe, implemented under authoritarian rule in Chile as well as under liberal-democratic government in New Zeeland, Scandinavia or Germany, has raised questions about the 'diversity of neoliberal arrangements' and the institutions and actors involved in those particular places. Finally, scholars have cautioned to pay attention to the 'actually existing neoliberalism', that is, the differences between the theoretic and intellectual foundations of neoliberalism and its eventual practical realization.¹³ Without proper definitions, demarcations and analysis, those scholars caution, 'neoliberalism' is bound to be adopted as 'a blanket swearword for everything critics despise, or a brainless synonym for modern capitalism',¹⁴ in other words as an 'ideological political battle cry' that is 'completely emptied from meaning'.¹⁵ Therefore, the academic research into 'neoliberalism' as both an ideology, a thought collective and as practical politics has induced intensive research throughout the last decades. Yet, while underlining its theoretical as well as political diversity and adaptability across time and space, scholars agree on three basic features of the history of neoliberalism as both a field of ideas and a political programme.

First, as an enacted political programme – in David Harvey's words – the neoliberal turn was inaugurated during the 1970s and 1980s in authoritarian Chile under Augusto Pinochet, in post-Cultural Revolution China under Deng Xiaoping, in Great Britain under Margaret Thatcher and in the United States of America under Ronald Reagan. While they have been interpreted as a direct political answer to the global challenges the Keynesian 'embedded liberal' economies faced by the 1960s and 1970s, when 'stagflation' called the post-war order of state-directed economies into question,¹⁶ by the 1990s the neoliberal turn was largely continued and adapted by 'third way' or 'new labour' social-democratic governments of Tony Blair in the UK, Gerhard Schröder in Germany, Bill Clinton in the United States and in various non-European countries under the *Washington Consensus*. Characteristically, these 'actual existing' neoliberal policies aimed, albeit local differences abounded, 'to curb the power of labour, deregulate industry, agriculture and resource extraction, and liberate the powers of finance'.¹⁷

Second, as an intellectual building among whose constructors the Austrian School around Ludwig von Mises and Friedrich August von Hayek, the German Ordoliberal School involving, for example, Alexander Rüstow and Wilhelm Röpke, and the Chicago School comprising again Hayek as well as Milton Friedman, Aaron

---

12. Philip Mirowski and Dieter Plehwe, 'Preface', in Mirowski; Plehwe, *The Road from Mont Pèlerin*, xii, xv.
13. Thomas Biebricher, *Neoliberalismus zur Einführung* (Hamburg: Junius, 2018), 17, 19.
14. Mirowski and Plehwe, 'Preface', xvii.
15. Biebricher, *Neoliberalismus*, 10, 14.
16. David Harvey, *A Brief History of Neoliberalism* (Oxford: Oxford University Press, 2010), 9–13; Biebricher, *Neoliberalismus*, 98, 111.
17. Harvey, *Neoliberalism*, 1; Biebricher, *Neoliberalismus*, 87–153.

Director and Richard Posner assume key roles, scholars largely agree about neoliberalism's character as a broader and deeper project to reconceptualize and reform government that cannot be reduced to 'free markets'.[18] In that perspective,

> [N]eoliberalism is in the first instance a theory of political economic practices that proposes that human well-being can best be advanced by liberating individual entrepreneurial freedoms and skills within an institutional framework characterized by strong private property rights, free markets, and free trade. The role of the state is to create and preserve an institutional framework appropriate to such practices. ... State interventions in markets once created must be kept to a bare minimum because, according to the theory, the state cannot possibly possess enough information to second-guess market signals.... In so far as neoliberalism values market exchange as 'an ethic in itself, capable of acting as a guide to all human action, and substituting for all previously held ethical beliefs', it emphasizes the significance of contractual relations in the marketplace. It holds that the social good will be maximized by maximizing the reach and frequency of market transactions, and it seeks to bring all human action into the domain of the market. This requires technologies of information creation and capacities to accumulate, store, transfer, analyse, and use massive databases to guide decisions in the global marketplace.[19]

In other words, neoliberalism – intellectually developed under the impression of both World Wars and the Shoa – does not seek to free markets of all intervention, as Quin Slobodian recently demonstrated. Rather, it aims to encase markets with global institutions that would protect the market – and capitalism – from lopsided 'irrational human behaviour' and indeed from democracy deemed capable of destroying human freedom, as the election of the Nazi regime had seemingly proven.[20] To this endeavour a reconceptualization of the market as the guardian of freedom, of a good society and of the common good is probably the most important intellectual feat especially of Hayekian neoliberal thought. In that perspective, the market represented an 'information processor more powerful than any human brain' and 'the market always surpasses the state's ability to process information' thus ensuring freedom, understood as 'the positioning of autonomous self-governed individuals ... striving to improve their lot in life by engaging in market exchange'.[21] Therefore, in a nutshell, neoliberal policy centres

---

18. Slobodian, *Globalisten*, 8.
19. Harvey, *Neoliberalism*, 2–3.
20. Slobodian, *Globalisten*, 8–16.
21. Philip Mirowski, 'Postface: Defining Neoliberalism', in Mirowski; Plehwe, *The Road from Mont Pèlerin*, 435, 437. As Slobodian also points out rightly, the key difference between Hayek and Polanyi is therefore only the philosophical interpretation between a dystopian and a utopian 'free market'. Whereas Polanyi considers it detrimental, Hayek sees in it the only possible producer of general freedom. See Slobodian, *Globalisten*, 13.

around enabling the market to unfold its mechanisms of freedom by liberating and framing – protecting – it at the same time as well as to expand this market mechanism onto parts of human life previously not geared by market forces to ensure freedom in as many aspects of life as possible.

Third, students of neoliberalism and economic history agree that both the intellectual construct and the political implementation of neoliberalism represent 'a revolutionary turning-point in the world's social and economic history'.[22] Historians of the twentieth century have labelled the 'rediscovery of the market' during the 1970s and 1980s a key watershed in political and economic history because the market became 'the dominant social metaphor of the age'. As 'a series of conjunctions between ideas, economic circumstances and patrons had joined to push a newly abstracted and idealized concept of "the market" into the center of social and economic analysis', 'a new idea of the market, cut free from the institutional and sociological relationships constitutive of earlier economic analysis ...] was being called on'.[23] Thomas Piketty has recently drawn a direct line between 'ideologies' and 'inequality regimes' in the longue durée, explicitly noting the 1980s and 1990s a key rupture,[24] a notion shared by David Harvey.[25] Similarly, Nancy Fraser and Rahel Jaeggi locate a 'clandestine' capitalist regime change from 'state-administered capitalism' towards a neoliberal, financialized, global capitalist regime during the 1970s.[26] This notion is also adopted by the food regime analysis developed by Harriet Friedman and Philip McMichael;[27] Bas van Bavel equally considers the 'revival of neo-liberal economic thinking' and its political implementation a cornerstone; and both Jürgen Kocka and Werner Plumpe also underwrite to such a periodization.[28]

Consequently, political scientists, sociologists and especially historians of the twentieth century have drawn attention not only to neoliberalism per se, but also to the impacts of the neoliberal turn and marketization since. Though massive

22. Harvey, *Neoliberalism*, 1.

23. Daniel T. Rodgers, *Age of Fracture* (Cambridge, MA: Harvard University Press, 2012), 41, 44, 76.

24. Thomas Piketty, *Kapital und Ideologie* (München: C.H. Beck, 2020), 14, 21, 41, 45, 52.

25. Harvey, *Neoliberalism*, 14–19.

26. Nancy Fraser and Rahel Jaeggi, *Kapitalismus: Ein Gespräch über Kritische Theorie* (Berlin: Suhrkamp, 2020), 114–15.

27. Ernst Langthaler and Fridolin Krausmann, 'Nahrungsregime und Umwelt in der Globalisierung (1870–2010)', in *Rohstoffe und Entwicklung: Aktuelle Auseinandersetzungen im historischen Kontext*, ed. Karin Fischer, Johannes Jäger and Lukas Schmidt (Wien: New Academic Press, 2016).

28. Bas van Bavel, *The Invisible Hand? How Market Economies Have Emerged and Declined since AD 500* (Oxford, UK: Oxford University Press, 2016), 237–50; Jürgen Kocka, *Geschichte des Kapitalismus*, 3., überarbeitete Auflage (München: Verlag C.H. Beck, 2017), 92–99; Werner Plumpe, *Das kalte Herz: Kapitalismus: die Geschichte einer andauernden Revolution* (Berlin: Rowohlt Berlin, 2019), 506–44.

differences in the interpretation of marketization remain within the academic community, many scholars have grown rather sceptic and have developed rather pessimistic notions towards 'the market', especially since 2008. Thomas Piketty's and David Harvey's work represent prominent sceptic evaluations of the economic consequences of neoliberalism on equality. Such a notion seems to be shared by other scholars perceiving that 'the market's reputation is damaged', as German historians Ralf Ahrens, Marcus Boick and Marcel vom Lehm found in a 2015 issue of *Studies in Contemporary History* on *Vermarktlichung* – marketization. Accelerated by the global financial crisis of 2008, they refer to a zeitgeist determined by a 'growing unease about the "economization" of labour relations, social security and education' as the 'dark side of a highly flexible supply of information and consumer goods'.[29] Defining marketization as a 'process of taking goods and services that had previously been provided under bureaucratic, political or professional means of resource allocation and transferring them to market arrangements', they seek to investigate the *Problemgeschichte* of a 'shift of balance from state to market, from society to the individual' that became the dominant form of societal organization by the 1990s. Centrally, they ask for the actors, practices and debates over marketization, for conflicts and struggles over and against its implementation, for diverging local, regional and national settings, and for the 'actual impacts processes of marketization have had on constellations of political power and inequality'.[30] Already a decade earlier, historians Hartmut Berghoff and Jakob Vogel edited a collective volume with various contributions on 'economic history as cultural history'.[31] Criticizing the failure of cultural historians to tackle the most important issues of the twenty-first century, such as the 'continuing economization of all aspects of life' and a general divergence of economic and cultural history since the 1970s, they call for a stronger dialog between both history subfields. Since 'every economic system and all economic actions are based on constructions of meaning and produce such meaning at the same time, hence they create culture', market cultures should be analysed more closely.[32] In one way or the other, all of the volume's contributions underline the interrelationship between the market

29. Ralf Ahrens, Marcus Böick, and Marcel vom Lehn, 'Vermarktlichung. Zeithistorische Perspektiven auf ein umkämpftes Feld', *Zeithistorische Forschungen/Studies in Contemporary History*, no. 3 (2015), 393.

30. Ibid., 395, 393, 401.

31. Hartmut Berghoff and Jakob Vogel, eds., *Wirtschaftsgeschichte als Kulturgeschichte: Dimensionen eines Perspektivenwechsels* (Frankfurt/Main: Campus Verlag GmbH, 2004). See also Eva Brugger et al., *Marktgeschehen: Fragmente einer Geschichte frühneuzeitlichen Wirtschaftens* (Frankfurt: Campus, 2023).

32. Hartmut Berghoff and Jakob Vogel, 'Wirtschaftsgeschichte als Kulturgeschichte. Ansätze zur Bergung transdisziplinärer Synergiepotentiale', in *Wirtschaftsgeschichte als Kulturgeschichte: Dimensionen eines Perspektivenwechsels*, ed. Hartmut Berghoff and Jakob Vogel (Frankfurt/Main: Campus Verlag GmbH, 2004), 12, 13, 25.

and societies, nations, religions, companies, science and expertise, or images and visions of society.

Drawing on such contemporary notions and experiences of a decisive socio-economic transition during the late twentieth century, historians especially of the eighteenth and nineteenth centuries have taken up the questions about the development and impacts of marketization before the twentieth century. Already by the late 1990s, Paul Nolte had cast an eye on a thematic shift of the US-American historical sciences in the late twentieth century. In the context of ongoing commercialization that included not only commodities but 'all areas of society and culture' and created a 'comprehensive culture, a life style of the market', a 'market paradigm' grew prominent in historical research and led to manifold studies that investigated both the 'culture of the market' and 'the market as culture', about which Nolte presents a historiographic overview.[33] After all, the neoliberal reconception of market and society has its roots in the enlightened liberal ideas and ideologies of the eighteenth and nineteenth centuries, as Helena Rosenblatt has recently highlighted.[34] The beginnings of an 'economic turn',[35] many historians agree that Reinhard Koselleck's *Sattelzeit* witnessed a great transformation when 'alternative and irreconcilable views of human order – one based on mutuality, the other on competition – confronted each other between 1815 and 1850', as eminent E.P. Thompson prominently diagnosed.[36]

Indeed, concepts of a great socio-economic transformation and the end of a social-economic order based on a certain set of morals around the turn on the eighteenth to the nineteenth century have become eminent reading material among social and economic historians. These are, of course, inherently bound to the names Karl Polanyi and E.P. Thompson, probably among the most influential scholars addressing the historic formation of marketization. Both Polanyi and Thompson have provided central narratives of a transformation of the relation between market and society and the commodification and marketization of central aspects of human life. While Polanyi focussed on land, labour and money, Thompson turned his attention towards food as a key good of human subsistence. In part fervently contested, in the last decades both Polanyi's and Thompson's ideas have created fields of historical research on their own that investigate and analyse phases of market revolution and commodification prior to the twentieth century and ask for the impacts of such alterations on the socio-economic fabric.

33. Paul Nolte, 'Der Markt und seine Kultur – ein neues Paradigma der amerikanischen Geschichte?', *Historische Zeitschrift* 264, no. 1 (1997), 332, 336, 347.

34. Helena Rosenblatt, *The Lost History of Liberalism: From Ancient Rome to the Twenty-First Century* (Princeton: Princeton University Press, 2020).

35. Sophus A. Reinert and Steven L. Kaplan, eds., *The Economic Turn: Recasting Political Economy in Enlightenment Europe* (London: Anthem Press, 2019).

36. E.P. Thompson, *The Making of the English Working Class* (Harmondsworth: Penguin Books, 1981), 226–7.

Rather informed by E.P. Thompson than by Karl Polanyi, both food and the city have been at the centre of such investigations into the relation between market and society. While commentators in 2022 and 2023 debated over 'Übergewinne' or 'greedflation' regarding both energy and food prices, eighteenth-century urbanites across Europe defended a moral economy of food as E.P. Thompson and his disciples have highlighted.[37] Building on Thompson's work and perceiving urban centres across both Europe and North America with their extensive market laws, regulated guild economies and quite frequent food riots as *loci classici* of moral-economy settings of the market,[38] historians have paid great attention to the changing market-politics of food supply in agglomerations as diverse as Paris and New York City over the course of the eighteenth and nineteenth centuries in order to describe and analyse the impacts of market transformation.

Whereas early modern cities across all of Europe had implemented strict and wide-ranging regulations to control and survey the production and retail of food and other important items of necessity in quite comparable manners, such restrictions were challenged by the eighteenth century. Consequently, liberalizations were introduced in New York City, Paris and other French urban centres as well as in Dutch and German cities alike during the nineteenth century to free the market from traditional containment. Attempting to understand the logics and judge the consequences of market liberalization and the commodification of food, the international investigations underline how politics affected the residents' access to and supply with food in general and how changes in the manners of food market regulation shaped such conditions. Therefore, departing from – though not negating – quite dominant approaches rather focussing on cultural aspects such as taste, ideology or representation as determinants of food consumption, this body of research has taken up the narration of a market revolution to underline how the political economy of food shaped and altered the daily provision with basic food items of European and American urbanites during the late eighteenth and nineteenth centuries.[39] While food inherently represents a product charged with

---

37. E.P. Thompson, 'The Moral Economy of the English Crowd in the Eighteenth Century', *Past and Present* 50, no. 1 (February 1971); John Bohstedt, *The Politics of Provisions: Food Riots, Moral Economy, and Market Transition in England, c. 1550–1850* (London: Taylor and Francis, 2016).

38. See e.g. Charlie Taverner, 'Moral Marketplaces: Regulating the Food Markets of Late Elizabethan and Early Stuart London', *Urban History*, 2020.

39. See e.g. Dennis de Vriese, 'Steering the Free Market through a Food Crisis? Fiscal Policy and Meat Consumption in Brussels during the 1840s', *History of Retailing and Consumption* 8, no. 1 (2022); Jan de Vries, *The Price of Bread: Regulating the Market in the Dutch Republic* (Berkeley, CA: University of California Press, 2019); Marcel Streng, *Subsistenzpolitik im Übergang: Die kommunale Ordnung des Brot- und Fleischmarktes in Frankreich 1846–1914* (Göttingen: Vandenhoeck & Ruprecht, 2017); Gergely Baics, *Feeding Gotham: The Political Economy and Geography of Food in New York, 1790–1860* (Princeton, Oxford: Princeton University Press, 2016); Steven L. Kaplan, *Bread, Politics and Political Economy in the Reign*

meaning, representation, taste or ideologies, it also remains an item produced and consumed within certain socio-economic frameworks that equally shape its making and consuming. The present book is situated in this intellectual environment.

Drawing on the research on other European and American cities as well as on the theoretical approaches presented by Karl Polanyi and E.P. Thompson, which are supplemented with works by Michel Foucault, this book analyses the transformation from moral to market economies of bread in Vienna between 1775 and 1885. Whereas bread remained the single most important staple of daily food supply throughout the eighteenth and nineteenth centuries, the city of Vienna as the capital of the Holy Roman Empire until 1806 and later of the Austrian Empire provides a fruitful case study for several reasons. Besides the striking absence of Austrian cities from an otherwise rich international school of research, the Habsburg capital represented not only an important political hub in Central Europe; it was also among the largest cities of the continent and the most important economic centre of the Habsburg realm. Moreover, Vienna's drastic population growth – the agglomeration grew from some 270,000 residents by 1800 to over one million by 1880 – represented a fierce challenge to meeting the food demands of quickly rising numbers of inhabitants. Indeed, not only that challenge was met with a decisive deregulation of both the imperial trade law and the urban supply system determined by guilds, market laws and the bread assize. Comparable to other cities, around the middle of the nineteenth century Vienna's urban economy was liberalized thoroughly from traditional limitations and regulations. Finally, the periodization follows the classification of Habsburg economic policies offered by other scholars. Establishing this book's starting point, John Komlos has argued that the imperial government began to rely 'more on free market forces, abandoning its exclusive dependence of mercantilist policies' since the 1770s.[40] Meanwhile, determining the end point, historians of the Austrian Empire quite unanimously agree that free-market policies came increasingly under pressure after the crash of Vienna's stock exchange in 1873, which inaugurated a 'transition from a free to a bounded economy', as Herbert Matis has put it. Usually characterized by the Taaffe government, which came to power in 1879, such a return to more interventionist

---

of Louis XV, Second edition (London, New York: Anthem Press, 2015); Roger Horowitz, Jeffrey M. Pilcher and Sydney Watts, 'Meat for the Multitudes. Market Culture in Paris, New York City, and Mexico City over the Long Nineteenth Century', *The American Historical Review* 109, no. 4 (2004), 1055–83; Judith A. Miller, *Mastering the Market: The State and the Grain Trade in Northern France, 1700–1860* (Cambridge: Cambridge University Press, 1999); Steven L. Kaplan, *Provisioning Paris: Merchants and Millers in the Grain and Flour Trade during the Eighteenth Century* (Ithaca: Cornell University Press, 1984).

40. John Komlos, *Nutrition and Economic Development in the Eighteenth-Century Habsburg Monarchy: An Anthropometric History* (Princeton, NJ: Princeton University Press, 1989), 143.

policies was expressed by the 1883 and 1885 amendments of the liberal trade code and the reintroduction of imperial tariffs on international commodity trade.[41]

Against that background, this book has several main tasks for the systematic analysis of the transition from moral to market economies of bread provisioning in Vienna between 1775 and 1885. My main aim is to investigate and trace such a transformation in the case of the Habsburg capital and to examine the effects the transition had on producing, selling and buying food. In order to analyse how a changing politico-economic regime affected the daily bread supply of Vienna's urban dwellers, the book is laid out as follows.

Part I presents a concept of market revolution based on the theories of Karl Polanyi and E.P. Thompson. In Chapter 1, I argue that both perceptions of the formation of self-regulated markets and the end of a moral economy are inherently related as theories of the reconsideration of certain kinds of food and the reconceptualization of the market and society. While I derive a theory of a transformation from a moral economy of bread to a setting in which food should be left over to a self-regulated market, I use Michel Foucault's concept of biopolitics, disciplinary and security mechanisms of government as well as technologies of the self to provide a more exact theory of the 'free' market and the revolutionary changes between a moral economy and biopolitics of food between the late eighteenth and late nineteenth centuries.

Following, Part II paints a picture of the organization of the moral economy of bread and the institutions embedding Vienna's bread market and analyses the politico-economic circumstances, developments and debates between the 1770s and 1850s that would lead to the wide-scale deregulation of Vienna's bread market in 1860. Chapter 2 describes how the bread market was embedded by regulating the people, products, places and prices connected to the bread trade; it is based on both existing research literature and a new analysis of archival sources concerned with the regulation of bread prices. Chapter 3 adopts a supply side-driven, spatial approach by mapping out and analysing Vienna's landscapes of bread production between the 1790s and 1860. The examination of the geographies of baking centrally draws on the spatial approach of geographic information system (GIS) research. Based on so far unused sources from the bakers' archives and the municipal archives, the infrastructural evolution of bread production and retail is mapped and reconstructed. This way, an important part of the food infrastructure of the Habsburg capital is systematically visualized and investigated for the first time. Based on trade statistics, newspaper reports, maps and both historical and present-day research literature on the grain trade and flour production in the Austrian Empire, Chapter 4 turns to the structural changes of the city's grain supply since the late eighteenth century and the consequences these would have with regard to the calculation of the assize.

---

41. Herbert Matis, 'Leitlinien der Österreichischen Wirtschaftspolitik', in *Die Habsburgermonarchie 1848–1918*, vol. 1, ed. Alois Brusatti, Adam Wandruszka and Helmut Rumpler (Wien: Verl. der Österr. Akad. der Wiss, 1973), 45, 47–51.

Finally, Chapter 5 discusses attempts at reforming the assize during the *Vormärz* period and highlights the debates over liberalization following the March Revolution of 1848 using early nineteenth-century reform attempts and debates from the municipal archives. Other main sources include heretofore disregarded protocols of the bakers' guild, protocols of the sittings of Vienna's city council as well as a number of contemporary newspaper reports. Besides research literature on the city's guild system and market laws, Part II rests on the evaluation of hitherto unused archival sources from both the municipal archives and the archives of Vienna's bakers' guild/association. For the purpose of describing the structural regulation of Vienna's bread market I draw on completely disregarded sources in the bakers' archives informing about various aspects of the profession, on sources in the municipal archives providing information about the trade's regulation and monitoring as well as on inventories of bakers in order to dive into the world of late eighteenth- and early nineteenth-century bread production.

Part III turns to the impacts of bread market liberalization after 1860. Chapter 6 continues the spatial analysis of the bread landscape based on both GIS mapping and trade statistics. Chapter 7 follows to the political debates and policies following deregulation. Here I describe the effects of market transition on the prices and qualities of bread as well as the political attempts to recreate institutional frameworks especially with regard to market transparency, product standardization and consumers' ability to negotiate a deregulated market. In order to do so, Chapter 7 is based on the analysis of available bread price materials as well as the hermeneutic reading of hitherto disregarded observations of Vienna's market department (Marktamt). These sources, preserved in the municipal archives, are supplemented by a vast number of newspaper articles to trace the public debates unfolding around bread after 1860.

Concluding, I will argue that the city of Vienna saw a notable shift from a regulated moral economy towards a largely free market economy of bread between 1775 and 1885. However, while a self-regulated market was installed around 1860, in the decades to come urban authorities came to judge a free market unfit to promote cheap and good bread for all as deregulation eliminated institutions of public solidarity and increased the inequality between poor and better-off inhabitants and between producers and consumers more generally. Although policies were debated and eventually passed to reintroduce legislation between 1860 and 1885, these were less a countermovement against a free market in the Polanyian sense. Rather, they represented more subtle biopolitical techniques to provide consumers with the ability to negotiate the self-regulated market on their own. This not only presented a sea change in the way market and society were conceptualized and governed, I argue, it also left its mark on the landscapes and bodies of bread.

Part I

FROM MORAL TO MARKET ECONOMIES

Part I develops the theoretical approach of this book. Based on the presentation of the theories of Karl Polanyi, E.P. Thompson and Michel Foucault in Chapter 1, I postulate a market revolution from moral to market economies over the course of the late eighteenth and nineteenth centuries comparable to the watershed of the intellectual formation and political implementation of neoliberal reforms during the twentieth century. By the eighteenth century, a moral economy that rested on a certain set of social norms and beliefs leading to strong intervention into the market was challenged by an emerging alternative idea of the market as the place in which norms and values should be developed in the first place. Chapter 1 draws on Karl Polanyi to derive the concept of a transformation from embedded to self-regulated markets and on E.P. Thompson to define the setting of the embedded market by the late eighteenth century. Additionally, I adopt Michel Foucault's theory of governmentality and biopolitics to sketch out both a more precise process of the turn towards the self-regulated market and a more fine-grained concept of the countermovement against such a disembedded market. Although various scholars have made the proximity of the ideas of Polanyi, Thompson and Foucault a subject of discussion, my combined reading of these three concepts offers a theory of a great transformation of the government of market and society that has to my knowledge not been framed in such a way.

Chapter 1

A GREAT TRANSFORMATION? KARL POLANYI, E.P. THOMPSON AND MICHEL FOUCAULT

Karl Polanyi: The disembedded market and fictitious commodities

In *The Great Transformation*, Karl Polanyi put forwards his theory of the transition from 'embedded' to 'disembedded' markets. Identifying a shift in Western Europe and North America 'from regulated to self-regulated markets at the end of the eighteenth century [that] represented a complete transformation in the structure of society', Polanyi found what he believed to be the 'birth of the market economy'.[1] Inspired by Marx's theories of alienation and the separation of politics and economics, Tönnies's *Gemeinschaft und Gesellschaft* and Weber's postulates 'that the dominant ethic in capitalism contrasted sharply with that of previous systems', Polanyi observed a general transformation of 'the relationship between "economy" and "society"' around the turn of the eighteenth and nineteenth centuries.[2] Central to his theory was the way in which societies organized the production and exchange of goods and services among its members. Emphasizing a diversity of socio-economic behaviours and organizations beyond 'the market', Polanyi held that prior to the ascent of the 'market society' in all societies the production and distribution of goods was built upon four general, though not mutually exclusive economic systems in which the exchange of goods and services was based on social relations.[3]

Drawing extensively on social-anthropological studies, in *reciprocity* and *redistribution* Polanyi identified two mayor 'principles of behaviour not primarily associated with economics' as fundamental lines along which societies were

---

1. Karl Polanyi, *The Great Transformation: The Political and Economic Origins of Our Time*, 2. Beacon Paperback (Boston: Beacon Press, 2001), 74.
2. Gareth Dale, *Karl Polanyi: The Limits of the Market* (Oxford: Polity Press, 2010), 189, 191.
3. Alexander Ebner, 'Karl Polanyi: The Great Transformation', in *Schlüsselwerke der Wirtschaftssoziologie*, ed. Klaus Kraemer and Florian Brugger (Wiesbaden: Springer VS, 2017).

organized.⁴ *Reciprocal* organizations of exchange were to be found principally among societies arranged around relations of family, kinship and mutual sustenance. These were characterized by patterns of symmetry and 'duality' in give-and-take relations of the exchange of goods and services such as the reciprocal distribution of gifts among inhabitants of the Trobriand Islands. In such an organization of exchange, 'the product is exchanged for the sake of the relationship' and transactions involved 'equivalently valued resources between correlative points of symmetrically arranged groups'.⁵ Redistribution, in turn, defined communities in which rule was monopolized under a central power. Here, exchange was determined by 'economic co-ordination through appropriational movements towards and away from a centre (a chief or state), organized through "custom, law or ad hoc central decision". [...] What is common to all these [redistributive systems] is a significant measure of "centricity": the concentration of power in central hands'.⁶

In such a system, goods were 'acquired, collected in a central place, then distributed for consumption' by 'a central individual or group that takes charge of the collection and reallocation of goods'.⁷ In *householding*, Polanyi defined a third, somewhat intermediate pattern of economic exchange in which, in the sense of Greek *oeconomia*, production and distribution of goods was geared towards the own use of a closed, self-sufficient unit such as 'the very different entities of the family or the settlement or the manor'.⁸

In the *market pattern*, Polanyi identified a fourth system of exchange. Both local and long-distance trade, he believed, 'are common in almost all types of primitive society [...]'.⁹ Crucially, however, the market pattern remained but *one* means of production and exchange that continued to be embedded into the other three types. 'Though the institution of the market was fairly common since the later Stone Age,' he conceded, 'its role [...] had remained, at best, a subordinate feature of economic life': 'In the same manner in which either reciprocity, redistribution or householding may occur in a society without being prevalent in it, the principle of barter also may take a subordinate place in a society in which other principles are in the ascendant.'¹⁰

One of the cornerstones of his thinking, philosophically disagreeing with Adam Smith's notion of 'man's "propensity to barter, truck and exchange one thing for another"'¹¹, Polanyi believed that

---

4. Polanyi, *Great Transformation*, 49.
5. Dale, *Karl Polanyi*, 116; Polanyi, *Great Transformation*, 77–8.
6. Ibid.
7. Dale, *Karl Polanyi*, 117.
8. Polanyi, *Great Transformation*, 55.
9. Ibid., 64.
10. Ibid., 45, 59.
11. Ibid., 45.

man's economy [...] is submerged in his social relationships. He does not act so as to safeguard his individual interest in the possession of material goods; he acts so as to safeguard his social standing, his social claims, his social assets. [...] Neither the process of production nor that of distribution is linked to specific economic interests attached to the possession of goods, but every single step in this process is geared to a number of social interests.[12]

This setting was, in Polanyi's view, the more or less 'natural' relationship between society and economy in which the market remained limited by such social relationships. 'In the vast ancient systems of redistribution,' he argued,

acts of barter as well as local markets were a usual, but no more than a subordinate trait. The same is true where reciprocity rules; acts of barter are here usually embedded in long-range relations implying trust and confidence [...]. The limiting factors arise from all points of the sociological compass: custom and law, religion and magic equally contribute to the result, which is to restrict acts of exchange in respect to persons and objects, time and occasion.[13]

Borrowing Tönnies's notion of *Gemeinschaft*, before the nineteenth century Polanyi considered 'the economy is embedded in non-economic institutions' that 'enmesh the economic system proper in social relations' and 'individual members tend to suppress egoistical behaviour in favour of their role within the collective whole'.[14] Generally, he claimed, 'all economic systems [...] up to the end of feudalism in Western Europe were organized either on the principle of reciprocity or redistribution, or householding, or some combination of the three'.[15] The 'production and distribution of goods was secured through a great variety of individual motives disciplined by general principles of behaviour. Among these motives gain was not prominent. Custom, and law, magic and religion cooperated in inducing the individual to comply with rules of behaviour which, eventually, ensured his functioning in the economic system.'[16]

Specifically, with regard to the production and exchange of food, 'regulation involved the application of such methods as enforced publicity of transactions and exclusion of middlemen, in order to control trade and provide against high prices'.[17]

To this classification, he argued, the Roman Empire or the early modern European mercantilist states 'represented no break'. In Polanyi's perspective, reciprocity and redistribution formed the main institutions of exchange in which

---

12. Ibid., 48.
13. Ibid., 64.
14. Dale, *Karl Polanyi*, 192.; Polanyi, *Great Transformation*, 55.
15. Polanyi, *Great Transformation*, 57, 45.
16. Ibid., 57.
17. Ibid., 67.

market transactions were embedded while 'markets played no important part in the economic system and other institutional patterns prevailed'.[18] 'As a rule, the economic system was absorbed in the social system, and whatever principle of behaviour predominated in the economy, the presence of the market pattern was found to be compatible with it.'[19] Regulated and controlled even stricter than before, to Polanyi mercantilist capitalism was not 'a market economy in statu nascendi', it continued to be 'immutably fixed by the traditional organization of society' and mercantilism 'thought of markets in a way exactly contrary to market economy'. 'Where markets were most highly developed, as under the mercantile system, they throve under the control of a centralized administration […]. Regulation and markets, in effect, grew up together. The self-regulating market was unknown.'[20] Before the late eighteenth century, 'regimentation' of the market, 'a main concern of government', aimed to stabilize the 'organization of society through the institutional regulation of markets'.[21]

Around the turn of the eighteenth to the nineteenth century, Polanyi claimed, in the course of the British Industrial Revolution this 'traditional organization of society' was forsaken. Preceded by a 'transitional society, torn as it was between "two mutually exclusive systems, namely a nascent market economy and a paternalistic regulationism"', the early nineteenth century brought a 'sudden change over to an utterly new type of economy'.[22] Essentially, the core development to this was the 'transition from a mercantilist capitalism to its free market liberal successor' that represented a conversion from regulated and limited to self-regulated markets.[23] Different from any socio-economic organization previously, to Polanyi this new type of economy was characterized by the 'dominating part played by markets'.[24] 'Out of […] regulated markets,' Polanyi believed, 'economic liberalism in 1830s Britain rapidly forged a new and unified market economy', to be defined later in this section.[25] As one 'step which makes isolated markets into a market economy, regulated markets into a self-regulated market',[26] the early nineteenth-century

18. Ibid., 57, 58.
19. Ibid., 71.
20. Ibid., 71.
21. Dale, *Karl Polanyi*, 51–2; Polanyi, *Great Transformation* 58, 86–7; Jens Beckert, 'The Great Transformation of Embeddedness: Karl Polanyi and the New Economic Sociology', in *Market and Society: The Great Transformation Today*, ed. C. M. Hann and Keith Hart (Cambridge: Cambridge University Press, 2009), 8. Cited in Ernst Langthaler and Elke Schüßler, 'Commodity Studies with Polanyi. Disembedding and Re-Embedding Labour and Land in Contemporary Capitalism', *Österreichische Zeitschrift für Soziologie* 44, no. 2 (2019), 212.
22. Dale, *Karl Polanyi*, 55; Polanyi, *Great Transformation*, 58.
23. Dale, *Karl Polanyi*, 51.
24. Polanyi, *Great Transformation*, 59.
25. Dale, *Karl Polanyi*, 52.
26. Polanyi, *Great Transformation*, 60.

British state was 'deprived of its former regulatory functions' and took on 'a narrow nightwatch man role as enforcer of the rules of the market'.[27] Accordingly, this was an entirely new relation between economy and society characterized by 'a distinct economic sphere' completely '*separate from the political*'.[28]

Less inclined to offer exact explanations, Polanyi roughly outlined two main drivers of the transition: technological improvements – 'the machine' – as well as politico-philosophical processes of the Enlightenment. Regarding the former, 'the application of elaborate machines to the production process gave rise to the self-regulating market'. As 'expensive equipment was not profitable unless continuously churning out goods; the smooth running of this circuit, in turn, required an assured supply of the factors of production, and this necessitated their commodification'. This required the state's withdrawal from interventionist policies regarding, for example, land and labour in order to make raw materials and workers constantly available.[29]

Meanwhile, the latter driver represented an underlying, longue durée ideational change of thought about the individual and society. Not very well elaborated by Polanyi, it might roughly be termed a transition from a pessimistic Hobbesian notion of the nature of man – homo homini lupus – necessitating oversight and control of society to a Smithian perception of man's moral sentiments and innate propensity to barter, truck and exchange, necessitating 'natural freedom' and economic deregulation. A turn from suspecting individual motives of gain as hurtful for society, such a new conception that all individual selfish acts combined would produce the common good gave rise to the idea that individual interests needed to be left unhampered with.[30]

From the middle of the eighteenth century, Polanyi diagnosed, enlightened intellectuals – 'the political economists Adam Smith, David Ricardo and Thomas Malthus' – contested the market's embeddedness. Notions of 'man's innate propensity to barter, truck and exchange' as well as concepts of the 'natural price' became the cornerstones of arguments that 'human laws that interfere with the market [...] could only be counterproductive' to produce the common good.[31] 'Economic liberalism and the "militant creed of laissez-faire [...] burst forth as a crusading passion"' to rid the market of societal regulations and subject production and distribution of goods to market rather than to human laws.[32]

Polanyi detected the golden spike of the transition to a market economy in the British debate about the Poor Laws and their eventual abolition in 1834.

27. Dale, *Karl Polanyi*, 50.
28. Ibid., 50. Italics in original.
29. Ibid., 52, 53.
30. Helena Rosenblatt, *The Lost History of Liberalism: From Ancient Rome to the Twenty-First Century* (Princeton: Princeton University Press, 2020), chapter 1; Hendrik Hansen, 'Adam Smith, Der Wohlstand der Nationen (1776)', in *Geschichte des politischen Denkens: Ein Handbuch*, ed. Manfred Brocker (Frankfurt am Main: Suhrkamp, 2007).
31. Dale, *Karl Polanyi*, 53–4.
32. Ibid., 59.

This year's drastic elimination of Speenhamland poor relief policies, parish relief programmes which since the 1790s had succeeded in 'buffering the rural poor against unemployment and the loss of other income sources that resulted from collapsing craft industries, land enclosures and falling demand for agricultural labour', 'did away with this obstruction of the labor market'.[33] In Polanyi's view, the abolition of that 'safety net [...] provided to protect workers from the threat of starvation [...] accounts for the introduction of the market economy in the 1830s' by creating a free market for labour.[34]

Although he recognized the commercialization of land as a longer, ongoing process since the fourteenth century connected to urbanization that 'induced landlords to produce primarily for sale on the market' and their 'mobilization of land for the market' through enclosures, to Polanyi the abolition of Speenhamland was key.[35] This '"released" the market economy' – 'out of separate and regulated markets, economic liberalism in 1830s Britain rapidly forged a new and unified market economy' in which 'all dimensions of human life [...] now had to be moulded according to the ends of the new system'. 'As soon as this drastic step was taken, the mechanism of the self-regulating market sprang into gear.'[36] By Polanyi's definition, this new nineteenth-century market economy was 'an economic system controlled, regulated, and directed by market prices; order in the production and distribution of goods is entrusted to this self-regulating mechanism' and 'ensured by prices alone'.[37] By actively withdrawing to the role of the night watch, the state assumed a key role in disembedding the market as lawmakers took on the view that 'nothing must be allowed to inhibit the formation of markets [...]. Neither must there be any interference with the adjustment of prices to changed market conditions [...]. Neither price, nor supply, nor demand must be fixed or regulated, only such policies and measures are in order which help to ensure the self-regulation of the market [...].'[38]

In this new, unprecedented market society – termed *Gesellschaft* – 'the sphere of economic exchange is "institutionally separate and motivationally distinct"'. 'All integral components, including land, labour, and money, are commodified' and the economy is 'directed by market prices and nothing but market prices'.[39] Social relationships 'were now embedded in the economic system' instead of an economy being enmeshed within society.[40] Contrary to every society before, Polanyi claimed, in a market society 'the relationship is entered into for the sake of

---

33. Ibid., 56; Polanyi, *Great Transformation*, 86.
34. Dale, *Karl Polanyi*, 57.
35. Ibid., 50.
36. Ibid., 52; 54–5; Polanyi, *Great Transformation*, 225.
37. Polanyi, *Great Transformation*, 71, 72.
38. Ibid., 72.
39. Dale, *Karl Polanyi*, 192, 49.
40. Ibid., 193.

the commodity',[41] meaning market exchange became the prime mean of exchange in contrast to reciprocal or redistribute relations. After 1834, he believed, not only the British 'society was determined by economics': 'The loci classici of market exchange are the capitalist societies of nineteenth-century Europe and North America, where economic intercourse centres upon goods and services changing hands in vice-versa movements amongst isolated actors within an economic realm that is "disembedded" from non-economic institutions.'[42]

To Polanyi, this represented the 'dissolution of the pre-capitalist embeddedness of land, labour, and money' and the 'birth of the market economy', in which 'neither price, nor supply, nor demand must be fixed and regulated'.[43] Rather, the market economy was 'directed by market prices and nothing but market prices'.[44] In the commodification of labour, land and money, Polanyi recognized the key process in the expansion of the market. These were *fictitious* as opposed to *genuine* commodities; while the latter are 'objects produced for sale on the market', the former are fundamentally not.[45] 'To allow the market mechanism to be sole director of the fate of human beings and their natural environment', Polanyi believed, 'would result in the demolition of society': 'For the alleged commodity "labor power" cannot be shoved about, used indiscriminately, or even left unused, without affecting also the human individual' while 'nature would be reduced to its elements, neighbourhood and landscapes defiled, rivers polluted, [...] the power to produce food and raw materials destroyed'.[46]

Assuming people and societies to recognize the 'disruptive effects of the "free market"', he further identified *countermovements* to processes of marketization aiming to 'retreat from the tenets of market self-regulation to protect society and environment'.[47] In this regard, to Polanyi the state came to occupy an ambivalent double function. On the one hand, it had actively contributed to the disembedding of the market; on the other hand, the state represented a main driver of countermovements against the unregulated market.[48] Accordingly, 'this shift from disembedding to (re-)embedding marks a "double movement"' between self-regulated markets and efforts to stabilize the 'organization of a society through the institutional regulation of markets'.[49]

---

41. Ibid., 116.
42. Ibid., 55, 115.
43. Langthaler and Schüßler, 'Commodity Studies', 212; Polanyi, *Great Transformation*, 72.
44. Dale, *Karl Polanyi*, 49.
45. Polanyi, *Great Transformation*, 75.
46. Ibid., 76.
47. Langthaler and Schüßler, 'Commodity Studies', 212.
48. Polanyi, *Great Transformation*, 71, 75.
49. Beckert, 'Great Transformation of Embeddedness', cited in Langthaler and Schüßler, 'Commodity Studies', 212.

E.P. Thompson: The moral economy

Polanyi's double movement between regulated and 'free' markets was, as E.P. Thompson suggested, one of the central politico-economic frameworks of food production and retailing during that period. Indeed, Polanyi was 'a key tributary' to Thompson's moral economy.[50] In his famous 1971 essay he elaborated his concept of 'epochal changes in marketing, economic thought and governance' at the end of the 1700s.[51] Thompson identified two complementary key constituents, a moral economy of the crowd and a paternalist moral economy of the ruling elite. On the one hand, he considered food riots 'triggered off by soaring prices, malpractices among dealers or by hunger' as 'rational' reaction against tendencies of commodification. Eighteenth-century English crowds were, he argued, 'informed by the belief that they were defending traditional rights or customs; and in general, that they were supported by the wider consensus of community'. They held 'notions of the common weal, notions which, indeed, found some support in the paternalist tradition of the authorities [...]. Hence this moral economy impinged very generally upon eighteenth-century government and thought. [...] It was [...] informed by general notions of rights [...].'[52]

This outlook of paternalists on the other hand, Thompson claimed, constituted the second pillar of the moral economy. The crowds' notions of the common weal 'operated within a popular consensus as to what were legitimate and [...] illegitimate practices in marketing, milling, baking, etc.' Rulers, governments and magistrates held ideas of a 'good government' or the 'good king' to be responsible for their subjects' well-being. They considered themselves responsible to 'enhance public and private welfare by creating conditions of equitability and reciprocity'.[53] They agreed with the crowd that in emergencies 'human subsistence must take precedence over property rights'.[54]

---

50. John Bohstedt, *The Politics of Provisions: Food Riots, Moral Economy, and Market Transition in England, C. 1550–1850* (London: Taylor and Francis, 2016), 10, footnote 31. See also Dale, *Karl Polanyi*, 59; Norbert Götz, '"Moral Economy": Its Conceptual History and Analytical Prospects', *Journal of Global Ethics* 11, no. 2 (2015), 154; Tim Rogan, *The Moral Economists: R. H. Tawney, Karl Polanyi, E. P. Thompson, and the Critique of Capitalism* (Princeton: Princeton University Press, 2017); Ute Frevert, 'Introduction', in *Moral Economies*, ed. Ute Frevert (Göttingen: Vandenhoeck & Ruprecht, 2019), 8. Indeed, Polanyi's work also centrally influenced Immanuel Wallerstein's work on commodity chains and his world-systems analysis at large as Wallerstein acknowledged. See e.g. Langthaler and Schüßler, 'Commodity Studies'.

51. Bohstedt, *Politics of Provisions*, 7.

52. E.P. Thompson, 'The Moral Economy of the English Crowd in the Eighteenth Century', *Past and Present* 50, no. 1 (February 1971), 78–9, 98.

53. Götz, '"Moral Economy"', 149; Bohstedt, *Politics of Provisions*, 10–11.

54. Bohstedt, *Politics of Provisions*, 9.

Thompson's dualism of a moral economy of the crowd and the paternalist model of provision can be interpreted as two sides of the same coin. Both 'conflated into' a more general societal concept in which 'the market remained a social as well as an economic nexus' based on senses of rights, duties and responsibilities; especially food remained a fictitious commodity.[55] 'This in turn was grounded upon a consistent traditional view of social norms and obligations, of the proper economic functions of several parties within the community, which, taken together, can be said to constitute the moral economy.'[56] In this setting, the interference in the market for foodstuffs, through expropriation or by price setting, was legitimized. 'Abstract markets did not set prices, people did [...]. When subsistence necessities stood between crowds and starvation, normal property laws must yield.'[57] In that sense, the people's riots and their toleration by the authorities were countermovements against tendencies of disembedding avant la lettre.

The ideology of moralized theories of trade and consumption was, in the very Polanyian sense, from the late eighteenth century superseded by a 'new model' that was 'disinfested of intrusive moral imperatives'.[58] After about 1770, Thompson argues, 'the customary order clashed increasingly with the emerging modern political economy that brought about "a de-moralizing of the theory of trade and consumption" and was associated with an abstract market mechanism [...]'.[59] In this new model, 'the natural operation of supply and demand in the free market would maximize the satisfaction of all parties and establish the common good. The market was never better regulated than when it was left to regulate itself.'[60] Although, Thompson concluded, the 'death of the old moral economy of provision' was a 'long-drawn-out process' during most of the eighteenth and well into the nineteenth century, the 'victory of the new political economy' eventually brought about 'the end of one tradition' and a 'different historical territory'.[61]

Michel Foucault: Disciplinary and security mechanisms and the birth of biopolitics

However, the 'free' market economy forged out of the moral economy was never free of societal intervention; the disembedded market had to be re-imbedded by other measures of enclosure. Instead of conceptualizing the transition as a move away from all public interference towards a fully self-regulated market-leviathan

---

55. Götz, '"Moral Economy"', 152; Thompson, 'Moral Economy', 135.
56. Thompson, 'Moral Economy', 79.
57. Bohstedt, *Politics of Provisions*, 3, 10; E.P. Thompson, *Customs in Common: Studies in Traditional Popular Culture* (New York: The New Press, 1994).
58. Thompson, 'Moral Economy', 90.
59. Götz, '"Moral Economy"', 152.
60. Thompson, 'Moral Economy', 90.
61. Ibid., 132, 128–9.

beyond all societal control, the introduction of liberal market policies was closely connected to the formation of a new form of governmentality and new techniques of governing, as Michel Foucault has suggested. Karl Polanyi and E.P. Thompson have presented closely related concepts of a late eighteenth- and early nineteenth-century transition from a regulated (food) market entrenched into 'moral' perceptions of fairness, justice and public welfare reached through reciprocity and redistribution to the notion that only 'free' markets liberated from such public interference would produce the common good. Much less appreciated especially by historians,[62] Thompson's and Polanyi's diagnosis of a major revolution in the governance of society and market was joined by Michel Foucault.

In his lectures on *Security, Territory, and Population* and the *Birth of Biopolitics* through 1977 to 1979, Foucault has outlined a transition of the mechanisms of power, the emergence of biopolitics and, effectively, the theoretical-ideological foundations of (neo-)liberalism in 'occidental societies' since the mid-eighteenth century.[63] In these addresses, Foucault laid out a comprehensive and complex sketch of this transformation that, unfortunately, remained in the state of a lecture. Given his premature death, Foucault could not elaborate and specify these ideas further. This caused not only the comparatively small reception of this major theoretical contribution to economic history; it also left his thoughts somewhat unfinished, sometimes apparently contradictory, in any case not easy to absorb.[64]

Defining three major ensembles and practices of power – the juridical/sovereign, the disciplinary and the security dispositive – Foucault offered a 'barren historical scheme' of these three 'arts of government'.[65] 'Since the middle ages', he argued, a juridical mechanism had dominated governing in the western world. A 'system of the code of law with a binary division between what is allowed and forbidden', in this 'archaic system of punishment' the legal code linked a 'type of forbidden action' to a 'type of penalty'. During the seventeenth and eighteenth centuries, the second, disciplinary mechanism was added, 'a whole range of police, medical, psychological etc. techniques which point to surveillance [and]

---

62. For an exception, see most importantly Patrick Joyce, *The Rule of Freedom: Liberalism and the Modern City* (London: Verso, 2003); for adoption of Foucault's theory with regard to food, see e.g. David Nally, 'The Biopolitics of Food Provisioning', *Transactions of the Institute of British Geographers* 36, no. 1 (2011); Aaron Bobrow-Strain, 'White Bread Bio-Politics: Purity, Health, and the Triumph of Industrial Baking', *Cultural Geographies* 15, no. 1 (2008).

63. Michel Foucault, *Sicherheit, Territorium, Bevölkerung: Geschichte Der Gouvernementalität I. Vorlesungen am Collège de France 1977/1978*, 5. Auflage (Frankfurt am Main: Suhrkamp, 2017); Michel Foucault, *Die Geburt der Biopolitik: Geschichte der Gouvernementalität II. Vorlesungen am Collège de France 1978/1979*, 6. Auflage (Frankfurt am Main: Suhrkamp, 2018).

64. Thomas Lemke, '"The Birth of Bio-Politics": Michel Foucault's Lecture at the Collège de France on Neo-Liberal Governmentality', *Economy and Society* 30, no. 2 (2001).

65. Foucault, *Sicherheit, Territorium, Bevölkerung*, 20.

diagnosis' and which aimed to ensure the observance of law and order. According to Foucault, this juridical-disciplinary set of mechanisms formed a governing complex determined by a system of lawfulness (*Legalitätssystem*) and a system of ordinance (*Verordnungssystem*) that was constituted 'not only to stop [...] but to prevent' crises that would challenge the power of government.[66] Third, over the eighteenth century, Foucault claimed, a new technique of power emerged that was 'not constituted by the code of law or the disciplinary mechanism'.[67] This new security dispositive, he defined, differed from the former juridical-disciplinary complex in three ways. It integrated a phenomenon in question into a series of probable events; the reaction of power regarding this phenomenon was integrated into a cost calculation; instead of a binary division between the permitted and the prohibited an 'optimal' mean was determined and the limits of the acceptable constituted.[68]

Illustrating this somewhat abstract notion, Foucault gave the examples of the medieval handling of leprosy, the early modern pest ordinances and the practices of vaccination since the eighteenth century. First, the statutory medieval exclusion of lepers into separate leprosaria constitutes the juridical-binary division, determining between sick and not sick. Second, the sixteenth and seventeenth centuries' pest ordinances 'had a very different purpose and different means'. Representing the disciplinary type, they were to establish a net of controls over the regions and cities hit by plague and regulations of daily life to prevent contagion. Third, with the practice of smallpox vaccination since the eighteenth century, the technique was not to enforce discipline in the form of quarantine, 'the fundamental problem is rather to know how many are infected, at what age, with which consequences, which mortality [...], what risk vaccination entails', about smallpox's 'statistical consequences on the population' and thus evaluate appropriate means of action. The difference in these practices was key. The juridical lepers' exclusion and the disciplinary quarantine of plague victims both aimed to contain crises from spreading while their origins and reasons were deemed 'natural' or 'divine', thus uncontrollable. In contrast, the security dispositive's aim of vaccination is to identify and know the reasons of the emergence of an epidemic in the first place and thus prevent such a crisis from developing at all.[69]

Different from the first two mechanisms, the security mechanism thus aims to gain a wide range of information about a whole *milieu*, understood as an ensemble of 'natural circumstances', 'artificial facts' and a 'number of mass effects directed at all individuals' within it. Consequently, the milieu appears as a nexus between a 'geographic, climatic, physical' milieu and 'mankind';[70] it

66. Ibid., 55.
67. Ibid., 19.
68. Ibid., 20, 21.
69. Ibid., 25–6, 54–5.
70. Ibid., 43.

is therefore 'a field of intervention where a population is targeted'.[71] Under the security dispositive, a 'historic-natural milieu becomes the object of intervention' if 'mankind shall be affected'.[72] The security mechanisms are thus a 'political technique directed at the milieu'.[73] Whereas disciplinary mechanisms targeted the governance, surveillance and control of a given territory – of space – security techniques should rather 'enable circulation: circulation of people, circulation of commodities'.[74] It was therefore crucially connected to a withdrawal of certain cruder forms of government intervening and limiting individual acts and a turn towards techniques of power that could allow greater levels of freedom and the transition to a 'security society'.[75]

Indeed, Foucault went on to specify his theory of a transition from disciplinary to security mechanisms by using the example of (urban) bread provision. In the second lecture on *Security, Territory, and Population* he analysed 'how a moral economy of hunger is gradually replaced by a political economy of food security that promotes market mechanisms as a better protection against scarcity' during the eighteenth and nineteenth centuries.[76] In his perspective, the moral-economy setting of the grain market – geared to prevent starvation and maintain societal justice – fundamentally represented 'the clearest and most dramatic motive for a government' to regulate the market. Closely related to E.P. Thompson's concept, to prevent 'revolt', urban administrators would set the prices of grain and bread through urban assizes; prohibit storage, engrossing and regrating; and impose other regulations of the production, trade and processing of cereals and bread. This represented a 'comprehensive political [and] moral' concept of crisis prevention before the background of 'the evil nature of man' which created or at least worsened supply crises through 'the people's greed – their desire for profit, their wish to earn ever more, their egoism' expressed in 'hoarding, foraging and withholding of goods'. These 'institutional means, the techniques of government of the political and economic administration' installed to prevent exactly such crises represented disciplinary mechanism par excellence, Foucault argued.[77] Disciplining people, this was 'a coercive system' forcing farmers, merchants, bakers and consumers to comply with the market laws created to prevent egoistical wrongdoing. A 'comprehensive system of surveillance', a 'disciplinary system of limitations, coercion and permanent observation' was created to monitor the trade and 'prevent circulation [of grain] from country to country, from province to province' in order to avert local hardship. Such an 'anti-food-shortage-system'

71. Ibid., 41.
72. Ibid., 43.
73. Ibid., 43, 44.
74. Ibid., 52.
75. Ibid., 26.
76. Nally, 'Biopolitics of Food', 37.
77. Foucault, *Sicherheit, Territorium, Bevölkerung*, 54–5.

prevailed in most of mercantile Europe in order to inhibit 'what was feared the most, namely that prices in cities skyrocketed and people revolted'.[78]

These disciplinary mechanisms, Foucault continued in his Polanyian-Thompsonian analysis, were increasingly criticized by the 'physiocratic doctrine' of the latter part of the eighteenth century, which centred on the 'freedom of trade and of grain circulation' as the best means to prevent dearth. This turn represented 'actually a complete change or rather a phase of great change of the techniques of government and part of the introduction of [...] what I call the security dispositive', Foucault pointed out. Thus, 'the principle of free grain circulation' characterized an 'episode in the transformation of power technologies and an episode of the implementation of the technique of security dispositives'.[79] With this emerging mechanism of governance, 'the main target of analysis is not the market, i.e. not the price of the product, rather, [the analysis] goes [...] several steps further' to include 'the history of grain', meaning everything that contributed to the price of grain. 'The unit of analysis is no longer the market with its nexus of shortage and price increases, but grain with everything that happens to it' and affecting its price – environmental conditions, agricultural techniques, supply, demand, etc. Thus, in this perspective, it was the milieu – the 'reality of grain' and the factors influencing provision – that became the target of governmental intervention rather than the mere (urban) marketplace.[80] Central to such a 'liberal solution' was the 'alleviation of the market' from uninformed regulation and the abolition of short-sighted limitations on trade, storage, etc., which would – very briefly put – eventually end shortages.[81] Refocussing the analysis on such a milieu and a less-limited market consequently required a 'broad expansion' of governmental attention. In order to govern the liberated market and ensure stable provisions and public welfare, the entire milieu of grain needed to be understood. Instead of setting prices and limiting trade, 'not only the marketplace, but the entire cycle' from producers to retailers needed to be known. 'Instead of forcing binding regulations on them', it was needed to 'learn, to understand, to recognize how and why' all protagonists of the grain trade acted and 'what calculations they make'.[82]

Contrary to the 'centripetal' character of the disciplinary mechanism which 'concentrates, centres, encloses' and focusses 'mainly on the market', the security mechanism is 'centrifugal', it has the tendency to expand, to include new factors like 'production, psychology, behaviour patterns' and allows 'always expanding circles'. 'Discipline regulates everything by definition. [...] The security dispositive, however, [...] permits.' It is based on 'laissez faire' exactly because only that way the crucial factors influencing the milieu can unfold and can be recognized.[83]

78. Ibid., 56–7.
79. Ibid., 58, 59.
80. Ibid., 62–3.
81. Ibid., 63, 64–6.
82. Ibid., 67.
83. Ibid., 73, 74.

Security mechanisms 'answer to a reality', as a means of liberalism they 'let things happen [...] so reality can unfold [...] according to the laws, the principles and the mechanisms of reality itself'.[84] Based on these intellectual assumptions, the milieu of grain – in other words a liberated grain market in the loosest and widest meaning of the word – became 'a natural phenomenon that cannot be changed by decree'. Therefore, any acts of government needed to be oriented towards acting upon what was not normal instead of what was not the norm. Reality could therefore only be governed with 'techniques of transformation that are enlightened, well-grounded, analytical, calculated, anticipatory'. It was thus not the 'obedience of the subjects' – the prime target of disciplinary measures – that needed to be achieved, but to influence 'more removed things of which it is known through calculation, analysis and reflection that they effectively influence the population'.[85] Governmental policies thus needed to turn from limiting to enabling individual acts.

> There remains neither legitimacy nor interest regarding attempts to implement regulating systems of request, order, and prohibition. It will be a basic principle of the role of the state and of the form of governmentality [...] to mind the natural processes [...] and let them play [...]. On the one hand, this means the state's governmentality shall be limited. [...] It will be administered, not regulated. This administration will not have the main target to prevent things, but to see that the necessary and natural regulations occur or to provide regulation that allows such natural regulation. [...] That means security mechanisms need to be implemented. Mechanisms of security or of state intervention, which have the core function to guarantee the security of natural phenomenon important to the population, like economic processes.[86]

Thus, Foucault considered the physiocratic ideas revolutionary because they allegedly acknowledged the complexity of factors influencing the growing, harvesting, trading, processing and retailing of grain and bread. 'This idea of a governing of people that foremost considers the nature of things instead of the bad nature of man, the idea of an administration of things that considers above all the freedom of people, what they want to do and what is most advantageous to them' was structurally completely different from the disciplinary techniques of governance, Foucault argued.[87] Most importantly, discipline establishes categories of 'normal and abnormal, healthy and sick, cheap or expensive, allowed and forbidden – 'disciplinary normalization means to create an optimal model', a norm according to which all acts are judged consequently. Meanwhile, allowing reality – the milieu, the market – to unfold, normalized. Instead of defining a 'moral'

84. Ibid., 77.
85. Ibid., 110, 111.
86. Ibid., 505–6.
87. Ibid., 78–9.

norm and then judging events, developments and actions against such a norm, the security technique of governing aimed to analyse a phenomenon, a milieu, a market in its entirety and thus led milieu or market constitute a normal, an average constructed empirically.[88]

Although not adopting either Polanyi's or Thompson's vocabulary, to Foucault exactly this intellectual reconsideration meant nothing else than the abolishment of the moral economy and the creation of a disembedded, self-regulated market, as the argued in his lectures on the *Birth of Biopolitics*.

> Within the functionality of government [...] since the Middle Ages there was an object of preferred intervention, of regulation by governments, a prime object of vigilance and intervention of governments. It was this place [...] that would become the location and the mechanism to constitute truth by the 18th century. It will be recognized that this location of establishing the truth can be left alone with as few interventions as possible instead of saturating it with continuous regulations, so it can formulate its truth and present it to the government as rule and norm. This location of truth is [...] the market. [...] The market, as it functioned during the Middle Ages, in the 16th and 17th centuries, was essentially a location of justice [...] in the sense that the [officially] settled retail price was [...] a just price, or at least a price that should be deemed just, i.e. a price that was in a certain ratio to the work performed, to the requirements of the merchants and of course to the needs and capabilities of consumers. [It was] a location of justice in the sense that the market represented a location of justice of distribution because [...] the regulation of the market [...] commanded a certain arrangement to enable the poor [...] to buy [basic necessities]. [...] What was to be ensured was the absence of fraud, in other words, the protection of buyers. [...] The regulation of the market thus aimed to ensure a just distribution of goods on the one hand, and the prevention of [...] offence on the other. [...] Say, the market was a location of jurisdiction.[89]

With the ideational reconsideration of eighteenth-century physiocratic thinking, the market became 'something that obeyed and should obey "natural" mechanisms', too complex to fathom by the individual and thus too complex to modify and regulate. Thus, the market 'becomes a location of truth' which 'reveals the natural mechanisms' and enables the creation of the '"natural" price' that will express the 'appropriate ratio between production costs and demand'.[90] If left free, the market will therefore 'present a standard of truth, which enables to distinguish right from wrong act of government [...] and to falsify and verify the regulations and measures issued'. This way, the market became 'a location of verification and falsification of government. Consequently, it is the market who [...] will determine

---

88. Ibid., 89–91.
89. Foucault, *Biopolitik*, 52–4.
90. Ibid., 54–5.

that a government needs to respect the truth to be a good government.' Thus, in the political economy of eighteenth century liberal thinkers 'from a location of justice [...] the market became [...] a location of veridiction. [...] His role of veridiction will henceforth order, dictate, prescribe the [...] juridical measures or the absence of such measures [...].'[91] With regard to commodities, such a self-regulated market as the location of veridiction would produce the 'natural price' of things and thus a win-win situation for both vendors and buyers. A 'maximum of mutual enrichment', the market free of disciplinary intervention would create the maximal price obtainable for retailers and the minimal price possible for consumers.[92]

As the market transformed from a location where justice needed to be guaranteed through intervention into a location that created truth, in the liberal-physiocratic thinking this implicated a see-change to the ways of economic governance. Foucault called this new way of politics the 'governmental reason of self-limitation' or a 'raison of the minimal state that finds its basic veridiction in the market'.[93] In other words, facing the market as loco of veridiction, the government was now bound to

> identify the economic mechanisms in their inner and complex nature. If [the government] has identified these, it needs to respect them. [...] It means that it will equip its policies with exact, continuous, clear, and sharp knowledge about what happens in the society, on the market, in the economic cycles so that the limitation of [governmental] power [...] is based on the certainty of economic analysis.[94]

Thus, it follows, such a self-limited government inherently needed to abstain from crude disciplinary mechanisms based on moral notions and assumptions intervening into the market. On the contrary, a governance of society and economy in the presence of a self-regulated, veridictative market required much more subtle, indirect, yet much broader efforts of regulation.

Such efforts of regulation remained fundamentally necessary. While a self-limited government 'executes freedom' through self-limitation and by enabling the market to become a place of truth, it simultaneously had to ensure and protect freedom – 'the new art of government is the management of freedom'. In such a position, Foucault followed the physiocratic-liberal reasoning, the government needed to ensure the 'production and organization of those conditions' necessary to 'be free'. It was thus in a constant 'problematic, always changing relation between

---

91. Ibid., 56.
92. Ibid., 84.
93. Ibid., 73, 84.
94. Ibid., 95.

the production of freedom' and that 'what limits freedom by producing it'. 'On the one hand, freedom has to be created, but this act implicates on the other hand that limitation, coercion, control, obligation are introduced.'[95] More precisely, freedom of trade for example was not possible without introducing 'a number of measures' overseeing and organizing that freedom, such as the introduction of certain standards or the prevention of monopolies, or the support of consumers so producers would find a market for their products. Therefore,

> the liberal art of government is forced to determine up to which point the individual interest [...] does not endanger the interests of all. [...] It will also be necessary to protect individual interests from impairment through collective interests. The freedom of economic processes must be no hazard to businesses or workers. The freedom of workers must not be a hazard for companies and production.[96]

In short, Foucault got to the heart of it, 'all these requirements [of freedom] need to be met through security strategies, which are the backside and the requirement of liberalism'. The inherent consequence of such a transformation is therefore the 'enormous expansion of procedures of control, of limitation, of coercion, which form the counterpart and counterbalance of freedom'.[97] To enable freedom, the presence of a self-regulated market necessitated the turn away from – though not complete abolishment of[98] – intervening disciplinary mechanisms in favour of security mechanisms framing the market and providing institutions, information, standards and many other factors that would enable both circulation and equal chances.[99]

Foucault considered exactly this transformation the *Birth of Biopolitics* as a 'constellation in which the modern human and natural sciences and the concepts of normality inform political action and determine the goals of politics'.[100] Closely linked to the liberal forms of government pushed forward by the French Physiocrats since the middle of the eighteenth century, biopolitics represented 'a fundamental transformation in the order of politics'.[101] It

---

95. Ibid., 97–8.
96. Ibid., 99–100.
97. Ibid., 100, 102.
98. Foucault, *Sicherheit, Territorium, Bevölkerung*, 20–3.
99. For a similar analysis of particularly neoliberal theory, see Quinn Slobodian, *Globalisten: Das Ende Der Imperien und Die Geburt des Neoliberalismus* (Bonn: bpb: Bundeszentrale für politische Bildung, 2020).
100. Thomas Lemke, 'From State Biology to the Government of Life: Historical Dimensions and Contemporary Perspectives of "Biopolitics"', *Journal of Classical Sociology* 10, no. 4 (2010), 429.
101. Ibid., 429–30.

refers to the emergence of a specific political knowledge and of new disciplines such as statistics, demography and epidemiology. These disciplines make it possible to analyse processes of life on the level of populations [earlier termed 'milieu'] and to 'govern' individuals and collectives by practices of correction, exclusion, normalization, disciplining, therapeutics and optimization. [...] The object of biopolitics is not singular human beings, but their biological features measured and aggregated on the level of populations. This procedure makes it possible to define norms, establish standards and determine average values. [...] Life ceases to be the always presumed but never explained counterpart of politics. It is separated from the singularity of concrete lives and becomes an abstraction, the object of scientific knowledge, administrative concern and technical improvement. Politics, too, is transformed by biopolitical rationalities and technologies. It depends on life processes that it cannot directly control, and it has to respect their capacities for self-regulation. However, this very limitation allows politics to expand its range of options for intervention and government. It does this because politics disposes not only of direct forms of authoritative command but also of indirect mechanisms for inciting and directing, preventing and predicting, moralizing and normalizing. Politics can prescribe and prohibit, but it can also incite and initiate, discipline and supervise – or activate and animate.[102]

This way, biopolitics 'is the positive power to establish the health and security of a population by creating new, responsible subjects [enabled to negotiate the veridictive market]. Yet bio-politics' protective measures require a carefully defended architecture of boundaries, divisions, and hierarchies among and within populations aimed at defining and eliminating "the biological threat to [...] the species or race".'[103]

To Foucault, such a creation of responsible subjects represented the key novelty brought about by the birth of biopolitics. As biopolitics primarily depended on life processes that could not be controlled directly and needed to be respected for their abilities of self-regulation, 'technologies of the self' became a core means of governmental security mechanisms. Biopolitics

> feature not only direct intervention by means of empowered and specialized state apparatuses, but also characteristically develop indirect techniques for leading and controlling individual subjects without at the same time being responsible for them. The strategy of rendering individual subjects 'responsible' [...] entails shifting the responsibility for social risks [...] and for life in society into the domain for which the individual is responsible and transforming it into a problem of 'self-care'.[104]

---

102. Lemke, 'From State Biology to the Government of Life', 429–31.
103. Bobrow-Strain, 'White Bread Bio-Politics', 35.
104. Lemke, '"The Birth of Bio-Politics"', 201, 202.

Therefore, biopolitics not only meant a change in the mechanisms of regulation, it rather formed a 'reorganization or restructuring of government techniques, shifting the regulatory competence of state onto "responsible" and "rational" individuals'. Rather than directly interfering into both individual acts and in the market through disciplinary mechanisms of government, more indirect security techniques aimed at '"supplying" individuals and collectives with the possibility of actively participating in the solution of specific matters and problems which had hitherto been the domain of state agencies specifically empowered to undertake such tasks'. Thus, the births of biopolitics centrally brought about the 'replacing (or at least supplementing) [of] out-dated rigid regulatory mechanisms by developing techniques of self-regulation' through security mechanisms framing market and society.[105]

A Great Transformation? Moral and market economies, disciplinary and security mechanisms and biopolitics of bread

The Polanyian-Thompsonian framework has been subject of, partly, severe critique. Historians have offered critical adjustments and rejections both regarding the notion of a dramatic rupture between pre-capitalist economies and capitalist market economies in general, its timing around the late eighteenth century and in terms of the interpretation of the allegedly new economic system. E.P. Thompson's concept of a moral economy was accused early on to overlook the 'moral sentiments', in Adam Smith's words, of economists arguing for the liberalization of markets.[106] A second strand of criticism rejected his English particularism which made the moral economy 'irrelevant and obsolete as global perspectives became dominant',[107] while at the same time others made adjustments by tackling his tendency to neglect 'both structure and dynamic' – that is economic, cultural, political diversity across spaces and changing compositions of motives and tactics over time.[108] Some critics remained deeply at odds with the consideration of the eighteenth century as an alleged rift between non-capitalist and capitalist economies, arguing 'the moral economy was a correction of capitalist trade, not a condemnation of it' rather than 'a radical populist protest on behalf of an alternative economy'.[109] Indeed, E.P. Thompson revised his original, Polanyian timeframe and conceded that the '"story of the free market" economy reached back into the eighteenth and seventeenth centuries' while elements of the moral economy 'extended through the nineteenth century into the present moment'.[110]

---

105. Ibid.
106. Rogan, *Moral Economists*, 26–8.
107. Ibid., 181.
108. John Bohstedt, 'The Moral Economy and the Discipline of Historical Context', *Journal of Social History* 26, no. 2 (1992), 276.
109. Ibid., 268.
110. Rogan, *Moral Economists*, 167.

While Thompson's moral economy has nevertheless enjoyed 'continuous relevance' and has become a major point of reference for the analysis of late eighteenth- and early nineteenth-century 'politics of provisions' and (urban) food provision in particular,[111] historians from the start have remained deeply sceptic about Karl Polanyi's broader account of an abrupt eighteenth- and nineteenth-century great transition towards capitalism.[112] In fact, however, this scepticism of the Polanyian timeframe has inspired manifold inquiries, especially by historians of the medieval and early modern periods, into the 'modernity' of markets for land, labour and money. These and others have thoroughly dismissed the empirical basis and the timeframe of parts of the narration in the Great Transformation.[113]

---

111. Rudi Batzell et al., 'E. P. Thompson, Politics and History. Writing Social History Fifty Years after the Making of the English Working Class', *Journal of Social History* 48, no. 4 (2015), 754; Bohstedt, *Politics of Provisions*. Among the many works using the moral economy concept, see e.g. Gergely Baics, *Feeding Gotham: The Political Economy and Geography of Food in New York, 1790-1860* (Princeton, Oxford: Princeton University Press, 2016); Cynthia A. Bouton, *The Flour War: Gender, Class, and Community in Late Ancien Régime French Society* (Pennsylvania: Pennsylvania State University Press, 1993); Courtney Fullilove, 'The Price of Bread. The New York City Flour Riot and the Paradox of Capitalist Food Systems', *Radical History Review*, no. 118 (2014); Steven L. Kaplan, *Bread, Politics and Political Economy in the Reign of Louis XV*, Second edition (London, New York: Anthem Press, 2015); Judith A. Miller, 'Politics and Urban Provisioning Crises. Bakers, Police, and Parlements in France, 1750-1793', *The Journal of Modern History* 64, no. 2 (1992); Marcel Streng, *Subsistenzpolitik im Übergang: Die kommunale Ordnung des Brot- und Fleischmarktes in Frankreich 1846-1914* (Göttingen: Vandenhoeck & Ruprecht, 2017); Helen Tangires, *Public Markets and Civic Culture in Nineteenth-Century America* (Baltimore: Johns Hopkins University Press, 2003); Sydney Watts, *Meat Matters: Butchers, Politics, and Market Culture in Eighteenth-Century Paris* (Rochester: Univ. of Rochester Press, 2006); Emma Hart, *Trading Spaces: The Colonial Marketplace and the Foundations of American Capitalism* (Chicago: The University of Chicago Press, 2019).

112. On contemporary critiques, see Dale, *Karl Polanyi*, e.g. 84-5; see also Marcus Gräser, 'Historicizing Karl Polanyi', *Österreichische Zeitschrift für Soziologie* 44, no. 2 (2019), 132-3.

113. Bas van Bavel, *The Invisible Hand? How Market Economies Have Emerged and Declined Since AD 500* (Oxford, UK: Oxford University Press, 2016), 8-18, offers a concise overview over the historiography; Dale, *Karl Polanyi*, 72-88, presents a more extensive critique of Polanyi's argument.

On the commodification of labour, see e.g. Marc W. Steinberg, *England's Great Transformation: Law, Labor, and the Industrial Revolution* (Chicago, London: The University of Chicago Press, 2016). On 'market mentality' and motives of gain, see e.g. Joyce Appleby, *Economic Thought and Ideology in Seventeenth-Century England* (Los Angeles: Figueroa Press, 2004); Jan de Vries, *The Price of Bread: Regulating the Market in the Dutch Republic* (Berkeley, CA: University of California Press, 2019), esp. chapter 2, and Karl Gunnar Persson, *Grain Markets in Europe, 1500-1900: Integration and Deregulation* (Cambridge: Cambridge University Press, 2005).

Therefore, large parts of the historical evidence in Polanyi's argument on a fundamental nineteenth-century transition towards self-regulated markets are certainly incorrect and need to be rejected.[114]

Rather than accepting the shaky story of Polanyi's birth of the market economy, E.P. Thompson's rather pessimistic-romanticizing and particularly British notion of the end of the moral economy and Foucault's somewhat abstract concept of regulative mechanisms and biopolitics individually, my approach is to combine these master narratives as well as to confront them in order to address both commonalities and contradictions. In the wake of a broader rediscovery of Polanyi's ideas in other social sciences and humanities, from his *Great Transformation* I take the ideas of the creation of a self-regulated market and the commodification and marketization of goods of first necessity. From E.P. Thompsons' moral economy, I extract the particular socio-politico-economic setting of market embeddedness with regard to bread in late eighteenth-century Europe. In this sense, my definition of the moral economy goes beyond E.P. Thompson's conceptualization. Here, with regard to food, it describes and represents the institutionalization of the embedded food market before the nineteenth century. Therefore, the moral economy is not only considered as a state of mind of the working classes, but – integrated into Polanyi's transition from an embedded to a disembedded market – as a particular state of the late eighteenth- and early nineteenth-century food market in Europe, in which food inherently remained a fictitious commodity. Instead of Polanyi's less-detailed theory of countermovements aiming to re-embed the market, from Foucault I adopt the much more fine-grained transition from relatively straightforward disciplinary mechanisms controlling and intervening into a thoroughly regulated market to much broader security mechanisms created specifically to provide 'technologies of the self' that frame and embrace a self-regulated market and 'responsible individuals', enabling freedom in the first place. By thus combining and contrasting Polanyi, Thompson and Foucault, I adapt the three theories into a picture of a great transformation of both the conception of the nature of man and the market within society, and consequently of its societal regulation in Europe since the eighteenth century.[115]

---

114. Note that Polanyi did not intend the book to be a historical account of the nineteenth century, but a diagnosis of the 1940s crisis of capitalism and liberal democracy. See Gräser, 'Historicizing Karl Polanyi', 131.

115. In so doing, I follow other scholars who have recognized and elaborated on the intellectual proximities and complementarity between Polanyi, Thompson, and Foucault. See Rogan, *Moral Economists*; Danielle Guizzo and Iara Vigo de Lima, 'Polanyi and Foucault on the Issue of Market in Classical Political Economy', *Review of Radical Political Economics* 49, no. 1 (2017); Nicola Short, 'Market/Society: Mapping Conceptions of Power, Ideology and Subjectivity in Polanyi, Hayek, Foucault, Lukács', *Globalizations* 15, no. 7 (2018); see also Nally, 'Biopolitics of Food'.

On this basis, I postulate a great transformation from moral to market economies of food, from the reconceptualization of food from a fictitious to a genuine commodity, from disciplinary to security mechanisms of market regulation unfolding from the latter half of the eighteenth century. I use this axiom 'as a heuristic lamp post that sheds light on the complicated relationship between morality and capitalist market economies'.[116] Thus, the perception of such a shift is not regarded as an epic-eternal struggle between non-capitalist and capitalist market economies. Rather, it is adopted as a main guideline of the book to follow the historic phases of transitions between regulative market regimes and to explore the consequences of this evolution during the late eighteenth and most of the nineteenth centuries.

---

116. Frevert, 'Introduction', 9. For the recent adoption of Polanyi in other social sciences, see Brigitte Aulenbacher, Richard Bärnthaler and Andreas Novy, eds., 'Karl Polanyi, "The Great Transformation" and Contemporary Capitalism', special issue, Österreichische Zeitschrift für Soziologie 44, no. 2 (2019).

Part II

BETWEEN MORAL AND MARKET ECONOMIES OF BREAD. ECONOMIC AND INSTITUTIONAL CHANGE, 1770s–1860

Making sure enough and healthy food was available at affordable prices year-round was among the main concerns of both municipal and state administrations to prevent social unrest and upheaval. Historians of various subfields have paid great attention to the provision of urban centres across Europe, North America, the Ottoman Empire and Asia.[1]

Comparable to other early modern urban centres like Paris, Brussels, New York City, Mexico City, Istanbul or Beijing, supplying and retailing food in Vienna was fundamentally organized within the framework of the moral economy until the

---

1. See e.g. Dorothee Brantz, *Slaughter in the City: The Establishment of Public Abattoirs in Paris and Berlin, 1780–1914* (2003) (Chicago: University of Chicago PhD Thesis); Steven L. Kaplan, *Provisioning Paris: Merchants and Millers in the Grain and Flour Trade during the Eighteenth Century* (Ithaca: Cornell University Press, 1984); Roger Scola, *Feeding the Victorian City: The Food Supply of Manchester, 1770–1870* (Manchester: Manchester University Press, 1992); Marcel Streng, *Subsistenzpolitik im Übergang: Die kommunale Ordnung des Brot- und Fleischmarktes in Frankreich 1846–1914* (Göttingen: Vandenhoeck & Ruprecht, 2017); P. J. Atkins, Peter Lummel and Derek J. Oddy, eds., *Food and the City in Europe Since 1800* (London, New York: Routledge, 2016); Piet van Cruyningen and Erik Thoen, eds., *Food Supply, Demand and Trade: Aspects of the Economic Relationship between Town and Countryside (Middle Ages – 19th Century)* (Turnhout: Brepols, 2012); Gergely Baics, *Feeding Gotham: The Political Economy and Geography of Food in New York, 1790–1860* (Princeton, Oxford: Princeton University Press, 2016); G. Billen et al., 'Grain, Meat and Vegetables to Feed Paris: Where Did and Do They Come From? Localising Paris Food Supply Areas from the Eighteenth to the Twenty-First Century', *Regional Environmental Change* 12, no. 2 (2012); Roger Horowitz, Jeffrey M. Pilcher and Sydney Watts, 'Meat for the Multitudes. Market Culture in Paris, New York City, and Mexico City over the Long Nineteenth Century', *The American Historical Review* 109, no. 4 (2004); Rhoads Murphey, 'Provisioning Istanbul. The State and Subsistence in the Early Modern Middle East', *Food and Foodways* 2, no. 1 (1987); Lillian M. Li and Alison Dray-Novey, 'Guarding Beijing's Food Security in the Qing Dynasty. State, Market, and Police', *The Journal of Asian Studies* 58, no. 4 (1999).

middle of the nineteenth century. Before the introduction of the *Gewerbefreiheit* in 1860, both state and municipal institutions assumed tight authority over the food supply system of the Habsburg capital. Abundant, cheap and healthy supplies were the 'guideline of all market regulations'.[2] To achieve that goal, Viennese moral economy institutions of embeddedness secured the wide-ranging public control and regulation of places, people, products and prices. These institutions rested upon disciplinary mechanisms: the guild system, urban market laws and both the municipal control over bread prices and the direction of a regulated landscape of bread ensured wide-ranging disciplinary measures that warranted oversight over most central factors of producing, selling and buying bread.

To understand and assess the changes, costs and benefits that liberalization introduced through the *Gewerbefreiheit* would bring, the development of the municipal landscape of bread under the officially regulated system before 1860 needs to be analysed first. Besides official intervention this landscape represented a complex interplay of both competing and fraternizing individuals, families and larger networks haggling about permits, procedures and profits and thus playing a crucial role in the reproduction of the municipal landscape from below. Starting, Chapter 2 introduces the main institutions of embeddedness that regulated Vienna's systems of provision within the framework of a moral economy of bread. Chapters 3–5 examine the political and economic-structural changes during the late eighteenth and first half of the nineteenth centuries that would crucially contribute to the elimination of institutional regulation by mid-century. Chapter 3 analyses the geographic and organizational modifications Vienna's bread landscape underwent between the late eighteenth and the late nineteenth centuries. Using geographic information system (GIS) mapping technology, it focusses on the built environment of baking and the channels of bread distribution to answer how a municipal landscape of bread performed in the bread provisioning of the growing numbers of the capital's residents.[3]

Following the analysis of the urban side of bread production and retail, Chapter 4 examines the consequences of both the changes of the political landscape and the economic, environmental and technological developments in the urban hinterland on the institutions of embeddedness.[4] On the one hand, the expansion

---

2. Rudolf Till, *Geschichte des Wiener Marktwesens* (Wien: Geitner, 1939), 24.

3. In so doing, Chapter 3 adopts a spatial-history approach as suggested e.g. in Baics, *Feeding Gotham* or Clé Lesger, 'Patterns of Retail Location and Urban Form in Amsterdam in the Mid-Eighteenth Century', *Urban History* 38, no. 1 (2011).

4. Earlier versions of Chapter 4 have been published as Jonas M. Albrecht, 'The Need for Wheat. The Pre-Industrial Expansion of Vienna's Grain Supply, 1800–1840', in *Stocks, Seasons and Sales: Food Supply, Storage and Markets in Europe and the New World, C. 1600–2000*, vol. 17, ed. Wouter Ronsijn, Niccolò Mignemi and Laurent Herment (Turnhout: Brepols Publishers, 2019) and as Jonas M. Albrecht, 'Brot für die Hauptstadt. Niederösterreich und die Nahrungsversorgung Wiens', in *Geschichte Niederösterreichs: Band 2. Gesellschaft und Gemeinschaft. Eine Regionalgeschichte der Moderne*, ed. Oliver Kühschelm, Elisabeth Loinig and Willibald Rosner (St. Pölten: Verlag NÖ Institut für Landeskunde, 2021).

of Vienna's grain hinterland since the 1700s fostered industrialization and product diversification and had most serious impacts on the institutional bread market regulation in Vienna during the first half of the nineteenth century. Covered in Chapter 5, these changes led to quite thorough reform debates during the 1820s and 1840s, and eventually to the final elimination of most of the institutions of embeddedness by 1860.

Chapter 2

INSTITUTIONS OF EMBEDDEDNESS

Regulating people and places

'As long as the institution of guild bakers persists, they can be compelled to provide for the consumers at all times, and if they will not comply obligingly, they can be impelled by the authorities because they are granted a privilege and protected against competition.'[5]

With this 1781 statement, the Imperial government summarized the underlying key assumptions of a regulated municipal landscape of bread in Vienna. Embedded into the central European guild system, by the late eighteenth and early nineteenth centuries Vienna's infrastructure of bread provision was the result of an ongoing expansion of the bread landscape that was regulated and directed by the municipality. While parts of the Habsburg guild system were reformed and liberalized during the eighteenth century,[6] a 'state guild organization' remained in place regarding everyday basic needs. In this political environment, besides the city's more general market laws that strictly prevented forestalling, regrating and engrossing before 1860,[7] guilds functioned as 'instruments of the state's social, economic and security policies' and became an 'integral part of the social and

---

5. Cited in Karl Přibram, *Geschichte der Österreichischen Gewerbepolitik von 1740–1860; auf Grund der Akten* (Leipzig: Duncker & Humblot, 1907), 458.

6. See John Komlos, *Nutrition and Economic Development in the Eighteenth-Century Habsburg Monarchy: An Anthropometric History* (Princeton, NJ: Princeton University Press, 1989), 131–4; Bernhard Hackl, 'Die Staatliche Wirtschaftspolitik zwischen 1740 und 1792. Reform versus Stagnation', in *Josephinismus als Aufgeklärter Absolutismus*, ed. Helmut Reinalter (Wien, Köln, Weimar: Böhlau, 2008); Herbert Matis, 'Leitlinien der Österreichischen Wirtschaftspolitik', in *Die Habsburgermonarchie 1848–1918*, vol. 1, ed. Alois Brusatti, Adam Wandruszka and Helmut Rumpler (Wien: Verl. der Österr. Akad. der Wiss, 1973).

7. Alexander Gigl, *Geschichte der Wiener Marktordnungen: vom Sechzehnten Jahrhundert bis zum Ende des Achtzehnten aus Urkunden entwickelt* (Wien, 1865), 109, 181–205; Ferdinand Opll, 'Studien zur Versorgung Wiens mit Gütern des Täglichen Bedarfs in der Ersten Hälfte des 19. Jahrhunderts', *Jahrbuch für Geschichte der Stadt Wien* 37 (1981).

economic dynamic of the 18th century'.[8] By the 1790s, they were still regarded as 'legitimate and relevant political representations' of interests within a system determined by both relatively strict regulation and continuous negotiations over – and adaptions of – corporate and individual market access in the embedded economy.[9] Rather than static or irrational, this constituted a 'flexible and ultimately very efficient means of regulating' the market.[10] It was created through constant, complex negotiations over 'an alignment of interests' and over the 'economy of interests' that 'generally ensured the interests of rich and poor were marshalled to meet the common good'.[11]

First officially mentioned in 1278, the Bakers' Guild was the backbone of the municipal landscape and functioned as the main component of the inhabitants' daily access to the most important food item, bread. It represented one of the crucial disciplinary mechanisms to maintain public oversight over people, places and products and facilitated the authorities' involvement into issues as varied as production processes, qualifications of artisans, working hours and wages as well as official specifications of shops' locations, commodity qualities and prices, retail guidelines, etc. Before the introduction of commercial liberty in 1859/60, Vienna's magistrate actively managed both the numbers of master bakers and the location of bakeries across the city. The underlying dualistic – and somewhat dialectic – aim of the regulated-landscape policy was to secure a ready access to the basic food item for residents all over the urban space while guaranteeing bakers what was deemed 'deserved' and adequate *bürgerliche* profits. In this sense, politically warranting the economic profitability of running a bakery – at least to some extent – made sure producers were constantly attracted into the trade, which in turn secured a comprehensive spatial network of bakeries covering the capital.

Becoming a guild master was a highly restricted and thoroughly regulated occupation; this was especially true for women, who were generally denied the formal job training and education within the guild structure. Rather unrepresented by official sources like master or apprentice directories, women nevertheless formed an integral part of social and commercial life and everyday procedures. Wives and daughters were usually involved in selling bread and bakery products both in the bakery shop and on the markets. Yet, women also assumed more important positions in everyday life. The conferment of formal widow's privileges

---

8. Annemarie Steidl, 'Silk Weaver and Purse Maker Apprentices in Eighteenth- and Nineteenth-Century Vienna', in *Learning on the Shop Floor: Historical Perspectives on Apprenticeship*, ed. Bert de Munck, Steven L. Kaplan and Solym Hugo (New York, NY: Berghahn Books, 2007), 134; Josef Ehmer, 'Zünfte in Österreich in der frühen Neuzeit', in *Das Ende der Zünfte: Ein europäischer Vergleich*, ed. Heinz-Gerhard Haupt (Göttingen: Vandenhoeck & Ruprecht, 2011), 112, 116.

9. Ehmer, 'Zünfte', 113.

10. Steidl, 'Silk Weaver', 133.

11. Emma Hart, *Trading Spaces: The Colonial Marketplace and the Foundations of American Capitalism* (Chicago: The University of Chicago Press, 2019), 44, 46.

in 1779 and an 1808 reform giving widows the right to legally carry on their husbands' businesses strengthened the position of female actors.[12] While denied to women, young men needed to go through and endure an intensive vocational training as well as years of working experience thereafter to become a licensed baker. For most of them, an apprenticeship in Vienna also involved the possibilities and challenges of migration.

Strict guidelines determined by both guild and magistrate dominated the lives of bakery workers. Having finished the years of job training and work experience becoming a master baker was still confined to only few artisans. While piety, church attendance at guild-sponsored services, marital birth and citizenship were among the personal requirements, candidates also needed to prove work experience of at least two years with a Viennese master. Such qualified candidates then had to prove their artistry in form of a master trial. Indeed, money probably represented the most important asset a qualified master baker needed. Owing to the restricted number of guild members and baking licences, by the late eighteenth and early nineteenth centuries a master bakers' title had become a valuable asset in form of the so-called *Realgewerbe*.[13] Titled *radiziert*, such a business licence was tied to a specified building rather than a personal concession and could be sold, let and inherited; in 1778 a government survey found there were 'nearly no craft and master titles not saleable'.[14] By the turn of the century, becoming a master baker essentially meant to ransom a fellow artisan at a price that had been rising throughout the 1700s. The sums required to purchase and run a licensed bakery would differ greatly across the city area, depending on the market position, the neighbourhoods' purchasing power and the size of the real estate. According to his bequest directory, Valentin Sauer, a widowed former master baker who died on 8 July 1817, owned a debt certificate from baker Johann Kleindienst and his wife Rosalia over 20,000fl., signed 24 April 1813. Equivalent to about 200 times the annual wage of the highest-paid rank of a baker's journeymen or to over 48,000-day wages of a mason' handyman,[15] although not explicitly stated this note almost certainly represented the price for Sauer's bakery.[16]

---

12. Sigrid Kretschmer, *Wiener Handwerksfrauen: Wirtschaft und Leben im 18. Jahrhundert* (Wien: Milena, 2000), 38. On the important role of women in Paris, see Steven L. Kaplan, *The Bakers of Paris and the Bread Question, 1700–1775* (Durham: Duke University Press, 1996), 321–36.

13. On a similar setting in Paris, see Kaplan, *Bakers of Paris*, 284–9.

14. Přibram, *Gewerbepolitik*, 289–318.

15. Robert C. Allen, 'Consumer Price Indices, Nominal / Real Wages and Welfare Ratios of Building Craftsmen and Labourers, 1260–1913. Prices and Wages in Vienna, 1439–1913', *International Institute of Social History data files*, accessed 5 May 2021, https://iisg.amsterdam/en/blog/research/projects/hpw/datafiles.

16. Wiener Stadt- und Landesarchiv, Zivilgericht, A2, Fasz. 2 – Verlassenschaftsabhandlungen: 1817–432. Verlassenschaftsabhandlung Valentin Sauer.

Furthermore, besides such an initial amount of investment necessary to buy into the trade, operating a bakery also required a remarkable amount of working capital, the disposability of which a prospective master baker also needed to prove to the authorities. Detected of lacking the funds to purchase the required monthly flour supplies each baker needed to have in stock as a security measure, bakers Ignatz and Elisabeth Kreutzer as well as Johann Rudolph were jailed in October 1771, their debts had to be cleared by the guild and their bakeries were given to other masters able to raise the funds necessary.[17] This way of continuous attempts to restrict the positions of master bakers to individuals who could muster enough capital to run the bakery without interruption and through times of crisis represented another important aspect of regulating people and places via the guild system. Being a guild baker was a privilege with more or less guaranteed income that fundamentally entailed obligations to supply urban dwellers constantly.

Vienna's master bakers thus formed a controllable and usable organization. Privileged and protected through the monopolistic policies in times of abundance, the authorities might turn to the city bakers to carry extra expenditures of increasing bread prices in times of hardship. Relying on the bakers' capital stocks to prefinance subsidies in critical periods was a rather common feature of the moral economy during the late eighteenth and first half of the nineteenth centuries. Viewing bakers as much as privileged and protected suppliers than as servants to the urban public, Vienna's authorities drew upon the guild to support bread weights throughout the Napoleonic Wars as well as during the supply crisis of 1848. In 1816, for example, the guild was granted a reimbursement over 27,000fl. for bread deliveries made during the French occupation in 1809 while in June 1851, the bakers claimed 35,000fl. of compensations for bread weight subsidies provided between 15 May and 15 August 1848.[18]

Besides the personal qualifications of master bakers, work and the processes of baking were among the main reasons for authorities and guild to maintain the strict and disciplining municipal landscape of bread. Baking good and healthy bread relied on good management, hard but well-organized labour and artisanal skills of both journeymen and master. Work in a bakery meant long hours of hard labour in conditions that were physically and psychically challenging and even dangerous. Often situated behind the shop or in basements without daylight and ventilation, apprentices, journeymen and bakers spent most of their days in confined, hot and sticky bake rooms. While affluent masters might run capacious shops and facilities, others would occupy 'basement bakerooms so confined that the baker could barely manipulate the peel, so hot that the dough "melted" during proofing, so dark that one could hardly see, and so stifling that one could barely find air for a deep breath'.[19] Workers had to lift heavy flour sacks and knead hundreds

---

17. Kretschmer, *Handwerksfrauen*, 63.

18. Landesinnung der Wiener Bäcker, ed., *700 Jahre Wiener Bäcker-Innung* (Wien: Verlag der Wiener Bäcker-Innung, 1927), 39, 43.

19. Kaplan, *Bakers of Paris*, 61.

of kilograms of dough with hands and feet, prepare the oven, chop wood, light a fire, draw and carry hundreds of litres of water, clean the bake room, sell bread in the shop and deliver rolls to customers. Working virtually day and night, labourers would get only little sleep, often in the bake room. Night work itself was 'morally as well as physically devastating'. Segregating them from the daily routines of others, apprentices and journeymen were sometimes considered a 'class apart', absorbed and contained by their work.[20]

Literally living at work, labourers might suffer very poor hygiene as they 'washed and even urinated in the pails they used to carry water to the flour'.[21] Bakers often suffered from respiratory illnesses, rheumatism, arthritis and eczema caused by the absorption of flour dust and yeast through the skin as well as from psychological disorders triggered through stress, strain and probably night work. Poor sanitations could also affect flour and bread as water might be contaminated, dirt from the walls could fall into the flour, insects might be mixed into the dough, rats would infest the flour stocks and the sweating workers would flavour the dough with perspiration and saliva.[22] Indeed, poor hygiene remained an issue throughout the entire nineteenth century, especially when consumers were informed how many bakery labourers working on the dough suffered from tuberculosis, gonorrhoea, chancroid, syphilis, scabies and other diseases.[23]

Though it depended on hard physical labour under sometimes detrimental conditions, producing good bread also required essential skills, knowledge and experience by both master and journeymen. Besides economic expertise, material knowledge was absolute key. While bakers needed to be able to tell good from spoiled flour and, at least rudimentary, fresh from polluted water, fermentation remained the 'soul of the bread-making process' as the 'preparation and insinuation of leaven into the dough required "the most care and skill" of all the stages' of baking.[24] Finally, the quality of bread would also depend on the processes of kneading, resting, forming and eventually baking the dough in a well-kept and correctly heated oven; bad handling along all these steps might negatively affect or even ruin the product.

While details of production varied with individuals and shops according to expertise, equipment and management, these facilities, business procedures and universal steps of baking were much the same for all bakers. To a certain degree, all producers were subject to the 'fragility of the bread-making enterprise, the manifold conditions that had to obtain for success, and the ease with which everything could fall and fail'.[25] A successful bakery thus relied heavily on both

20. Ibid., 227, 228.
21. Ibid., 229.
22. Ibid., 227–49.
23. *Arbeiter-Zeitung. Zentralorgan der österreichischen Sozialdemokratie*, 'Die Brotwucher in Wien', 22 November 1895, 321.
24. Kaplan, *Bakers of Paris*, 65.
25. Ibid., 80.

physical and psychical demanding yet qualified labour in order to produce healthy bread and secure the consumers' access to satisfying amounts and qualities of bread as well as to ensure public tranquillity. Therefore, an average late eighteenth- and early nineteenth-century guild bakery represented a complex urban craft business that, to be successful, needed to command a wide range of both artisanal and managerial expertise as well as financial assets to secure continuous production. Often, though doubtlessly not always a highly skilled and complex occupation and generally a crucial role for the city's bread supply, being a master baker was among the most lucrative positions of the pre-industrial urban economy.[26]

Similar to New York's council regulating butchers Vienna's urban authorities were very keen to manage the numbers and locations of licensed bakeries in any given part of the city closely. Assuming direct and sole control to award the rank of a master artisan and grant baking licences in 1775 the magistrate aimed to balance both an extensive infrastructure of bread supply securing the inhabitants' equal access to food and adequate, monopolistic outlets for all bakers to guarantee them what was deemed a *bürgerlicher* profit. The authorities limited the number of licensed master bakeries and determined which applicant was granted to take over an existing workshop or open a new production site. In the latter case, the magistrate also determined the city area with the most urgent demand and straightforwardly directed the infrastructural development for the common good.[27] Next to regulating the landscape of bakeries, the magistrate equally limited and directed the numbers and locations of bread stalls the bakers were allowed to set up across the city, an important auxiliary infrastructure that ensured the consumers' access to bread and enabled the bakers to geographically expand their outlets. Thus exercising a 'massive right to interfere' into the trade the magistrate created a 'landscape of municipal food access' over the last third of the eighteenth and the first half of the nineteenth centuries.[28]

In this tightly regulated environment, individual bakers and families as well as the guild, interlopers and the authorities constantly quarrelled over market access,

26. Andreas Weigl, 'Gewerbepolitik', in *Wien. Geschichte einer Stadt: Band 2. Die Frühneuzeitliche Residenz (16. Bis 18. Jahrhundert)*, vol. 2, ed. Peter Csendes and Ferdinand Oppl (Wien/Kön/Weimar: Böhlau, 2003).

27. Andreas Baryli, 'Gewerbepolitik und gewerbliche Verhältnisse im vormärzlichen Wien', in *Wien im Vormärz*, ed. Renate Banik-Schweitzer, Forschungen und Beiträge zur Wiener Stadtgeschichte 8 (Wien: Jugend und Volk, 1980).

28. Baics, *Feeding Gotham*, chapter 2. On Vienna, see Jonas M. Albrecht, '„Das Ringen des Freihandels mit dem Prohibitivsystem". Politische Ökonomie und Infrastruktur der Brotversorgung Wiens, 1815 – 1847', *Österreichische Zeitschrift für Geschichtswissenschaften* 30, no. 2 (2019); Weigl, 'Gewerbepolitik'; Günther Chaloupek, Michael Wagner and Andreas Weigl, 'Handel im Vorindustriellen Zeitalter: Der Kanalisierte Güterstrom', in *Wien Wirtschaftsgeschichte 1740–1938*, ed. Günther Chaloupek, Peter Eigner and Michael Wagner, 2 vols. (Wien: Jugend und Volk, 1991); Till, *Geschichte des Wiener Marktwesens*, 24–42; Přibram, *Gewerbepolitik*, 43–5, 245–65, 280–8, 452–508.

individual privileges, business conducts and many other aspects that could arouse small and large disputes. Therefore, besides regulative interventions from above, the municipal landscape of provision was equally produced and reproduced through constant and complex negotiations, conflicts and impulses from below. This can be highlighted through the many cases of competition and rivalry over baking licences and retail permits, which also underline the important role of women.[29]

The complexity of the production and reproduction of the municipal landscape of baking is corroborated by the innumerable requests for permissions to sell bread, infringements against regulations and many other issues that are documented in the guild registers before 1860. Though much less profound, these sources contain hundreds and hundreds of tiny actions of daily negotiations and acts of regulation, like widow Katharina Witschkin's request to sell *Kollatschen* and Catharina Feichtinger's plea to sell 'bakery products' on Josephstadt district's Lange Gasse, which were both rejected among many others not only in January 1807. In April 1807, Johann Igers was reported by *Brodbeschauer* Joseph Wolf. Only licensed to produce 'potato bread', Igers had apparently violated his baking permission by offering 'gusto' baked goods. Having presumably refused to abide, the baker was again reported in June 1807 for his 'rude behaviour' towards the inspector, and another prohibition to bake gusto products was reissued. Maybe some form of a family habit, one Phillip Igers was reported to illicitly produce 'luxurious' baked goods twenty-three years later.[30]

Concluding, these examples outline the relevant structures of the disciplinary measures embedding the baking trade during the late eighteenth and early nineteenth centuries. First, under the moral economy regime both guild and political authorities issued disciplinary rules and regulations that heavily intervened into the bakers' trade. On paper, guild statutes rigidly regulated who was allowed entrance into the baking industry, under which conditions and at what times. Second, the magistrate exerted manorial power to geographically direct the baking infrastructure over the developing urban area. Fundamentally, the authorities did answer both micro-spatial settings of supply and demand and broader moral considerations about individual meritoriousness determined through moral, artisanal and financial capabilities. While officials thus acted to provide deserving bakers with the means to make a living, they also made sure no individual baker would come to monopolize the market and fostered competition where and when needed. In this setting, apprentices, journeymen and bakers were

29. Kretschmer, *Handwerksfrauen*.

30. Archiv der Bäckergenossenschaft in Wien, HS 15: Innung der bürgerl. Bäckermeister in der k.k. Haupt- und Residenzstadt Wien. Protocollum uiber merkwürdige Gegenstände, als: Volksaufruhr gegen die Bäcker anno 1805; die den bürgl Bäckermeister geleisteten Vergütungen; mehrere Backproben; Consignation über die Ausgaben eines mitleren Bäckermeisters; dann der vom Jahre 1807 bis 1830 ergangenen Verordnungen und Rathschläge, January 1807 and 22.4.1830.

mobile in geographical and to some extent in social terms. Bakers changed, traded, bought, rented and sold workshops – or failed to do all this – over the urban area due to official intervention as well as for socio-economic reasons. Third, while these frameworks appear relatively straightforward, this was still a system of decisive flexibility and agency from below. Individuals constantly haggled, bickered and negotiated with the authorities and among each other over permits, places, conducts and putatively morally grounded prerogatives. Negotiations, disputes and likely even hostility between rivalling individuals, families and interest groups together formed the complex municipal landscape of provision.

For many of these actions, the decisive role and agency of women need to be underlined as a fourth characteristic. Female actors were not only engaged in the trade as mothers or daughters with charitable duties and retailing tasks, they were involved as business owners, representatives before the law, landlords and authorities. Wives, widows and daughters could not only come into the situation to defend businesses and secure generational transfers when the husband died, they might also have had the skills to run bakeries themselves, be successful artisans, fend off male rivals, provide a living for existing families or start new ones. In that position, via marriage they could also open a door into the trade for men who for some reason or the other lacked the skills, connections or funds to become a master on their own. Generally, while women remained marginalized systematically, the powerful positions some female actors could occupy within a business, a family and probably the broader bakers' community should not be underestimated. All in all, despite these complex daily negotiations and options to produce and reproduce the municipal landscape of bread from below, both the market laws and the guild system represented a body of comprehensive institutionalized disciplinary measures aimed to oversee the production and retail of bread in general and discipline the behaviour of retailers, producers and customers.

Regulating products: The assize

Besides regulating people and places, regulated and standardized bakery products represented the second pillar of the moral economy of bread. Since the thirteenth century, Viennese authorities controlled the production of the urban bakers by defining and regulating a certain number of bread types and qualities bakers were imperatively obliged to produce at officially settled prices. By the late seventeenth century, these compulsory products were fairly standardized. From the 1720s until 1849/60, clerks and authorities continued to set the prices and weights for a relatively stable set consisting of two kinds of rolls, two kinds of bread and two kinds of pastries. The *Mundsemmel* or *Rundsemmel* represented the finest wheat roll, followed by the *ordinari Semmel* as second-grade roll. With the so-called *Pohlenbrot* an unbolted wheat bread was equally regulated besides large loaves of rye bread. *Eyernes* and *schmalzenes Gebäck*, yeast bread pastries usually baked into crescent-shaped forms, and leached *Kipfel* complemented the list. Until the early decades of the nineteenth century, such more luxurious bakery products remained highly seasonal; their production was only allowed during certain times of the year, for example Easter or Christmas, and production permits were drawn by lot, giving extra income opportunities only to a restricted number of guild masters.[31]

While pastry products assumed a special position among a baker's product range, the two types of rolls and the two types of bread formed the absolute backbone of the bread supply of Vienna's inhabitants. All bakers were compelled under threat of penalty to always produce sufficient amounts of all of those bakery goods at satisfying qualities to secure the consumers' uninterrupted access to basic bread products. In late March 1819, for example, master baker Johann Wagner pleaded to have a 25fl. fine waived, a penalty for the 'failure to produce rolls and rye bread'.[32] Bakers were also compelled to keep a month's supplies of flour. Their adherence to both quantitative and qualitative requirements was ensured through disciplinary measures of control and penalty; inedible bread or insufficient production of any of the four types of bakery goods could be reported and penalized with fines, public shaming, arrests or even occupational ban. The so-called *Bäckerschupfen*, a public humiliation during which offending bakers were put into a cage-like ducking stool and ducked into the river, represented a common form of punishment well into the late eighteenth century.[33] Additionally, bakers were regularly publicly 'remembered' to adhere to quality and quantity standards.[34] To prevent fraudulent behaviour every licensed bakery, regardless of the artisan occupying it, was assigned an individual number for identification. Called *Brotstupfer*, the products of every bakery had to be marked with the shop's individual number. This allowed consumers and authorities to clearly identify the producer of every loaf of these standardized bakery products sold in Vienna and trace both good and spoiled bread.[35]

Without doubt, infringements especially against quality standards were manifold, regular and probably omnipresent. Answering complaints about bad rye bread in early March 1762, baker's widow Barbara Fischer blamed one of her journeymen for the faulty products. Having undergone bloodletting several days earlier, his wound had opened at work and contaminated the dough. The journeymen was punished with fourteen days of arrest.[36] In late 1797, a decree by the government prompted the magistrate to make sure bakers would not use retail outlets that were 'too low, too small, and damp' and that the sales person would

31. Alfred Francis Pribram, *Materialien zur Geschichte der Preise und Löhne in Österreich.*, with the assistance of Rudolf Geyer, and Franz Koran (Wien: Ueberreuter, 1938), 194-8, see also Přibram, *Gewerbepolitik*, 454-5.

32. Bäckerinnung, *Protocollum 1807-1830*, 31 March 1819.

33. Max Kratochwill, 'Ein Bäckerschupfen in der Roßau (1728)', *Jahrbuch des Vereins für Geschichte der Stadt Wien* 21, no. 22 (1965/1966).

34. Opll, 'Versorgung Wiens', 59.

35. Albrecht, 'Ringen des Freihandels', 77.

36. Kretschmer, *Handwerksfrauen*, 62.

not live in the same room where the bread was kept.[37] Put-up announcements kept requesting bakers to maintain cleanliness in the bake rooms and reminded journeymen of the prohibitions to sleep, shave, comb or wash in the bakery or do anything else that could 'arouse disgust'.[38] Yet, when *Wiener Zeitung* reporter L.F. visited Vienna's first steam bakery in January 1849, he admired not only the bakery's technical equipment but explicitly highlighted its cleanliness accomplished through the 'removal of the workers' accommodation from the baking room', a fact he apparently thought extraordinaire.[39] Having discovered journeymen with 'eczema of higher or lower grades, and even with scabies' as well as a general lack of cleanliness, in March 1851 the magistrate instructed the market commissioner to control all bakeries 'often' and 'at short intervals' to report all infringements immediately.[40] A year later, the authorities ordered to ensure that workers would not climb into the baking troughs and knead the dough with their feet.[41] A proverbial fight against windmills, the availability of these sources nevertheless underlines the existence and efforts of disciplinary techniques to keep fraud and infringements at bay.

However, while adherence to the rules of baking was secured through these disciplinary techniques of control, the definitions and regulations of bread themselves were created through much more comprehensive measures to safeguard the provision of good and cheap bread. While city authorities were readily able to intervene into procedures of buying and selling on urban marketplaces and processes of baking in local shops, another major factor of the urban bread supply was beyond their regulatory reach: grain prices. Indeed, intervening into the grain market by keeping prices on urban marketplaces artificially low would have entailed the danger of distracting merchants and provisions in the first place. Therefore, besides the thick fabric of disciplinary measures of regulation and control spun around Vienna's marketplaces and woven into the procedures of bakers, profound measures were erected around the bread market in order to 'protect the poor and promote public tranquillity'.[42] These mechanisms opened up

37. Wiener Stadt- und Landesarchiv, Marktamt A2/1 – Bäcker: sanitäre Vorschriften, 18.11.1797.

38. Wiener Stadt- und Landesarchiv, Marktamt A2/1 – Bäckergewerbe: Kundmachungen Nr. 18188, 13.02.1850: Magistrat der Stadt Wien. The same announcement was published on 12 June 1845, see Magistrat der Stadt Wien, Kundmachung über Beobachtung der Reinlichkeit in den Bäckhäusern.

39. L.F., 'Die Erste Wiener Dampfbäckerei. Panem et Circenses', *Wiener Zeitung*, 19 January 1848, 19.

40. Wiener Stadt- und Landesarchiv, Marktamt A2/1 – Bäcker: sanitäre Vorschriften Z. 21091, 26.03.1851: Magistrat der Stadt Wien.

41. Wiener Stadt- und Landesarchiv, Marktamt A2/1 – Bäcker: sanitäre Vorschriften, 08.07.1852: Magistrat der Stadt Wien.

42. Judith A. Miller, *Mastering the Market: The State and the Grain Trade in Northern France, 1700–1860* (Cambridge: Cambridge University Press, 1999), 39.

a much wider horizon of intervention epitomized by the remaining factor urban authorities could regulate: bread prices.[43]

The main institution to protect the city's inhabitants from supply shortfalls and dearth was, like in other cities across Europe, the assize for bread under which the urban authorities settled the costs of a range of defined and regulated bread items. Since 'affordable bread prices underlay any hopes for urban tranquillity' and 'reflected the city's sense of fairness to both bakers and consumers',[44] the overarching goal was to make sure that bread prices and grain prices stood in the 'right' proportion and millers and bakers would not profit immorally from the basic needs of large numbers of urban consumers. Therefore, the management of prices represented one of the central institutions of the moral economy and echoed a 'broadly shared set of beliefs (an ideology) about the proper economic roles of market actors and regulators'.[45] As a 'regulatory system that keyed the price of bread directly to the price of its chief cost component, that made these prices public, and that inspected the weight and quality of the product to ensure honest dealings', it answered the two-sided idea of the *just price*, attributed to Thomas Aquinas, and the *Nahrungsprinzip*, coined by Max Weber.[46] Hence, 'the assize-type regimes did address the "moral economy" notion that elites should be seen to be actively superintending the food economy – tracking prices, monitoring quality, restraining the avarice of bakers and millers' while they 'allowed magistrates to present themselves as guardians of the public weal'.[47] This way, 'the thinking behind the assize of bread is also fully consistent with […] ideals of social structure, justice, and morality' in which 'the baker's social responsibilities for the common good' remained a key principle. 'Bakers were expected to sell for the common good, not for unilateral profit.'[48] From a different perspective highlighted by Charles Tilly, the assize was an essential tool of governance to prevent public disorder and to implement 'effective strategies to manage public expectations in order to achieve

43. Michel Foucault, *Sicherheit, Territorium, Bevölkerung: Geschichte der Gouvernementalität I. Vorlesungen am Collège de France 1977/1978*, 5. Auflage (Frankfurt am Main: Suhrkamp, 2017), 40–2.

44. Miller, *Mastering the Market*, 35, 36.

45. Jan de Vries, *The Price of Bread: Regulating the Market in the Dutch Republic* (Berkeley, CA: University of California Press, 2019), 19.

46. Ibid., 17, 18; James Davis, 'Baking for the Common Good: A Reassessment of the Assize of Bread in Medieval England', *The Economic History Review* 57, no. 3 (2004), 484–6. By *Nahrungsprinzip*, Weber recognized the craft guild's philosophy to hold the idea that all producers should charge what it takes to maintain their proper station of life but not to seek more, which would mean committing the sin of avarice. Jan de Vries interprets this philosophy as 'the just price seen from the perspective of the producer rather than the consumer'. See de Vries, *Price of Bread*, 19.

47. de Vries, *Price of Bread*, 21.

48. Davis, 'Baking for the Common Good', 480, 482, 485.

a polity with the institutional capacity to actually govern'.[49] Either way, 'the assize provided a legal basis for food regulation, couched in accepted moral and social terms' and thus presented 'standardized information to consumers' as well as protecting bakers 'from inaccurate accusations of infringements that might lead to corporal punishment'.[50]

As a complex institution that derived from the Roman *Annona*, this 'regulatory regime' was shared by many towns across Europe since the high Middle Ages and throughout the early modern period; it represented 'a set of practical rules that endured to define a key component of Europe's political economy until the early nineteenth century'.[51] Developing in many cities from the thirteenth through the fifteenth centuries, these systems differed from the *Annona*-model in three ways. They left the trade in grain and grain inventories largely in private hands; they accepted the price of grain as exogenous and focussed instead on the constitution of proper bread prices; and they did not consider bread price stability as significant but rather turned towards product quality and 'the maintenance of clear "rules of the game" between producers and consumers'. Therefore, the authorities 'no longer aspired to a command economy' and 'the objective shifted from sheltering consumers from the volatility of the market to the enforcement of rules' that embraced relatively freer grain markets while maintaining the assize as a disciplinary measure to produce 'a market price that both buyer and seller were willing to accept'.[52]

Although described as a crude and inflexible system despised by market-liberal critics who considered the assize as antiquated, market-hostile and an issue of premodern 'big government',[53] this was a highly sophisticated system that 'recognized the centrality of the market and set about regulating the terms in which the bakers [...] carried out their critical function of supplying bread to the community. Public authority [...] sought to enforce a practical regulation of a primarily market economy'.[54]

In this setting, 'bread prices in the assizes were based upon competitive wholesale market prices of grain plus a stable, fixed profit margin for the baker'.[55] Rather than being oblivious towards market forces, this system required the price-setting authorities to '*discover* the market' and to know the costs of making

---

49. de Vries, *Price of Bread*, 20.
50. Davis, 'Baking for the Common Good', 491, 492.
51. de Vries, *Price of Bread*, 21, 22, 7–17; Miller, *Mastering the Market*, 35–9.
52. de Vries, *Price of Bread*, 17. Davis, 'Baking for the Common Good', 484.
53. Crude translation of 'Vielregiererei' which literally translates into 'too much governance', see Landesinnung der Wiener Bäcker, *700 Jahre*, 42; Pribram, *Materialien*, 809. On international critiques see e.g. de Vries, *Price of Bread*, Ch. 15, esp. 408–25; Miller, *Mastering the Market*, 107–13, 282–4.
54. de Vries, *Price of Bread*, 17.
55. Davis, 'Baking for the Common Good', 485.

bread.⁵⁶ To know these costs, authorities not only needed to discover the market, they also had to discover nature and the technologies with which grain was turned into food. Essentially, setting bread prices was a technique that required deep knowledge of the milieu of grain, the 'ensemble of interdependent natural and artificial circumstances' that come together and result in the final product concerned, bread.⁵⁷

Discovering and knowing nature and the market meant that roughly since the thirteenth century cities across Europe made increasing efforts to 'arm themselves with the intimate knowledge of the bread making' processes in order to develop 'elaborate and continuous information gathering, recordkeeping, and monitoring' and to establish 'a rational basis for price regulation'.⁵⁸ While these schemes remained rather rudimentary in many parts of Europe until 'well into the eighteenth century', a more complex system developed in the Dutch Republic since the late 1500s.⁵⁹ Similar efforts to reform the basic price designs were undertaken in Vienna around the same time.⁶⁰ The norms of price regulations, dating back to the fourteenth century, were refined since 1534 and especially during the 1580s and 1590s in order to calculate bread prices more precisely. While market price observation had already been a central part of the 'old system' assize during the fourteenth and fifteenth centuries, from the late sixteenth and especially during the late seventeenth centuries a rather 'rigid frame' of the assize was further reformed.⁶¹ The key innovation was the reform of the baker's finances by introducing a more precise distinction of a baker's expenses. Including average expenses for taxes, non-grain inputs, labour or wages, rents and capital costs as well as the expenses required for a master baker's respectable lifestyle, by institutionally determining and settling these costs the authorities essentially pulled a significant part of the baker's operational expenses including personal revenue into the political sphere of the moral economy. With the introduction of the reformed bread assize authorities 'delivered a tangible and substantial benefit' to the urban customers and 'were visibly fulfilling their sworn duty to serve their communities as good regents.'⁶²

By the middle of the eighteenth century, Vienna's assize system was relatively similar to the Dutch way of *broodzetting*.⁶³ Institutionally, the city council assumed sole authority over the assize system around 1690. Over the course of the following

---

56. de Vries, *Price of Bread*, 84. Italics original.

57. Foucault, *Sicherheit, Territorium, Bevölkerung*, 40–2, 73, 75–6.

58. Kaplan, *Bakers of Paris*, 508; de Vries, *Price of Bread*, 65, 22.

59. For description of the older system of calculation see de Vries, *Price of Bread*, 35–6, 58–60.

60. Werner Berthold, 'Brotsatzungen – Weizenpreis und Brotgewicht in Wien und Niederösterreich vom Spätmittelalter bis um 1600', *Jahrbuch für Landeskunde von Niederösterreich* NF 72, no. 74 (2006–8), 33–5.

61. Pribram, *Materialien*, 797–8, 805–8.

62. de Vries, *Price of Bread*, 60–2.

63. Berthold, 'Brotsatzungen', 27, 34–6.

years, the municipal authorities expanded the mechanisms and regulations that would remain the frameworks of price surveys and calculations until the assize's dissolution in 1849/60.[64] By the eighteenth century, aspects of that improved way of price-setting had been adopted to varying degrees in other parts of the continent like Belgium, England or Prussia and less so in France.[65] Considering the milieu of grain, the improved way of price setting was much more sensitive to the various factors along the commodity chain that shaped bread and its prices. Reconsidering and improving the assize security mechanism thus implicated an enormous surge of administrative efforts to arrive at suitable information to calculate bread prices. Cities adopting these changes

> took upon themselves a significant new administrative burden, which included itemizing and measuring the admissible constant costs, drafting the new price schedules, and establishing the true yield from a measure of grain. In return for this effort they secured a tangible benefit: by tethering the bakers to a fixed amount of revenue to defray their constant costs, the bread price rose less rapidly […] than the grain price.[66]

To arrive at suitable prices for both bakers and consumers to subsist in times of abundance and scarcity, royal and urban governments needed to gain and negotiate expertise on a number of interlocked key issues of the bread trade. Involving 'tedious arithmetic and an ongoing commitment to monitoring the costs of baking' they had to systematize and regulate the natures, materials, techniques, people and procedures in question.[67] These acts of knowledge production remained constantly contested and fought over – 'however much the new system demystified bread pricing and established a rational basis for the price regulation, [officials] could never hope to remove their function entirely from the realm of debate and controversy.' In the last instance, settling the price of bread always 'involved some element of discretion and judgement and had the potential to spark controversy'.[68] Therefore, new-system bread prices were but the tip of the iceberg of complex and contested efforts to collect knowledge and introduce regulation on a wide range of socio-economic and natural-technical aspects regarding the trading, milling and eventually baking of grain and flour. Essentially, settling the price of bread required authorities to know and regulate both nature and the market in its societal embeddedness at the same time.

64. Opll, 'Versorgung Wiens', 52; Přibram, *Gewerbepolitik*, 454–5; Pribram, *Materialien*, 797–808.

65. de Vries, *Price of Bread*, 376–83; Kaplan, *Bakers of Paris*, 493–520; Miller, *Mastering the Market*, 35–40, 93–107; Christian Petersen, *Bread and the British Economy, c. 1770–1870* (Aldershot: Scolar Press, 1995), 97–124.

66. de Vries, *Price of Bread*, 60.

67. Ibid., 61.

68. de Vries, *Price of Bread*, 65.

Knowing and regulating nature and the market

As a crucial precondition to settle bread prices, Viennese authorities had to know how much flour a given quantity of grain would yield, and how much bread could be baked from that flour. Simply expressed – but cumbersome to achieve – officials had to establish the true bread yield of grain and flour. This represented a major task because it required four essential, albeit extensive intermediate steps.

For one, producers and administrators needed to establish the quality of grain, which decisively influences the amount and quality of flour and bread produced from it. Short-term fluctuations could affect the entire system of milling and baking, which made relatively regular observations of the material conditions of grain a necessity. Vienna's *Metzenleihamt* gave increasing attention to grain qualities and weights at least since the second third of the eighteenth century. Using a stonewalled vessel erected on the city's flour market, administrators, buyers and sellers could weigh out cereals and determine high-, medium- and low-quality standards.[69]

Second, the flour output of wheat and rye had to be tested. To determine the milling grade of wheat and rye, commissioners, millers and bakers would visit the first of two major laboratories of the trade, a mill. The choice of the laboratory, the procedure of milling and the results were themselves contested issues, especially between the three parties that all had very distinctive interests. The standards set through a trial would not only depend on the grain used but also on the mill's technological equipment, its techniques of grinding, the source and availability of power and the craftsmanship of the miller. Consequently, the representativeness of the mill and miller chosen always remained a matter of dispute that was often solved by choosing the 'neutral' ground of a mill belonging to an ecclesiastical institution. Therefore, milling trials were as much an issue of determining material and technical standards as they were a balancing of socio-economic interests.[70] Test millings in and around Vienna were conducted at least since the middle of the fifteenth century.[71] Usually multi-day events, clerks, millers and bakers would meet in the mill(s) chosen for trial, for example, in July 1769 under the auspices of

---

69. Pribram, *Materialien*, 800. The name *Metzenleihamt* derives from this agency's function in keeping and renting-out the city's official grain volume measure, the *Metzen*, containing 61.5 litres of grain.

70. For a detailed description see Kaplan, *Provisioning Paris*, chapter 6; Kaplan, *Bakers of Paris*, 508–15; on mills in and around Vienna, see Friedrich Hauer, Severin Hohensinner and Christina Spitzbart-Glasl, 'How Water and Its Use Shaped the Spatial Development of Vienna', *Water History* 8, no. 3 (2016); Christina Spitzbart-Glasl, 'Feste Wassermühlen und Schiffsmühlen als Bestandteil der Wiener Gewässerlandschaft', in *Donau-Stadt-Landschaften. Danube-City-Landscapes*, ed. Máté Tamáska (Berlin: LIT, 2016).

71. Pribram, *Materialien*, 798.

secretary Hägelin at Vienna's clerical-owned Dominicaner and Dorotheer mills.[72] Based on the results of such test millings, bakers, millers and authorities would constitute flour qualities and establish how much flour could be produced from a given quantity and quality of grain and would thus produce the first crucial information on which bread prices would eventually rest upon. Having settled that issue the amounts and qualities of bread that could be obtained from a given quantity of flour needed to be elaborated. Turning to bread production, this time the laboratory was a bakery.

Authorities and bakers needed to elaborate how much bread could be produced from a given quantity and quality of flour. This required urban authorities and bakers to 'organize more or less elaborate laboratory trials' in bakeries aimed to represent 'real-life conditions'.[73] Similar to production trials conducted in the mill, baking trials were equally complex issues. The bread yield would depend on material qualities, the baker's skills, the size and equipment of the workshop, other ingredients used, the baking processes and procedures adopted as well as the kinds of bread and rolls formed. Since the baker's profits were also elaborated during trials, they represented an extremely critical step for the entire structure of the baking trade on which both the survival of the city's bakers and the customers' access to cheap, good bread depended. Therefore, comparable to test millings, the details of baking try-outs remained controversial. Among the issues of dispute were the site of the trial; the technical representativeness of the bakery; the individual skills and credit of the master baker selected; the choice and ratios of flour, water, salt and herbs used; as well as the processes adopted to bake bread. Bakers and officials would often use the bakeries of ecclesiastical or military facilities as more or less neutral ground, though bakers continued to protest about 'artificial, unrepresentative, and unrealistic' conditions in such institutions.[74] Moreover, since these 'laboratory reports' were attempts by the authorities to 'demystify' baking and to 'turn art into science', bakers usually had a keen interest not to share their intimate knowledge on bread production which usually gave them an important advantage in negotiating the material and financial conditions of their craft with city officials.[75] Consequently, rather than representing 'neutral' material and technical standards, test bakings constituted a lowest common denominator between the interests of the authorities and those of the bakers.[76]

Finally, what remained to be done was to establish the costs of these processes. Knowing nature was only one of two crucial steps to determine bread prices.

---

72. Wiener Stadt- und Landesarchiv, Alte Registratur A2 – Berichte: 210/1770, 29.07.1769: N.Ö. Regs. Secretär Hägelin. Nota Die von mir Endes gefertigte aufgetragener Massen abgeführte Mahl- und respective Back Probem betreffend.

73. Kaplan, *Bakers of Paris*, 508.

74. de Vries, *Price of Bread*, 73.

75. Ibid.

76. For a Vienna baking trial, see Bäckerinnung, *Protocollum 1807–1830*, 28–9.

2. Institutions of Embeddedness 59

Knowing the market, that is, the prevalent market prices of grain, the costs of milling and the expenses required to turn flour into bread was equally important. To settle the prices of various bread rolls and loaves authorities needed to know the expenditures that went into bread production. From the baker's point of view these included market prices of grain or flour, the baker's actual expenditures of running a bakery, hiring labour, purchasing ingredients and expenditures to make ends meet. Consequently, these costs were as much an issue of surveying as they were subject to detailed negotiations between producers and authorities.

As the basis of the entire structure, the system-relevant market price of grain – be it local, regional, national or in some cases even international – had to be established and continuously documented, requiring authorities to create extensive institutions of market oversight and price collection. Similar to their Dutch, French or English counterparts, the collections of market prices constituted the absolute fundament of the Viennese *Satzungen* and represented a 'flexible indicator answering market conditions' that were captured by urban authorities since the 1400s.[77] From 1691, the city council continuously collected wholesale and retail grain and flour prices and reported them to the provincial government; since 1727 reports were submitted on a monthly basis. Showing the authorities' investedness in market procedures, these grain protocols documented all purchases on any market day, listing the names of sellers and buyers, individual contract volumes and the kinds of cereals purchased as well as prices. Since 1727, weekly surveys on transactions beyond official market days including volumes and prices were added. The same protocols were kept for flour so that grain and flour prices could be used interchangeably as the basis for assize calculations, though this remained a contested question among authorities, bakers and millers.[78]

While at first limited to the city's own marketplace, in 1708 price observations were extended to the surrounding markets of Stockerau, Fischamend and Mistelbach to mitigate local fluctuations. Between 1731 and 1736, the market of Langenlois was also consulted, that of Himberg in 1734/5, Bruck an der Leitha was added during 1776–9 and Großenzersdorf's grain market was implemented between 1802 and 1835. All these adaptions mirror the system's reaction to short- and medium-term market changes and highlight the city's regional supply system during much of the eighteenth century. By the early 1800s, Vienna's *Metzenleihamt* continued to require millers and bakers to deliver receipts of daily grain purchases on those markets. These receipts provided the bureau with comprehensive, though likely not perfect information on market transactions.[79] Based on this extensive gathering of documentation and information the official administrators would establish a week's highest, medium and lowest price for wheat, rye, barley and

---

77. Pribram, *Materialien*, 797, 809. See also Berthold, 'Brotsatzungen'.
78. Berthold, 'Brotsatzungen'.
79. See e.g. Wiener Stadt- und Landesarchiv, Hauptregistratur A24, Dep. G – Marktsachen, 1812. Schachtel 1.

oats. They also noted such prices for various flour qualities.[80] With the collection of either figure authorities effectively established how much a baker needed to spend on flour, the main ingredient and expenditure to bake bread. The last effort required was to determine the baker's costs of turning flour into bread, or rather, the expenses allowed to be included into the price of bread.

Usually settled for longer periods until changes in the economic situation required a revision, negotiating the expenses represented a final major issue of conflict between administrators and bakers. The 'true' costs of bread production were negotiated in the baking trials, during which authorities not only collected knowledge of the natural-technological, but also on the economic aspects of baking by surveying the costs of several main components: excise taxes, the costs for non-grain ingredients like fuelwood, salt, milk, yeast or herbs, labour expenses such as employees' wages, rent and, importantly, the baker's fee. This fee was 'intended to compensate the baker for all labour costs and for the capital value of the bakery' and basically represented the master baker's remuneration to make a living.[81]

Determining these expenditures was as crucial to the entire system as using correct market prices, and bakers and administrators continued to haggle about the circumstances of trials. Both parties might hold very different opinions on what changes in market conditions were sufficient to hold a trial and adapt the system of bread prices and baker's fees. In times of rising prices and costs, bakers were quick to demand a revision of the costs and fixed profits allotted to them while urban officials might choose to delay adaptions to grain market changes for a short time to cushion consumers from very high prices. Conversely, officials might defer to lower the calculated costs after the crisis was over to compensate bakers for the losses suffered.[82]

Equally important as the timing of adjusting the cost calculations was the general composition of the list of expenses allowed into the account. Deliberately excluding important factors and thus setting costs very low would reduce prices for customers but undermine the bakers' subsistence, which might even threaten the inhabitants' access to a bakery. In contrast, setting costs higher than necessary would make bread more expensive.[83] Consequently, establishing the costs of bread making and 'setting the baking fee was not simply an innocent or purely technical activity; a larger public policy objective – or set of possibly conflicting policy goals – was affected by this decision'.[84] Including policy goals and interests like low bread prices, ready access to bakeries, a certain range of products as well as high food quality standards 'the bread price commissioners not only affected the wellbeing of consumers, they affected the very economic fate of a large, organized

---

80. Pribram, *Materialien*, 193–4.
81. de Vries, *Price of Bread*, 180.
82. Miller, *Mastering the Market*, 39.
83. de Vries, *Price of Bread*, 184.
84. Ibid., 184.

artisanal group' consisting not only of bakers, but of their families, employees and a number of ancillary trades and services.[85]

Therefore, determining appropriate bakery expenses was crucial to the entire bread supply of the city. Similar to their Dutch counterparts Viennese authorities and bakers negotiated and elaborated an artificial 'medium-sized' bakery with the objective to model an average business that would represent the baker's guild in its entirety.[86] Obviously, this involved not only detailed observations but also persistent negotiations of the expenses bakers could include into the costs of baking, which would affect their overall profitability. Moreover, like millers and milling try-outs, bakers did have a keen interest to inflate these theoretical production costs and thus drive up bread prices in order to profit from expenses that were lower in reality. Meanwhile, authorities aimed to keep estimates balanced.[87] In essence, the average bakers' expenses elaborated and negotiated represent a compromise between bakers and commissioners rather than a 'real life' bakery in operation.

The just price of bread

Eventually, having collected complementary knowledge on nature and the market, authorities could finally settle bread prices. They now knew what general costs of bread making needed to be divided among which amounts of bread. In Vienna a system prevailed that determined variable weights at standardized prices. While concealing small weight variations to consumers, this way of price setting represented a 'crude form of rationing, common all over Europe'.[88] Since cash wages tended to remain stable over long periods, with fixed prices and variable weights the consumers' ability to purchase fixed-price loaves at the expense to eat less was ensured under this system. More importantly, according to Jan de Vries selling fixed-price bread was inherently connected to the monetary system of early modern cities and states. In systems of moving prices, small changes in grain prices could hardly be expressed accurately in bread prices because they would have corresponded to fractions of the smallest coin in circulation. This was a very impractical solution as only larger changes in grain prices could be implemented into whole-coin modifications of the costs of bread, leading to a constant over- or underpricing of loaves and rolls. In reality, 'only the largest loaves were sold at prices sufficiently high to allow their price to vary promptly by whole units of the smallest coins as grain prices changed'. Therefore, 'early modern societies resorted to weight-variable bread pricing in order to adjust the price of bread to changing grain prices with an accuracy that exceed the practical limits of the circulating coinage. […] The loaves varied by weight because weight could be adjusted more

---

85. Ibid., 186.
86. Ibid., 199.
87. Ibid., 183, 190–200.
88. Ibid., 31.

readily than price to small fluctuations in the price of grain.'[89] Simply put, a rise in market prices for grain would be expressed in diminished bread weights and vice versa.

Although probably more exact to calculate, setting weights instead of prices created the problem that bakers needed to implement very small changes in bread weights at small price variations, resulting in a very inconvenient practical solution for producers. Therefore, authorities tended to adapt assize weights only at certain intervals of grain price changes to simplify procedures and to allow bakers certain weight ranges within which their products had to move.[90] In Vienna, the prices for standard assize Mundsemmeln, ordinari Semmeln, Pohlenbrot and rye bread were fixed while these products' weights would vary with market prices of grain. For example, in the assize calculated during a baking trial in 1805 the price of Mundsemmeln and ordinari Semmeln was fixed at one Kreuzer per piece while loaves of coarse wheat Pohlen and rye bread would cost three and six Kreuzer, respectively. A stable system, these prices changed only rarely and remained constant over decades until the systems' abolishment, except for minor changes in periods of crisis.[91]

While authorities thus calculated bread weights instead of prices, the actual sizes and weights of various rolls and bread loaves differed decisively for the more expensive products were baked into smaller units. Therefore, in practice average costs needed to be divided not into a general across-the-board yield of average production figures but into the differing amounts of different individual products the bakers were required to produce. As a consequence of the need to divide the total costs over a range of various products, like urban authorities in other parts of the continent, Vienna's *Metzenleihamt* ran complicated and complex catalogues of bread price calculations which 'listed all the possible prices for grain, and indicated the corresponding rates for which bread loaves could be sold'.[92] 'At every grain price, the city magistrates calculated the number of loaves into which the [amount] of bread dough was to be divided in order to generate revenue equal' to the total production costs.[93] These calculations provided Vienna's *Metzenleiher* with detailed instructions how much a piece of what kind of bread would weigh at which grain prices, and to what extent weights needed to be altered for every one-Gulden-change in grain prices.[94] These sources reveal a third factor that, though largely hidden in this complex system, probably represented the most important asset of the moral economy system of assize prices: cross-subsidization.

When allocating the total costs of baking over a range of diverse products in order to settle their weights Vienna's early nineteenth-century bread

---

89. Ibid., 32.
90. Ibid., 35.
91. Pribram, *Materialien*, e.g. 381ff.
92. Miller, *Mastering the Market*, 36; de Vries, *Price of Bread*, 34.
93. de Vries, *Price of Bread*, 34.
94. See e.g. Bäckerinnung, *Protocollum 1807–1830*, 30–8.

commissioners followed a practice similar to one conducted in the Netherlands before the abolishment of the *broodzetting* system in 1855.[95] As central feature of cross-subsidization, the authorities would distribute the sum of production costs and the baker's fee unequally over the various assize products. At the core of this procedure higher-quality wheat products became relatively more expensive to refinance lower prices settled for rye bread. With this measure,

> the regulatory regime shifted a portion of the joint production cost onto the consumers of wheat bread by burdening the price of such bread with a larger portion of the costs of general bakery operation. Correspondingly, they removed some of that burden from the consumers of rye bread. [...] Wheat consumers paid for a part of the cost of producing rye bread, allowing the latter to be sold at a lower price than would otherwise have been the case.[96]

While this was a common practice in the Dutch Republic the assize prices settled in 1805 in Vienna highlight that a very similar mechanism was in place in the capital of the Habsburg Empire.[97] By allocating losses on the production of rye bread and cross-subsidizing the baker's earnings on wheat rolls and thus allowing the bakers a larger profit on high-end products, reductions in the weight of rye bread loaves, the 'stuff of life' for most of the urban consumers, were prevented. As a core purpose of the moral economy assize this core function shifted costs from poorer to better-off consumers who directly subsidized larger rye bread loaves. In so doing, Vienna's bread price supervisors 'used their regulatory authority to advance a public purpose: in assigning the [...] costs for wheat and rye they acted to reduce the price of rye bread at the expense of wheat bread'. Comparable to policies in Dutch towns of Kampen, Amsterdam or Rotterdam, 'they kept the baker's fee for rye bread low' and 'sought to compensate the bakers for these unremunerative fee levels by raising the baker's fee for wheat bread. [...] Nearly everywhere, the regulatory regime defined the non-grain costs attributable to the production of wheat bread in such a way that it cost far more' than it would have without the measure to subsidize rye bread consumption.[98] In Vienna and various French cities such as Caen or Rouen alike 'this meant that there were higher profits overall to be made on white loaves in comparison to "working class" loaves. Thus, wealthier customers paid more per pound for bread than the poor' and the price systems 'were structured to transfer the weight of rising grain prices progressively onto those more prosperous consumers. [...] All of this cushioned the poorest consumers from the worst effects of rising grain prices.'[99] This way, as comprehensive disciplinary mechanisms, 'assize price policies were in harmony

---

95. de Vries, *Price of Bread*, 224–48.
96. Ibid., 209.
97. See e.g. Bäckerinnung, *Protocollum 1807–1830*, 30–8.
98. de Vries, *Price of Bread*, 246, 248.
99. Miller, *Mastering the Market*, 37–8.

with the requirements of justice and the common good [...]; while controlling food prices helped to preserve the governing hierarchy, peace, and order [...] the assize of bread kept prices to a minimum for [poor] consumers, but also enabled producers and traders to maintain a "reasonable" livelihood'.[100]

Therefore, these vast efforts to regulate the selling and buying of bread in Vienna represented the results of magistrate policies to create a 'landscape of municipal food access'.[101] While this process remained a complicated, complex and partly messy struggle between authorities, corporations, individuals, families and networks over rights and resources with many infringements against restrictions of production and retail, the political direction of the bread infrastructure was nevertheless a comparatively straightforward policy of disciplinary measures that managed to adapt the bread market to the needs of a growing city.

---

100. Davis, 'Baking for the Common Good', 495.
101. Baics, *Feeding Gotham*.

Chapter 3

THE MUNICIPAL LANDSCAPE OF BREAD, 1790s–1859

'A population of 300,000 would be supplied by and thus be depended on only 70 bakers in Vienna with regard to their prime needs, that is flour and bread', *Metzenleiher* Wolfgang Sittenberger summarized one baker Johann Maria's extensive proposal for a regulative assize reform by the late 1820s, which also included a reduction of the number of bakers in the capital from 185 to 70 in 1829. 'What if some bakers do not have enough flour in case of an emergency?', the chief official responsible for the city's bread supply asked remembering the French siege and occupation in 1805/6 and 1809. In any case, he continued, 'since the population is rather growing than decreasing, the opening of new bakeries needs to be ensured at all times'. Then, Sittenberger cautioned, 'if the numerous residents of the capital were supplied by only 70 bakers', this would mean the 'elimination of all competition' among bread producers and surrender the customers into the hands of monopolistic producers.[1]

Metzenleiher Wolfgang Sittenberger's opinion in this case was surely a particular answer to a specific question asked during the very late 1820s and early 1830s. However, to some degree his answers represent the mainstream of the magistrate's policy towards the bread infrastructure during the late eighteenth and the first half of the nineteenth centuries. Ensuring continuous and steady access to bread for a quickly growing population as well as keeping up a certain level of competition among bakers to prevent monopolies somewhat outweighed the officials' other concern – providing bakers with a reasonably and reliably profitable income. Before the liberalization of mid-century, accelerating population growth and urbanization proved to be a major impetus of change to the system of a regulated municipal bread infrastructure. Vienna had already witnessed high rates of population growth since the military conflicts with the Ottoman Empire had ended by the early 1700s and grew particularly quick during the century after the Seven Years' War. While around 175,000 inhabitants had called the capital their home

---

1. Wiener Stadt- und Landesarchiv, Hauptregistratur A24, Dep. G – Marktsachen, 1829, Schachtel 19, 04.05.1829: Wolfgang Sittenberger. Schriftliche Aeusserung des gehorsamsten Metzenleiheramte Uiber den Vorschlag des Bürgers Johann Maria hinsichtlich eines neuen Mehl und Gebäck-Satzungs Regulatives für die kais.könig. Residenzstadt Wien.

by the 1750s, some 190,000 people crowded the city's streets two decades later. Slowed down by the Napoleonic Wars, growth recommenced after 1815, driven largely by immigration. By 1820, Vienna's population stood at about 260,000 and the city was among the continent's quickest-growing agglomerations. Growth continued throughout the *Vormärz* era; by the late 1850s, when liberalization was introduced broadly, the Habsburg capital counted more than 500,000 residents and represented the largest European agglomeration after London and Paris.[2] Therefore, before the large-scale political reorganization of the supply system came to affect Vienna's municipal landscape of bread provision after 1860, like in New York City population growth and urbanization presented an eminent need to adapt the infrastructure to the demographic development.[3]

How did the regulated landscape of bread production change facing the drastic population growth of the decades between the 1770s and 1850s? Was the regulated municipal system able to adapt to these challenges, and what would be its legacies when it was abolished around 1860? The development of the numbers of guild bakeries highlights that Vienna's magistrate satisfied that need and continually raised the numbers of licensed guild master bakers throughout the century after the 1770s.[4] While around 124 guild bakers had held shop in the urban area

---

2. Jonas M. Albrecht, 'The Need for Wheat. The Pre-Industrial Expansion of Vienna's Grain Supply, 1800-1840', in *Stocks, Seasons and Sales: Food Supply, Storage and Markets in Europe and the New World, C. 1600-2000*, vol. 17, ed. Wouter Ronsijn, Niccolò Mignemi and Laurent Herment (Turnhout: Brepols Publishers, 2019), 106; Andreas Weigl, *Demographischer Wandel und Modernisierung in Wien* (Wien: Pichler, 2000), 53-6.

3. See Jonas M. Albrecht, '„Das Ringen des Freihandels mit dem Prohibitivsystem". Politische Ökonomie und Infrastruktur der Brotversorgung Wiens, 1815-1847', *Österreichische Zeitschrift für Geschichtswissenschaften* 30, no. 2 (2019), 81.

4. The analysis is based on Vienna's official guild registers, which include only a certain, though arguably the most important part of bread producers and retailers negotiating the city's landscape of bread. Therefore, only guild members, licensed bakers as well as registered retailers and intermediaries are covered in the following sections. Illicit producers, interlopers and others acting on the fringes or outside these official infrastructures largely evade capture and this kind of investigation. Moreover, the city's central marketplaces are also not covered. The role of marketplaces has been intensely researched, especially in the British context. See e.g. the classic David Alexander, *Retailing in England during the Industrial Revolution* (London: Athlone Pr, 1970). More recent studies partly contesting Alexander include Ian Mitchell, *Tradition and Innovation in English Retailing, 1700 to 1850: Narratives of Consumption* (London: Taylor and Francis, 2016); Robyn S. Metcalfe, *Meat, Commerce and the City: The London Food Market, 1800-1855* (London: Routledge, 2016); Jon Stobart and Ilja van Damme, 'Introduction: Markets in Modernization. Transformations in Urban Market Space and Practice, c. 1800-c.1970', *Urban History* 43, no. 3 (2016), 358-71; Jon Stobart and Lucy Bailey, 'Retail Revolution and the Village Shop, C. 1660-1860', *The Economic History Review* 71, no. 2 (2018). See also Emma Hart, *Trading Spaces: The Colonial Marketplace and the Foundations of American Capitalism* (Chicago: The University of Chicago Press, 2019).

within the *Linienwall* by 1775 the city listed 138 in 1793. Two decades later, 161 guild bakers supplied the participants of the Congress of Vienna; there were 175 masters in 1827; 186 by 1833; 198 in 1840; 214 before the March Revolution and 229 in 1854. By the late 1850s, the figure surpassed the 250-mark.[5] Although slowed down by a royal order to halt the granting of new licences in various trades during the early 1830s, roughly twenty new permits were granted per decade between 1815 and 1850.[6] This policy of expanding the baker's trade from above was met with lasting resistance from the guild throughout the entire period. In the words of their early twentieth-century archivist 'the guild lodged appeals against every new business license', for example, in 1819 against one Martin Weickart of Nr. 60 An der Wien, whose permit was actually withdrawn after exhaustive negotiations.[7] Yet, Weick(h)art was again listed a master baker in the same area by 1827 and continued to appear in the guild registers at least into the late 1840s, illustrating that in the medium and long run the urban authorities pushed through their policy of expanding the bread infrastructure against guild resistance.[8] By 1860, compared to 1775 the authorities had about doubled the numbers of guild bakeries steadily and almost held pace with the growth of the urban population inside the *Linienwall*, which increased approximately by the factor 2.4. Consequently, while each stationary bakery in Vienna had catered on average about 1,700 residents during the last third of eighteenth century, this hypothetical ratio approached approximately 2,000 customers per workshop in the middle of the nineteenth century and thus maintained a relatively steady relation between the population and the stationary guild infrastructure of baking.

While these average numbers of residents per baker allow only for a limited assessment of the performance of the municipal landscape, an analysis of how that increase of guild master bakeries between the 1770s and 1850s played out spatially yields better-suited results to answer that question. What patterns can be observed

5. Sources: Wienbibliothek im Rathaus, A-83171: Hans Rotter. Die Wiener Bäcker von 1400 bis 1814; Wiener Stadt- und Landesarchiv, Marktamt A2/1: Bäckergewerbe: Dekrete, 1793. Verzeichnis der gesamt-hiesigen Bäcker und Ausweiß wie viel jeder derselben an monathlichen Mehlvorrath haben soll; Archiv der Bäckergenossenschaft in Wien: Innung der bürgerl. Bäckermeister in der k.k. Haupt- und Residenzstadt Wien. Kalender für das Gremium der bürgerl. Bäckermeister in der k.k. Haupt- und Residenzstadt Wien 1815, 1827, 1833, 1840, 1847, 1854; 1858; *Bericht der Handels- und Gewerbekammer für das Erzherzogthum Oesterreich unter der Enns an das k.k. Ministerium für Handel und Volkswirthschaft über die Verkehrsverhältnisse des Kammerbezirkes in den Jahren 1857 bis 1860* (Wien, 1861), Table I, 238-9.

6. See Albrecht, 'Ringen des Freihandels', 81.

7. Landesinnung der Wiener Bäcker, ed., *700 Jahre Wiener Bäcker-Innung* (Wien: Verlag der Wiener Bäcker-Innung, 1927), 43.

8. Bäckerinnung, Kalender, 1827, 1833, 1847. See also Albrecht, 'Ringen des Freihandels', 81-2.

regarding the urban topography against the background of a decisive numerical expansion of the bread infrastructure? How did the municipal landscape of food access unfold?

Geographies

Map 1 visualizes the expansion of Vienna's geography of bread production and retail between 1775 and 1847. For reasons of comprehensibility and comparability as well as for reasons of digital availability the stable map depicting the built-up structure of the city around 1820 fails to highlight the notable changes in the developed structures. Yet, the expansion of bakers across the urban fabric is evident. In this regard, Map 1 highlights three patterns that characterized the municipal landscape of bread during the late eighteenth and early nineteenth centuries: expansion, duration and centrality.

Regarding expansion, the municipal landscape of baking spread into the developing urban areas; all over town the new bakeries settled both along main streets – especially on the arterial roads leading into and out of the city – and followed the consolidation of established and the development of new residential, artisanal and commercial quarters. Like their colleagues on Landstraße high street, four masters opened new bakeries on the main street of Wieden parish to the south. Whereas by 1775 several bakers had clustered at the centre-near and centre-far ends of the road, the new bakeries provided shopping opportunities all along Wieden's high street for both passers-by and the growing number of residents in the neighbourhood. By 1815, along almost the entire length of the street the network of bakeries had grown so close that a bakery could be reached within a short walk from virtually all points of departure along the road. Equally, two bakers opened shop along both Gumpendorferstraße north and Margarethenstraße south of the Wien River. Other thoroughfares in the densely settled western suburbs had already boasted a relatively dense baking infrastructure when the last third of the eighteenth century began. Especially Mariahilferstrasse, connecting the city not only directly with Schönbrunn Palace but also with the important trade route running westwards, and Neustiftgasse, a thoroughfare that led commuters out of the city into Neulerchenfeld parish just outside the *Linienwall* famously described as the 'Holy Roman Empire's largest tavern', featured a close-knit network of bakeries.[9] These western parts of the city inside the *Linienwall* became the spectacular hubs of Vienna's developing silk industry, which occupied several tens of thousands of workers by the early 1800s. As the area was increasingly built up at the expense of agricultural plots from the first decade of the new century bakers also moved swiftly into these artisanal-residential areas. By 1815, six bakeries were opened alone in the area where until about a decade ago the namesake *Schottenfeld*

---

9. Karl Ziak, *Des Heiligen Römischen Reiches grösstes Wirtshaus: Der Wiener Vorort Neulerchenfeld* (Wien: Jugend und Volk, 1979).

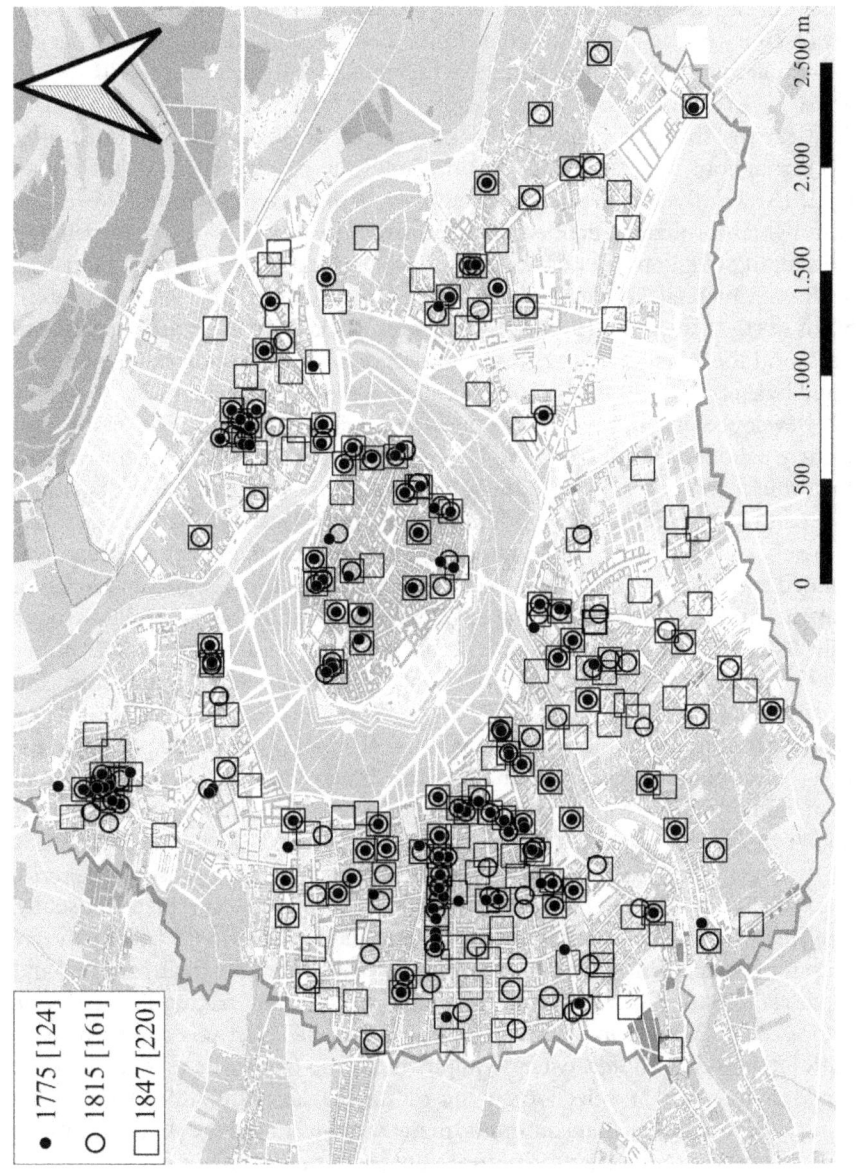

Map 1 Bakeries in Vienna, 1775–1847.[10]

10. Sources: Bäckerinnung, Kalender, 1775, 1815, 1847.

had been used as a major source of urban agricultural production. Thus, at the time of the Vienna Congress a quite close-knit comprehensive network of bakeries covered this part of town, too. Usually, a baker could be reached within just a few walking minutes. A similar expansion of the municipal landscape of bread production can be observed in the parishes of Michelbeuern to the northwest and those of Thury in the north as well as in the Leopoldstadt district east of the old town and across the Danube channel, where bakers clustered in the old suburb centres.

The expansion of the municipal landscape of bread access continued after 1815 throughout the Vormärz period. Granting nearly sixty more licences after 1815 and thus increasing the number of bakers by a third, the urban government thoroughly directed the infrastructure's extension into expanding or developing neighbourhoods across the city. Especially the hubs of population growth, commercial activities and housing construction such as the western suburbs north of the Wien River or the parishes marked-off by Belvedere palace to the east and the Wien River in the north saw a decisive expansion in the numbers of guild bakers. There, eighteen bakeries alone were founded until 1847 to supply newly developed quarters like *Elisabethviertel* bordering the *Linienwall* just east of Belvedere palace. Expansion can also be observed in Leopoldstadt parish northeast of the Danube Canal branch or in the suburbs of Althan and Thury at the northern fringe of the agglomeration while the number of bakeries in the old town city centre rose only slightly. Strikingly, while the regulated landscape of bread was expanded into the quickly growing suburbs after 1775, the number and location of bakeries in the very centre of the agglomeration within the city walls changed hardly. As the number of the residents of the old town steadily hoovered just above 50,000 after the 1770s, the number of twenty-four bakers was not increased but held steady.

While expansion was one of the major forces producing the municipal landscape after 1775, duration represented another key dimension in the old town and in the surrounding suburb parishes. In the city proper, almost no spatial changes in the geography of existing bakeries occurred between 1775 and 1815, and the same is largely true for the agglomeration's entire area. Though some bakeries moved, albeit typically not far, very few sites were abandoned completely. Usually, where there had been a bakery by the former date, there would be one by the latter point in time. This might not be very surprising given the legal, artisanal and commercial circumstances of running a bakery. *Radizierte* baking licences were tied to specified houses, and bakeries themselves needed relatively comprehensive facilities like storage rooms, ovens, equipment and so forth. Then, as bakers were inclined to maintain, or indeed to purchase a stable relationship to customers that was partly secured by spatial continuity, many short-term changes in the locations of larger numbers of bakeries seem unreasonable in the first place.

The third citywide pattern, centrality, is understood as the occupation of shop locations that were arguably central to everyday life and movements of people across the city in social, cultural or economic terms. By the notion of centrality, or rather, central places, historians have adopted Walter Christaller's central place theory on city networks for the urban space in order to 'study the spatial patterns of commercial activities within cities'.[11] Central place theory applied on the locational patterns of different kinds of market activities assumes different levels of centrality according to the economic reach or range of a product – i.e. the maximum distance consumers are willing to travel – and the conditions of entry or threshold requirement – that is the minimum demand needed to keep a business profitable in a specific location. In this regard, central place theory distinguishes between two kinds of commodities: convenience and comparison goods. Whereas the former are relatively cheap, bought frequently as often as daily, the latter are more expensive and bought occasionally. Consequently, the theory's assumption holds, businesses selling comparison goods can supply a whole city while retailers catering basic needs cater smaller communities and neighbourhoods. Since bakers and other food retailers sell convenience goods par excellence – commodities for which consumers are not willing to travel larger distances daily – food vendors can be expected to disperse across the urban space due to the high demand and small range of their goods. They can be assumed to move near to customers, to seek to minimize competition, to disperse evenly and seek privileged locations within the urban fabric.[12]

The expansion of the municipal landscape until 1847 largely secured bakers' central locations for customers in the sense of a quite comprehensive dispersion of shops across the city, thus keeping distances for consumers to bakeries low. At the same time, bakers sought to occupy privileged spaces in the urban fabric as a business tactic. On the one hand, situated in direct vicinity of the k.k. Infantry barracks and of Vienna's infirmary declared General Hospital by Joseph II during the early 1780s, in 1815 bakers Valentin Nerber and Joseph Kreuzer presumably not only sold bread to doctors, visitors or patients of the hospital but might also have catered some of the military personnel next door – besides welcoming walk-in customers strolling down Alserstraße. On the other hand, situated off main street on the other roads of the neighbourhood various master bakers apparently chose business locations that offered some levels of centrality, too. Franz Stachler held shop on Piaristengasse facing the square in front of lavish Maria Treu Piarist Church. Meanwhile, a customer following the alley north would have found the bakeries of Joseph Kasimir and Johann Regenhart nearby, who both occupied workshops on street corners where traffic was likely most vivid.

While bakers could be found 'just' along streets, everywhere across town they would choose houses close to churches, on intersections and near traffic bottlenecks like bridges or the *Linienwall* city gates, and in positions that might

11. Gergely Baics, *Feeding Gotham: The Political Economy and Geography of Food in New York, 1790–1860* (Princeton, Oxford: Princeton University Press, 2016), 69. For other similar approaches, see e.g. Clé Lesger, 'Patterns of Retail Location and Urban Form in Amsterdam in the Mid-Eighteenth Century', *Urban History* 38, no. 1 (2011).

12. Baics, *Feeding Gotham*, 69–71; Jan de Vries, *The Price of Bread: Regulating the Market in the Dutch Republic* (Berkeley, CA: University of California Press, 2019), 194–5.

combine several aspects of centrality. For example, k.k. court purveyor Joseph Eberl, located on the corner of Strausgasse and elite Herrengasse, held shop directly vis-à-vis the Estates House of Lower Austria housing the province's estates general. There, his bakery was generally just a stone's throw away from the political centres of the realm like the k.k. Haus-, Hof- und Staatskanzlei or even Hofburg palace.[13] Less prominently, yet also attempting to maximize their levels of centrality, bakers Kurzmeyer and Eberl also occupied positions that where both close to institutions of daily life such as St. Rochus church and the market held on the namesake square.

Yet, bakery locations disagree with the assumptions of central place theory regarding the producers' seeking of monopolized places to minimize competition. Master bakers held shop in immediate vicinity of a competitor. Ludwig Beyerl and Nikolaus Willmy on Servitengasse in Althan parish directly competed in shops just opposite of each other. The same applies to Franz Keppler and Franz Held on the head of Ferdinandsbrücke connecting city centre and Leopoldstadt or to Michael Wagner and Michael Keppler at the *Linienwall* gates of busy Mariahilferstraße. In the old town, bakers Regenhart, Schimpf and Krehan all clustered in or around Schottenstift monastery at the northern fringe of the city centre. Whereas guild bakers thus occupied privileged places all over town, one very central space of the capital exhibited a striking lack of bakeries. No bakeshop could be found in the busy commercial core area of Stephansplatz, Graben, Fleischmarkt and Hoher Markt in the centre of the old town. While bakers were present in these streets' markets with many mobile stalls, they apparently avoided these streets as locations of proper shops.[14]

Continued durability as well as the bakers' choosing of central spaces remained key for the regulated landscape of bread. Generally, bakeries that had existed in 1775 or 1815 continued to serve their respective neighbourhoods by 1847. Like their predecessors, bread producers continued to pursue workshops located centrally in the urban fabric. Among the few newly founded bakeries in the city centre, Carl Gerber opened his rather noble shop behind *Peterskirche* to provide his elite customers with fresh rolls after services and with Christmas fruit bread and 'Leipzig stollen' during the winter season. Mentioned earlier, Martin Weickhart's bakery was just one hundred metres removed from Theater an der Wien, already a famous theatre and opera house by the early years of the nineteenth century. The only city guild baker outside the *Linienwall* by 1847, Joseph Stiechler secured an arguably favourable business location at the site of Vienna's Raaber Bahn railway station, opened in 1846.[15]

---

13. Eberl's business location retains some of its prominence until today; Vienna's famous tourist attraction Café Central is just next door.

14. See also Ferdinand Opll, 'Markt im Alten Wien', *Wiener Geschichtsblätter* 34, no. 2 (1979), 49–73.

15. See Albrecht, 'Ringen des Freihandels', 86.

3. The Municipal Landscape of Bread, 1790s–1859

By the end of the *Vormärz* period, Vienna's urban authorities had expanded the municipal landscape of bread into areas of development and increasing population density. At the same time, within the system heavily regulated by guild and assize that provided bakers with relatively solid incomes while compelling them to supply their customers at all times, the locations of bakeries remained stable in the central and already densely populated areas of the suburb parishes around the capital's old town centre. Some consumers would find a less comprehensive network of guild bakeries in some areas of the less densely inhabited parts of town, especially north and south of the city centre in spaces where aristocrat palaces continued to shape the urban fabric. In most neighbourhoods, however, a baker was just a short walk away, securing the residents' bread supply in terms of geographic accessibility. Analysing bakers' locations in the urban fabric and the territorial expansion of the municipal landscape of bread provision highlights the authorities' efforts to warrant a comprehensive network of bakeries across town that ensured close access points for residents almost everywhere in the city. However, the spatial analysis yields no information whether the municipal landscape of bakeries could satisfy the demand of customers in quantitative and qualitative terms. Did bakers offer enough and good bread, rolls and pasty to meet the demands of residents, shoppers and the authorities alike, and what changes can be observed over time?

Business structures

Part of these questions are almost impossible to answer. The production of bakery goods and the range of products a guild baker was allowed to bake and sell was regulated and monitored extensively by city and guild officials. Therefore, theoretically consumers all over town could expect to find a certain range of standard wheat bread and rye bread as well as finer roll products and qualities in every bakery in the city. Yet, individual differences in the qualities of bread and the adherence of bakers to quality standards set in the assize are impossible to analyse systematically over longer periods of time due to both the multiplicity and the lack of sources. On the one hand, there is an overall lack of relevant sources on what, how and how much Vienna's guild bakers produced actually; neither the guild archive nor the city archives hold systematic sources on bakery business figures or comparable documents, a problem other authors also face.[16] On the other hand, the guild registers pass down many instances of bakers' violations of quality requirements such as the case of one master baker Brendel who was publicly shamed at the pillory for repeated infringements of assize requirements in 1812. Several years later, on 12 October 1819, the magistrate fined no less than forty-seven guild bakers in one go for producing low-quality bread.[17]

---

16. See de Vries, *Price of Bread*, 191–201.
17. Landesinnung der Wiener Bäcker, *700 Jahre*, 43.

Yet, what can be approximated – at least to some extent – with the sources available is the matter of quantity and, though very roughly, the question of the assortment bakeries offered in different parts of town. Regarding the former, information on assigned trade taxes of about 1,000 bakers between 1828 and 1871 allows for a rough assessment of business sizes. As *Klassenerwerbssteuer*, throughout the entire period trade taxes were raised based on different tax classes. Tax officials estimated an artisan's annual business turnover and categorized her or him in lump-sum tax classes between 5 and 500fl. per annum.[18] Although these sources do not permit a direct assertion of a baker's turnover, they still allow for a broad estimation of the general scope of bakery operations across town and the differences between producers. Since the tax registers before 1852 are largely lost, the only sources available for tax information on the first half of the century are the *Grundbücher 1. Reihe*, started in 1852. Although fortunately recording 'all still existing' businesses, this source only offers very limited data on trade taxes before the late 1840s.[19]

The trade taxes assigned to several hundred bakers during approximately the second third of the nineteenth century paint a relatively clear picture that is not particularly different from the situation during the middle of the 1700s.[20] Throughout the 1830s, 1840s and 1850s, the lion's share of Vienna's tax paying bakers was categorized into medium tax classes. While around 1 per cent of the 340 cases documented paid the 5fl. tax levied on workshops currently not in operation, a tenth of the bakers was taxed with 30fl. or less, indicating rather small turnovers. Simultaneously, a full-blown 75 per cent was assigned between 40fl. and 80fl. of trade taxes per annum; most shops were situated at the lower end of this range. Another tenth of producers formed the baking elite paying 100fl. per year or more. On the lonely top stood two bakers taxed with 300fl. by the 1850s, respectively: k.k. court baker Anton Schachtner with his bakery in the city centre and Josef Mittermeyer, who ran a large industrial steam bakery that employed some thirty workers.[21] According to this data, most bakers remained small- and medium-sized businesses that likely produced roughly comparable quantities of baked goods arguably for neighbourhood customers and passers-by and, given the strong standardization of products and prices, competed in terms of quality rather

18. Andreas Weigl, 'Gewerbepolitik', in *Wien. Geschichte einer Stadt: Band 2. Die Frühneuzeitliche Residenz (16. bis 18. Jahrhundert)*, vol. 2, ed. Peter Csendes and Ferdinand Oppl (Wien/Kön/Weimar: Böhlau, 2003).

19. See the archive's source description regarding the *Erwerbsteuerbücher* more generally and the *Grundbuch 1. Reihe* in particular, available online through the archive directory at https://www.wien.gv.at/actaproweb2/benutzung/archive.xhtml (19.11.2020).

20. See Weigl, 'Gewerbepolitik'.

21. Source: Own calculations based on Wiener Stadt- und Landesarchiv, Serie 1.1.3.2.B1003 (prov.) alt: 301–307 – Erwerbsteuer: Grundbuch 1. Reihe 1828–1861. Erwerbsteuerbücher.

than quantity and prices. In any case, the data on assigned trade taxes remain only an indirect measure of bakers' turnovers. While indicating a rather balanced environment of relatively small- and medium-sized bakeries, the tax data largely fails to yield more detailed information about differences across the urban space in terms of quantities and qualities customers would find in the shops of bakers.

The broad although limited data on trade taxes can be supplemented with two most valuable sources that provide a rare glimpse into individual production numbers of Vienna's guild bakers. On the one hand, a comprehensive 1793 survey on the bakers' compulsory flour storages raised by the city's officials offers detailed information on 138 bakeries. On the other hand, a similar yet even more thorough survey was undertaken between *c.* 1855 and 1865 that investigated not only the guild bakers' obligatory flour stocks but also the number of ovens fired in each bakery as well as the numbers of journeymen and apprentices employed at that point in time.

As there are no enclosed documents or further information on both the 1793 and the 1855-65 registers it is impossible to tell to what extent bakers could report misleading or false numbers or to judge the margin of error handed down in these sources. Given the guild's extensive documentation of journeymen and apprentices, the numbers of workers reported might be rather trustworthy. However, if these sources were put together for reasons of taxation bakers might have attempted to underreport the numbers of ovens in operation as an indicator of overall production. Furthermore, the flour storages stated almost certainly did not represent a baker's actual turnover but rather a bottom-line stock he or she had to keep officially as a measure to prevent supply crises. Finally, neither can quality and handling differences regarding ingredients and work processes be assessed. Thus, while these sources also come with important limitations they are the only spotlights into the municipal landscape of bread on an individual basis throughout the late eighteenth and most of the nineteenth centuries.

Map 2 presents the compulsory flour storages reported for 138 guild bakers in 1793. It highlights significant differences in the raw material stocks held by bakers all over town. Generally, the amounts these artisans were obligated to keep each month ranged from as little as 4 Muth per month – roughly 2.5 tonnes – with the smallest producer to ten times that amount in the largest bakery, whose 45 Muth storage corresponded to approximately 27 tonnes per month. On average, a baker was bound to keep 8 tonnes of flour supplies as an emergency stock, the equivalent of probably about 10 tonnes of bakery products assuming an average flour-to-bread yield of 1.2.[22] However, while a bakery was only a few minutes

---

22. Archiv der Bäckergenossenschaft in Wien, HS 15: Innung der bürgerl. Bäckermeister in der k.k. Haupt- und Residenzstadt Wien. Protocollum uiber merkwürdige Gegenstände, als: Volksaufruhr gegen die Bäcker anno 1805; die den bürgl Bäckermeister geleisteten Vergütungen; mehrere Backproben; Consignation über die Ausgaben eines mitleren Bäckermeisters; dann der vom Jahre 1807 bis 1830 ergangenen Verordnungen und Rathschläge.

walking distance away from most places in town, consumers would find bakeries and bread shops of quite different sizes across the urban space. Comparable to the situation in the Netherlands, the overwhelming number of Viennese bakeries in 1793 remained rather small businesses arguably supplying a rather limited number of customers within a limited geographic range that would usually not greatly exceed neighbourhood boundaries and short walking distances.[23] Of the 138 shops, 48 held less than 10 Muth of flour, *c.* 6,000 kilograms per month or 200 kilograms per day.

By the early 1790s, these very small bread producers were to be found mainly in parts of the city under development such as the Schottenfeld close to the *Linienwall* in the western suburbs, still an agricultural area at that time, and the western suburbs as centres of immigration and population growth more generally. Especially in these parts of town, many bakers of that class settled on smaller north-south oriented neighbourhood alleys instead of the arterial roads. Meanwhile, sixty-two guild members ran medium-sized businesses with official flour stocks from 10 to 16 Muth, corresponding to between 6 and 10 tonnes a month. Exhibiting a somewhat different geographic profile, many of them could be found either in the city centre, along the major arterial streets of the city, in positions even more central for traffic such as on bridge heads or in areas where the larger roads ran into the *Glacis* dividing suburbs and old town. The same is true for the twenty-five bakers holding between 16 and 26 Muth of compulsory stocks each month – almost all of them could be found on main streets, in monopolistic positions or in the suburbs' core areas. Three bakeries championed the trade around 1793 holding stocks much larger than most of their counterparts. Two of them were located in the city's buzzing commercial und cultural centre. To its west end, Eva Eberlin represented the Eberl family, which held the title of a k.k. court baker. In the east, one baker Tratner occupied the bakery located in the vicinity of St. Stephen's Cathedral. Yet, both these workshops were bested in terms of flour stocks by the bakery occupied by one Karl Nagowitz in Gumpendorf parish to the southwest. Holding 45 Muth – 27 tonnes – per month, this was the largest guild bakery in town around 1793. Just next door of the *Hof-* or *Dorotheermühle*, one of the mills located along the Wien River, a close connection between bakery and mill might explain this workshop's high turnover. Therefore, while by 1793 most bakeries across town remained rather small- and medium-sized workshops consumers would nevertheless encounter notable differences in the quantities of bread and rolls offered by bakers. Whereas small shops prevailed in areas less developed, larger representatives of the trade usually settled on major roads and other central places where passers-by would raise the numbers of possible customers.

However, turnover measured as compulsory flour storages was not the only difference consumers would encounter at various bakers, the range of products

---

23. de Vries, *Price of Bread*, 196–9.

3. The Municipal Landscape of Bread, 1790s–1859

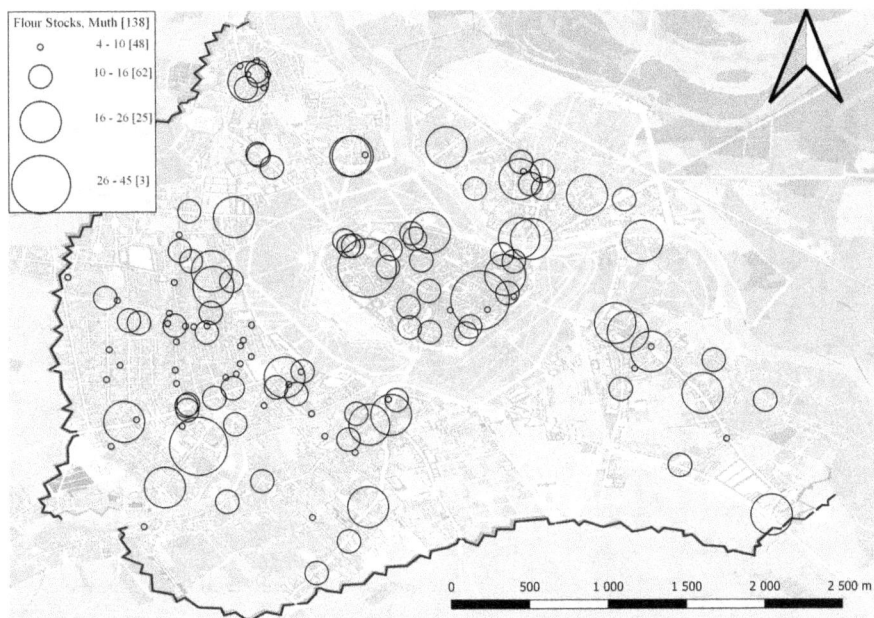

Map 2 Bakers' Compulsory Flour Stocks 1793, in Muth.[24]

and their qualities could equally be divergent as Maps 3 and 4 demonstrate. Categorizing stocks into the kinds of flour regulated under the assize, *Mundmehl*, *Semmelmehl*, *Pohlmehl* and rye flour, an even more detailed picture of the municipal landscape of provision by 1793 can be painted. Map 3 depicts a first distinction of these stocks in wheat and rye flour as share of the respective total stocks of each bakery. It highlights that most of Vienna's bakers at the close of the eighteenth century overwhelmingly used wheat flour as their main ingredient for bread production. Although some bakers held almost equal stocks of wheat and rye flour, most kept more of the former than the latter, partly close to 90 per cent. Especially those masters running shops in the city centre tended to process mainly wheat flour, and many of their counterparts in the suburb parishes did so, too; small masters stored more wheat as a percentage of their total stocks than larger producers did. Moreover, larger bakers located along the busy arterial high streets tended to stock more rye than bakeries that might rather have functioned as neighbourhood providers.

Since these were compulsory stocks that attempted to mirror consumer demand it can be argued that they represent the bakers' product ranges, at least to some degree. In any case, while individual differences are noticeable, there are

24. Verzeichnis 1793.

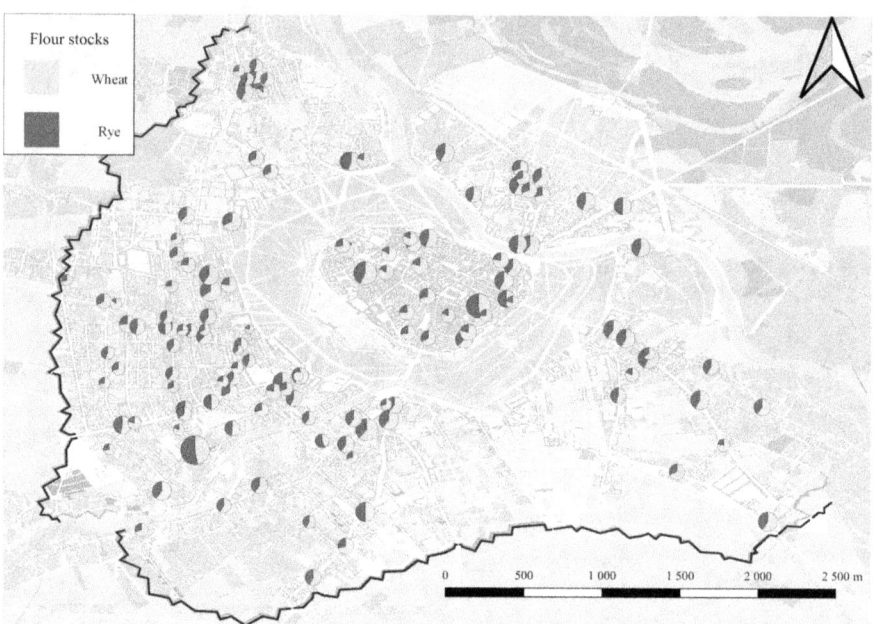

Map 3 Composition of Bakers' Flour Stocks, 1793.[25]

almost no disparities between different parts of the city. Whereas wheat and rye bread consumption surely remained a matter of income, it appears to have been no matter of space. Although bread production and quality will have been different between individual bakers, in all parts of town residents would find bakers predominantly selling products made of, or mainly made with, wheat.

Diving even deeper into the municipal landscape of bread at the close of the 1700s, Map 4 details the bakers' stocks into the four major types of flour distinguished by the assize as share of their respective total inventories. While it is not easy to distil a general image of the picture composed of 138 individual cases, some conclusions can be drawn nevertheless. For one, all bakers used amounts of rye flour that were often close to half of their stocks, or not much less. Where this was not the case, usage of *Pohlmehl*, the coarsest sort of wheat flour, usually increased as a share of overall stocks rather than the finest two kinds of wheat flour. In most bakeries across town the finest wheat *Mund-* and *Semmelmehl* represented roughly a quarter of stocks held. While differences can be observed elsewhere bakers in the city centre were most likely to deviate from this pattern. Producers in the city proper tended to use more fine sorts of flour; usually between one and two quarters of their stocks consisted of the top varieties.

25. Source: Verzeichnis 1793.

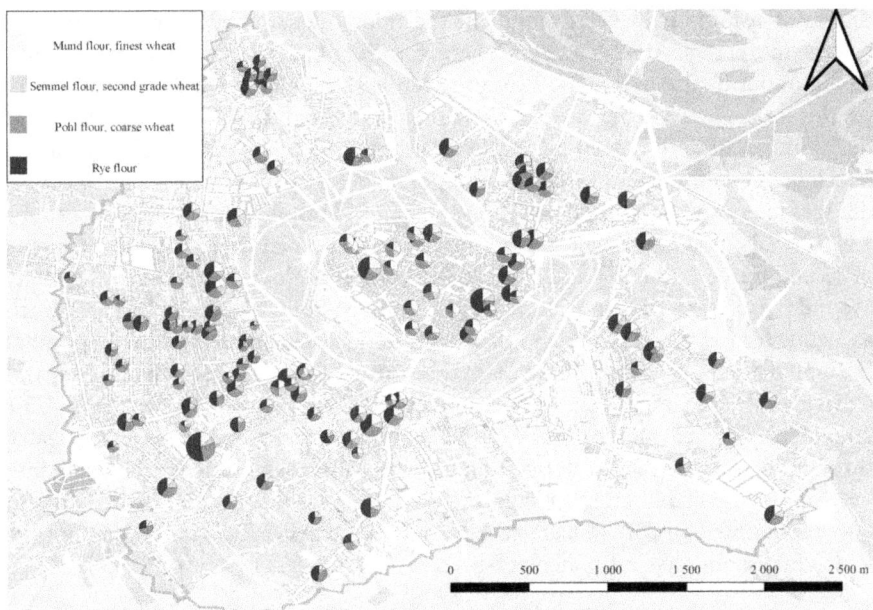

Map 4 Detailed Composition of Flour Stocks, 1793.[26]

We have seen earlier that the geographic expansion of the municipal landscape of bread across the capital of the Habsburg Empire since the late eighteenth century ensured a comprehensive network of bakeries covering most parts of the city. Yet, we have equally noted that the ratio between residents and bakers increased after 1848, from roughly 1,700 inhabitants per baker to approximately 2,000, and that bakeries differed in production volumes and, though to a lesser degree, in the composition of the sorts of flour used. Thus, while bakeries remained easily accessible in spatial terms in most parts of the city, on average guild masters had to satisfy the needs of a generally rising number of customers, and customers in developing parts of town might find rather smaller bakeries nearby. In the face of, hypothetically, rising numbers of consumers per bakery, could bakers satisfy the urbanites' increasing demand for bread? What patterns of development can be observed during the first half of the century besides the municipal landscape's spatial expansion?

Before turning to a visual analysis, a comparison of the amount and composition of obligatory flour stocks held by 138 bakers in 1793 and by 233 guild masters half a century later yields several important developments the municipal landscape of baking and the baker's trade underwent between both points in time. Illustrated in Table 1, between 1793 and 1857 the monthly flour stocks bakers were obliged to keep changed notably both in terms of quantity, composition and probably quality.

26. Source: Verzeichnis 1793.

The total volume held each month in the numerous storage rooms of Vienna's bakers more than doubled from slightly over 1,000 tonnes to approximately 2,600 tonnes by the latter date. Not only caused by the increase in the number of producers, on average the rise in flour stocks translated to a 30 per cent growth in the amounts of flour stored per bakery. Whereas a late eighteenth-century baker needed to keep some 8 tonnes of flour as an emergency supply their successors six decades later would maintain an average stock of 11 tonnes per month. Roughly, by 1793 the city's 138 guild bakers combined kept an annual emergency flour supply of 13,000 tonnes, almost half of the 30,000 tonnes of flour imported into the city around these years. In comparison, in 1857, the 233 guild members stored as much as 32,000 tonnes of wheat and rye flour in their facilities, still approximately half of the *c.* 60,000 tonnes of flour that passed the *Linienwall* gates into town in that year.[27] Corresponding to an average of 59 kilograms of flour per resident in 1793 and 67 kilograms sixty years later, these emergency supplies remained impressively stable throughout a time of quick population growth. Moreover, crudely translating into between 70 and 80 kilograms of bakery products per capita and annum, they might have represented more than half of the average urban per capita bread consumption, which historians have estimated at between 100 and 150 kilograms.[28]

Table 1 Compulsory Monthly Flour Stocks, 1793–1857

Year	1793			1857		
Bakers	138			233		
Total flour stocks	in Muth	in Tonnes	in %	in Muth	in Tonnes	in %
Wheat, finest	323	202	18	1,245	778	28
Wheat, middle	226	145	12	445	286	10
Wheat, lower	596	352	33	2,056	1,214	46
Wheat, subtotal	1,145	699	63	3,746	2,277	84
Rye	678	377	37	700	389	16
Total	1,823	1,075	100	4,446	2,666	100
Average monthly stock per baker	13	8		19	11	
Average annual stock per baker	159	94		229	137	

Sources: Wiener Stadt- und Landesarchiv, Marktamt A2/1: Bäckergewerbe: Dekrete, 1793. Verzeichnis der gesamthiesigen Bäcker und Ausweiß wie viel jeder derselben an monathlichen Mehlvorrath haben soll; Wiener Stadt- und Landesarchiv, Innungen und Handelsgremien 1/B1: Bäcker: Bücher. Bäckerverzeichnis 1.

27. See Albrecht, 'Need for Wheat'; see also Friedrich Hauer, ed., *Die Versorgung Wiens 1829–1913: Neue Forschungsergebnisse auf Grundlage der Wiener Verzehrungssteuer* (Innsbruck/Wien: StudienVerl., 2014).

28. See de Vries, *Price of Bread*, 310–33; Yves Segers, 'Oysters and Rye Bread: Polarising Living Standards in Flanders, 1800–1860', *European Review of Economic History* 5, no. 3 (2001), 320–1; Sabine Barles, 'Feeding the City: Food Consumption and Flow of Nitrogen,

However, while those compulsory stocks appear to have been raised to meet the rising (emergency) demand induced by urbanization it remains unclear if the increase in flour stocks also signals a growth in the production volumes of bakeries, which would probably have been needed to feed rising numbers of customers. In *Das Kapital*, Karl Marx was famously sceptic about the development of baking, which he thought had 'preserved up to the present a method of production as archaic, as pre-Christian' as no other industry.[29] Yet some evidence indicating a certain growth in the size of businesses can be drawn from the guild archives in order to tackle the question if the municipal landscape of bread was able to meet the rising demand of a growing urban population. The guild's official and extensive documentation of hired and discharged apprentices represents one of the few sources that allow at least a cautious estimate of the development of bakery sizes. Available until 1858, when the register was discontinued, this collection offers another profound insight into the working world of Vienna's bakers, documenting when, with which master and how long over 4,000 apprentices were trained. While this source would allow for a much more fine-grained analysis, Figure 1 is content to depict the annual numbers of apprentices starting their three-year training and those being discharged. Generally, apprentices would enter the trade each quarter-year, known as *Quatember* in contemporary language.

As Figure 1 indicates, the numbers of apprentices hired by Vienna's guild bakers grew significantly from the early 1840s, after a notable stagnation during the previous decade. Had the city's master bakers hired roughly between 70 and 120 boys during the late 1820s and 1830s, these numbers would have risen to 170 in the early 1850s and peaked at about 250 in 1854. Whereas an average baker had employed approximately 0.5 apprentices around 1824, that number had doubled three decades later. After 1840, more apprentices tended to stay on their jobs than during the previous twenty years. This observation would need closer attention to explain. It might point out several developments, such as increased need for and use of cheap labour by bakers, decreasing motivation or ability to take to the road as a journeymen during the 'hungry forties', or declining economic perspectives to find other employment. In any case, the rough analysis of apprentices employed with guild bakers suggests a rise in the number of workers in the city's bakeries that is supported by information on the number of journeymen working Vienna's ovens. Josef Ehmer has estimated that around 700 journeymen were employed by

---

Paris, 1801–1914', *Science of The Total Environment* 375, no. 1 (2007); David R. Ringrose, *Madrid and the Spanish Economy 1560–1850* (Berkeley, CA: University of California Press, 1983), 75; Albrecht, 'Need for Wheat', 109. According to estimates made by Vienna's chamber of commerce, around 1860 the city's inhabitants consumed around 100 kilograms of flour and pulses on average per annum. See Roman Sandgruber, *Die Anfänge der Konsumgesellschaft: Konsumgüterverbrauch, Lebensstandard und Alltagskultur in Österreich im 18. und 19. Jahrhundert* (Wien: Verlag für Geschichte und Politik, 1982), 137.

29. Cited in de Vries, *Price of Bread*, 358.

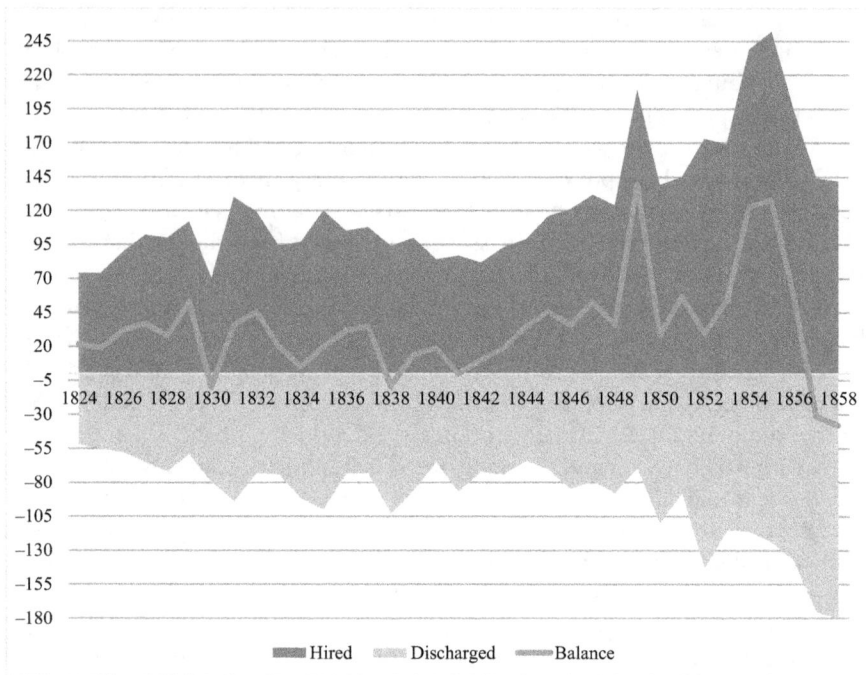

Figure 1 Hired and Discharged Apprentices by Vienna's Guild Bakers, 1824–58, per annum.
Source: Own calculations based on Archiv der Bäckergenossenschaft in Wien, HS 2: Innung der bürgerl. Bäckermeister in der k.k. Haupt- und Residenzstadt Wien. Aufding- und Freisprech-Protokoll 1824–1858.

the guild during the late 1830s; by 1857, 1,115 journeymen were counted in the *Bäckerverzeichnis*. Corresponding to a ratio of about three journeymen per baker at the earlier point in time, by 1857 a baker employed almost five labourers on average, thus also indicating a growth in the labour force employed to produce bread.[30]

Another factor to judge if bakers would have been able to cope with rising demand is technology. Technologic improvements in the processes of baking, especially regarding the preparation of the dough and the bakers' ovens, represented a possible key driver to improve a bakery's productivity and its daily turnover. Unfortunately, this issue is especially hard to grasp besides the prominent though solitary attempt to industrialize baking by Leopold Wimmer's founding of a steam bakery around 1848.[31] Following that example, several other steam bakeries were

30. Josef Ehmer, 'Produktion und Reproduktion in der Wiener Manufakturperiode', in *Wien im Vormärz*, ed. Renate Banik-Schweitzer, Forschungen und Beiträge zur Wiener Stadtgeschichte 8 (Wien: Jugend und Volk, 1980), 116; Wiener Stadt- und Landesarchiv, Innungen und Handelsgremien 1/B1: Bäcker: Bücher. Bäckerverzeichnis 1.

31. L.F., 'Die Erste Wiener Dampfbäckerei. Panem et Circenses', *Wiener Zeitung*, 19 January 1848, 19; *Fremden-Blatt*, 'Echtes Kornbrod', 10 January 1857, 7, 11.

planned – and some of them eventually constructed, although mostly since the early 1860s. Generally, like elsewhere, mechanization and industrialization of the baking trade remained an expensive and, given the comparatively low wages paid to bakery workers, often untenable option for most of the rather small- and medium-sized master bakers. They, in tandem with consumers, might even have met the application of machines to the food trade with scepticism rooted in their views on work culture and ethics, artisanal skills, honesty and, probably, product quality.[32] Reporting of early attempts to install coal-heated ovens by the turn of the century, chairman Roman Uhl celebrated the acceleration of endeavours to replace traditional ovens with industrial so-called *Kunstöfen* and the application of kneading machines since the 1860s.[33] Yet, Eben Norton Horsford continued to describe the intensive manual labour that still characterized baking by the early 1870s. Horsford knew the dough in Vienna's bakeries remained to be mixed 'with the aid of the naked hands and arms' and formed into small portions by hand in order to be inserted and taken out of the oven using 'the same long-handled, thin, flat, wooden shovel'. While ovens remained to be 'made of brick', there was 'nothing of complexity to challenge attention' about them, Horsford thought to continue 'the ovens in the city were built substantially on the same simple plan'. Fired 'eight times in the twenty-four hours with dry light wood', bakers had apparently resisted to replace wooden fuel with coal, which burns hotter than wood and therefore would require ovens differently constructed and the baking process to be adapted to both stoves and fuel, an issue the bakers were well aware of: 'Our ovens are not suited to be heated with coal, which also remains more expensive than firewood. [...] Firing with coal would necessitate refurbishing our ovens', baker Rudolf Plank argued when asked whether he would prefer one to the other in the 1870 *Enquête* concerning Vienna's food supply.[34] Detailing his concerns, the baker continued

32. Aaron Bobrow-Strain, 'White Bread Bio-Politics: Purity, Health, and the Triumph of Industrial Baking', *Cultural Geographies* 15, no. 1 (2008), 19–40; John Burnett, 'The Baking Industry in the Nineteenth Century', *Business History* 5, no. 2 (1963), 98–108; de Vries, *Price of Bread*, 201.

33. Roman Uhl, 'Brodbereitung', in *Beiträge zur Geschichte der Gewerbe und Erfindungen Oesterreichs von der Mitte des XVIII. Jahrhunderts bis zur Gegenwart*, ed. Wilhelm F. Exner (Wien: Wilhelm Braumüller, 1873).

34. k. k. Handelsministerium, *Enquête über die Approvisionirung Wiens: II: Theil, Lebensmittel (Ausgenommen Fleisch), Brennholz und Mineralkohle*, 2 vols. (Wien: Kaiserlich-königliche Hof- und Staatsdruckerei, 1871), 8, 12.

More generally, see Johann Carl Leuchs, Vollständige Brod-Bak-Kunde Oder Der Europäische Bäkermeister. Wissenschaftlich-Praktische Darstellung Der Bäkerkunst in Ihrer Größten Vollkommenheit und Nach Ihrem Zustande in Allen Ländern Der Welt (Nürnberg: C. Leuchs und Comp., 1832), 308–27; Jim Chevallier, *August Zang and the French Croissant: How Vienneroiserie Came to France* (North Hollywood, CA: Chez Jim Books, 2009).

to reason that 'coal produces too much soot spoiling the baked goods, it equally produces too hot a flame that would damage the oven construction quickly' and thus cause an increase of repair costs. Moreover, Plank added, 'our ovens cost 3, 4, or 500fl. [sic!] whereas a Wochenmeyer [coal-fired] oven is 2 or 3,000fl., and we don't know yet how long it lasts. Possibly, it needs to be refurbished in 1 or 2 years.'[35]

Therefore, this kind of finance-intensive technological improvement largely remained somewhat of an elite gimmick rather than a widespread opportunity for bakers to improve productivity. 'As promising as the increasing pursuit of mechanization in the baking trade is, the actual results remain unsatisfying', Roman Uhl reported from the 1867 Paris *Exposition Universelle* in his function as member of the jury of the Products of Bread and Cake Baking. 'All known industrial ovens produce too intense a heat, bake unevenly, consume too much fuel and their construction and maintenance is too expensive and time-consuming'; not even the large military bakery in Vienna used such a facility. Moreover, Uhl lamented, 'kneading machines [...] remain advantageous only for large bread factories. Machines dividing the dough still leave too much to the whims and vigour of the worker.'[36] Exciting technological improvement involving coal, iron and steam remained an issue of genteel masculine fascination rather than a widely available option to enhance productivity until the latter part of the nineteenth century. Therefore, it seems likely that the rise of the workforce occupied by Vienna's bakers during the first half of the 1800s in combination with increasing compulsory flour stocks can be interpreted cautiously as indicators of a certain growth of production and distribution capacities in the city's bakeries. Created through the intensification of labour, bread producers appear to have been able to respond to the rising demand for bread, rolls and pastry between the late eighteenth and mid-nineteenth centuries, at least to some degree.

Maps 5 visualizes the municipal landscape of bread in 1857 to produce an even more detailed glimpse into the landscape of baking and the residents' provision with bakery products in quantitative terms across the city.

Compared with 1793, six decades later the spatial situation of small and larger bakeries had changed markedly when measured by the compulsory flour stocks held. Most notably, the small shops, which had pioneered the municipal landscape's expansion into the growing western suburbs by the late eighteenth century, had mostly grown into medium bakeries by the middle of the 1850s. At that time a densely settled commercial, artisanal and residential part of town home

---

35. F. Klamminger, 'Bericht über die von einer Commission der löbl. Bäckerinnung in Wien an Wochenmayr's Patenofen vorgenommenen Prüfung', *Kremser Wochenblatt*, 21 April 1866, 16; Handelsministerium, *Enquête*, 13.

36. Roman Uhl, 'Producte der Brot- und Kuchen-Bäckerei', in *Officieller Ausstellungs-Bericht, 7. Lieferung: Nahrungsmittel und Getränke auf der Welt-Ausstellung zu Paris im Jahre 1867*, ed. k.k. Österreichisches Central-Comité (Wien: Braumüller, 1868), 30.

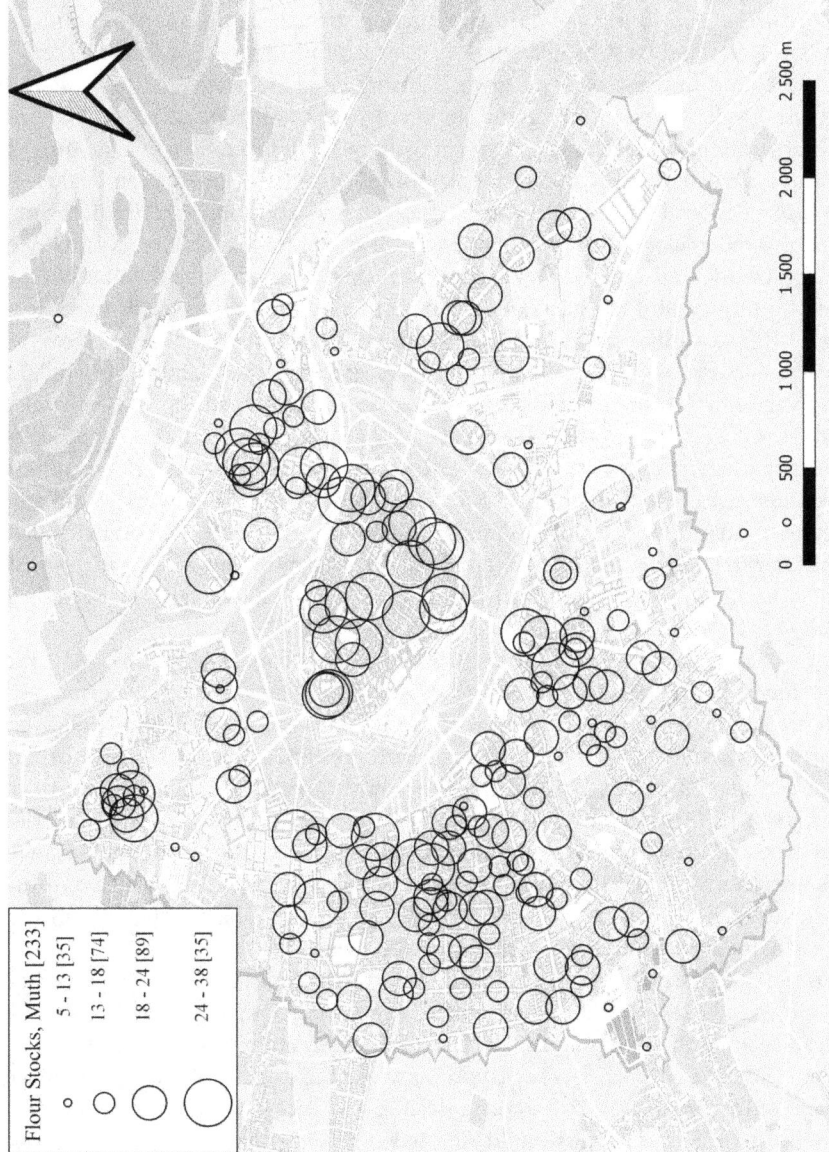

Map 5 Bakers' Compulsory Flour Stocks 1857, in Muth.[37]

37. Source: Bäckerverzeichnis 1.

to close to 200,000, this area that had become Vienna's sixth, seventh, eighth and partly ninth districts in 1850 was covered mostly by bakeries of the larger categories in terms of flour stocks.

Meanwhile, answering the quick population growth in the suburbs south of the Wien River and west of Belvedere Palace, around 1857 the smallest bakeries could be found in these parts of town. Turning large areas covered by fruit and vegetable gardens into housing development, the total population of Wieden and Margarethen districts had grown from some 30,000 souls around the turn of the century to just over 100,000 residents in 1857, providing newly found bakeries with ample demand for bread. As Map 5 indicates, while those bakeries in the old centre of Wieden close to the city centre as well as along the high streets remained the largest workshops, many smaller producers opened shop along the roads of the unfolding though still less densely inhabited former parishes towards the urban fringe. While a similar pattern of the founding of small pioneer bakeries can be observed across town and even in areas located within the Danube's floodplain in the very north, the largest bakers tended to hold shop in the old town city centre. Besides few exemptions these bakers all belonged to the class of producers keeping the largest amounts of flour in their stores, like k.k. court baker Albert Schachtner, who held a stock of 38 Muth. Yet, other bakers in town were able to compete in quantitative terms; Valentin Nerber opposite to the General Hospital on Alserstrasse kept some 34 Muth of flour each month, and Adam Mittermair was supposed to hold 32 Muth in the famous steam bakery next to Belvedere palace.

On a general level, measured by their flour stocks maintained, by 1857 the dispersion of bakers across various size classes had changed notably, as visualized in Figure 2. Whereas in 1793, 110 out of the 138 bakers – 80 per cent – had been required to store less than 16 Muth per month, by 1857 most of the guild bakers stored between 18 and 24 Muth of flour monthly. Moreover, about 15 per cent of all bakers in 1857 held stock larger than 25 Muth, a figure that only three bakeries had reached six decades ago. These changes signal a decisive shift from many small producers to mostly medium-sized bakeries between the late eighteenth and the mid-nineteenth centuries. By 1857, an average Viennese bakery would employ roughly half a dozen hands and fire one or two ovens.[38]

Dominated largely by small- and medium-sized bakeries and complemented by some petty and a few larger, partly industrial endeavours, this regulated landscape of bread secured the access to usually an artisanal neighbourhood bakery for most residents across town, where they could purchase their needs of daily subsistence and sometimes satisfy more exquisite desires. Certainly, the numerous masters belonging to Vienna's bakers' guild differed regarding their overall production volumes and therefore their individual reach and sales tactics. On a more general level, however, most bakeries that constituted the municipal landscape of bread had grown in size and expanded production, albeit within the limits of artisanal,

38. Bäckerverzeichnis 1.

3. The Municipal Landscape of Bread, 1790s–1859

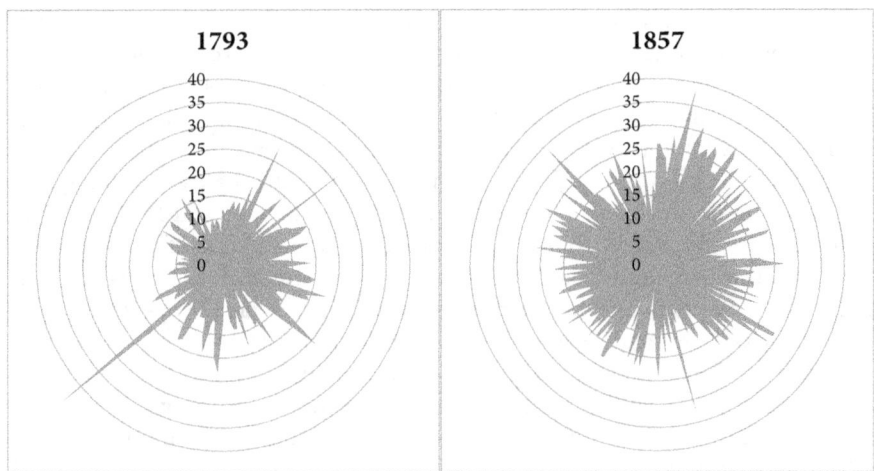

Figure 2 Dispersion of Bakers across Size Categories according to Flour Stocks, 1793 and 1857, in Muth.

Sources: Wiener Stadt- und Landesarchiv, Marktamt A2/1: Bäckergewerbe: Dekrete, 1793. Verzeichnis der gesamt-hiesigen Bäcker und Ausweiß wie viel jeder derselben an monathlichen Mehlvorrath haben soll; Wiener Stadt- und Landesarchiv, Innungen und Handelsgremien 1/B1: Bäcker: Bücher. Bäckerverzeichnis 1.

hardly mechanized frames of handicraft production to accommodate growing demand induced by quick population growth. Therefore, compared to the late eighteenth century, by 1857 the regulated landscape of bread production had not only unfolded in spatial terms but also expanded in terms of overall production capacities to answer the increase of the urban population during the half century since. It thus continued to secure the basic provision of the capital's residents, at least in quantitative terms.

Wheatification

However, quantity was not the only change that characterized the development of the municipal landscape of bread throughout the first half of the nineteenth century. Quality mattered, too. Returning to Table 1, the analysis of the composition of bakers' flour stocks underlines the striking alteration of the sorts of flour mainly used by Vienna's bakers after 1793. Inseparably connected to an increasing inflow of hard red steppe wheat and the concurrent improvements of milling techniques and product diversification described subsequently in Chapter 3, by 1857 Vienna's bakers processed much more wheat relatively to the sorts of flour they had turned into bread sixty years earlier. Whereas wheat and rye flour imports into the capital had been roughly equal until as late as the early 1830s, by the middle of the century wheat assumed two thirds of the urban flour supplies.³⁹ Applied to the bakers' obligatory flour storages shown in Table 1, the combined share of various qualities of wheat rose from about two thirds to over four fifths of the total volumes of flour in storages; the amount of rye flour held in stores decreased by half, from one third to only one sixth. Moreover, the upsurge of wheat flour was driven by an increased use of both the finest and the lowest qualities, whereas the share of middling sorts remained almost unchanged in relative terms. Between 1793 and 1857, the share of finest wheat flour rose from about 18 to 28 per cent and that of lower qualities from one third to almost half of the total volume stored in the city's bakeries, indicating a sea change in the composition and quality of bread consumers would find on the counters and shelves of the city's bakeries.

Historians have highlighted the superior meaning attributed to wheat and wheat bread consumption in the nineteenth century and the general pursuit for an increase of the eating of white bread, which Fernand Braudel termed a 'wheat bread revolution'.⁴⁰ In this more general context, Vienna's supply with food grains experienced a comparative *wheatification* already during the decades of the *Vormärz* period. Despite of the rather hesitant application of industrial technologies of bread production, various aspects of baking underwent important changes apart from exciting steam-driven machines.

Yeast represented one major aspect of improvement. Comparable to bakers in Paris, Vienna's bread producers started to replace sourdough with brewer's yeast as their favourite leavening agent. Hastening the dough's fermentation, barm was therefore not only a major driver of dough fermentation, it also drove the productivity increase in the city's bakeries before the 1850s as 'bakers sought to produce bread in greater quantities and reduced time to feed' the growing numbers of customers.⁴¹ Equally important, yeast affected the bread's taste and form, too. Labelled 'sweet fermentation', well-done barm-fermented bread carried less of the rather sour taste of bread leavened by sourdough and hops starter and produced a lighter and airy body. Not only Parisian and Viennese contemporaries noted that it yielded 'a light and better-tasting bread',

---

39. Albrecht, 'Need for Wheat', 110–11.

40. Fernand Braudel, *Civilization and Capitalism, 15th – 18th Century, Vol. 1: The Structures of Everyday Life* (New York: Harper & Row, 1981), 137–8; E. J. T. Collins, 'Dietary Change and Cereal Consumption in Britain in the Nineteenth Century', *The Agricultural History Review* 23, no. 2 (1975), 97–115; Sandgruber, *Konsumgesellschaft*; E. J. T. Collins, 'Why Wheat? Choice of Food Grains in Europe in the Nineteenth and Twentieth Centuries', *Journal of European Economic History* 22, no. 1 (1993), 7–38; Bobrow-Strain, 'White Bread Bio-Politics'; Christian Petersen, *Bread and the British Economy, c. 1770–1870* (Aldershot: Scolar Press, 1995), 15–26; Segers, 'Oysters and Rye Bread'; de Vries, *Price of Bread*, 328–33.

41. Carolyn A. Cobbold, 'The Rise of Alternative Bread Leavening Technologies in the Nineteenth Century', *Annals of Science* 75, no. 1 (2018), 22.

the production of which became more common during the early decades of the 1800s – although many of Vienna's *Vormärz* bakers continued to be scolded for the bad quality of their products.[42] Yet, top-fermented traditional brewer's yeast remained 'notoriously unreliable and unpredictable, varying in its availability, price and effects according to weather conditions and other factors outside of the bakers' control'.[43] When entrepreneur Adolf Ignaz Mautner industrialized his St. Marx brewery and reconfigured production from top-fermented to bottom-fermented lager beer by the 1840s a serious yeast shortage was the consequence. Since 'not enough' top-fermenting barm was produced and bottom-fermented yeast needed 'a time-consuming treatment to eradicate its bitterness for usage in the bakery' the city's bakers issued a price of 1,000fl. C.M. for the production of press yeast.[44] In 1850, Mautner himself won the bakers' price with an industrial press yeast that, in his own words, enabled 'perfect fermentation of the dough' and yielded bread 'not only preferable in flavour, but also light in volume, and great in demand'.[45] Very effectively used in combination with high-milled hard red steppe wheat Mautner's *Presshefe* was cultivated on rye, barley and malted corn to be compacted hydraulically and became an internationally renowned product by the 1870s.[46] The increasing adoption and subsequent standardization of brewer's yeast as means of fermentation, inherently tied to the ever-growing use and consumption of wheat, therefore contributed crucially to both the accelerated processes inside the bakery and a change in taste and form of the products that would come out of the bakers' ovens.

While barm changed the taste and volume of bread, steam changed its outer appearances. However, it was steam *inside* the oven that was crucial to this

---

42. Steven L. Kaplan, *The Bakers of Paris and the Bread Question, 1700–1775* (Durham: Duke University Press, 1996), 67; Uhl, 'Brodbereitung', 181–2; Gustav Pappenheim, 'Geschichte der Österreichischen Müllerei 1848 bis 1898', in *Geschichte der Österreichischen Land- und Forstwirtschaft und ihrer Industrien: 1848–1898: Festschrift zur Feier der am 2. December 1898 erfolgten Fünfzigjährigen Wiederkehr der Thronbesteigung Sr. Majestät des Kaisers Franz Joseph I. Supplementband I* (Wien: Moritz Perles, 1901), 279; Landesinnung der Wiener Bäcker, *700 Jahre*, 74; Cobbold, 'Alternative bread', 36.

43. Cobbold, 'Alternative bread', 22.

44. *Wiener Zeitung*, 'Industrie und Gewerbe. Nieder-Oesterreichischer Gewerb-Verein', 31 January 1847, 31, 258; *Wiener Zeitung*, 'Nied. Oesterr. Gewerb-Verein. Ausschreibung eines Preises für die inländische Erzeugung einer vollkommen brauchbaren Kunsthefe (eines künstlichen Gährungsmittels)', 11 June 1847, 159, 1286.

45. Georg J. E. Mautner-Markhof, *Von Irgendwo in alle Welt – Geschichte der Familie Mautner Markhof* (Wien: Guardaval Verlag, 1998), 69.

46. Cobbold, 'Alternative bread', 37; Gerhard A. Stadler, ',Es Hat Fürchterlich Gestunken, Grauenhaft!' Bürgerprotest gegen Umweltbelastungen aus der Hefefabrik', in *Technik, Arbeit und Umwelt in der Geschichte*, ed. Torsten Meyer and Marcus Popplow (Münster: Waxmann Verlag, 2006).

development. 'It had long been noticed in Vienna', French chemist Anselme Payen noted by the early 1840s,

> that in cleaning the floor of the oven with a plug of moist hay the batch was finer and the crust of the bread more glazed. It was thought correctly that this result must be attributed to the steam which, in condensing, fell on the loaves. Since then, [...] once the item was in the oven, the opening of the oven kept closed with a pad of moist hay; this arrangement allows the steam to fall on the loaves and to obtain a glazed and shiny crust as if it had been first covered with a solution of egg yolk. This is what makes up the steam cooking of so-called Viennese breads.[47]

Spreading apparently quickly in France from the 1850s,[48] by the middle of the century the process of steam cooking bread and rolls seems to have been well known and proven as the 1848 description of the opening of Leopold Wimmer's steam bakery exemplifies:

> A special device is used to feed the steam produced in the boiler into the oven, from which it can again be removed via two valves. The purpose of this device is no other than the distribution of moisture into the air that surrounds the bread in the oven, thus the bread's crust remains soft until the bread has risen and obtained the popular and pleasant finish.[49]

Speaking of the bread's 'popular and pleasant finish', the author's wording might support Anselme Payen's notion that those procedures and results were not unfamiliar to Viennese customers by the 1840s. Two decades later Wochenmayr's model steam oven, inspected by Vienna's bakers in the town of Krems, featured a similar function through which water from reservoir r could be introduced into the oven room b via tube s by using valve n to moisten and steam-cook the bread.

The actual adoption of improved yeast and steam-cooking procedures and techniques among bakers in Vienna cannot be proven for a want of sources. The bakers' general turn towards wheat, however, can be. Visualized in Map 6, by 1857 in every bakery across town the compulsory flour stocks consisted of three quarters of wheat; in some bakeries nine out of ten sacks of flour processed would contain wheat instead of rye. Compared to 1793, this represented a drastic change in the products and qualities costumers would find on the shelves of Vienna's bakeries. Moreover, *wheatification* was a citywide phenomenon. Although bakers located at the urban fringes might have tended to use slightly

---

47. Anselme Payen, *Manuel du Cours de Chimie organique appliquée aux Arts Industriels et Agricoles* (Paris, 1842), 312–13, cited in: Chevallier, *August Zang*, 31.
48. Chevallier, *August Zang*, 31–2.
49. L.F., 'Dampfbäckerei', 83.

3. The Municipal Landscape of Bread, 1790s–1859

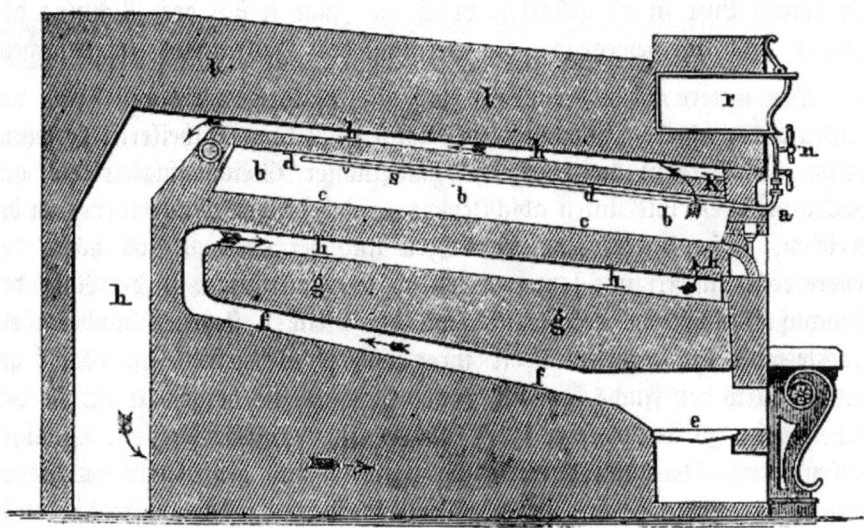

Image 1 Wochenmayr's Steam Oven.
Source: 'Wochenmayr's Backofen. Mit Einer Abbildung', *Polytechnisches Journal* 185, LVI (1867).

more rye vis-à-vis more centrally located competitors, these differences were relatively insubstantial. Across town bakers had come to offer baked good primarily made of wheat.

The shift from rye to wheat was driven by the increased use of both the finest and the coarsest sorts of wheat flour. Shown in Map 7, especially bakers in the city centre tended to use the largest amounts of finest *Mund* flour. Storing slightly less *Mund* flour in relative terms, many of the bakeries assuming central positions on bridgeheads and main streets also tended to hold larger amounts of premium flour compared to their neighbouring guild fellows. For most of Vienna's bakers and consumers across town, however, *wheatification* rather meant substituting rye for coarse wheat *Pohl* flour. Probably the most striking driver of changes in consumption habits, compared to 1793 Vienna's bakers had largely replaced the former with the latter. On average coarse wheat flour assumed almost half of the total flour storage a baker was obligated to keep. Thus, whereas some affluent inhabitants would have enjoyed almost exclusively fine wheat products most of Vienna's urban dwellers rather improved – in contemporary notions – their bread consumption modestly, though visibly by this replacement. Moreover, substituting rye through coarse wheat was a pattern observed all over the capital. Although differences remained between individual bakeries, judging by the flour stocks bakers held consumers would have access to a relatively equal range of overwhelmingly wheat bread products across the entire urban area of the Habsburg capital within the *Linienwall* by 1857.

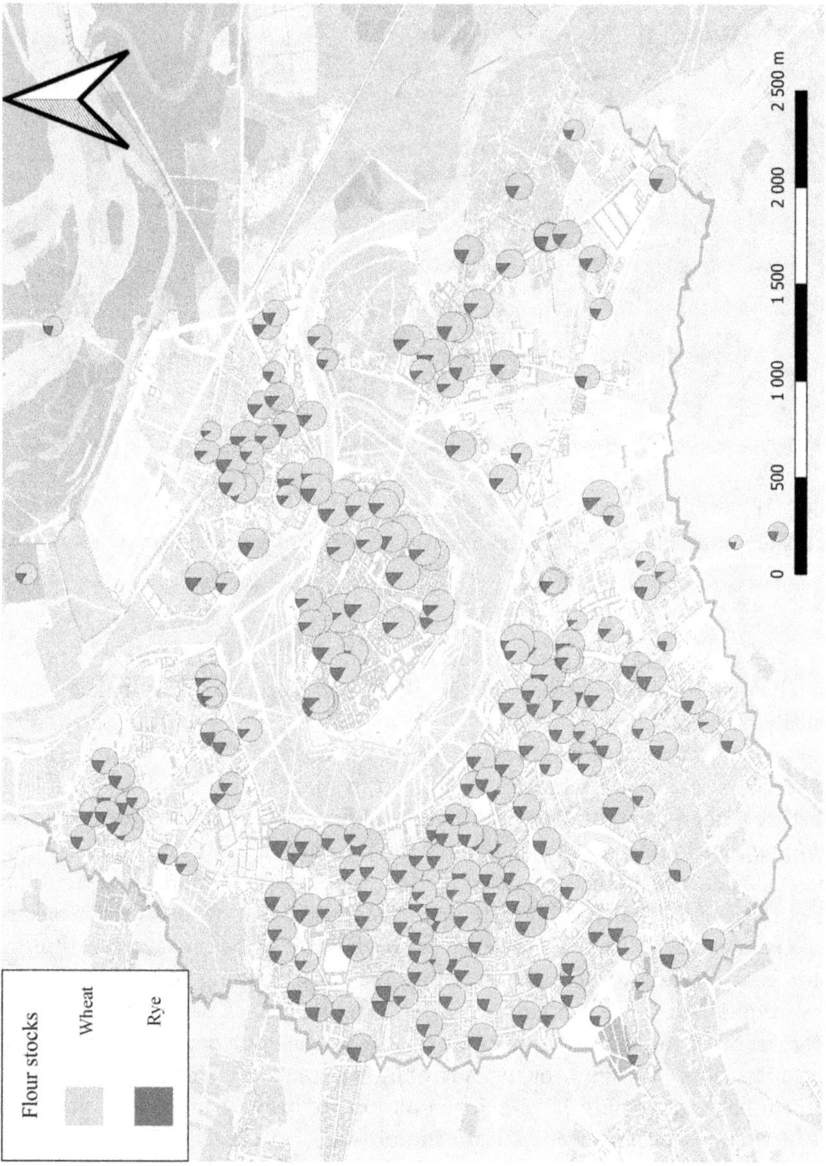

Map 6 Composition of Flour Stocks, 1857.[50]

50. Source: Bäckerverzeichnis 1.

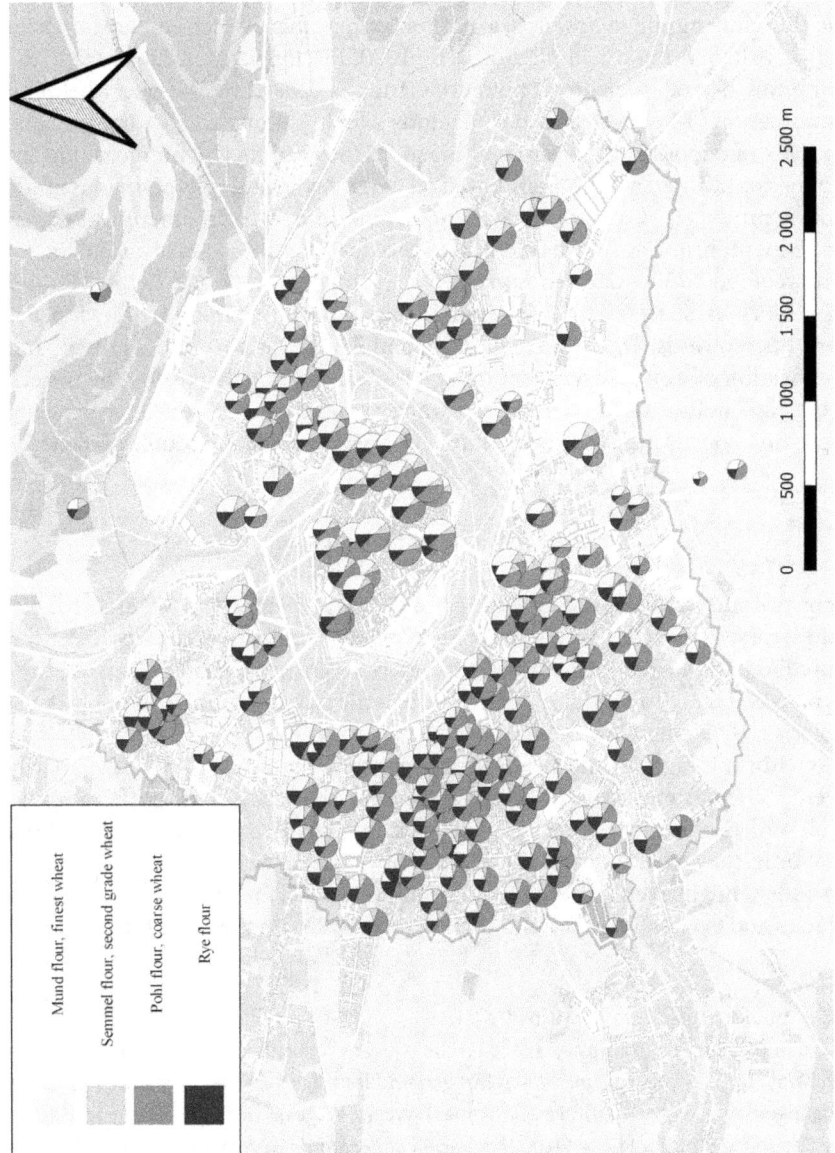

Map 7 Detailed Composition of Flour Stocks, 1857.[51]

51. Source: Bäckerverzeichnis 1.

Compared to 1793, in the face of the doubling of Vienna's urban population, by 1857 the municipal landscape of bread had certainly expanded in space to offer plenty access points across town. It had grown in terms of production and supply capacities, and modified towards a product range increasingly made of wheat widely considered the cereal of choice. By 1870, the *Enquête's* findings read, 'the striking low use of [rye] bread flour in Vienna is caused by the overwhelming consummation of fine, yet stale baked goods which, sold up to 75% cheaper, the large mass of people prefer over [rye] bread'.[52] However, this by no means meant everyone could afford a diet largely based on wheat bread and rolls of various grade of finesse produced by a master baker and her workforce. As in other parts across the continent, historians have underlined the dear conditions many residents of and newcomers to Vienna lived in especially during the 1830s and 1840s.[53] Rather than a glorious success story of good regulation and prudent artisanship the bakers' turn towards labour intensification and wheat was part of the growth and diversification of a rival infrastructure of bread supply largely outside the bakers' and the city's authority. Specializing on wheat was thus an answer to the growing competition constituted by a rising number of new players: the country bakers.

Competing circuits of bread provision

Authorities and city bakers alike referred to the rural members of Vienna's bakers' guild as *country bakers*. Bakers in Vienna's wider rural surroundings had been required to join the guild since at least the early seventeenth century because they were assumed to 'sell all kinds of baked good in the city and thus harm the [urban] bakers' as a 1629 craft code put it.[54]

Notwithstanding juridical disadvantages,[55] country bakers customarily delivered Vienna's markets with bread and pastry products. Many of them would find an outlet for ordinary bread and rolls on the busy urban marketplaces of the capital or in the buzzing streets of the suburbs; some of them, like Johann Gerber from Baden, might even achieve a certain amount of acclaim with more prominent delicacies and eventually move into the metropolis.[56] With the abolition of various

---

52. Handelsministerium, *Enquête*, CXVI.

53. Among many examples, see e.g. the various contributions in Renate Banik-Schweitzer, ed., *Wien im Vormärz,* Forschungen und Beiträge zur Wiener Stadtgeschichte 8 (Wien: Jugend und Volk, 1980); see also Tomas Cvrcek, 'Wages, Prices, and Living Standards in the Habsburg Empire, 1827–1910', *The Journal of Economic History* 73, no. 1 (2013), 1–37 and Wolfgang Maderthaner and Lutz Musner, *Die Anarchie der Vorstadt: Das andere Wien um 1900* (Frankfurt/Main: Campus-Verl., 2000).

54. Cited in Gustav A. Ressel, *Das Archiv der Bäckergenossenschaft in Wien: Ein Beitrag zur Geschichte des Wiener Handwerkes* (Wien: Gerlach & Wiedling, 1913), 21.

55. Ibid., XXVII–XXVIII, 42.

56. Wiener Stadt- und Landesarchiv, Zivilgericht, A2, Fasz. 2 – Verlassenschaftsabhandlungen: 1829–720. Verlassenschaft Johann Gerber.

disciplinary mechanisms regulating and limiting food and raw material imports into Vienna during the first wave of free-competition politics under Joseph II, these country bakers gained more economic freedom to drive their produce into town.[57] However, whereas rural bakers were permitted to bring bread into the city 'on every workday of the week' they had to adhere to Vienna's assize and were forbidden to sell their produce 'other than from their carts'. To tackle the shortages induced by war and the French occupation regulations were lifted further in 1809. Country bread was exempted from any assize regulations and, in the context of lasting population growth, remained so since despite the urban bakers' continuous protests.[58] Adding to this politico-economic setting the rapid rise in the numbers of both urban dwellers and new residents of the growing outskirts beyond the *Linienwall* during the decades after 1815 crucially contributed to the increase of the numbers of bakers beyond the tax wall.[59] Map 8 visualizes the number of country guild bakers per parish across the capital's immediate hinterland during the first half of the century.

Around 1815, various towns in the wine-growing areas around Mödling southwest of the city, well-known as summer resorts not only to Ludwig van Beethoven, had a rather developed infrastructure of official guild bakers who provided delicate baked goods for both the capital's marketplaces and well-off customers escaping from the heat and chaos of the city. Meanwhile, many other smaller villages in southern environs of the metropolitan area also registered one or two master bakers like the village of Simmering, where two guild members held shop by the end of the Napoleonic Wars. Three master bakers settled in the town of Schwechat just a few kilometres to the east along the imperial highway frequented by grain waggons and cattle tracks arriving from Hungary. The parish with the largest number of guild-incorporated country bakers by 1815, the famous Neulerchenfeld leisure area right beyond the Linienwall to the west of the city had four official bread workshops.

Half a century later, the rural landscape of baking had changed significantly. Driven by the increasing population growth not only within the city limits but also beyond the *Linienwall* the number of country bakers belonging to the guild grew quickly. While the population of the villages and hamlets around the capital on today's urban territory not quite tripled from about 66,000 in 1815 to some

---

57. See Jonas M. Albrecht, 'The Struggle for Bread. The Emperor, the City and the Bakers Between Moral and Market Economies of Food in Vienna, 1775–1791', *History of Retail and Consumption* 5, no. 3 (2019), 276–94.

58. Alexander Gigl, *Geschichte der Wiener Marktordnungen: Vom Sechzehnten Jahrhundert bis zum Ende des Achtzehnten aus Urkunden entwickelt* (Wien: Kais. Kön. Hof- und Staatsdruckerei, 1865), 189–90; Innung der bürgerl. Bäckermeister in der k.k. Haupt- und Residenzstadt Wien, *Darstellung der Gewerblichen Zustände der Wiener Bäcker-Innung* (Wien: Ferd. Jahn, 1848), 7; Landesinnung der Wiener Bäcker, *700 Jahre*, 45; Albrecht, 'Ringen des Freihandels', 78–82.

59. Hauer, *Versorgung Wiens*.

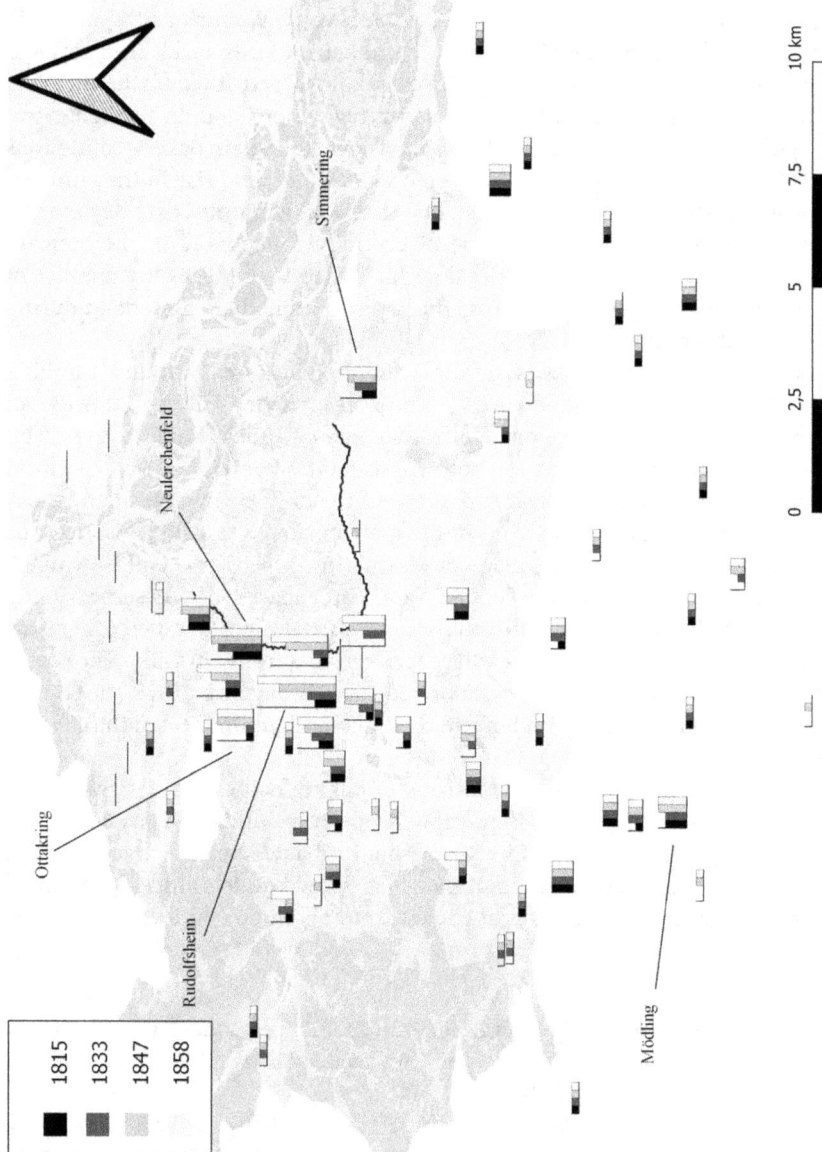

Map 8 Country Bakers per Parish, 1815–58.[60]

60. Source: Bäckerinnung, Kalender, 1815–1858.

170,000 by 1858 the number of country bakers in this area increased more than twofold, from 68 to 154.[61]

Between both dates the lion's share of new bakeries was clearly founded in those villages located just at the urban fringe outside the *Linienwall*. The parishes to the southwest located directly outside the *Linienwall* remain the unrivalled epicentres of the expansion of the rural landscape of baking. Meanwhile, other villages to the north-west where *Vormärz* immigration and urbanization began to change the hamlets' faces and paces experienced comparable growth in bakeries. Regulated by the parish authorities subject to the Lower Austrian provincial government the foundation of new bakeries in the outskirts of Vienna thus followed suit to provide rising numbers of immigrant workers.

However, the increase in bakers just outside the *Linienwall* was proportionally much higher when compared with the urban area inside the tax wall. Between 1815 and 1858 the population outside the densely developed urban area rose by the factor of 2.5 while the number of bakeries increased by a factor of 2.3. Meanwhile, the twofold rise of urban dwellers inside the *Linienwall* was met with an increase of guild bakers by roughly the factor 1.6. For example, by the end of the 1850s the twenty-four bakers of Rudolfsheim, Fünfhaus and Sechshaus combined would have supplied that area's roughly 36,500 residents. By comparison, the 55,000 inhabitants of the Landstraße, Weißgerber and Erdberg parishes combined could also visit twenty-four local bakers and similar ratios can be observed for other parts of town.[62] Proportionally, there were more guild bakers in the much less densely populated, partially poorer and overwhelmingly rural outskirts than inside the densely developed, quickly growing urban area of the Austrian capital. When accepting these ratios as measure of the people's access to a bakery of the regulated landscape of bread both in the city and around it rural residents appear to have found better conditions of bread supply.

However, this conclusion is misleading. Rather than a more expansive supply infrastructure for inhabitants outside the city the slightly disproportionate increase of country bakeries especially in localities close to the developed urban area was mostly a result of the diversification of the baking landscape between city and country bakers. Whereas their urban counterparts increasingly focussed and specialized on the production of baked goods primarily made of wheat the country bakers grew to become a complementary, albeit still competing rye supply infrastructure. Like in other towns across the continent the bakers in the city's rural surroundings and smaller towns formed 'competing circuits of bread provisioning' that challenged the urban bakers' monopoly.[63] Like in the city of Leuven in

---

61. Bäckerinnung, Kalender.

62. Own calculations based on Bäckerinnung, Kalender and Weigl, *Demographischer Wandel*.

63. Brecht Dewilde and Johann Poukens, 'Bread Provisioning and Retail Dynamics in the Southern Low Countries. The Bakers of Leuven, 1600–1800', *Continuity and Change* 26, no. 3 (2011), 408.

Vienna both the urban and the country bread circuits of provision had their 'own characteristics in terms of product and price'.[64] Since the *Verzehrungssteuer*, collected at the *Linienwall*, was levied on a much wider range of products within the urban area baking in the countryside was considerably cheaper. Whereas the assize prices in the city needed to include *Verzehrungssteuer* tolls on flour, wood and almost all other raw materials needed for bread production especially flour and wood came free of that urban extra charge outside the city limits.[65] Additionally, country bakers could pay lower wages and would remit lower trade taxes compared to guild members with shops inside the *Linienwall*.[66] The country bakers around Vienna could thus undersell the urban bakers. Like in Leuven, where bread sold by rural competitors 'was kneaded from the less expensive rye',[67] Vienna's country bakers did so increasingly in the category of *Landbrot*, large loaves of bread baked with rye and probably some coarse wheat.[68] Reinforcing the city bakers' turn towards wheat country bakers had largely taken over Vienna's supply with cheaper rye bread loaves by the middle of the century, also taking advantage of relatively ample amounts of bread allowed to be imported free of tax by individuals.[69] This is mirrored in the *Verzehrungssteuer* registers documenting the amounts of goods imported into the urban area within the *Linienwall*. Already in 1829 some 1.3 million kilograms of 'black bread' passed the tax border compared to about 43,000 kilograms of 'white bread'.[70] Whereas wheat and rye had assumed about one third of total urban cereal supplies by the late eighteenth and early nineteenth centuries, rye imports stagnated since whereas the provision of wheat had grown almost threefold. Around the mid-1850s, wheat assumed approximately two thirds of registered imports while the volumes of rye driven into Vienna had barely changed.

In 1848, the bakers within the *Linienwall* complained that 'the vendors of *Landbrot* heed neither the market days nor the places assigned to them, they bring their bread to Vienna every day, drive it from street to street in order to make a sale, and carry it in sacks and baskets from house to house'.[71] By 1857, the Lower Austrian Chamber of Commerce noted that since 1809 'the complete liberalization of bread deliveries [...] induced a great number of *Schwarzbäcker*

---

64. Ibid., 410.
65. On the Verzehrungssteuer see the contributions in Hauer, *Versorgung Wiens*.
66. Albrecht, 'Ringen des Freihandels', 90.
67. Dewilde and Poukens, 'Bread Provisioning', 411.
68. Albrecht, 'Ringen des Freihandels', 90.
69. See Hauer, *Versorgung Wiens*.
70. See Friedrich Hauer et al., 'Die Wiener Verzehrungssteuer. Auswertung nach einzelnen Steuerposten (1830–1913)', https://boku.ac.at/wiso/sec/publikationen/social-ecology-working-papers. See also Friedrich Hauer, *Die Verzehrungssteuer 1829–1913 als Grundlage einer umwelthistorischen Untersuchung des Metabolismus der Stadt Wien* (2010), Social Ecology Working Paper 129.
71. Innung der bürgerl. Bäckermeister in der k.k. Haupt- und Residenzstadt Wien, *Gewerbliche Zustände*, 10.

Table 2 Composition of Cereal Supplies, 1780–1870

	Five-Year Averages/ Estimates				
Period	Total Supply, in tonnes			Share of Total Supplies, in %	
	All Cereals	Wheat Flour	Rye Flour	Wheat Flour	Rye Flour
1782–6	45,137	17,750	14,944	39	33
1802–7	77,219	25,892	22,228	34	29
1808–12	57,341	24,116	14,867	43	26
1813–15/17	54,253	24,464	22,660	36	34
1828–30/32	50,030	14,273	12,624	28	25
1850–4	69,847	54,000	15,000	70	20
c. 1870	217,000	108,000	32,000	50	32

Source: Jonas M. Albrecht, 'The Need for Wheat. The Pre-Industrial Expansion of Vienna's Grain Supply, 1800–1840', in *Stocks, Seasons and Sales: Food Supply, Storage and Markets in Europe and the New World, C. 1600–2000*, vol. 17, ed. Wouter Ronsijn, Niccolò Mignemi and Laurent Herment (Turnhout: Brepols Publishers, 2019). Note: 1782–1850s: Vienna within Linienwall; 1870 estimate for Vienna and surroundings, including wheat, rye and barley.

[rye bread bakers] to settle in the parishes just outside the Linien[wall] who seek their outlets in Vienna'.[72] 'It is known,' a member of the city's magistrate argued in the large-scale *Enquête* about the capital's food supply in 1870 'that most of Vienna's demand for [rye] bread is supplied by so-called country bakers'.[73] Also consulted, chair of Vienna's Danube ship millers offered a similar opinion: 'The flour is not made of wheat, the 60 ship mills only produce rye flour. [...] It is sold to our *Schwarzbäcker* who take it to bake country bread.' When asked to give more details where the ship millers' rye flour was transported, he explained it was delivered to the bakers 'outside the Linien[wall]. Inside the Linien[wall] one cart of rye is sufficient for one month; this is not the case beyond the Linen[wall].' Moreover, he added, Floridsdorf – across the Danube – was too far removed from the urban marketplaces for ship millers to bake themselves and transport the bread into the city; 'it would not pay to keep a horse and drive to market because the gentlemen in Fünfhaus find themselves much closer [to the city] and supply their customers three times a day with fresh goods'.[74] 'We bakers in the city produce only little [rye] bread', agreed Ferdinand Boos who ran a bakery in the city centre while chairman Rudolf Plank confirmed that 'the country bakers close to Vienna [...] largely produce the city's [rye] bread supply'.[75] Master baker Gaugusch of 20 Kirchengasse

72. *Bericht der Handels- und Gewerbekammer für das Erzherzogthum Oesterreich unter der Enns an das K.K. Ministerium für Handel und Volkswirthschaft über die Verkehrsverhältnisse des Kammerbezirkes in den Jahren 1857 bis 1860*, 53.
73. Handelsministerium, *Enquête*, 31.
74. Ibid., 57–61.
75. Ibid., 6, 17, 22.

in Rudolfsheim equally highlighted that 'great amounts of bread are imported, and even some wheaten goods from the parishes directly outside the suburbs, though not much'.[76] Hence, by 1870 the *Enquête's* final report constituted what had been a day-to-day reality for several decades: 'with regard to [rye] bread the country bakers assume a considerable and increasing share in Vienna's provision. They import those baked goods in masses, they partly send them to customers or go hawking.'[77]

Thus, the *wheatification* of bread consumption in Vienna was accompanied by a diversification of the retail infrastructure of bread. However, *wheatification* was also centrally connected to large-scale developments of the grain trade and milling sector in the Habsburg Empire since the late eighteenth century, which represented major drivers for changing consumption habits and eventually challenged the regulatory setting of Vienna's assize system.

---

76. Ibid., 74.
77. Ibid., 445.

Chapter 4

THE CONQUEST OF CORNUCOPIA

'The Banat is the cornucopia not only of Hungary but of the whole Austrian Empire [...]', reported British diplomat, traveller and author Andrew Archibald Paton in 1861 from his journeys in Central Europe.[1] Paton was neither the first nor the only nineteenth-century observer of the 'division of labour' between the industrializing Austrian territories of the monarchy and agrarian Hungary.[2]

Indeed, contemporaries concerned with the economic development of the empire had noted the importance of Hungarian wheat for the provision of the capital for several decades. 'The bakers in Vienna', wrote famous geographer and statistician Wenzel Blumenbach in 1835, 'strongly prefer flour made of Banat wheat [...]'.[3] While economic historians have underlined the growth of agricultural exports from Hungary to Austria especially during the second half of the nineteenth and early twentieth centuries,[4] Pannonian grain deliveries to Vienna gained eminent

---

1. Andrew Archibald Paton, *Researches on the Danube and the Adriatic: Or, Contributions to the Modern History of Hungary and Transylvania, Dalmatia and Croatia, Servia and Bulgaria*, II (Leipzig: F.A. Brockhaus, 1861), vol. II, 28, cited in: Ortrun Veichtlbauer, 'Zwischen Kolonie und Provinz. Herrschaft und Planung in der Kameralprovinz Temeswarer Banat im 18. Jahrhundert' (Institute of Social Ecology Vienna (SEC), 2016), 40.

2. Historians have contributed a lot of research and different interpretations on the question of the relationship between the Austrian and Hungarian parts of the empire. For an exemplary introduction, see e.g. Andrea Komlosy, 'Innere Peripherien als Ersatz für Kolonien? Zentrenbildung und Peripherisierung in der Habsburgermonarchie', in *Zentren, Peripherien und Kollektive Identitäten in Österreich-Ungarn: Kultur-Herrschaft-Differenz*, ed. Endre Hárs et al. (Tübingen, Basel: Francke, 2006).

3. Wenzel Carl Wolfgang Blumenbach, *Neueste Landeskunde von Oesterreich unter der Ens, Zweiter Band* (Güns: Reichard, 1835), 40.

4. See, among many other, e.g. Scott M. Eddie, 'The Terms and Patterns of Hungarian Foreign Trade, 1882–1913', *The Journal of Economic History* 37, no. 2 (1977), 329–58; Mariann Nagy, 'The Regional Structure of the Hungarian Agriculture in the Beginning of the 20th Century', *Zgodovinski časopis (Historical Review)* 67, nos. 3–4 (2013); Ernst Langthaler, 'Vom Transnationalen zum Regionalen Hinterland – und Retour. Wiens Nahrungsmittelversorgung vor, im und nach dem Ersten Weltkrieg', in *Erster Weltkrieg*

importance already by the late eighteenth and early nineteenth centuries. In the context of fast population growth both in the province of Lower Austria and in the city of Vienna this development was part of a substantial reorganization and expansion of cereal production in the agglomeration's more traditional hinterland and a simultaneous expansion of the supply area into the Hungarian Pannonian Plain. Addressing the 'energy and resource scarcities in the core area', the capital's grain hinterland expanded into the rural peripheries to the east, where it 'deeply influenced massive and growing human-induced environmental change'.[5]

The notable rise of demand for food and fuel was facilitated by the significant expansion of wheat production in the urban hinterland since the late eighteenth century.[6] This expansion was an integral part of the spatial spread and intensification of land use in the province of Lower Austria during the eighteenth century, as the growing population 'put intensifying demands on scarce natural resources – especially food and energy'.[7] Just like 'population pressures drove the expansion of arable land in Tudor and Stuart England', when 'woodlands, forests, moors, heaths, fens, and other lightly inhabited tracts were colonized, reclaimed, and settled', urban and rural population growth induced the expansion of agricultural land use in Lower Austria after 1750.[8] Between the 1780s and 1850s, the province's 'unproductive' land was almost extinguished, declining from about one fifth of Lower Austria's total area to merely 4 per cent. By the middle of the nineteenth century, the area under any form of cultivation nearly equalled the province's total surface of 1,982,500 hectares. Formerly non-productive soils were turned into areas devoted to either forestry, food or fodder production.[9]

As 'war against untamed nature was being waged' in Frederician Prussia, the Austrian state's settlement policy with regard to agricultural expansion

---

Globaler Konflikt – Lokale Folgen: Neue Perspektiven, ed. Stefan Karner and Philipp Lesiak (Innsbruck/Wien: Studien-Verl., 2014); Jennifer Alix-Garcia et al., 'Tariffs and Trees. The Effects of the Austro-Hungarian Customs Union on Specialization and Land-Use Change', *The Journal of Economic History* 78, no. 4 (2018).

5. John F. Richards, *The Unending Frontier: An Environmental History of the Early Modern World* (Berkeley, Los Angeles, London: University of California Press, 2005), 4. See also R. C. Hoffmann, 'Frontier Foods for Late Medieval Consumers: Culture, Economy, Ecology', *Environment and History* 7, no. 2 (2001); Jason W. Moore, 'Sugar and the Expansion of the Early Modern World-Economy: Commodity Frontiers, Ecological Transformation, and Industrialization', *Review (Fernand Braudel Center)* 23, no. 3 (2000), 409–33.

6. Jonas M. Albrecht, 'The Need for Wheat. The Pre-Industrial Expansion of Vienna's Grain Supply, 1800–1840', in *Stocks, Seasons and Sales: Food Supply, Storage and Markets in Europe and the New World, C. 1600–2000*, vol. 17, ed. Wouter Ronsijn, Niccolò Mignemi and Laurent Herment (Turnhout: Brepols Publishers, 2019).

7. Richards, *Unending Frontier*, 11.

8. Ibid., 123.

9. Albrecht, 'Need for Wheat', 112.

and modernization, market access and the removal of trade barriers assumed a leading role in agricultural expansion from above.[10] While in Russia 'the tsarist state had extended its fortified frontier lines to make new areas safe for pioneer settlement and cultivation' during the eighteenth century,[11] emperors Maria Theresa and Joseph II sent out large numbers of settlers to plough the black earth of the Hungarian and the sandy soils of the Lower Austrian frontiers.[12] With expansion came new settlements, like Theresienfeld (1763) or Oeynhausen (1773) in Lower Austria and many other new villages in the Banat.[13] The draining of marshlands, construction of irrigation works and other measures to expand the surface available to agriculture followed these new foundations. Like Golden Age Dutch waterworks engineers accomplished 'the land reclamation that literally changed the face and shape of whole regions',[14] the enlightened Austrian state administration and Austro-Hungarian landlords developed plans and made efforts to gain more control over the empire's rivers and wetlands, especially the Danube.[15]

10. David Blackbourn, *The Conquest of Nature: Water, Landscape, and the Making of Modern Germany* (New York, NY: Norton, 2007), 46.

11. Richards, *Unending Frontier*, 272.

12. Ernst Bruckmüller, 'Eine "grüne Revolution" (18.-19. Jahrhundert)', in *Agrarrevolutionen: Verhältnisse in der Landwirtschaft vom Neolithikum zur Globalisierung*, ed. Markus Cerman, Ilja Steffelbauer and Sven Tost (Innsbruck: Studien-Verl., 2008); Helmuth Feigl, ed., *Die Auswirkungen der Theresianisch-Josephinischen Reformen auf die Landwirtschaft und die ländliche Sozialstruktur Niederösterreichs: Vorträge und Diskussionen des ersten Symposiums des Niederösterreichischen Institutes für Landeskunde, Geras, 9. – 11. Oktober 1980* (Wien Selbstverl. d. NÖ Inst. für Landeskunde, 1982, 1982); Karl Gutkas, *Geschichte Niederösterreichs* (Wien: Verl. für Geschichte u. Politik, 1984).

13. Márta Fata, *Migration im kameralistischen Staat Josephs II: Theorie und Praxis der Ansiedlungspolitik in Ungarn, Siebenbürgen, Galizien und der Bukowina von 1768 bis 1790* (Münster: Aschendorff, 2014); Horst Haselsteiner, 'Cooperation and Confrontation between Rulers and the Noble Estates, 1711-1790', in *A History of Hungary*, ed. Peter F. Sugar (Bloomington: Indiana Univ. Pr, 1990), 142–3.

14. Jan de Vries and A. M. van der Woude, *The First Modern Economy: Success, Failure, and Perseverance of the Dutch Economy, 1500–1815* (Cambridge: Cambridge University Press, 2008), 27.

15. Horst Glassl, 'Der Ausbau der ungarischen Wasserstraßen in den letzten Regierungsjahren Maria Theresias', *Ungarn-Jahrbuch - Zeitschrift für die Kunde Ungarns und verwandte Gebiete* II, no. 2 (1970); Severin Hohensinner et al., 'Two Steps Back, One Step Forward: Reconstructing the Dynamic Danube Riverscape under Human Influence in Vienna', *Water History* 5 (2013), 121–43; Viktor Thiel, 'Geschichte der Donauregulierungsarbeiten bei Wien II. Vom Anfange des XVIII. bis zur Mitte des XIX. Jahrhunderts. Von der Mitte des XIX. Jahrhunderts bis zur Gegenwart', *Jahrbuch d. Vereins f. Landeskunde von Niederösterreich*, 4–5 (1905/1906).

One of the largest attempts at land reclamation was the partial drainage of the Hanság marsh at Lake Neusiedl southeast of Vienna. Begun by Count Esterházy in the 1770s, drainage schemes were developed and partly carried out. Between 1777 and 1780, a three-kilometre road with twenty bridges, allowing up to four wagons to drive side by side, was constructed to improve transportation through the swamp. By the 1820s, 'huge amounts of hay' grown on soils claimed from the marsh could be transported via the Hegedus Canal, built 1795–1813, to Lower Austria and Vienna.[16] As a result, the area devoted to the production of basic food and feedstuffs in Lower Austria grew by almost a third during the early nineteenth century. Compared with the late 1700s, when cereal production had occupied around one fifth of Lower Austria's total surface, the incorporation of frontier soils lifted this share to about a quarter by the 1850s. Moreover, additional room to grow cereals was not only gained by making land arable but also by giving already cultivated plots over to grain cultivation.[17]

The product of frontier expansion in Lower Austria was a decisive increase in cereal output. Compared to the province's total annual grain production of some 300,000 tonnes around 1790, by the early 1850s yearly harvests approached half a million tonnes. Although rye and oats remained more important in terms of the actual area under cultivation and total harvest output, wheat and barley became ever more significant to the regional agriculture. Like their Belgian counterparts Lower Austrian farmers, landowners and agronomists 'saw the way the wind was blowing'.[18] Indeed, wheat cultivation directly replaced rye growing to some extent, just as contemporary observers would have it.[19] By the late 1780s, Lower Austria produced some 25,000 tonnes of wheat and some 150,000 tonnes of rye per annum. Sixty years later, wheat harvests had more than doubled to about 55,000 tonnes, while rye crops grew by about half to 225,000 tonnes annually.

However, between the major grains, output increases were generated quite differently. Wheat was among the main objectives of frontier expansion – and

16. Gergely K. Horvarth, 'Rendi Autonómia És Fiziokratizmus. Kísérlet a Hanság Lecsapolására Az 1820-30-as Években (2. Rész)', *Soproni szemle*, no. 62 (2008); Gergely K. Horvárth, 'Rahmen des bäuerlichen Handelns im Wieselburger Komitat (Ungarn) in der ersten Hälfte des 19. Jahrhunderts. Modell der Kommerzialisierung einer west-ungarischen Region', in *Bauern als Händler: Ökonomische Diversifizierung und Soziale Differenzierung Bäuerlicher Agrarproduzenten (15. -19. Jahrhundert)*, ed. Frank Konersmann and Klaus-Joachim Lorenzen-Schmidt (Berlin: Walter de Gruyter GmbH, 2016), 164.

17. Albrecht, 'Need for Wheat', 112–13.

18. Yves Segers, 'Oysters and Rye Bread: Polarising Living Standards in Flanders, 1800–1860', *European Review of Economic History* 5, no. 3 (2001), 322.

19. Johann Burger, 'Ueber die Vortheile der Vergrößerung der Cultur des Weizens, und die Anwendung der Schaufelpflüge', *Verhandlungen der k.k. Landwirtschaftsgesellschaft in Wien, und Aufsätze vermischten ökonomischen Inhalts*. Neue Folge, Zweyter Band, no. 1 (1833), 57–79.

pushing out the boundaries of the wheat frontier was the single most important response to growing demand. Within the Lower Austrian agriculture gains in wheat harvests were almost exclusively generated through the extension of cultivation before the 1860s. By mid-century, the area under wheat had grown more than twofold compared with the situation around 1790 while little or no gains in area productivity were achieved on the overall provincial level.[20] Barley cultivation followed a similar pattern, but the production of both oats and rye exhibited a different behaviour. For the latter types of grain, the intensification of production, that is the increase in yields per hectare, was much more important. Whereas the wheat and barley frontiers widened during the first half of the nineteenth century, both the rye and oat frontiers deepened.

Yet, the regional widening of the wheat frontier was not enough to satisfy the growing urban appetite. A comparison of average wheat harvests with average wheat imports into Vienna shows how large the capital's demand loomed. The city required nearly 18,000 tonnes of wheat in flour each year on the eve of the French Revolution. Since wheat delivered in the form of grains and supplies for the royal court are excluded in this figure, the actual demand was probably even higher. On this scale, Vienna's consumption of wheat was almost as high as the total annual wheat output of the entire province of Lower Austria. Despite the great extension of the cultivated area, there was no real change in this ratio before the middle of the following century. Hypothetically, Vienna would still devour almost all wheat grown in the province by the 1850s.

Early nineteenth-century observers were quite aware of Lower Austria's chronic deficit in wheat supplies as agronomist Johann Burger commented around 1830: 'Considerable amounts of grain need to be imported from Hungary. [...] We have to be grateful that we are provided with our neighbours' abundance, who themselves would be seriously embarrassed if we were capable to satisfy Vienna's demand ourselves.'[21] Thus, the agricultural expansion across Vienna's traditional

---

20. Ernst Bruckmüller, *Sozialgeschichte Österreichs* (Wien, München: Verl. für Geschichte und Politik; Oldenbourg, 2001), 209–12; Roman Sandgruber, 'Die Agrarrevolution in Österreich', in *Österreich-Ungarn als Agrarstaat: Wirtschaftliches Wachstum und Agrarverhältnisse in Österreich im 19. Jahrhundert*, ed. Alfred Hoffmann and Roman Sandgruber (Wien: Verl. für Geschichte und Politik, 1978), 210. To be sure, agricultural modernization, such as summer stall feeding and increased use of manure, abolition of fallow and implementation of leguminous crops were essential parts of the physiocratic programme during the 'transition from traditional to advanced organic farming'. Indeed, they were highly important locally, especially on large estates. See e.g. Dino Güldner and Fridolin Krausmann, 'Nutrient Recycling and Soil Fertility Management in the Course of the Industrial Transition of Traditional, Organic Agriculture: The Case of Bruck Estate, 1787–1906', *Agriculture, Ecosystems & Environment* 249 (2017).

21. Burger, 'Vergrößerung der Cultur des Weizens', 62.

Table 3 Lower Austrian Average Wheat Harvests and Vienna's Average Wheat Supplies 1789–1857, in Tonnes

Year	Wheat Harvest	Vienna Wheat Supply	Period
1789	25,000	17,750	1782–6
1851	56,000	54,000	1850s

Source: Albrecht, Need for Wheat, 2019, 114.

hinterland was insufficient to satisfy the capital's ever-growing need for white bread. As Burger noted, the solution was to be found in the east.

Wheat from the western parts of Hungary had been important for Vienna's provision since the Middle Ages. In late eighteenth-century descriptions of the capital 'Hungary' is mentioned regularly as a source of grain supplies.[22] According to scattered data on grain transactions in Hungarian markets in 1772/3, the largest amounts of grain changed hands in markets in the western provinces of Hungary, and especially markets distinctly located close to Vienna. Neusiedel, a small border village just 45 kilometres east of Vienna, held the largest grain market in all of Hungary with nearly 1,500 tonnes of cereals sold in that year.[23] Due to the incapability of the Austrian hinterland, population growth and wartime demand during the Seven Years' War and the Napoleonic Wars had been a major incentive for Hungarian landlords to convert wastelands into arable soils, especially in the border districts of Moson and Sopron. Consequently, not only 'Esterházy estates close to the Danube and the Austrian border produced grain for the Vienna market' since the eighteenth century.[24]

By 1820, Moson county was considered 'one of the granaries of Vienna and Austria'.[25] However, before the turn of the century 'profits from [...] estates less favourably situated, further south in Vas and Somogy counties and far down the Danube, were limited by economic handicaps common to most of

---

22. Ignaz de Luca, *Wiens Gegenwärtiger Zustand unter Josephs Regierung* (Wien: Georg Philipp Wucherer, 1787), 105, 399.

23. Deszö Dányi, "*Az Élet Ára*": *Gabona És Élelmiszerárak Magyarországon, 1750–1850* (Budapest: Központi Statisztikai Hivatal Könyvtár és Levéltár, 2007), 177–88.

24. Rebecca Gates-Coon, *The Landed Estates of the Esterházy Princes: Hungary during the Reforms of Maria Theresia and Joseph II* (Baltimore: Johns Hopkins University Press, 1994), 88; see also István Kállay, *Management of Big Estates in Hungary Between 1711 and 1848* (Budapest: Akad. Kiadó, 1980).

25. Andr. Grailich, 'Die Wieselburger Gespannschaft in Ungern', *Erneuerte Vaterländische Blätter für den Österreichischen Kaiserstaat*, 1 April 1820, 27, 108.

Hungary: difficult, costly transportation and dependence on a weak local market.[26] Cereal transports from central Hungary remained unprofitable, except for times of dearth like 1771/2, and these districts were much less important for the supply of the Habsburg capital by the late 1700s. Before the turn of the century, this would change. Following the rise in grain prices 'demand for Hungarian grain – in the hereditary provinces and the army – grew steadily from the middle of the century and especially the final twenty or thirty years. When this could no longer be satisfied by the feudal manors of the Lesser Hungarian Plain, grain started to be transported from the Great Plain.'[27]

This expansion of the frontier was greatly facilitated by the state. Settlement programmes to colonize the fertile plains of the Banat and Bačka provinces and boost agricultural production had been at the heart of the imperial policies of both Maria Theresa and Joseph II since the middle of the 1700s.[28] At first mainly the areas along the Danube and Tisza rivers accessible by ship were incorporated.[29] However, since the 1750s it became obvious that it was not enough to colonize only the land – it was also necessary to conquer the water. Simultaneous to the settlement endeavours the navigability of the Danube started to receive serious attention with respect to the natural, technological and legal conditions of water transport. The systematic navigation and mapping of the entire river between Engelhartzell and Belgrade was begun under the auspices of a court commission in 1771, resulting in extensive plans to tackle the main obstacles of shipping, particularly ship mills, bridges, overgrown riverbanks and floods. For that purpose, the *Navigationsdirektion* appointed engineers for certain sections of the river who were to recruit labourers locally in order to chop down trees and other vegetation overgrowing the towpaths, remove obstacles in the current, construct bridges at confluences, build dams, drain swamps and fill side arms where necessary.[30] At the same time, other frontier waterways also received accelerating attention.[31]

Secondly, the state actively facilitated technological improvements of water transportation. By offering a price of 1,000fl. to anyone who would 'navigate the

26. Gates-Coon, *Landes Estates*, 88. See also Jerome Blum, *Noble Landowners and Agriculture in Austria, 1815 – 1848: A Study in the Origins of the Peasant Emancipation of 1848* (Baltimore: Johns Hopkins University Press, 1948), 92–5, and András Vári, *Herren und Landwirte: Ungarische Aristokraten und Agrarier auf dem Weg in die Moderne (1821–1910)* (Wiesbaden: Harrassowitz, 2008), 25.

27. Lajos Rácz, *The Steppe to Europe: An Environmental History of Hungary in the Traditional Age* (Cambridge: White Horse Press, 2013), 217.

28. Fata, *Migration*.

29. Zsolt Pinke, 'Modernization and Decline: An Eco-Historical Perspective on Regulation of the Tisza Valley, Hungary', *Journal of Historical Geography* 45 (2014), 92–105; Vári, *Herren und Landwirte*, 25.

30. Glassl, 'Wasserstraßen'.

31. Pinke, 'Modernization and Decline'.

Danube with the best sailing ship and reduce the present freight rates',[32] Maria Theresa sought to introduce up-to-date shipbuilding technologies to her empire and modernize Danube shipping.[33] A third public measure concerned the legal circumstances of river transportation. Beginning in 1770, the *Navigationsdirektion* was to elaborate how the complex system of navigation taxes and fees could be simplified to ease trade and transportation. In this context the state attempted to regulate the trade by creating a shippers' organization with professional codes and qualification guidelines, as well as wage and tariff regulations for apprentices and drivers.[34]

Besides these direct, though in their success somewhat limited state attempts private encounters also tried to grab a slice of the pie and invested into ventures aiming to generate profits from the increasing amounts of frontier goods that literally flowed westwards. From the 1750s through the 1840s, piecemeal regulation works were carried out in the Tisza Valley where 'rises in grain prices in the late eighteenth century led landowners to convert waste lands, pastures, forests and marshes [...] into arable land'.[35] The most prominent and probably most important of these endeavours was the construction of the *Franzenscanal* by the k.k. priv. ung. *Schifffahrts-Gesellschaft* between 1793 and 1801, which shortened the route from Timisoara to Vienna by 250 kilometres. Cut into the soil by a workforce of several thousand partly forced labourers, its construction necessitated the draining of swamplands and other serious interventions in the local environment, displaced migratory people from their lands and sparked intense conflict with various settler colonies.[36] In the first year of operation, some 10,000 tonnes of grain passed through the waterway, largely shipped towards Austria. These numbers reached 40,000 to 60,000 tonnes at the height of the Napoleonic Wars, declined to about 30,000 tonnes in the years afterwards and again reached 60,000 to 70,000 tonnes by the 1820s and 1830s.[37]

Liberalized from trade restrictions in 1817 and a reaction to the outbreak of the Tambora volcano and the 'year without a summer', the supply of frontier wheat as the prime cereal of choice to Vienna's flour and bread producers was ensured by vast grain trading networks unfolding eastwards. Partly controlled by Jewish

---

32. Glassl, 'Wasserstraßen', 56.

33. Friedrich Slezak, 'Zur Geschichte der Donauschiffahrt (1765–1829)', *Der Donauraum* 19, nos. 1–2 (1974).

34. Glassl, 'Wasserstraßen'.

35. Pinke, 'Modernization and Decline', 95.

36. Nikola Petrović, *Die Schiffahrt und Wirtschaft im mittleren Donauraum in der Zeit des Merkantilismus: Der Bau des Donau-Theiß-, des Franzens-Kanals und die Bestrebungen gegen Ende des XVIII. Jahrhunderts, den mittleren Donauraum mit dem Adriatischen Meer zu verbinden* (Novi Sad: Akademie der Wissenschaften und Künste der Wojwodina, 1982), 89–90; 153–4; 372–81; 399–407.

37. Sources: see Albrecht, 'Need for Wheat', 117.

wholesale firms that almost all did at least 'a little business in grain',[38] within these networks merchant firms in Vienna, Bratislava or Budapest had very close business links to the grain growing regions through intermediaries, itinerant merchants, shopkeepers or innkeepers, who were centrally involved in the local and regional grain trade. Bought by agents in the producing regions the grain was shipped westwards via the Tisza and Danube rivers. Having passed the *Franzenscanal* the caravans of *Kelheimer* barges mainly used in grain transportation entered the Danube near Bezdan. Up to forty metres long and seven metres wide these ships had carrying capacities of 300 to 500 tonnes. Each needed up to eight boatmen, thirty drivers and forty horses to be hauled upriver as well as pioneers, cooks and other staff to be operated. Usually, a caravan consisted of three to four barges, each with three to four additional steering boats, making these shipments the endeavour of several hundred men and horses.[39] After months of perilous journey and several pit stops in trade ports such as Baja, Dunaföldvár or Pest along the Danube, the caravans would reach the town of Győr situated east of Vienna on a side arm of the Danube. There, the large barges could go no further. Called 'bad waters', in this area the main branch of the Danube was fragmented into several shoal, winding arms with unpredictable winds, currents and sandbanks that made the journey onwards dangerous and long.[40] Consequently, in Győr the cereals bound for Vienna and Lower Austria were reloaded into smaller ships and carried on the river's side arm to Moson. There, water transport finally ended. The ships were unloaded and the grain eventually driven towards Vienna, less than a two-day journey by horse cart.[41]

Given these circumstances, during the early nineteenth century Moson and Győr became epicentres bundling the growing streams of frontier wheat. Whereas around 1820 some 300 ships unloaded about 60,000 tonnes of grains into Moson's granaries, those figures grew to more than 220,000 tonnes and about 2,000 ships by the early 1840s. By that time, most of the town's population was involved in the trade as agents, brokers, drivers, accountants or by simply renting out their basements as grain store facilities.[42] Moson's position had become so important

---

38. Peter Hanak, 'Jews and the Modernization of Commerce in Hungary, 1760-1848', in *Jews in the Hungarian Economy 1760-1945: Studies Dedicated to Moshe Carmilly-Weinberger on His Eightieth Birthday*, ed. Michael K. Silber (Jerusalem: Magnes Press, Hebrew University, 1992), 65-8.

39. Blumenbach, *Landeskunde*, 182; Ernst Neweklowsky, *Die Schiffahrt und Flößerei im Raume der oberen Donau* (Linz: Linz [Donau] Oberösterr. Landesverl., 1952), 181, 291-330.

40. Friedrich Hauer, Severin Hohensinner, and Christina Spitzbart-Glasl, 'How Water and Its Use Shaped the Spatial Development of Vienna', *Water History* 8, no. 3 (2016).

41. Horvárth, 'Rahmen des bäuerlichen Handelns', 182; Johann Winkler, 'Wien und die Entwicklung des Donauhandels', *Mittheilungen der k.k. geographischen Gesellschaft in Wien* 15 (1872), 87-90.

42. See Albrecht, 'Need for Wheat', 117.

that only about one tenth of Vienna's grain supplies arrived directly in the city via the Danube waterway.[43] Furthermore, the town had developed storage facilities large enough to make separate granaries in Vienna virtually unnecessary and unprofitable, a fact often bemoaned by Viennese merchants and politicians.[44] As traveller-geographer Johann Georg Kohl noted in 1842, Moson, 'Raab [Győr] and Timisoara can be called the endpoints of a great shipping line, of which Raab lies near to an area in need (Vienna) whereas Timisoara is located in the centre of a grain-growing country'.[45]

From the Moson and Győr magazines merchants and agents would bring grain samples to Vienna, where they met on Wednesdays and Saturdays with millers, brewers and other traders at the *Mehlgrube* and a small number of other distinctive taverns, the business's informal meeting points.[46] After sales were agreed upon, instructions were sent back to local hauliers contracted to transport the purchases to the mills in Vienna's hinterland or, in the case of international purchases, to Nußdorf north of Vienna, where the cargo would be reloaded on ships bound northwards.[47]

Thus triggered, Hungarian grain production grew significantly. Cereal outputs more than doubled in Moson County between 1769 and 1844, grew more than tenfold in the counties of Pest and Bács-Bodrog and more than fivefold in Békés County.[48] Decisive tendencies towards market integration between Austria and Hungary appeared during the *Vormärz*. Wheat prices in Hungarian and Austrian markets converged rapidly between 1811 and 1826 and there was a significant wheat price correlation between Vienna and Hungarian as well as Banat markets already before 1847.[49] As the growth of Hungary's agricultural sector 'was contingent on exports to Vienna' steppe wheat gained importance for the capital's supply system.[50] When the *Vormärz* era ended, Vienna's hinterland expanded deep into the Pannonian Plain. Hungarian grain exports towards the Austrian

---

43. Simone Gingrich, Gertrud Haidvogl, and Fridolin Krausmann, 'The Danube and Vienna: Urban Resource Use, Transport and Land Use 1800–1910', *Regional Environmental Change* 12, no. 2 (2012), 288.

44. See Albrecht, 'Need for Wheat', 117.

45. Johann Georg Kohl, *Hundert Tage Reisen in den Oesterreichischen Staaten: 4. Teil, Reise in Ungarn, Zweite Abtheilung* (Dresden: Arnoldische Buchhandlung, 1842), 205–6.

46. Victor Heller, *Der Getreidehandel und seine Technik in Wien* (Tübingen: Mohr, 1901), 13.

47. Albrecht, 'Need for Wheat', 118.

48. John Komlos, *The Habsburg Monarchy as a Customs Union: Economic Development in Austria-Hungary in the Nineteenth Century* (Princeton, NJ: Princeton University Press, 1983), 54.

49. Tomas Cvrcek, 'Wages, Prices, and Living Standards in the Habsburg Empire, 1827–1910', *The Journal of Economic History* 73, no. 1 (2013), 15; Dányi, „Az élet ára", 32–4.

50. Komlos, *Habsburg Monarchy*, 89.

lands had increased from around 90,000 tonnes by the 1780s to 130,000 tonnes in the early 1830s and reached more than 300,000 tonnes before mid-century.[51] The sheer, constantly growing quantities of Pannonian frontier wheat floating *up* the Danube helped to ease the pressures of rising demand after the financial and supply turmoil of the first fifteen years of the century.

By the 1820s, advertisements for 'real, good flour made from famous Banat wheat' produced by local mills appeared in Vienna's major newspapers.[52] In 1836, a trade report from Bratislava, an important intermediate market, remarked, 'in the last two years local harvests failed, but Hungary's great granary, the Banat, helped out everywhere',[53] and by 1848, a petition of Vienna's bakers' guild argued:

> The four markets [of Vienna, Stockerau, Enzersdorf and Fischamend] together do not supply the twelfth part of rye and wheat needed [...]. Surely, the quality of cereals sold on these markets does not suffice to produce the kind of flour that satisfies the requirements of local authorities and customers. As a matter of fact, Hungarian wheat sold in Wieselburg [Moson] or Raab [Györ], [is] largely covering Vienna's flour demand.[54]

As an 1855 evaluation of the city's supply system by the Lower Austrian Board of Trade reads, around mid-century Vienna's reliance on frontier food was taken for granted: 'Wheat, the major article of Vienna's demand, is mainly delivered from Banat, because, as is generally known, regarding fineness and quality Banat wheat is the most excellent in the entire Monarchy.'[55]

Highlighted in Map 9, by 1865 Györ/Raab was among the most important and largest train depots of the entire Danube area, syphooning much of the cereal production of the Hungarian Plains westward. The largest trade ports along the Danube-Tisza-Maros water system – Mako and Szegedin – turned over volumes of about 2.8 and 2.5 million centners of grain in that year. Most of the grain was sent either via the Kupa and Save rivers towards the Adriatic or via the Danube upriver towards Pest, Raab and Vienna. The third-largest port, Raab's 1865 grain

---

51. Herbert Hassinger, 'Der Aussenhandel der Habsburgermonarchie in der Zweiten Hälfte des 18. Jahrhunderts', in *Die Wirtschaftliche Situation in Deutschland und Österreich um die Wende vom 18. zum 19. Jahrhundert: Bericht über die erste Arbeitstagung der Gesellschaft für Sozial- und Wirtschaftsgeschichte in Mainz 4. – 6. März 1963*, ed. Friedrich Lütge (Stuttgart: Fischer, 1964), 87; Komlos, *Habsburg Monarchy*, 60, 75–6.

52. Albrecht, 'Need for Wheat', 119.

53. Ibid., 119.

54. Innung der bürgerl. Bäckermeister in der k.k. Haupt- und Residenzstadt Wien, *Darstellung der Gewerblichen Zustände der Wiener Bäcker-Innung* (Wien: Ferd. Jahn, 1848), 3.

55. Niederösterreichische Handels- und Gewerbekammer, *Statistische Übersicht der wichtigsten Productionszweige in Oestereich Unter der Ens* (Wien: L. Sommer, 1855), 19.

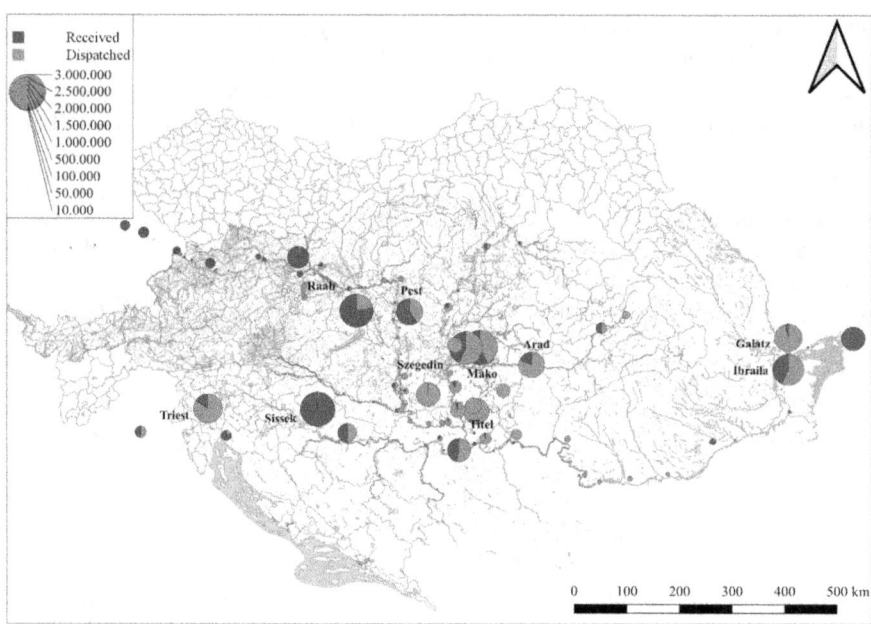

Map 9 Grain Trade by Ship on Major Rivers of Austria-Hungary, 1865, in Centners.[56]

water transport volume just surpassed 2.5 million centners of grain while Vienna received about 1.1 million centners by ship transport.

The result of the conquest of cornucopia, by the first half of the nineteenth century the urban consumption of bread in Vienna was essentially bound to the fate of distant people and environments. Furthermore, the fruits of cornucopia proved a major reason for the *wheatification* of bread consumption in Vienna and for political reforms of the capital's regulated bread market.

The fruits of cornucopia: Hard reds and the coming of 'good bread'

Foreigners visiting the Austrian capital find at every hotel and restaurant the *Kaiser-Semmel*, a smooth, irregularly-rounded, small, wheaten-flour loaf, or roll, of uniform weight, and always fresh, but not warm. It presents a rich, reddish-brown crust, and a delicately-shaded, yellowish, almost white, interior. [...] This wheat-bread of Vienna has long been famed for its excellence. As produced at the Paris International Exposition in 1867 it elicited universal admiration. The

---

56. Source: K.K. Statistische Central-Commission, ed., *Schifffahrt und Verkehr auf der Donau und ihren Nebenflüssen im Jahre 1865,* Mittheilungen aus dem Gebiete der Statistik 13, IV. Heft (Wien, 1867) Johann Winkler, 247.

products of the French bakery were, at their best, plainly inferior to the steady, uniform achievements of the Vienna bakery. The proprietors of the latter, when asked what their secret was, replied: "We have none; we use Hungarian flour and press yeast". [...] The uniformity of the product demonstrates that the problem of making good bread has been solved.[57]

A member of the US scientific commission to the 1873 Vienna World's Fair, Eben Norton Horsford was an expert in the evolving food sciences around the middle of the nineteenth century. A trained mathematic and chemist, Horsford had left the United States during the 1840s and worked with Justus von Liebig in Giessen, Germany, before returning to his home country to assume the Rumford Chair of Physics at Harvard University in 1847. Besides a fruitful academic career Horsford co-founded Rumford Chemical Works in 1854, successfully producing an industrial baking powder he had patented in 1856.[58] Equally recognized by various mid-century observers, not only the quantitative importance but also the qualitative impacts of Hungarian wheat and flour for Vienna's bread crafts had become commonplace by the 1850s. 'Only in Austria, namely in Vienna,' another author claimed already in 1846, 'do the millers choose hard, vitreous, brown Banat wheat as the best quality, they rightly gauge it to produce strong and rich flour.'[59] During the 1867 Paris *Exposition Universelle* various flour products from millers from Vienna and the vicinity were awarded silver and gold medals. According to the Austrian report it was 'generally recognized that the flour products of the entire Austrian milling industry are not only excellent, but that the Hungarian and Austrian mills produce the absolute best, finest, purest and whitest flour [...]'.[60] While maybe a little biased this judgement was indeed shared by Horsford several years later when he found that the 'berry from which the best Hungarian flour is made, is for the most part, of reddish color' and 'reminds one of our best so-called southern wheat. [...] Besides being rich in flour of extraordinary keeping quality it contains more gluten than other varieties of wheat. [...] The Hungarian flour produced by high milling is, in the points of purity, whiteness, yield and keeping qualities, not equaled by that of any other country [...]'.[61]

57. Eben Norton Horsford, *Report on Vienna Bread* (Washington: Government Printing Office, 1875), 1.

58. Charles L. Jackson, 'Eben Norton Horsford', *Proceedings of the American Academy of Arts and Sciences*, no. 28 (1892), 340–6; Samuel Rezneck, 'The European Education of an American Chemist and Its Influence in 19th-Century America: Eben Norton Horsford', *Technology and Culture* 11, no. 3 (1970), 366–88.

59. Lochner, 'Bericht über die Probemahlung in der neuen Leykower Mühle', *Encyklopädische Zeitschrift des Gewerbewesens*, November 1846, 1077.

60. H. Zichy, 'Cerealien und Mehl', in *Officieller Ausstellungs-Bericht, 7. Lieferung: Nahrungsmittel und Getränke auf der Welt-Ausstellung zu Paris im Jahre 1867*, ed. k.k. Österreichisches Central-Comité (Wien: Braumüller, 1868).

61. Horsford, *Vienna Bread*, 16, 76.

In his prosaic retrospect also written on the occasion of the 1873 World Fair, chairperson of Vienna's Baker's Association and president of the Produce Exchange Roman Uhl looked back appraisingly:

> In the years 1814–1815 Banat wheat was ground in Lower Austrian mills for the first time. The flour samples established the superior quality and the bakers' demand for this sort of flour became more and more urgent. [...] When the '30s began, [...] diligence and knowledge had made arable the Hungarian steppes and pusztas, and the rich yields of this blessed soil poured into all mills in Vienna's vicinity. Trading firms were created in Wieselburg [Moson] to reload wheat delivered on large ships from the Banat. We see carters with countless wagons bringing Hungary's harvests in mighty caravans to the Lower Austrian mills, and Vienna and her vicinity are flooded with the best grains. Hungary became the granary of Vienna.[62]

Harvesting the fruits of cornucopia surely helped to sustain a growing population in the industrializing core region around Vienna and to prevent food shortages and price crises throughout the Vormärz period.[63] Equally important, between the late eighteenth and mid-nineteenth centuries wheat from the Pannonian Steppe helped transform the economic and technical conditions of flour production in the Viennese hinterland. An exclave of the Eurasian Steppe in geographic terms, the environmental conditions of the Pannonian Plain are comparable to those of the Russian Steppes, the North American Great Plains or parts of the South American Pampas.[64] With a semi-arid to arid climate, cold winters, hot summers, relatively low precipitation over the year and humus-rich black chernozem earth, like her American and Eurasian relatives the Pannonian Puszta offers a very suitable environment for grain cultivation.[65] Wheat grown on the most ideal soils of the steppe feature a reddish-brown, vitreous appearance; the kernels are harder and thus tougher to break and contain higher amounts of protein and gluten than those of softer wheat varieties grown in regions that are more humid across

62. Roman Uhl, 'Mühlen-Industrie', in *Beiträge zur Geschichte der Gewerbe und Erfindungen Oesterreichs von der Mitte des XVIII. Jahrhunderts bis zur Gegenwart*, ed. Wilhelm F. Exner (Wien: Wilhelm Braumüller, 1873), 176–7.

63. See Albrecht, 'Need for Wheat'.

64. Rácz, *Steppe*; Güldner and Krausmann, 'Nutrient Recycling and Soil Fertility Management'; Pinke, 'Modernization and Decline'.

65. Alan L. Olmstead and Paul W. Rhode, 'The Red Queen and the Hard Reds: Productivity Growth in American Wheat, 1800–1940', *The Journal of Economic History* 62, no. 4 (2002); David Moon, 'In the Russians' Steppes: The Introduction of Russian Wheat on the Great Plains of the United States of America', *Journal of Global History* 3, no. 2 (2008), 203–25; David Moon, *The Plough That Broke the Steppes: Agriculture and Environment on Russia's Grasslands; 1700–1914* (Oxford: Oxford University Press, 2013); Courtney Fullilove, *The Profit of the Earth: The Global Seeds of American Agriculture* (Chicago: University of Chicago Press, 2017).

Europe.[66] Recognized by experts like Horsford or Uhl, by the 1870s and 1880s such knowledge was of fundamental commercial interest as the superior bread-making qualities of wheat and flour became scientifically tied to glutinous hard wheat and detailed information on wheat qualities in the various regions of the Hungarian half of Austro-Hungary became widely available.[67]

Whereas knowledge on wheat became ever more widespread not only among exchange agents after mid-century, the millers in Vienna's surroundings had gained practical experience with Pannonian steppe wheat since the turn of the century, when hard reds had started to arrive in ever-growing amounts. Experimenting with the 'new' raw material, the superior quality of Hungarian grain enabled and induced millers, technicians and businessmen alike to invest into and implement changes in the techniques and processes of milling. Adapting the techniques to ground hard reds into flour, under the developing procedure of 'high milling' the millstones were set wider apart from each other than it was done under the 'old' system of 'low milling'. As the hardness of hard red steppe wheat allowed grinding and peeling the grain kernels in successive rounds instead of crushing them in just one pass 'high milling' enabled to mill the same load of kernels repeatedly. Lowering the upper millstone with every round and setting it closer to the lower millstone the results of each step could be sifted and sorted. This made possible the production of various flour qualities of different fineness and colour from the same load of grains. In comparison, 'low milling' would yield fewer and coarser sorts of flour as well as more bran in general.[68] Famed by academics and engineers of the latter half of the century, one Ignaz Paur of Vöslau was allegedly among the first pioneers to introduce 'high milling' in the Vienna region. Having created

66. B. Belderok, J. Mesdag, and D. A. Donner, *Bread-Making Quality of Wheat: A Century of Breeding in Europe* (Dordrecht: Springer Netherlands, 2000); Anneleen Pauly et al., 'Wheat (Triticum Aestivum L. And T. Turgidum L. Ssp. Durum) Kernel Hardness: I. Current View on the Role of Puroindolines and Polar Lipids', *Comprehensive Reviews in Food Science and Food Safety* 12, no. 4 (2013), 427–38. See also Horsford's 1870s analysis in Horsford, *Vienna Bread*. On the milling capacities of hard and soft wheat and varietal shifts in nineteenth-century Britain, see also Aashish Velkar, *Markets and Measurements in Nineteenth-Century Britain* (Cambridge: Cambridge University Press, 2012), 185, 191–3. On the importance of, and problem with, grain qualities elsewhere, see e.g. Liam Brunt and Edmund Cannon, 'Variations in the Price and Quality of English Grain, 1750–1914: Quantitative Evidence and Empirical Implications', *Explorations in Economic History* 58 (2015).

67. On the perception of gluten's nutritive value, its use as a quality measure for wheat and the creation of standardized flour quality denominations, see Velkar, *Markets and Measurements*, 195–6. On the production and dispersion of commercial grain quality knowledge, see e.g. grain agent Johann Treyer's 1878 and 1885 maps on wheat qualities on the Pannonian Plain available at Österreichische Nationalbibliothek, Weizen-Qualitäten-Karte von Ungarn, AB 9A 56, https://digital.onb.ac.at/RepViewer/viewer.faces?doc=DTL_7250626&order=1&view=SINGLE (29 March 2021).

68. On the techniques of low and high milling, see e.g. Friedrich Kick, *Die Mehlfabrikation: Ein Lehrbuch des Mühlenbetriebes*, 2nd ed. (Leipzig: Arthur Felix, 1878), Horsford, *Vienna Bread*.

and built a sifting apparatus with a regional carpenter Paur was said to have installed his wind-powered machine at his own mill around 1810 and introduced a similar construction to another mill in Lichtenwörth by 1826.[69] Apparently, the products of high milling enjoyed growing demand early on as especially the fine premium grits allegedly 'sold like hot cakes' and 'high-milling was implemented and perfected in the 25 years after the turn of the century.[70]

While nature facilitated technological change, politics enabled the large-scale implementation and adaption of new techniques in the milling sector, especially in Vienna and its southern environs. Having again liberalized the trade in grain in 1817 as a reaction on Tambora-induced harvest failures the Napoleonic era had already done away with various regulations of the milling trade. To smooth the city's food supply Vienna's assize on flour had been abolished in 1809. Five years later, the ending of thirlage (Mühlenzwang) and the introduction of a new *Mühlenordnung* freed millers from wide-ranging commercial and geographic restrictions while the city also eased the quality requirements for flour brought to the urban marketplaces in 1817. A wide-ranging liberalization of milling, this policy freed the sector of previously existing restrictions regarding outlet markets, locations, techniques, products and sales prices and opened flour production fundamentally to more capitalistic and market-oriented activities.[71]

Together, the coming of hard reds and economic liberalization created a different market situation for millers and fostered the implementation of technological changes. This again was linked to the beginning industrialization and concentration of the trade. Further speeded up by a drought that left many of the region's millers without waterpower during much of the 1830s the energy problem induced the increasing installation of steam engines.[72] By the 1820s, larger 'trading mills' processing mainly Hungarian wheat were founded at the rivers flowing down the Vienna Woods south of the city. Around 1846, Franz Spuller of Guntramsdorf operated a 'rational, great business' at the Badner Bach, where he processed some 60,000 Metzen of flour – almost 37,000 hectolitres per annum.[73]

69. Gustav Pappenheim, 'Geschichte der Österreichischen Müllerei 1848 bis 1898', in *Geschichte der Österreichischen Land- und Forstwirtschaft und ihrer Industrien: 1848–1898: Festschrift zur Feier der am 2. December 1898 erfolgten Fünfzigjährigen Wiederkehr der Thronbesteigung Sr. Majestät des Kaisers Franz Joseph I. Supplementband I* (Wien: Moritz Perles, 1901), 274; Kick, *Mehlfabrikation*, 295.

70. Pappenheim, 'Geschichte', 270–1; Gustav Pappenheim, 'Die Müllerei im 19. Jahrhundert', *Oesterreichisch-Ungarische Müller-Zeitung*, 31 December 1899, 53, 2.

71. Christina Spitzbart-Glasl, 'Feste Wassermühlen und Schiffsmühlen als Bestandteil der Wiener Gewässerlandschaft', in *Donau-Stadt-Landschaften. Danube-City-Landscapes*, ed. Máté Tamáska (Berlin: LIT, 2016), 269.

72. Uhl, 'Mühlen-Industrie', 178; Kick, *Mehlfabrikation*, 295.

73. This and the following are derived from Jonas M. Albrecht, 'Brot für die Hauptstadt. Niederösterreich und die Nahrungsversorgung Wiens', in *Geschichte Niederösterreichs: Band 2. Gesellschaft und Gemeinschaft. Eine Regionalgeschichte der Moderne*, ed. Oliver Kühschelm, Elisabeth Loinig and Willibald Rosner (St. Pölten: Verlag NÖ Institut für Landeskunde, 2021).

4. The Conquest of Cornucopia

At that time, however, Georg Volk was the trade's regional champion. Already in 1825 he had equipped his mill in Wienerherberg, located at Fischa River, with a 'paternoster' that transported the cereals into the engine-driven grinding gears. Commanding eleven grinders and eighteen workers producing some 73,000 litres of grain per week Volk extended his 'flour fabric' to twenty grinders and a capacity of nearly 185,000 litres per week until 1847. Though the establishment fell victim to a 'terrible fire' that also cost one life on 7 February 1847 Volk's insurance covered the losses. By 1861, his mill had thirty-two grinding gears and was considered the 'largest water mill in the empire'.

A noteworthy investment, introducing high milling, sifting machines and other technical changes to a mill was not cheap as can be taken from ads for mill sales during the early 1820s. Whereas the asking prices for the presumably smaller rural 'Luka mill' in Deutschbach was 1,600fl. and the 'Friedel mill' in Türnitz was advertised for 11,000fl., the Grammatneusiedl 'Laden mill' and an Obersievering mill, both in the capital's immediate vicinity, were offered for 50,000fl. and 100,000fl., respectively. Raw-material and capital-induced industrialization of the milling sector reached a first peak in 1840 with the founding of the *k.k. aussch. privil. Dampfmühlen-Actien-Gesellschaft in Wien*. Four years earlier, merchant Carl Markowitz had secured a five-year privilege on the foundation of a steam mill in Vienna. By 1839, he had sold these rights to a joint stock company. Selling shares worth 500,000fl. in total through Wertheimstein wholesale merchant house the Actien-Gesellschaft bought up convenient grounds at the Donaukanal and placed an order with the Liège machine factory of English-Belgian industrialist John Cockerill over a 100,000fl., 60-horsepower steam engine to power the mill. Rallying prominent financiers like Salomon Meyer Rothschild, Alexander von Schöller, Daniel von Eskeles or Heinrich von Wertheimstein as well as economic and technically learned investors like professors Joseph von Kudler, Adam von Burg and miller Augustin Preuß, Vienna's first steam mill opened its doors to customers on 1 July 1842. Three years later, its coal-driven machines ground close to 18,500,000 litres of solely Banat wheat per annum, outperforming all other players by far. Selling these premium sorts of flour through various retail shops across the city and in branded sacks only the Dampfmühle quickly became a behemoth of flour production that not only supplied the Vienna market but also delivered to outlets in other Habsburg cities. Yet, it did not go completely unchallenged, as the von Schöller family attempted to gain more of the cake through the foundation of a second steam mill in Ebenfurth, south of Vienna, in 1853.

While many smaller, mainly water-driven mills remained in business and secured no small market shares until the last third of the century industrialization also meant concentration. Though reliable numbers are hard to come by the number of mills in Lower Austria was declining since the late seventeenth century; by the 1850s almost a thousand mills less were counted than two centuries earlier. Until the 1890s, the province's milling sector was reduced by another 400 sites. Many mills in the more densely developed urban area of the capital had already been closed by the mid-1850s.[74] Underlining this trend narratively,

---

74. Spitzbart-Glasl, 'Wassermühlen', 276–7.

by 1848 Vienna's baker's guild was worried that 'regardless of the population growth during the last 50 years the number of mills has not increased, on the contrary, in the same period of time many were reconstructed into factories or other industrious [sic!] enterprises'.[75] Thus, between the 1770s and 1850s, nature, politics, capital and technology changed the circumstances of buying, producing and selling flour in Vienna decisively. Rippling down the food chain these altered market conditions brought two major ramifications to the bakers in and around the capital: a noteworthy expansion of the range of flour products available, and a critical change in their business relations with millers.

With the growing availability of hard red Banat wheat and high milling the range of flour qualities available to both the metropolitan bakers and urban consumers diversified significantly. Famed as *Auszugsmehl* (pull-out flour), again Ignaz Paur was credited with the invention of a premium, extra-fine and extra-white wheat flour named after the way it was produced. Sifted – in contemporary language, pulled out – from the coarser amounts of flour during successive rounds of grinding *Auszugmehl* was considered the finest possible kind of grits during the early decades of the century.[76] While the test millings and bakings of the late eighteenth and early nineteenth centuries indicated only a relatively straightforward number of different sorts of flour to be produced and used by bakers,[77] by the 1850s and 1860s, fostered by accelerating technological innovation, the flour market looked quite different.[78] In 1863, for example, Vienna's exchange for agricultural products noted prices for five more or less standardized qualities of wheat flour from various regional water mills as well as both steam mills. Distinguishing between numbers zero through five, between premium *Kaiserauszug* grits, a 'baker's Auszug', three sorts of *Mund-* and *Semmelmehl* as well as coarse *Pohlmehl*, these compilations of flour prices also reveal the notable differences between flour qualities produced. Whereas a centner of Number Five quality sold for between four and six Gulden, Number Zero premium *Auszug* was almost three times more expensive regardless of its producer. In addition, the finer two numbers milled in Vienna's steam mill were both more expensive than those of their competitors, although not by far.

75. Innung der bürgerl. Bäckermeister in der k.k. Haupt- und Residenzstadt Wien, *Gewerbliche Zustände*, 6.

76. Kick, *Mehlfabrikation*, 294–5.

77. Wiener Stadt- und Landesarchiv, Alte Registratur A2 – Berichte: 210/1770, 29.07.1769: N.Ö. Regs. Secretär Hägelin. Nota Die von mir Endes gefertigte aufgetragener Massen abgeführte Mahl- und respective Back Probem betreffend.

78. R. Perren, 'Structural Change and Market Growth in the Food Industry: Flour Milling in Britain, Europe, and America, 1850–1914', *The Economic History Review* 43, no. 3 (1990), 420–37.

Table 4 Vienna Exchange Wheat Flour Prices, January 1863, per Wiener Centner

Mill/Flour	Kaiserauszug, Tafelgries Nr. 0	Bäckerauszug extra fein Nr. 1	Griesler Mundmehl Nr. 2	Mundmehl, Griesler Semmelmehl Nr. 3	Semmelmehl Nr. 4	Pohlmehl/ lange Pohl Nr. 5
Various mills	12fl 25kr -	10fl 10kr -	9fl 50kr – 10fl 75kr	6fl 50kr -	5fl 25kr -	4fl -
	13fl 25kr	12fl 25kr		7fl 50kr	6fl 50 kr	5fl 25kr
Wiener Dampfmühle	13fl 50kr	12fl 50kr	10fl 25kr	7fl 50kr	6fl	5fl
Ebenfurther Dampfmühle	13fl 25kr	12fl 25kr	10fl 25kr	7fl 25kr	6fl 25kr	5fl 75kr

Sources: *Gemeinde-Zeitung. Unabhängiges, politisches Journal*, 'Fruchtbörse', 22 January 1863, 4.

A decade later, product diversification had created an even more differentiated flour market.[79] By 1875, Friedrich Kick identified eight kinds of wheat flour, from numbers 00, *Kaiser-Auszugsmehl*, through 0, *Auszugsmehl* to number 6, *black Pohlmehl*, the darkest and coarsest wheat flour made in Vienna mills. While 'these eight sorts are trade items, however, there are many intermediate nuances', as Kick himself observed. The Hungarian mills of Pest would classify their products into between nine and eleven numbers at the same time. By the 1870s, Austrian and Hungarian steam mills, and increasingly, steam roller mills, obtained much finer and more diverse sorts of flour from grinding hard reds than their predecessors had a century earlier.

Nature and technology changed the range and qualities of baker's mayor ingredient; capital and politics altered their business relation with millers. Although few sources are available to analyse these relations some indications can be found that suggest bakers might have grown as dependent on and indebted to industrial flour producers as their London or Paris counterparts did during the early decades of the nineteenth century.[80] Even though this might have also been the case by the eighteenth century, industrialization and concentration appear to have accelerated this development after the turn of the century. In December 1830, a petition by the guild to prohibit turning any of the region's 'mills at the larger creeks into factories' was rejected by the provincial government.[81] Over the following decades, the guild continued its opposition against concentration among millers. Welfare through competition, the corporation argued in 1848, 'would only be achieved if the number of mills in Vienna's vicinity and their production capacities were high enough to supply more flour than required by the city's bakers. [...] Vienna's bakers are completely in the hands of the millers, who benefit the most from the lack of competition.'[82]

Indeed, in January 1849 the authorities assessed the bakers' debts with the *Dampfmühle* at 300,000fl. plus another 600,000fl. with 'other mills'.[83] In late April,

79. On the process of flour standardization in Britain, see Velkar, *Markets and Measurements*.

80. On bakers' dependency on industrial millers in London, see John Burnett, 'The Baking Industry in the Nineteenth Century', *Business History* 5, no. 2 (1963); on Paris see Steven L. Kaplan, *The Bakers of Paris and the Bread Question, 1700–1775* (Durham: Duke University Press, 1996), 377–422; esp. 381.

81. Archiv der Bäckergenossenschaft in Wien, HS 15: Innung der bürgerl. Bäckermeister in der k.k. Haupt- und Residenzstadt Wien. Protocollum uiber merkwürdige Gegenstände, als: Volksaufruhr gegen die Bäcker anno 1805; die den bürgl Bäckermeister geleisteten Vergütungen; mehrere Backproben; Consignation über die Ausgaben eines mitleren Bäckermeisters; dann der vom Jahre 1807 bis 1830 ergangenen Verordnungen und Rathschläge, 14.12.1830.

82. Innung der bürgerl. Bäckermeister in der k.k. Haupt- und Residenzstadt Wien, *Gewerbliche Zustände*, 6–7.

83. Wiener Stadt- und Landesarchiv: Gemeinderat der Stadt Wien. Protokolle der III. Sektion, 1848–1852, 18 January 1849.

the manager of the Vienna steam mill filed a lawsuit against master baker Georg Putz of Nr. 12 Lichtenthal over 1,043fl. and 46 Kreuzer plus extra charges for flour deliveries. However, Putz's whereabouts were unknown. Indicating that this was no singular event the steam mill equally sued master baker Fanz Eder of Nr. 98 Neubau for flour deliveries over 1,674fl. and 30kr. in April 1851. Like his confrere earlier Eder was not to be found.[84] What is more, when the milling company went into economic turbulences in the late 1860s leading to its bankruptcy by June 1872, 'uncollectable claims' over 136,000 Gulden were one, though not the most important reason of failure.[85]

To conclude, compared to the late 1700s by the middle of the nineteenth century the commercial, technological and the political landscape of baking bread in Vienna had changed decisively. The flour products bakers could obtain were different, and had been produced differently from a rather different raw material that had reached the region's mills from different soils via different ways of transport and locations of commerce. These overall changes had most serious impacts on the capital's institutions of embeddedness, most prominently on the bread assize.

---

84. *Wiener Zeitung*, 'An Herrn Georg Putz', 28 April 1849, 101, Amtsblatt, 796; *Wiener Zeitung*, 'Aufforderung an Franz Eder, Bürgerl. Bäckermeister', 11 April 1851, 87, Amtsblatt.
85. *Neue Freie Presse*, 'Wiener Dampfmühlen-Gesellschaft', 25 May 1869, 1701.

Chapter 5

REFORMING THE ASSIZE?

If one bears in mind that anno 1696 the milling and baking system was constituted with all accuracy and love for justice and notes that it remains in practice for more than 130 years, one is carried away by reverence for its makers, whose inspiration and spirit – with only limited means – created a building that, although here and there a little rotten, stands upright until the present day. What proves useless and harmful of this system today is the result of developments of the last 50 years.[1]

Evidenced by his nineteen-pages 1828 ideas for a reform of the assize, to which he added a 16-pages addendum two years later, Johann Maria of Nr. 27 An der Wien was beyond doubt a vivid supporter of bread price regulation. What is more, a master baker turned urban clerk his plans for a reform of Vienna's bread assize calculations were as bold as they were extensive. Granted a private audience with Emperor Franz I on 31 December 1828 he presented detailed estimates of the costs of milling and baking, the quality of flour and bread obtainable from given quantities of wheat, the numbers of millers and bakers necessary to supply the capital and the level of taxation tolerable for poor consumers. He deemed his reform proposal not only fit for Vienna but 'even to be established in all provinces of the great Austrian Empire'. According to Maria, it was high time for reform. Written in 'the hours of regrettably compelled idleness' the former baker apparently intended to speed up a process that had been stalled for quite a while. After 'seven empty promises by the administration which assured the Vienna and Brünn bakers' guilds the speedy implementation of a new milling and baking regulation' he 'had been waiting for 10 years for the consultation of various experts familiar with the demands and moods of the consumers'.

However, a quick solution was necessary since 'the improved agriculture and milling mechanisms of the last decades' had rendered the basics of assize calculation 'unsuitable'. Banat wheat, Maria explained, had 'due to its glue more advantageous

---

1. Wiener Stadt- und Landesarchiv, Hauptregistratur A24, Dep. G – Marktsachen, 1829, Schachtel 19, 1828: Johann Maria. Ideen zu einem, dem Geist der Zeit angemeßenen neuen Mehl und Gebäcks Satzungs Regulativ als Provisorium für die k.k. Residenz Stadt Wien.

baking qualities than traditionally known' and was heavier per unit of volume than the locally grown varieties. Therefore, he argued for the standardized introduction of weight volumes – centners – instead of the volume measure of *Metzen* for market sales to establish the quality of cereals. Additionally, the 'improved mill structure compared to the old, simple techniques enable the production of more of the fine sorts of flour' from a given quantity of cereals. Yielding 'more *Mund-Semmel* flour' compared to traditional grinding methods, 'through the improvement of mill structures every kind of flour is much better, whiter and freer from brans and other impurities, which leads to higher flour qualities'. Consequently, 'the inhabitants of Austria enjoy more beautiful flour and better bread'. To Maria, this left the present assize calculations in need of adaption to the improved material and technological circumstances. Calculating such new rates the reform-minded former baker went on to suggest the founding of a *Pistorey*, which should be built at the harbour of the Wiener Neustadt Canal near the city centre.

Incorporating a public test mill and bakery 'for both of these trades of public interest' the *Pistorey* was intended to be something of an early municipal institute of food security, protected by a ten-foot wall and a k.k. military guard. Carrying out test millings as well as baking trials it was to establish grain, flour and bread quality standards to which the region's millers and the city's bakers were to adhere. While its products should be given to the city's orphanages and schools Maria also created detailed instructions for the *Pistorey*'s director, who was to become something like the city's superintendent of bread provision. Though he should not dispose of direct financial resources to prevent corruption, such a director would purchase representative qualities of grain via municipal promissory notes, oversee test millings and bakings and thus establish product standards with the help of chosen millers and bakers. Furthermore, he was to enforce very strict limits of the numbers of bakeries in the city, which should be reduced from 185 to 70, to examine prospective journeymen and masters, visit mills and bakeries to ensure adherence to food standards, and to observe grain trade activities and prices on the respective marketplaces.

Next to that implementation of a public institute adapting, standardizing and overseeing food qualities the reform also stipulated alterations regarding the system of market price surveys as the basis for assize calculation. In general, on the marketplaces surveyed assize officials should note whether transactions were realized in cash or on credit since this produced 'a significant difference in sales prices'. Moreover, with the liberalization of the grain trade the proponent deemed it necessary to not only register transactions on the four public marketplaces but it was also necessary to 'report all substantial grain sales by private individuals and from manorial granaries'. Most important, however, was a more general adaption of the system of grain price survey regarding the marketplaces consulted. 'Regarding the residence's demand', Maria continued,

> the ratio between the quantity of grain sold on the marketplaces considered for Vienna's assize and the amount of cereals bought in Wieselburg [Moson] stands at 1 to 3. Therefore, the Wieselburg grain prices including costs for transportation

to the mills should also be taken into consideration for the calculation of the assize, even more so since the market of Fischamend is insignificant.[2]

Johann Maria's ideas for a reform of Vienna's bread assize system were not purely altruistic. To 'fulfil his civic duties' Maria continued to underline his own expertise and offered himself as a member of the reform commission he thought genuinely overdue and thus apparently attempted to foster his very own career as a municipal clerk. Yet, his extensive proposal, addressed and presented to the emperor in person, was more than an individualistic act. Rather, it needs to be interpreted as both a sign for the quite urgent need to adapt the assize system to the general changes described above, and as a loud plea for a regulatory reform instead of liberalization. Although hard to capture due to the lack of sources Maria's was a contribution to a more general *Vormärz* debate over the course of economic reforms: adapt institutions of embeddedness or abandon them altogether. While imperial, provincial and local administrations tried rather unsuccessfully to negotiate the juxtaposition of economic liberal reformers and sceptics of laissez-faire in regard of the empire-wide *Gewerbefreiheit* throughout the 1830s and 1840s,[3] Viennese officials fought similar battles over the city's bread assize throughout the first half of the nineteenth century.

Signed 18 April 1810 by three unnamed 'proponents' an earlier modification proposal represents the explicitly mentioned point of reference for Maria's 1828 intervention. Apparently interrupted by the French invasion in 1808, around that time a court commission led by president of the Lower Austrian government Ferdinand von Bissingen-Nippenburg and Vienna's *Stadthauptmann* Joseph Paul Gottlob von Lederer had already debated over the necessity to reform the assize. Contrary to Johann Maria's rather anti-liberal recommendations two decades later these 1808 deliberations were much more liberal-minded. Not only did the commission members favour a wide-ranging reform of the assize and bread market regulations, they also issued loud scepticism over the guild system more generally. Debating over the assize and the calculation of bread weights and prices, thirteen of the fourteen members supported a proposal to alter the way by which bread was sold. Contrary to the traditional fixed-price system the large majority voted to set 'the weight of bakery goods constant and assess the prices variable according to the price of grain'. Then, it would only be necessary to 'survey which baked goods are to be subjected to the assize and which fixed weight needs to be constituted for each kind'. Moving on, it ought to be evaluated if not 'everything that is called craft or guild should, as in England or France, be abolished altogether'. Since the guild would only nominate master bakers who supported guild instead of consumer

---

2. Maria, Ideen.

3. Andreas Baryli, 'Gewerbepolitik und gewerbliche Verhältnisse im vormärzlichen Wien', in *Wien im Vormärz*, ed. Renate Banik-Schweitzer, Forschungen und Beiträge zur Wiener Stadtgeschichte 8 (Wien: Jugend und Volk, 1980); Andreas Baryli, *Konzessionssystem Contra Gewerbefreiheit* (Frankfurt am Main: Lang, 1984).

interests the state should give rather unlimited business licences to bakers 'without regard of their capabilities or fortune' because 'both of these properties are the only and main attributes to run a business, without them, it cannot be started or sustained'.

Thus largely accepting the Josephinian free-competition-position of the 1780s and departing from the moral-economy point of view 'the nature of a master [must] be no requirement for a trade license' in the future. The regulated system of closed numbers, the commission argued, 'by no means advantages the skilled, diligent and courteous tradesman but only the sluggish, inapt producer who exploits the consumers to his benefits'. Generally, the statement went, 'it is impossible for the government, and can thus not be required from it, to determine the numbers of producers of any kind in such a way that [...] there will never be too much or too little of the respective food items.' While otherwise agreeing that the assize remained a useful institution to guide and steer the bread market and the bakers 'to concentrate more on the production of bread instead of rolls and pasties, as they do now', in regard of the number of bakers with these statements the commission blatantly declared the market, not the government to be responsible for the regulation of the numbers of bakeries. Based on this outspokenly pro-deregulation reasoning the proponents of 1808 and 1810 introduced a detailed new way of assize calculation that would not 'treat the bakers for their services to the consumers like public officials with fixed incomes' and end the 'general cheating' of the customers.[4]

In some way or the other Maria seems to have been involved in this earlier reform movement. Directly commenting on the proposal in June 1811 he strongly argued that the new way of calculating bread prices and further deregulation would hurt the bakers and leave them to use 'self-defence and other prohibited tricks'. In such a case, he urged, 'even the most impartial person recognizes that this ever-important craft either needs to be reformed or – not advisable – left over to free competition'. Unfortunately, the results of the 1808 court commission remain obscure; there are no archival sources of the debate between 1811 and Johann Maria's reiterated address in 1828. Clearly, whereas milling and flour regulations were abolished during the 1810s, neither were the proposals towards a system of fixed bread weights and variable prices implemented nor was the baker's guild abolished. However, a March 1830 supplement written by Maria 'in the spirit of those stringent principles which take for granted a governmental paternalism towards all inhabitants of the residence' is well in line with a suggested struggle between reformers from above and below over the kind of action necessary to

---

4. Wiener Stadt- und Landesarchiv, Hauptregistratur A24, Dep. G, 1829, Schachtel 19, 1810/1811: Johann Maria. Auszug über das von drey Proponenten verfasste ganz neue Vermahlungs und Verbackungs System für die Residenzstadt Wien 808 [Abschrift genommen]. On the generally liberal-minded position of various members of the high bureaucracy, see e.g. Alois Brusatti, *Österreichische Wirtschaftspolitik vom Josephinismus zum Ständestaat* (Wien: Jupiter-Verl., 1965), 27–8.

improve the current system. Although he adopted the 1808 demand to change the bread retail system to variable prices and fixed weights, 'many liberal modifications', the supplement continued, 'crept into the flour and bread trades during the last 15 years and have reduced these strict principles to the minimum'. Wondering if the government was to maintain principles of a 'strict economy' or if adaptions and modifications based on liberal developments would be taken the baker-clerk repeated his plea for 'no striking innovation but only modifications according to current circumstances'.[5]

Though not easy to reproduce – this collection of the municipal archives has been discarded excessively – Maria's initial 1828 reform proposal had been passed down to other government and municipal authorities to comment and assess. Unfortunately, only the May 1829 reply by Vienna's Metzenleiher Wolfgang Sittenberger, the city's grain and flour market overseer survived in this collection. Yet, as the city's prime clerk responsible for assize collection, and indeed the person who would have been directly replaced by the proposed *Pistorey* director if Maria's ideas were realized, his is for both reasons a crucial statement. Unsurprisingly, Sittenberger opposed Maria's reform. To be precise, he crushed it into pieces. 'The tendency of this innovation is mainly selfishness, and the means to it, the ruin of many others', he wrote after having summarized the proposal: 'Despite feigned honesty the hidden hostility is too prominent to conceal the man, what he is and what he wants. He who deifies a 130-year-old system and its makers seeks to destroy it at the same time, although with weak hands, and without ever having known or comprehended it.'

Treating each topic of Maria's proposal successively Sittenberger rejected all of them. 'How many clerks would be needed' to measure 'the massive stream of grains arriving each year?', he wondered about the integration of the Wieselburg/Moson market into Vienna's assize price surveys. While the same was arguably true for the control of grain transactions in private granaries the Metzenleiher did also find no benefit in the founding of a *Pistorey* test mill and bakery. Furthermore, neither was an afresh regulation of milling preferable since the abolition of the flour assize in 1813 had 'granted the miller free movements since. To find buyers, his produce needs to be fine and qualitative. The competition between him and others by itself forces him' to be competitive and thus provide good flour for the city's marketplaces.

Continuing, he was especially aghast about Maria's plan to reduce the numbers of bakeries from 185 to 70. A 'loveless and inhuman behaviour of the proponent as former baker against 115 of his colleagues', from Sittenberger's point of view this would mean the 'elimination of all competition' among bakers and jeopardize the inhabitants' cheap provision. In addition, he argued, 'retired bakers don't pay taxes'. Neither did the proposed change towards a sale of bread by fixed weights and variable prices find any appreciation with the city's chief assize administrator. Not beneficial for consumers due to their 'pecuniary condition' he

---

5. Maria, Auszug, Anmerkung Johann Maria, 7 und 11 Juni 1811.

made a point that would continue to be repeated from several sides throughout the century. Not only was 'this application against the customs and habits of the customers': 'Most will not recognize 1 or 2 Lot of bread more or less' while any monetary price increases would render 'the purchase of bread impossible' for many. Offering a final opinion, any new calculations of assize prices would only be 'inappropriate' and hurt millers, bakers and consumers alike. Sittenberger was confident that 'this 130-year-old system, resting on approved principles, will endure for a long time'.[6]

While rather fragmentary, considered as documents produced within the same larger politico-economic debate the proposals of 1808/10, Johann Maria's 1828 reform ideas, and *Metzenleiher* Wolfgang Sittenberger's commentary outline the quite complex and sometimes ambivalent juxtaposition of various interest groups attempting to shape and modify Vienna's bread assize before 1848. For one, the 1808 court commission, staffed with members of the capital's higher bureaucracy, represented a rather liberal-leaning, physiocratic-inspired interest group that aspired a relatively wide-ranging deregulation and abolishment of state intervention after French and English examples. Still, while outspokenly supporting the abolition of official limitations of the numbers of producers, the commission yet maintained a certain support for assize regulation to direct producers and balance individual-corporate interests with those of consumers.

In contrast, Johann Maria, who had been a member of Vienna's baker's guild at least until 1815, rather embodied a position much more in favour of strict regulation and the preservation of guild privileges to which only few masters – 70 instead of 185 – should be granted access. Yet, Maria also made concessions to demands for liberalization in supporting changes to bread retail systems. Meanwhile, as the public clerk responsible for the entire day-to-day functioning of the assize system *Metzenleiher* Sittenberger occupied a middling position that was equally shaped by both liberal and pro-regulation aspects. Outspokenly in favour of liberalized flour trade and only loosely limited numbers of bakers his aim was the largely unhindered and reliable flow of food from producers to consumers to secure a steady supply for the capital. However, to guarantee such a provision at affordable prices for all Sittenberger strongly rejected any meddling with the system of assize calculations.

This was a general setting in which the complex juxtaposition of diverse interest groups with quite different aims between relatively wide-ranging liberalization and quite thorough regulation shaped the debate. Yet, though occupying different poles on such a scale, none of these groups assumed a totalitarian position, all parties encompassed contrary arguments in favour of either regulation or deregulation, too, making this a very complex conflict situation during the

---

6. Wiener Stadt- und Landesarchiv, Hauptregistratur A24, Dep. G – Marktsachen, 1829, Schachtel 19, 04.05.1829: Wolfgang Sittenberger. Schriftliche Aeusserung des gehorsamsten Metzenleiheramte Uiber den Vorschlag des Bürgers Johann Maria hinsichtlich eines neuen Mehl und Gebäck-Satzungs Regulatives für die kais.könig. Residenzstadt Wien.

Vormärz period. Given the overall political circumstances, such a complicated issue remained unsolved before 1848.

Although grossly dismissed by Vienna's Metzenleiher by September 1830, Johann Maria, now a member of the city's *Äußerer Rat*, was very optimistic that his proposal might be realized eventually. Allegedly having survived the 'ordeal by the fire of evaluation' through other government bodies he again expressed his hope that Emperor Franz would found another commission to finally settle the matter and added his most subservient plea 'for gracious use of his own usability' in such a panel.[7] However, despite his efforts, Maria's high hopes were in vain. Historians largely agree on the reform-averse position of the Metternich government, a period when 'the Habsburg regime maintained its centralizing efforts, but did not return to the socially transformative agenda of the eighteenth-century reform monarchs. Even in a time of greater peace and stability, and despite their continued interest in institutional rationalization, Emperor Franz I and his most influential advisors shied away from experimentation with socially significant changes.'[8]

While 'middle-class and noble Austrians initiated new forms of activism in order to solve local social problems that the paralyzed government seemed unwilling to address', 'the regime treated such initiatives with caution and often with suspicion'. Although 'they tolerated and occasionally encouraged independent civic engagement that worked to solve expensive social problems' the overall political climate among the highest levels of government was rather less fertile for wide-ranging and complex reforms. Despite the fact that 'Austrian society itself took upon the challenges of creating social and economic change', like Johann Maria, no consensus could be found, and no reform measures agreed upon between adherents of liberalization and supporters of regulation and status quo.[9]

Between the roughly three decades after 1815, various comprehensive attempts involving court authorities and an empire-wide array of provincial administrations, city councils and local guilds were started to unify the diverse landscape of craft and trade regulations across the realm under one increasingly liberalized roof. Yet, before 1848, none of these attempts to introduce commercial liberty were successful. In early 1835, Emperor Franz I dismissed the draft of a trade code written 'in the tendency of a greater freedom' he had commissioned himself two years earlier. Some eighteen months later, liberal-minded court councils Weiß, Heß and Kübeck decided to put a revision of the 1835 draft back into the shelf because they considered it not liberal enough and feared it might be approved by emperor Ferdinand I precisely for this reason. By April 1841, Kübeck pleaded

---

7. Wiener Stadt- und Landesarchiv, Hauptregistratur A24, Dep. G, 1829, Schachtel 19, 1.9.1830: Johann Maria. Allerunterthänigste Bitte: für den täglich dringender werdenden Fall der Retablierung einer allerhöchsten Hofcommaon in Mahl und Bakgeschäften; um allergnädigste Verwendung seiner diesfälligen Brauchbarkeit.

8. Pieter M. Judson, *The Habsburg Empire: A New History* (Cambridge, MA, London, England: The Belknap Press of Harvard University Press, 2016), 103–5.

9. Ibid., 103–5.

the emperor to be allowed yet another overhaul of the 1836 concept. Though debates among the highest court chambers were subsequently resumed Kübeck failed to convince the sceptics of deregulation among *Staatsrat* and *Hofkammer* and the reform movement was again halted. Another four years later, tireless Kübeck asked Ferdinand I to allow him to send the 1841 document to various provincial governments to collect their opinions on the draft. He was granted to do so by July 1846 after extensive arguments amid the court authorities over which of the rather liberal-leaning Italian and rather anti-liberal Czech, Hungarian and German provinces were to be consulted – a decision that could decisively influence the result of the consultation. While he received answers from Styria, Illyria, Lower Austria, Upper Austria, Moravia-Silesia, Tyrol-Vorarlberg and Lombardo-Venetia between late 1846 and early 1847 those of Galicia, the Austrian Littoral and Bohemia never arrived. Anyhow, encompassing very mixed results mirroring the divided positions among the empire's elites over trade liberalization the outcome of this poll did not represent the support Kübeck had hoped for. With such results, any implementation of a new, liberal commercial code remained impossible. Since 'the entire attempt had failed', it again vanished in the drawer until the revolution of 1848 would change the political circumstances for good.[10]

Just like concerning the *Gewerbefreiheit*, the debates on the reform of Vienna's assize remained equally stalled throughout the Vormärz period due to such contrary positions among different interest groups. Already by 11 July 1830, when Johann Maria's suggestions were still discussed by administrators, the k.k. Lower Austrian government had reminded the capital's bakers to adhere to traditional assize regulations, produce voluminous bread of good quality and sell them at regular assize prices.[11] Several years later, in 1837 the bakers' guild addressed both government and governor with comprehensive accounts of their misery caused by the want for reform, but again without much success.[12] Alarmed by beginning price increases in 1845 the guild again directly appealed Emperor Ferdinand I to regulate the flour price system and reform the bread assize in tandem since millers could freely raise flour prices in this time of crisis while bakers remained tied to fixed retail prices for bread. This time, reform-minded mayor Ignaz Czapka, who also recognized the misalignment of the assize system, aided the corporation.

Arguing that bakers were often indebted vis-à-vis millers due to faulty price surveys and the imbalance between free-market flour and regulated bread prices Czapka largely repeated the reasoning brought forward by various actors for several decades. However, different from the guild of bakers the mayor was strongly in favour of a liberalizing solution of the issue. Deeming an assize-like

10. Baryli, *Konzessionssystem*, 13, 36.

11. Innung der bürgerl. Bäckermeister in der k.k. Haupt- und Residenzstadt Wien, *Darstellung der Gewerblichen Zustände der Wiener Bäcker-Innung* (Wien: Ferd. Jahn, 1848), 10–11.

12. Landesinnung der Wiener Bäcker, ed., *700 Jahre Wiener Bäcker-Innung* (Wien: Verlag der Wiener Bäcker-Innung, 1927), 45.

re-regulation of flour prices unfeasible he outspokenly supported both to foster a greater competition among millers and the altogether abolishment of the bread assize, thus fundamentally irritating the guild. Furthermore, having travelled to Germany, Belgium and France to observe the food policies of other cities he proposed to found a *Mehlkassa* after the ideal of the Paris *caisse de service de la boulangerie* to clear the bakers' debts in late 1845.[13] Indeed, in March 1846 the guild was informed about a royal resolution to modify the assize system. However, facing a continuous price increase by late July the confreres still debated over the same adaptions of the municipal system of grain price survey.[14] Paralysed by the immediate need to police and regulate the speculation and trade in grain, mayor Czapka still repeated the same policies necessary to correct the system of bread provision in August 1847: a revision or complete repeal of the bread assize, changes in the system of grain price surveys and the foundation of a *Mehlkassa* to clear the bakers' debts.[15] Yet, again to no avail. Seven months later, the revolution swiped away parts of the old order and its institutions, especially in the city of Vienna. While the first major liberal revolution in Europe had in fact prevented the lasting, thorough liberalization half a century earlier,[16] the March Revolution of 1848 would set the tracks to change the political fate of Vienna's bread assize.

'Free competition is the magic phrase of our time'

'Today, the nearly 200 year-old bread assize has become void' reads an almost stoic two-line second-page announcement of the 1 November 1860 issue of *Das Vaterland*.[17] Over the course of a mere decade following the March Revolution of 1848 the economically liberal-minded bourgeois Viennese bureaucracy forged 'balanced dynamic transformation with authoritarian control' under the new, neoabsolutist institutional setting.[18] Indeed, while judged 'balanced' in some areas in various arenas of the economy the reforms introduced between 1848 and 1860 were very much imbalanced. 'In fact, however, as in other European states from France to Prussia, a modernizing program in the 1850s accomplished quite a lot of exactly what liberal reformers in the Habsburg Monarchy had desired in 1848.'[19]

---

13. Karl Weiß, *Rückblicke auf die Gemeineverwaltung der Stadt Wien in den Jahren 1838–1848* (Wien: Manz, 1875), 79–86, 88.

14. Landesinnung der Wiener Bäcker, *700 Jahre*, 47.

15. Weiß, *Rückblicke*, 86.

16. Jonas M. Albrecht, 'The Struggle for Bread. The Emperor, the City and the Bakers between Moral and Market Economies of Food in Vienna, 1775–1791', *History of Retail and Consumption* 5, no. 3 (2019), 276–94.

17. *Das Vaterland. Zeitung für die österreichische Monarchie,* 'Satzung', 1 November 1860, 55, 2.

18. Judson, *Habsburg Empire*, 219.

19. Ibid., 219.

In that way, the brief episode of Neoabsolutism under young Emperor Franz Josef I 'completed reforms initiated by Maria Theresa and Joseph II but interrupted by the *Vormärz* regime' under Franz I, Ferdinand I and Prince Metternich.[20] What is more, the economic policies implemented over the middle decade of the nineteenth century largely followed Manchesterian laissez-faire and free-market ideals both on the imperial and on the municipal level, hammered home 'in a politically absolutist fashion'.[21] 'The new regime confirmed the final establishment of capitalist relations in the countryside by abolishing what remained of the feudal system' and thus 'subjected agriculture to market laws'.[22] With the elimination of the customs border between Cis- and Transleithania in 1850 and free-trade treaties with the German *Zollverein* in 1853 as well as with France and Great Britain in 1865 the monarchy 'was opened to the competition of the world market'.[23] By 1859, the *Gewerbefreiheit* 'ended the medieval guild system', which similarly meant a 'shift from the principle of monopolies towards free competition'.[24] On a general level, after 1848 a drastic economic reform process aimed to 'subject society to a "natural" process of selection' in which competition would produce the 'natural order'.[25] On the municipal parquet of the capital, simultaneous large-scale modernization policies, reforms and infrastructures with regard to the city's administration, public health and education, water supply, sanitation and street lighting were quickly commenced after 1848.[26] Among these, the termination of the bread assize was accomplished with impressive speed since

> free competition is the magic phrase of our time. Demands to abolish all privileges of individual trades and crafts grow louder by the day. If this *zeitgeist* principle will guide the reforms of the trade laws and the guild privileges rooted in ancient times are to be repealed, this cannot be objected as long as the common good does not suffer. However, there can be no such half-hearted measures like those introduced to the baker's trade since 1809.[27]

---

20. Herbert Matis, 'Leitlinien der Österreichischen Wirtschaftspolitik', in *Die Habsburgermonarchie 1848–1918*, vol. 1, ed. Alois Brusatti, Adam Wandruszka and Helmut Rumpler (Wien: Verl. der Österr. Akad. der Wiss, 1973), 36.

21. Judson, *Habsburg Empire*, 219; Matis, 'Leitlinien', 39.

22. Judson, *Habsburg Empire*, 219; Matis, 'Leitlinien', 32.

23. Matis, 'Leitlinien', 40; Judson, *Habsburg Empire*, 230. See also David F. Good, *The Economic Rise of the Habsburg Empire, 1750–1914* (Berkeley, CA: University of California Press, 1984), 74–95.

24. Matis, 'Leitlinien', 40.

25. Ibid., 38.

26. For a brief overview, see e.g. Betrand M. Buchmann, 'Dynamik des Städtebaus', in Csendes; Opll, *Wien. Geschichte einer Stadt*.

27. Innung der bürgerl. Bäckermeister in der k.k. Haupt- und Residenzstadt Wien, *Gewerbliche Zustände*, 7.

With that statement, by July 1848 Vienna's bakers' guild hastened to position itself within the altered political environment of the – still ongoing – revolution. Upheaval and the founding of new governmental institutions introduced a strikingly different political environment to the city of Vienna that 'created spaces for a new politics in which the revolutionaries could negotiate with the state and influence its policies more effectively'.[28] The *Gemeindeausschuss* represented one such new space. Already on 17 March 1848, the government had ordered the provisional *Bürgerausschuss*, summoned by mayor Czapka two days earlier, to form a new representative body elected by the city's citizens. Laid down over the following weeks, the thus founded *Gemeindeausschuss* acted as de facto municipal government over the summer and prepared the transition to and very first election of Vienna's *Gemeinderat* in the autumn of 1848. Splitting the massive workload of the revolutionary reorganization of the city's administration over nine sections the *Approvisionirungssektion* [sic!] became responsible for most issues regarding the provision of food, water and other items of first necessity.[29]

'Invited by the *Gemeindeausschuß* to deliver proposals for a contemporarily adaption of the bread assize system' with their above-cited July manifest Vienna's bakers 'hurried to inform the *Gemeindeausschuß* exhaustively about the conditions of the bakers' trade' and to secure a place on the conference table set up in these new political circumstances.[30] The guild's eighteen-page endeavour surely represented a quest to maintain a certain amount of influence on the newly rolled-out political debate during the summer of 1848. Already by mid-May the corporation had submitted another petition for a 'modification of the bread assize form' to which they added an exemplary assize calculation.[31] While taking on to shape the political transition in general the *Gemeindeausschuss* equally engaged to take up necessary economic reforms at about the same time. The assize was among the prime topics of interest. Already on 13 June, the assembly's *Approvisionirungssektion* had calculated the bread prices for the following fortnight under supervision of the bakers' chairpersons Elsässer and Kuhn. Both certified the computed bread prices were 'in full accordance with the existing legal principles' of assize calculation. However, they 'could not help mention that the assize system originates from old times, is not appropriate in the actual circumstances, and could be called

---

28. Judson, *Habsburg Empire*, 156; on the administrative changes of the city government, see e.g. Betrand M. Buchmann, 'Politik und Verwaltung', in Csendes; Opll, *Wien. Geschichte einer Stadt*.

29. Maren Seliger and Karl Ucakar, *Wien, Politische Geschichte 1740–1934: Entwicklung und Bestimmungskräfte Großstädtischer Politik* (Wien: Jugend & Volk Verl.-Ges, 1985), 213–14, 223–6, 238–41.

30. Innung der bürgerl. Bäckermeister in der k.k. Haupt- und Residenzstadt Wien, *Gewerbliche Zustände*.

31. Archiv der Bäckergenossenschaft in Wien, HS 16: Innung der bürgerl. Bäckermeister in der k.k. Haupt- und Residenzstadt Wien. Protokolle über die bei der Bäckerinnung eingelangten Aktenstücke 1834–1868, 17 May 1848.

inadequate; regulation is necessary, however, it would come with multiple inquiries and required some time'. Having had no time 'to gain exact knowledge on the multiple ramifications of this highly important matter' the section members ordered the city's chief market wardens and the guild's chairpersons 'as experts' to hand in reports about the 'ailment of the assize system as well as the methods of remedy'.[32] On its meeting on 27 June, the *Ausschuß* had probably received the *gewerbliche Zustände* report the guild published in press about ten days later since committee member Burg requested that the drafting of a new municipal code, the reorganization of the police and the repeal of the assize were determined as the committee's most important tasks. According to the newspaper coverage future mayor Johann Kaspar Seiller reported about several drafts of a 'radical modification of the assize' in the same sitting, which received the assembly's 'highest attention' and sparked a lively debate over the pros and cons.[33] Only a few days later, on 30 June, committee member, master baker and industrial entrepreneur Leopold Wimmer reported over public complaints of small bread loaves as well as the 'root cause of high prices and the means of remedy'.[34]

Fundamentally, the guild's 1848 report about the bakers' economic situation largely mirrored the arguments ventilated over the preceding decades. Describing the misalignment of the assize system regarding free-market flour prices and regulated bread prices, the incorrect calculation of bread prices due to altered market and raw material conditions, the overwhelming concentration within the milling sector and unfair competition by rural bakers not subjected to the assize, the guild again reasoned 'the very first and most important aim of the monitoring of the bread trade is to secure Vienna's provision at all times, and especially with respect to the poorer inhabitants'. Requesting, again, the modification of assize calculations, the re-regulation of the flour market and the renewed limitation of the urban bread retail largely deregulated since the 1790s the corporation explicitly expressed the need for regulative reform and offered its cooperation for such a 'difficult task'.[35] There is no evidence how the *Gemeindeausschuß* received the baker's manifesto, but it appears that the corporation's standing with the new administration was not predominantly fortunate.

In any case, the aftermath of the revolution in Hungary presented a major impetus for the introduction of reformatory measures during the last months of the year. Caused by military conflicts of the Hungarian War of Independence

32. Wiener Stadt- und Landesarchiv: Gemeinderat der Stadt Wien. Protokolle der III. Sektion, 1848–1852, 13 June 1848.

33. *Wiener Zeitung*, 'Gemeinde-Ausschuß der Stadt Wien. Sitzung vom 27. Juni', 3 July 1848, 182, 30.

34. *Wiener Zeitung*, 'Ausschuß der Bürger, Nationalgarde und Studenten für Sicherheit, Ruhe, Ordnung und Wahrung der Volksrechte. (Vormittags-Sitzung vom 30. Juni)', 2 July 1848, 181, Abendausgabe, 356.

35. Innung der bürgerl. Bäckermeister in der k.k. Haupt- und Residenzstadt Wien, *Gewerbliche Zustände*, 14, 18.

the *Wiener Zeitung* reported on 17 November that 'the marketplaces used for assize calculation have been obstructed' and informed readers that grain prices were unusually high and thus would assize prices for bread be. According to the newspaper the *Gemeinderat*, having taken over municipal administration from the *Gemeindeausschuß* by early October, discussed for wheat rolls to be 'baked free of the assize temporarily' for the rest of November.[36] A day later, under the impression of similar problems with the city's meat supply, a *Gemeinderat* commission for the 'regulation of the bakers' conditions' was founded with the assignment to elaborate reform proposals regarding the bread assize.[37] Unfortunately, the proceedings of the commission are not preserved. On 27 November, however, chair of the *Approvisionirungssektion* Johann von Watzdorf followed the bakers' request to continue to exempt wheat roll 'Semmelgebäck' prices from the assize for the first two weeks of December; only rye and mixed bread prices were calculated according to the assize. As the section signalled it would 'continue to contemplate about the bakers' conditions in general and the assize regulation' more specifically in early December the *Wiener Zuschauer* assumed the abolition of bread the assize 'seems to be initiated slowly'.[38]

By December 13, the *Gemeinderat* had received the commission's reform proposal and started its deliberation. While the suggested modifications had already been sent to the Ministry of Trade, which also needed to comment, the municipal assembly decided to further elaborate the needed regulations of bread retail and the assize and a schemed public loan over 175,000fl. to clear the bakers' debts and align its findings with those of the ministry at a later point in time.[39] Two weeks later the *Wiener Zeitung* reported about the ministry's plans to found an official grain and flour exchange that should function as the fundament for a reform of the assize calculations. Additionally, the report reinforced the need for reform since the system of assize prices was misaligned because 'circumstances changed considerably in the last years', having 'sustained influence on the bread production in Vienna' by making bakers dependent on the 'free milling sector'.[40]

Over the following months the debate accelerated notably. By late January 1849, the trade ministry had, Watzdorf told the *Gemeinderat*, agreed to grant a 200,000 Gulden bailout to the bakers' guild in light of its 'hard-pressed situation'. Suggested by the guild the loan should be secured by a ten-Kreuzer surcharge on every centner of flour the bakers bought, 'even if the assize would be eliminated

---

36. *Wiener Zeitung*, 'Kundmachung', 17 November 1848, 309, 1112.

37. *Wiener Zeitung*, 'Gemeinderaths-Protokoll', 24 November 1848, 315, 1159.

38. Gemeinderat der Stadt Wien, Protokolle der III. Sektion, 1848–1852, 27 November 1848.

39. *Wiener Zeitung*, 'Protokoll der Sitzung des Gemeinderathes Vom 13. Dezember 1848', 19 December 1848, 337.

40. Gemeinderat der Stadt Wien, Protokolle der III. Sektion, 1848–1852, 18 January 1849.

eventually'. Additionally, the sum would be secured by the property values of the bakers' businesses and equipment, too.[41] Yet, bailing out bakers would only make sense if the assize was reformed, too, making a change in the bread price system a precondition of the loan. While wheat roll prices were left unregulated throughout January and February 1849, on 1 February some members of the council demanded a reintroduction of the flour assize 'as it had been in place until 1809'.[42] Since the 'initiated foundation of a grain exchange could enable the realization of the request' this was to be reviewed 'in due time'. It was, however, 'kept until then' and the attempt to counter further liberalization failed quickly.[43] Less than a week later Watzdorf continued to present a more extensive report about the commission's results and their motion for a 'contemporarily regulation of the assize'. Whereas the project of a grain and flour exchange was still evaluated by ministry and chamber of commerce Watzdorf as chairperson of the bread assize commission took the initiative and proposed to terminate regulated bread prices altogether. Supported by the magistrate, which rejected the baker's 1848 manifest, and vice-mayor Bergmüller, who thought that 'now is the time to eliminate the assize by way of trial' as well as backed up by various other councils considering the timing good to abolish the assize except for rye bread, the *Gemeinderat* accepted Watzdorf's motion.[44] With this decision of 7 February 1849 Vienna's 150-year-old assize was basically done with.

Over the course of the first half of 1849, much of the age-old disciplinary mechanism of Vienna's bread assize went quietly, and it went quickly. Effectively debated between the summer of 1848 and early 1849, the political agreement within the *Gemeinderat* to eliminate the bread assize instead of reforming it had materialized with a speed this very issue had not seen for decades. Yet, it took some time to turn the political consent into law. Two weeks after its momentous decision the *Gemeinderat* drafted an announcement informing the city's inhabitants that 'the calculations of the bread assize are based on false foundations', that the council had not yet been equipped to implement reform due to a want for final conclusions how 'the provision of the consumers with cheap bread and the demand of the bakers for a *bürgerliche* profit' could be equally secured, and that the assembly would do everything 'to bring permanent order to the production, prices, retail and control of bread'.[45] While Watzdorf referred to the 'intermediately made decision to abolish the assize for all kinds of bakery goods except rye bread' by

41. Ibid., 25 January 1849.
42. *Wiener Zeitung*, 'Protokoll der Sitzung des Gemeindrathes vom 1. Februar', 18 February 1849, 42, 489.
43. Gemeinderat der Stadt Wien, Protokolle der III. Sektion, 1848–1852, 19 February 1849.
44. *Wiener Zeitung*, 'Protokoll der Sitzung des Gemeinderathes vom 7. Februar', 21 February 1849, 44, 511.
45. *Wiener Zeitung*, 'Kundmachung', 23 February 1849, 46, 530.

late February the bakers appear to have been largely excluded from the debate within the city council and other authorities. On March 6, the Ministry of the Interior hosted a meeting to 'thoroughly examine the proposals to ease the bakers' hard-pressed situation and the provisional reform of the bakers' trade', to which councils von Watzdorf, J. Schmid, Würth and Kuhn were invited.[46] Seemingly, Watzdorf and his colleagues successfully presented and defended their motion to terminate Vienna's bread assize before the other participants. When the guild appealed the *Gemeinderat* to 'quickly settle the regulation of the assize' in late March it was told the decision was 'already made'.[47] Four weeks later, still waiting for the Ministry of Trade to approve liberalization, the assembly voted not to include the bakers' guild into still pending negotiations about the bailout fund.[48] On 25 April, Watzdorf and the council's *Aprovisionirungssection* pressed again to 'discontinue assize prices for wheat rolls and *Pohlenbrot* during the first half of May', a motion the *Gemeinderat* again passed.[49] On its meeting on 27 April, it was informed about the ministry's approval of the 'provisional reform of the baker's trade'. The suitability of that 'provisional reform' seems to have been confirmed in the course of further deliberations between the *Gemeinderat* and the Lower Austrian Provincial Government on 1 May, in which neither party expressed any worries 'a lack of grain or flour' might occur.[50] Two days later, on 3 May 1849, the Ministry of Trade announced the decree of the 'repeal of the assize except for rye bread'.[51] While the city council tried to seize the opportunity and swiftly recommended the abolition of the meat assize on the following day, in its issue of 11 May *Die Presse* knew that 'the assize on all bakery goods except rye bread will be eliminated on 16 May'.[52] 'According to the *Gemeinderat*'s announcement, the assize on all kinds of bakery goods, except for rye bread, is repealed effective from 16 May', the *Fremden-Blatt* told its readers on that very day.[53]

However, the municipality did not withdraw completely from intervention into the prices of wheat products. To ensure the affordability for all consumers, the bakers were ordered to 'maintain the present prices of rolls and Pohlenbrod', the weights of which bakers could now freely change.[54] At the same time, Watzdorf

---

46. Wiener Stadt- und Landesarchiv, Vertretungskörper, Gemeinderat B6: Gemeinderat der Stadt Wien. Sitzungsprotokolle: Öffentliche Sitzungen 7.10.1848–8.5.1919, 2.3.1849.

47. *Wiener Zeitung*, 'Protokoll der Sitzung des Gemeinderaths der Stadt Wien vom 21. März 1849', 4 April 1849, 80.

48. *Wiener Zeitung*, 'Protokoll der Sitzung des Gemeinderaths der Stadt Wien am 20. April 1849', 27 April 1849, 100.

49. Gemeinderat der Stadt Wien, Sitzungsprotokolle 1848–1919, 25 April 1849.

50. *Wiener Zeitung*, 'Protokoll der Sitzung des Gemeinderaths der Stadt Wien am 2. Mai 1849', 11 May 1849, 112.

51. Bäckerinnung, Protokolle 1834–1868, 3 May 1849.

52. *Die Presse*, 'Wien. Brodsatzung', 11 May 1849, 112, 3.

53. *Fremden-Blatt*, 'Tages-Neuigkeiten', 16 May 1849, 116, 2.

54. Ibid.

informed the *Gemeinderat* that the magistrate was to enquire 'after some time' into the effects and consequences of the assize abolition on the 'commercial conditions of the bakers and the provision of Vienna more generally'.[55] Therewith, on 16 May most parts of Vienna's bread assize were effectively repealed. The guild apparently protested against the decision, but the Ministry of Trade rejected the 'various proposed measures for the improvement of the Innung' in the following days.[56] The guild was, however, appeased by the Trade Ministry's approval of the 175,000fl. bailout fund for the bakers on 25 May, each of whom received an advance of 892 Gulden and 51 ¼ Kreuzer around mid-July.[57] While rye bread remained subject of official price regulation, with these decisions all other kinds of bread and rolls were subjugated to the market laws of supply and demand, representing a massive blow to the moral economy of bread in Vienna.

Though staggering, the moral economy of bread did not go down just yet. Over the 1849 summer period, the *Gemeinderat* continued to evaluate the consequences of liberalization. By 13 June, Watzdorf informed the board no price increases, meaning reductions in roll and loaf sizes, had been observed during the last month; seven days later, he reported the grain and flour exchange had been set up and was 'a success'. Keeping up the positive feedback throughout July, the president of the *Gemeinderat* honoured Watzdorf for his work and efforts on the matter of the assize.[58] In light of such a success story, the assembly grew optimistic this kind of liberalization-until-further-notice worked and could safely be realized completely. Already on 1 September, the magistrate discussed the elimination of the remaining assize on rye bread, 'if the gained experience allowed' for it.[59] By early October, it filed a motion for total liberalization in the *Gemeinderat* arguing 'after evaluation, the abolition of the assize on finer bakery products has proven beneficial'.[60] Instructing the *Aprovisionirungssection* to comment section chair Watzdorf demonstrated an echo of the moral economy prevailed in his application 'to uphold the rye bread assize considering the indispensability of this kind of bread to the poorer classes [...] and the short duration of only a few month during which the advantages of the liberalization could prove themselves'.[61] On 12 October 1849, the *Gemeinderat* passed Watzdorf's motion. In doing so, it effectively kept

55. Gemeinderat der Stadt Wien, Protokolle der III. Sektion, 1848–1852, 12 May 1849.
56. Bäckerinnung, Protokolle 1834–1868, 21.5.1849.
57. *Wiener Zeitung*, 'Protokoll der Sitzung des Gemeinderaths der Stadt Wien vom 25. Mai 1849', 8 June 1849, 135; Wiener Stadt- und Landesarchiv, Innungen und Handelsgremien 1, A1: Akten. Vorschüsse der Stadt an einzelne Meister, 1849–1855.
58. *Wiener Zeitung*, 'Protokoll der Sitzung des Gemeinderaths der Stadt Wien am 20 Juni 1849', 30 June 1849, 154, 1816.
59. Gemeinderat der Stadt Wien, Protokolle der III. Sektion, 1848–1852, 1 September 1849.
60. Gemeinderat der Stadt Wien, Sitzungsprotokolle 1848–1919, 5 October 1849.
61. Ibid., 12.10.1849.

rye bread prices within the regulated sphere of the moral economy while wheaten products now almost completely belonged to the free market. While, in the opinion of Vienna's urban authorities, the latter could be commodified, the former fundamentally remained a good that was not to be left to the unfettered market. In the bakers' words, abolishing wheat product regulation while maintaining official calculation of rye bread can be interpreted as another 'half-hearted measure'. While the legislation of 1849 presented a decisive step of deregulation towards a 'free' market, overall baking remained between moral and market economies of bread.

Total liberalization

Although obviously not all bodies of the urban government agreed on such different notions of wheat and rye bread, this rather pragmatic solution to the assize issue represented a compromise that accommodated the interest of most of the included parties, at least for the moment. While maintaining a baseline disciplinary mechanism for the fundamental food needs of the poorer strata of the urban society, the liberalization of white bread and wheat products enabled bakers to earn higher profits and make good on losses induced to regulated rye bread production. Through continued efforts to survey both wheat and rye prices over the following years, the *Gemeinderat* showed its satisfaction with the introduced measures. In July 1851, for example, it constituted that both wheat rolls and mixed *Pohlenbrot* had been baked in larger weights during April, May and June than the assize would have required. Therefore, the assembly found 'the abolition of the assize has produced no disadvantage to the customers'.[62] In spite of periodical criticisms by the bakers, who, for example, complained in late 1853 and early 1854 – during the Crimean War – about high prices and that the issue of misaligned unregulated rye flour and regulated rye bread prices remained unsolved under the new regulation,[63] the Gemeinderat apparently viewed the assize question as settled. Though assuring the survey of grain and flour prices remained a 'constant subject of attention' to the *Approvisionirungssektion*,[64] for the better part of the decade bread almost vanished from sight with next to no newspaper coverage or *Gemeinderat* debates covering it. This does not mean that urban lawmakers lost their interest in politics of provision. While very occupied with Vienna's territorial expansion and the integration of the city's former suburbs

---

62. *Wiener Zeitung*, 'Protokoll der Sitzung des Gemeinderaths der Stadt Wien am 30. Juli 1851', 13 August 1851, 192, 2336.

63. Archiv der Bäckergenossenschaft in Wien, HS 9: Innung der bürgerl. Bäckermeister in der k.k. Haupt- und Residenzstadt Wien. Handwerksprotokolle vom Jahre 1850 bis 1855, 3 December 1853 and 20 January 1854.

64. *Wiener Zeitung*, 'Protokoll der Sitzung des Gemeinderaths der Stadt Wien am 4. November 1851', 20 November 1851, 277.

into the municipality's administration after 1850, both *Gemeinderat* and magistrate were heavily concerned with the regulation of the capital's meat supply. Throughout most of the early 1850s, the abolition of the meat assize, the construction of public slaughterhouses and cattle markets, the spatial centralization of butchering into those establishments as well as the founding of a *Fleischkassa* after the ideal of Paris's *Caisse de Poissy* consumed much of the municipality's attention and produced major public institutions overseeing and guarding Vienna's provision with meat.[65]

Given these – very expensive – public projects and the city's poor financial situation large-scale municipal ventures into the provision with bread faded to the background. Already in late March 1850, the *Gemeinderat* acknowledged a Watzdorf motion to build a public grain mill providing the bakers with cheap flour a 'useful mean to help the bakers and create an advantage for the population'. However, the estimated costs of 800,000fl. were considered to overburden the strained public finances and the assembly declared the city not capable of financing the project.[66]

Whereas the municipal administration was either satisfied with the settlement of the bread assize or too occupied for further regulatory efforts, the issue remained a hot topic among other political institutions throughout the 1850s. Especially the economic-liberal Lower Austrian *Gewerbeverein* and the chamber of commerce, both important consulting bodies to the imperial government and largely staffed with members of the commercial elite, continued to press for the final elimination of the bread assize and the formation of a 'free' food market. Giving a talk on the 'relief of the lower classes through cheap bread and meat', already in April 1850 one *Gewerbeverein* member Franke argued for the society to push for the abolition of the assize on rye bread because 'just as the abolishment of the [wheat] bread and flour assize has led to better and cheaper products, it will also be the case in this instance'.[67] Supporting this request, the society heard a quite similar talk several months later. In the sitting of 22 January 1852, baker and founder of Vienna's first steam bakery Leopold Wimmer lectured on the 'means to obtain cheaper bread'. Highlighting the, in his opinion, poor quality of rye bread produced by the city's bakers – caused among other reasons by the misalignment of flour and bread prices inducing bakers to adulterate rye loaves – he equally thought the assize needed to be modified and recommended the creation of large-scale industrial bakeries.[68]

At the same time as institutions like the *Gewerbeverein* issued their dissatisfaction with the 1848/9 legislation, the liberal-minded press joined the chorus of voices

---

65. See Lukasz Nieradzik, *Der Wiener Schlachthof St. Marx: Transformation einer Arbeitswelt zwischen 1851 und 1914* (Wien: Böhlau, 2017), chapter 5.

66. *Wiener Zeitung*, 'Protokoll der Sitzung des Gemeinderaths der Stadt Wien vom 26. März 1850', 6 April 1850, 83, 1056.

67. *Die Presse*, 'Tagesneuigkeiten', 14 April 1850, 90, 2.

68. *Wiener Zeitung*, 'Kleine Chronik', 24 January 1852, 21.

demanding further deregulation – sometimes quite animatedly. Debating over the causes of high cattle and meat prices and haggling over a solution, Gustav Heine, younger brother of Heinrich Heine and editor of the moderate *Fremden-Blatt* newspaper, clashed with liberal *Die Presse* in June and July 1852. While Heine had argued for a political intervention into the prices of meat – the assize had already been abolished two years earlier – *Die Presse* published a fervent sweeping blow against any interventions in a sequence of heated opinion pieces. 'Like Herr Heine, we sincerely whish that [railway] ticket prices to Baden are reduced by half, that the price of beef is six Kreuzer like in 1824, and that the Kaisersemmeln have a weight of Five-Groschen loafs', it polemicized on 20 June. 'However, under no condition will we accept the ignorance […] to terrorize one tradesman today and another tomorrow and prevent him from the free exercise of his trade […]', the author held to conclude 'the government has, after ineffable efforts to find a just assize, reached the conclusion that it is not possible'.[69] 'The consumers can thank Herr Heine for the price increases', the newspaper added nine days later, claiming that 'the provocative language of the Fremden-Blatt' induced political intervention and eventually the butchers' unanimous raising of meat prices. To the *Presse* it was crystal clear: 'The local authority only has to guarantee every butcher can, unhindered by external influences, sell his wares at a price convenient to his business. Competition will do the rest in the interest of the consumers.'[70]

While baker Leopold Wimmer repeated his demands to abolish the rye bread assize in May 1856 arguing that it was 'incorrect, incomprehensible, and untenable',[71] the chamber of commerce, too, supported termination because 'with regard to the grain and flour trade, free competition is worshipped', as *Die Presse* put it by 1858.[72]

The accelerated reform programme regarding the empire-wide freedom of commerce, prepared during the very late 1850s and pushed through by trade minister Georg von Toggenburg against stark opposition from most Austrian and Czech provincial administrations as well as laissez-faire-critical members of the imperial government in 1859, poured a great amount of water on the mills of those in favour of complete assize termination.[73] When the Ministerrat started to debate over the proposed *Gewerbefreiheit* law in January and February 1859, parts of the liberal press and the chamber of commerce intensified their efforts to push for liberalization. 'We are debating over the total abolition of the bread assize for years', the *Morgen-Post* exasperatedly told its readers in early April: 'The abolition

69. *Die Presse*, 'Wien, 19. Juni', 20 June 1852, 144, 3.

70. *Die Presse*, 'Wien, 28. Juni', 29 June 1852, 151, 3.

71. *Morgen-Post*, 'In der letzten Sitzung des hiesigen Gewerbevereins', 7 May 1856, 1252, 2.

72. *Die Presse*, 'Müller und Bäcker in Wien', 29 January 1858, 23, 5.

73. Baryli, *Konzessionssystem*; Taras von Borodajkewycz, 'Gewerbefreiheit und konservativer Geist', in *Festschrift Walter Heinrich: ein Beitrag zur Ganzheitsforschung* (Graz: Akad. Druck- u. Verl.-Anst, 1963).

of the bread assize, deemed impractical by all experts [...], will have the same fortunate outcome like the termination of the meat assize in Vienna has had. [...] Certainly, the success would be even more brilliant if the bakers' trade in general was deregulated', the author eagerly promised.[74]

By late May, the chamber of commerce presented a detailed analysis of Vienna's bread provisioning that covered the commodity chain from the grain trade down to issues concerning baking. Contrary to the *Morgenpost*'s demands, the chamber held that 'the assize on rye bread should be maintained'. Upholding that notion in the sitting on 21 September, it voted to abolish the fixed wheat roll and loaf prices, which had been maintained since 1849, because 'the chamber has repeatedly argued against any assize regulation in principle [...] except for rye bread'.[75]

The *Reichsrat*'s approval of the introduction of freedom of commerce in the Austrian Empire in late November and its legislation on 20 December 1859 finally turned the tide in favour of full deregulation. Announcing the expected repeal of the bread assize in Bohemia and Moravia, by late February 1860 the *Morgenpost* knew deregulation would soon be introduced in Vienna and 'the consumers of bread will finally be freed of that fraud and the competition of unhindered production will provide better and cheaper bread'.[76] Having kept completely silent on the matter throughout 1859, on the sitting of 27 April 1860 vice-mayor Andreas Zelinka proposed the termination of the rye bread assize before the *Gemeinderat*. While such plans had been debated already by 1852 among the *Approvisionirungssektion* without results, he recounted, 'the introduction of the *Gewerbefreiheit* as well as the abolition of the forced prices for all kinds of baked goods in various provinces has led the magistrate to resume these debates. [...] The magistrate takes the view that the weight and quality of bakery goods have to be left to the producer, or rather to competition.'[77]

Following Zelinka's motion, the *Gemeinderat* voted to authorize the magistrate to propose the repeal of the bread assize to the superordinate authority of the *Statthalterei*. While a decision was 'still awaited' and the rye assize for the first half of August was publicized by late July, two months later the decision had been made. On 17 September 1860, the k.k. Lower Austrian Government's announcement No. 42069 proclaimed the abolition of the bread assize in Vienna and the surrounding counties from 1 November 1860.[78] Two days later, the eminent *Wiener Zeitung* as

---

74. *Morgen-Post*, 'Die Aufhebung der Brodsatzung', 3 April 1859, 92, 2.

75. *Wiener Zeitung*, 'Aus den Verhandlungen der Handels- und Gewerbekammer für das Erherzogtum Oesterreich unter der Enns, Am 21. September 1859', 13 October 1859, 255, 4316.

76. *Morgen-Post*, 'Aufhebung der Brodtaxe', 26 February 1860, 57, 3.

77. *Wiener Zeitung*, 'Sitzungsberichte. Protokoll der 209. Sitzung des Gemeinderathes der k.k. Reichshaupt- und Residenzstadt Wien am 27. April 1860', 25 May 1860, 125, 2187.

78. Wiener Stadt- und Landesarchiv, Marktamt A2/1: Brot und Gebäcksverkauf nach Gewicht, 17.09.1860: K.K. nö. Statthalterei.

the approved organ of the Austrian government explained the move to the city's inhabitants. Reminding of the assize's abolition on wheat products in 1849, the author went on to declare 'the necessity of a particular protection of the consumers' interest through the determination of an assize on bread has lapsed because those interests receive the best and most effective protection through free competition, introduced by the new *Gewerbe-Ordnung* of 20 December 1859, which is the most secure means against unjustified price increases'. Free competition, the article detailed,

> in connection with the great progress in agriculture and technology, the quick improvement of the means of communication and the great boom of the grain and flour trade are completely adequate to drive away all worries in that regard. Moreover, while maintaining the assize is therefore unnecessary, it appears even more untenable because the basic key of its calculation proves imperfect and detrimental to justice and fairness.[79]

For that reason, the government 'has arrived at the conviction that finding such a key, which represents the interest of consumers and producers alike, is very difficult, indeed nearly impossible'. Since the experience of the last decade, the *Wiener Zeitung*'s report closed, had shown no price increases in wheat bread, both *Statthalterei* and the Ministry of the Interior had agreed over the 'modern measure as a further step on the tracks laid out' by the *Gewerbefreiheit* to 'entirely abolish the assize on all kinds of baked goods from 1 November' and 'leave the determination of the prices of all bakery products to free competition'.[80]

On the following day, the *Morgenpost* benevolently presented its readers a full reprint of the *Wiener Zeitung*'s article because it 'stressed the principle of free competition'. 'Young institutions', it continued, 'which are opposed by old prejudices, sometimes need a word of explanation, and it is not trivial for the official organ to use the opportunity to support this modern development born by the latest period of reforms'. Presenting the assize as an improper 'intervention of the authorities into matters that are best taken care of by those directly involved', the author applauded that 'the assize will be repealed, which means the intervention of the authorities into the price of bread will cease'.[81]

Conclusion

Over the course of the late eighteenth and first half of the nineteenth centuries, institutions of embeddedness ensured that disciplinary mechanisms regulated how bread was produced, sold and bought in Vienna. On the one hand, the municipal

---

79. *Wiener Zeitung*, 'Wien', 19 September 1860, 220, 3696.
80. Ibid.
81. *Morgen-Post*, 'Aufhebung der Brodsatzung', 20 September 1860, 261, 2.

landscape's expansion during the late eighteenth and early nineteenth centuries with its network of guild bakeries unfolding across town under official control answered the quick rise of the urban population. This landscape was expanded over the entire developed urban area since the late eighteenth century to answer the construction of new neighbourhoods and the development of old ones to house the many newcomers to the city. Master bakers belonging to Vienna's guild attempted to occupy central positions within the urban fabric, which arguably maximized their accessibility; most of the bakers once founded remained in place and business for the entire period. Therefore, besides significant expansion and a pattern of centrality the municipal landscape of bread was equally determined by the duration of bakery locations during the first half of the nineteenth century.

Besides the spatial development this chapter has investigated whether the municipal landscape of bakeries could satisfy the demand of customers in quantitative and qualitative terms in the face of the significant rise of the numbers of mouths to feed in the Austrian capital. Between 1793 and 1857, bakery operations and their scales of production had grown to some degree, albeit not spectacularly. By 1857, Vienna's bakers combined kept more emergency stocks their predecessors six decades ago had and this increase translated to a 30 per cent growth of average emergency supplies available per resident. Without dramatic improvements of productivity gained through the adoption of industrial technologies, bakers secured growth in turnover through rising numbers of workers employed and the increasing adoption of brewer's yeast as driver of accelerated fermentation. Secured through labour intensification bread producers were able to respond to the rising demand for bread, rolls and pastry between the late eighteenth and mid-nineteenth centuries.

Indeed, Vienna's urban guild bakers' increase in overall bread production responded not only to general demand, but to a special demand, wheat. This was the result of the development of a second, competing as well as complementary rural landscape of bread production beyond the urban boundaries. The country bakers not only provided access points in the expanding settlements outside the *Linienwall* but gradually took over the arguably lower end of the product range of baked goods Viennese would consume. By the late 1850s, the country bakers largely supplied the capital with rye bread loaves sent into the city and sold via rather mobile channels of distribution. Meanwhile, the bakeries of the municipal landscape of bread increasingly turned towards the production of bread and rolls that would contain more wheat and much less rye compared to the 1790s. Largely driven by substituting rye with coarse wheat flour the *wheatification* of bread consumption was interwoven with the use of improved and, later, standardized industrial barm as well as a turn towards steam-cooking the products by incepting moisture into the oven in order to lend bread and rolls a pleasant appearance.

On the other hand, three major strands of political, commercial and technological changes unfolded that would be of fundamental importance to the institutions of embeddedness regarding Vienna's system of bread provision. First, while late eighteenth-century liberal politics had begun to question and partly to abolish a wide range of regulations, the huge demand for supplies during the Napoleonic Era and the Tambora-induced ecological crisis of 1817 were decisive factors of afresh acts to liberalize parts of the bread food chain, that is, the trade in grain and the production and retail of flour. Although the urban assize on bread items was maintained, liberalization introduced laissez-faire to these steps upstream and created a momentous imbalance in the commodity chain of bread between much less and clearly more regulated sectors.

Second, the conquest, colonization and commercial penetration of formerly barely cultivated fertile steppe environments to the east presented Vienna and the Austrian provinces more generally with a gradually growing and increasingly reliable inflow of hard red wheat since the late eighteenth century. Having created a noteworthy royal programme to colonize and cultivate the Pannonian Plain since the early 1700s, by the last decades of the century serious attempts were made to improve the conditions of Danube water transport and other infrastructures obstructive to trade and transport that led to growing human interventions into downstream environments. As the fruits of cornucopia were hauled upriver by hundreds and thousands of men, women and animals, the conditions of water transport made the towns of Moson and Győr buzzing hubs of the empire's grain trade. By the 1840s, they were among the largest grain entrepots of the entire Central European Danube area, channelling hundreds of thousands of tonnes of grain towards the west each year.

Third, as politics fostered commercial expansion, nature facilitated technological change. From the early 1800s, hard red steppe wheat from the Pannonian Plain began to induce adaptions to the techniques of milling in Vienna and its southern environs. Under the name of 'high milling', millers began to take advantage from the harder, gluten-rich kernels of the improved raw material that became ever more available. Through partly large capital investments and beginning industrialization, they started to refine the processes of flour production that led to the widening and diversification of the range of different qualities of flour over the course of the following decades. At the same time, capitalization, industrialization and concentration in the milling sector also appear to have affected the business relations between now large-scale flour producers and smaller-scale bakers, who likely grew economically more dependent on their suppliers over this period.

These significant changes of the commodity chain upstream the bakeries had dear consequences on the institution of the assize in Vienna. Contemporary experts and politicians alike recognized relatively quickly that improvements in agriculture and flour production as well as product diversification challenged the current way of calculating the assize both regarding the internal ways of calculating outputs and the external factor of price collection. However, the political debate which route a reform should take – liberalization or regulative reform – continued throughout the *Vormärz* period between economic-liberal and economic-conservative reformers. This was quite in line with the more general *Vormärz* debates in Austria over the course of economic reforms like the imperial *Gewerbefreiheit*. Situated in a quite complex and sometimes ambivalent juxtaposition of various interest groups attempting to shape and modify Vienna's bread assize before 1848, the complicated and extensive issue of the assize remained unreformed, and thus unsolved before 1848.

Only the March Revolution would set the tracks to change the political fate of Vienna's bread assize for good. Over the course of a mere decade following the Revolution of 1848, the economically liberal-minded bourgeois Viennese bureaucracy implemented economic policies that largely followed Manchesterian laissez-faire and free-market ideals both on the imperial and on the municipal level. In this altered political environment, the termination of the bread assize, now rendered an inadequate system of old times, was accomplished with impressive speed. Over the course of the first half of 1849, much of the age-old disciplinary mechanism of Vienna's bread assize went quietly, and it went quickly. Effectively debated between the summer of 1848 and early 1849, the political agreement within the *Gemeinderat* to eliminate the bread assize instead of reforming it had materialized with a speed this very issue had not seen for decades. Still, pragmatic rather than ideological considerations prevailed during the last years of the 1840s. When revolution in Hungary obstructed the grain trade in late 1848, Vienna's assize on fine wheat products was paused by way of trial rather than terminally ended. However, the municipality abstained to withdraw completely from intervention into the prices of bread. On the contrary, the assize on rye products was continued to secure access to bread for the city's poor inhabitants. In doing so, it effectively kept rye bread prices within the regulated sphere of the moral economy while wheaten products now almost completely belonged to the free market. While, in the opinion of Vienna's urban authorities, the latter could be commodified, the former fundamentally remained a good that was not to be left to the unfettered market.

This rather pragmatic solution to the assize issue represented a compromise that accommodated the interest of most of the included parties, at least for the moment. While maintaining a baseline disciplinary mechanism for the fundamental food needs of the poorer strata of the urban society, the liberalization of white bread and wheat products enabled the bakers to earn higher profits on this part of their product range. However, over the following decade liberal-leaning institutions like the *Gewerbeverein* issued their dissatisfaction with the 1848/9 legislation and the liberal-minded press joined the chorus of voices demanding further deregulation. Yet, whereas the topic was hardly touched upon by the municipal authorities throughout the 1850s, the *Reichsrat's* approval of the introduction of freedom of commerce in the Austrian Empire in late November and its legislation on 20 December 1859 finally turned the tide in favour of deregulation that rendered Vienna's bread assize incompatible with imperial law. With its appeal in November 1860, the assize and the comprehensive disciplinary mechanisms weaved into the bread market of the Habsburg capital were abandoned and a free market for food was created.

Part III

THE BREAD QUESTION, 1861–85

In March 1858, workers began to demolish the medieval city walls around Vienna's old town. Removing the structure both symbolized 'economic, social, and cultural renewal' under the 'liberal empire' at large and inaugurated the construction of the great bourgeois project of Austrian urban modernity: the *Ringstraße*.[1] In the years following the beginning of the removal of that nuisance of bygone times, the abolition of two more institutions that enclosed the city was made into law. This time, however, it was the urban economy, not the urban space that was liberated from containment. On 20 December 1859, Imperial Patent No. 227 announced the introduction of freedom of trade to most territories of the Habsburg Empire, including the city of Vienna. Effective with 1 June 1860, the *Gewerbefreiheit* turned baking and many other crafts into 'free' trades. Only a few months later, on 17 September 1860, the k.k. Lower Austrian Government proclaimed the abolition of the bread assize in Vienna and the surrounding communities. From 1 November, deregulation left the 'determination of the prices of all products of the baking industry to free competition'.[2]

These laws, issued within just a few months, wiped away almost all regulatory frameworks of bread production and distribution that had governed the bread supply of the residents of the Habsburg capital for centuries. Abolishing the major institutions of embeddedness that regulated entering the bread trade, its geography, its products and prices as well as its systems of retail, these laws did away with the embedded food market. A dramatic market revolution, over the course of the year

---

1. Pieter M. Judson, *The Habsburg Empire: A New History* (Cambridge, MA, London, England: The Belknap Press of Harvard University Press, 2016), 218. On the social, economic and cultural circumstances of mid-century reform and urban renewal, see Judson, *Habsburg Empire*, chapter 5 more generally, as well as, still eminent, Carl E. Schorske, *Fin-de-Siècle Vienna: Politics and Culture* (New York, NY: Vintage Books, 1981), chapter II. See also Franz Baltzarek et al., *Wirtschaft und Gesellschaft der Wiener Stadterweiterung* (Wiesbaden: Steiner, 1975); Karlheinz Rossbacher, *Literatur und Liberalismus: Zur Kultur der Ringstrassenzeit in Wien* (Wien: J&V, 1992).

2. Wiener Stadt- und Landesarchiv, Marktamt A2/1: Brot und Gebäcksverkauf nach Gewicht, 17.09.1860: K.K. nö. Statthalterei.

1860 the deregulation of Vienna's food market created a disembedded market for basic food items.

As tearing down the mediaeval city walls symbolically liberated Vienna from spatial containment, eliminating the assize freed the urban economy from legislative enclosure. Whereas either had originally been created as a means of control, security and governance, such functions were now regarded outdated, redundant and confining. Historians of various fields have highlighted how releasing the city from its spatial entrenchment had most significant consequences for the urban space, urban architecture and urban culture, epitomized by the *Ringstraße* and the buildings evoking a new age – University, Parliament, Town Hall, *Burgtheater* and Opera, to name but a few. Much less examined, liberalizing the bread market from its disciplinary confinement through the assize had similarly significant implications on the way bread was produced, sold and bought in Vienna after 1860. The following part analyses the consequences of this most significant institutional revolution.

Whereas the story of the *Gewerbefreiheit* has been subject of interest for several historical studies,[3] the consequences of deregulation on the landscape of bread in Vienna have not been analysed at all. Chapters 6 and 7 aim to fill this gap by analysing the effects of deregulation on Vienna's landscape of bread, on the prices of bakery products, and on the public debates and market policies concerning bread during approximately the quarter-century following the introduction of freedom of commerce. In the very pointed words of Gergely Baics, 'how did the free-market geography of food distribution differ from the municipally managed one, and what where the costs and benefits?'[4]

Chapter 6 turns to the free-market landscape of bread between 1860 and the 1880s. Continuing the spatial analysis using historical GIS mapping of bakeries, it examines how liberalization affected the landscape of bread. Subsequently, Chapter 7 draws on available price collections to analyse the consequences of liberalization on price movements and cross-subsidization and employs hitherto unused archival materials from the municipal archives and newspaper articles to examine the comprehensive debates over the interconnected issues of bread prices, product standards, retail practices and knowledge about bread making processes that came to be known as the 'bread question' between *c*. 1860 and 1885.

3. See Karl Přibram, *Geschichte der Österreichischen Gewerbepolitik von 1740 – 1860; auf Grund der Akten* (Leipzig: Duncker & Humblot, 1907); Alois Brusatti, *Österreichische Wirtschaftspolitik vom Josephinismus zum Ständestaat* (Wien: Jupiter-Verl., 1965); Andreas Baryli, 'Gewerbepolitik und gewerbliche Verhältnisse im vormärzlichen Wien', in *Wien im Vormärz*, ed. Renate Banik-Schweitzer, Forschungen und Beiträge zur Wiener Stadtgeschichte 8 (Wien: Jugend und Volk, 1980); Andreas Baryli, *Konzessionssystem Contra Gewerbefreiheit* (Frankfurt am Main: Lang, 1984).

4. Gergely Baics, *Feeding Gotham: The Political Economy and Geography of Food in New York, 1790–1860* (Princeton, Oxford: Princeton University Press, 2016), 10.

It argues that liberalization eliminated both the regulated relation between cereal, flour and bread prices and cross-subsidization as a means of societal solidarity in general, as well as a guideline for consumers and authorities to judge and compare prices. Termed 'bread question' by contemporaries, at the heart of the debates were two interconnected agendas: a struggle over the ways and forms bread should be produced and sold on the one hand, and issues of standardization and control concerned with both public health and with market transparency on the other hand. Both centrally involved struggles between politicians, bakers and eventually customers over knowledge, conventions, transparency and bargaining power within a free-market environment of baking, selling and buying bread.

Chapter 6

A FREE MARKET LANDSCAPE OF BREAD, 1860-80s

Mobilization and continued diversification

On 19 August 1860, *Fleischselcher* Georg Breitenbücker acquired a trade licence to operate the bakery in 951 Karolinengasse, a recently developed area near Belvedere Palace in Vienna's fourth district, Wieden. Although he named one Johann Friedrich Gerlinger to run the business in his name, Breitenbücker's is an early documented precedent of the new, liberal era. The butcher was probably neither the only nor the first to access the bread trade without being trained a baker, but he is the first person explicitly identified as such in the guild's registers.[5] While further information on his business is unavailable, his case represents one of the main effects of liberalization in the Austrian capital: the decisive mobilization of the bread landscape.[6]

Like in Paris or New York City,[7] the elimination of entrance regulations opened the trade and enabled the infrastructure of baking to expand decisively. While a total just short of 400 urban and rural guild bakers had provided the city with bread by the late 1850s, this number grew quickly after 1860 and reached nearly 650 by the late 1870s. A total of just under 160 workshops had been added to the ranks of guild masters during the four decades after 1815; some 250 bakeries joined

---

5. Archiv der Bäckergenossenschaft in Wien, HS 16/2: Innung der bürgerl. Bäckermeister in der k.k. Haupt- und Residenzstadt Wien. Gesetze und Verordnungen von 1853 bis 1868. Exhibiten Mag. Dekret 19.8.1860 Nr. 50. A *Fleischselcher* was a butcher licensed only to produce sausages and smoked (*geselchtes*) meat. See Lukasz Nieradzik, *Der Wiener Schlachthof St. Marx: Transformation einer Arbeitswelt zwischen 1851 und 1914* (Wien: Böhlau, 2017), 72.

6. Chapters 6 and 7 represent a revised and extended version of Jonas M. Albrecht, 'Surprising Similarities? Food Market Deregulation and the Consequences of Laissez-Faire in Vienna, Paris and New York City, C. 1840–1880', *Geschichte und Region/Storia e regione* 30, no. 1 (2021), 19–54.

7. On Paris, see Anne Lhuissier, 'Cuts and Classification. The Use of Nomenclatures as a Tool for the Reform of the Meat Trade in France, 1850–1880', *Food and Foodways* 10, no. 4 (2002), 183–208. On New York City, see Baics, *Feeding Gotham*.

the bakers' association in the quarter century following 1860. More precisely, the largest increase of bread producers did not take place in the urban area proper, but rather in the city's outskirts. Whereas the number of urban bakers grew rather slowly from about 160 to a peak of 320 by the late 1860s, most new production sites were opened in areas of fast population growth beyond the *Linienwall*. Continuing the growth in the numbers of country bakers of the previous decades, in the three years after 1858 alone over one hundred bakeries were started in Vienna's surroundings. By 1870, 120 more had started business.[8]

Returning to the example of Georg Breitenbücker, liberalization not only opened the trade in terms of sheer numbers, it also opened baking to actors who had previously been hindered to become a baker. Most obvious, this was especially true for women. In contrast to slaughtering, the abolition of guild-related job training and education requirements and the decentralized character of the trade opened female producers a window that had not existed for at least the previous half-century (Table 5). Although women's share as bakery owners during the 1830s and 1840s had risen formally, it remains to be analysed whether female entrepreneurs were really enabled to operate a bakery under the tight, male-dominated structure of the guild at that time. In any case, free commerce did offer new prospects for women to take over sometimes long-established bakeries both in the city proper and outside of it. This appears to be especially true for the period after 1860, when the share of women as shopkeepers in the city doubled from about 5 to over 10 per cent. Examples like Anna Liebig in the city centre, Christina Franz in Vienna's fourth district or Franziska Luckner in the northern area of the ninth district, all of whom were registered as shopkeepers in 1864, are all cases in point.

Concurring with the fast increase of population growth, the opening of the trade enabled the bread infrastructure to expand into the evolving immigration hotspots outside the densely populated area. As the city outgrew its former urban limits, the deregulated baking industry followed suit, providing crucial bread access points to the new residents in the expanding settlements in Vienna's environs. As indicated in Maps 10 and 11, liberated from municipal spatial regulation and retail limitations, the geography of baking expanded, especially outside the traditional urban core area. Inside the taxed area surrounded by the *Linienwall* almost seventy new bakeries were opened after 1847, particularly in the developing parts of the south-west (districts four and five) and north-east (districts two and twenty) as well as in the wake of the development of the *Glacis* and the construction of the *Ringstrasse* around the medieval city centre.

8. Sources: *Bericht der Handels- und Gewerbekammer für das Erzherzogthum Oesterreich unter der Enns an das k.k. Ministerium für Handel und Volkswirthschaft über die Verkehrsverhältnisse des Kammerbezirkes in den Jahren 1852–1885* (Wien); Archiv der Bäckergenossenschaft in Wien: Innung der bürgerl. Bäckermeister in der k.k. Haupt- und Residenzstadt Wien. Kalender für das Gremium der bürgerl. Bäckermeister in der k.k. Haupt- und Residenzstadt Wien, 1818–1885.

Table 5 Share of Women Named as Shopkeepers, 1815–82

	Within the Linienwall						
Year	1815	1833	1847	1858	1864	1870	1882
Men	157	171	200	220	247	250	254
Women	4	15	15	8	14	32	32
Total	161	186	215	228	261	282	286
Women, %	2	8	7	4	5	11	11
	Outside the Linienwall						
Year	1815	1833	1847	1858	1864	1870	1882
Men	65	90	113	142	244	263	311
Women	3	5	18	12	17	19	41
Total	68	95	131	154	261	282	352
Women, %	4	5	14	8	7	7	12

Source: Archiv der Bäckergenossenschaft in Wien: Innung der bürgerl. Bäckermeister in der k.k. Haupt- und Residenzstadt Wien. Kalender für das Gremium der bürgerl. Bäckermeister in der k.k. Haupt- und Residenzstadt Wien, 1815–82.

At the same time, a strong continuity of bakery locations is visible. Although the *Gewerbefreiheit* of 1860 ended the municipality's control over where a new bakery could be opened, deregulation had little effects on the topography of the *existing* landscape of bread. Many of the places that had hosted a bakery in 1847 continued to do so by 1882. Additionally, by the latter year some seventeen bakers had quickly opened shop in industrial Favoriten district outside the tax wall. In many parts of the capital, customers in 1882 might have visited the same bakery they had bought their bread at for several decades. Given the large investment needed to build a bakery, this is not surprising. By the early 1880s, one author estimated the price to buy an average operating bakery at 12,000 to 16,000fl., a sum that might have purchased over 20,000 working days of a mason's handyman at an average daily wage of 0.62 fl.[9]

Meanwhile, outside the tax border the growth of the numbers of bakers was the largest, and it was the quickest after 1858. Continuing the development of the first half of the century, bakeries were set up in the unfolding industrial area of Meidling with the communities of Gaudenzdorf, Rudolfsheim, Fünfhaus and Sechshaus close to the Wien River just to the southwest of the urban core. Whereas

---

9. J. Matern, *Licht in der Brodfrage und der sichere Weg zur Lösung derselben* (Wien: Karl Matern, 1885), 26; wages from Robert C. Allen, 'Consumer Price Indices, Nominal / Real Wages and Welfare Ratios of Building Craftsmen and Labourers, 1260–1913. Prices and Wages in Vienna, 1439–1913', International Institute of Social History data files, accessed 5 May 2021, https://iisg.amsterdam/en/blog/research/projects/hpw/datafiles.

154 *The Moral and Market Economies of Bread*

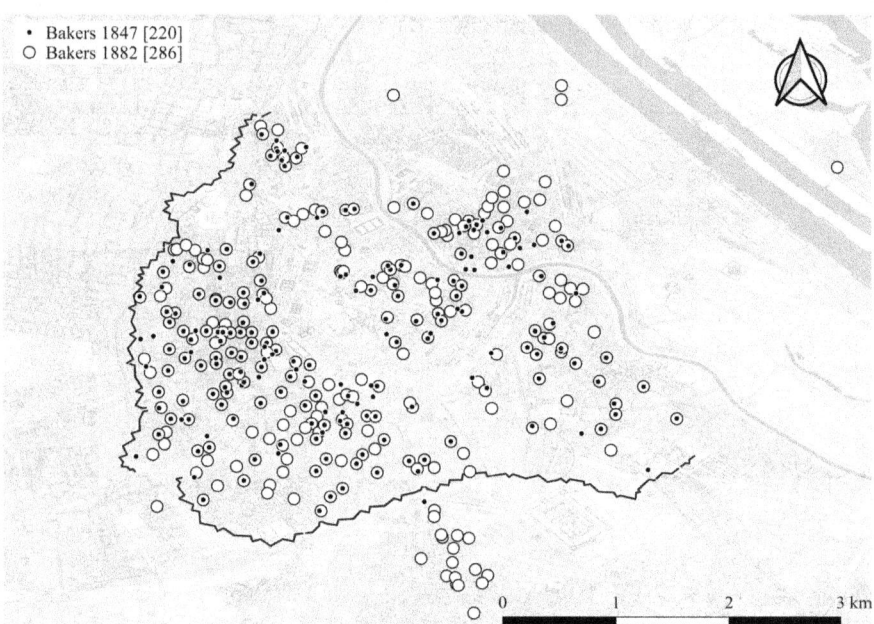

Map 10 Urban Bakers 1847 and 1882 within the *Linienwall* and in Favoriten district.[10]

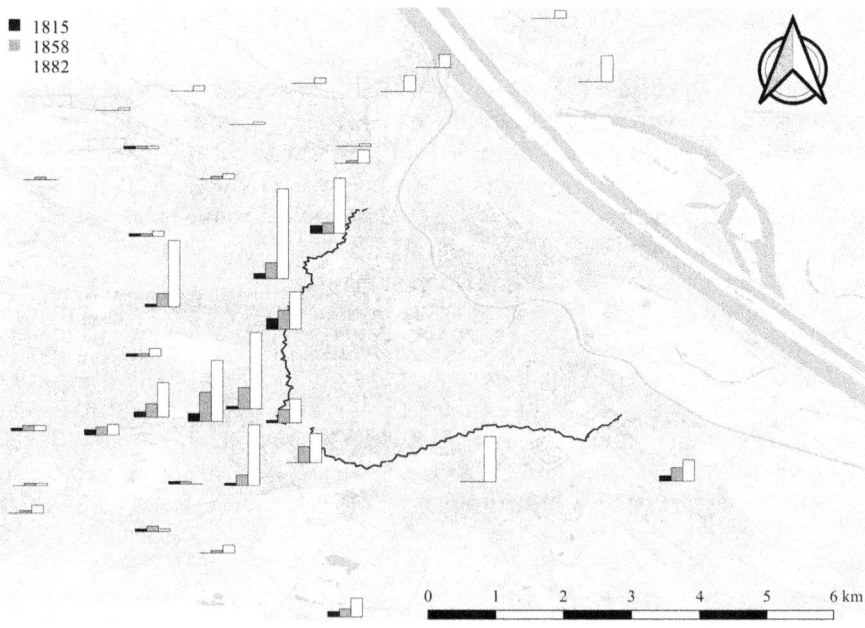

Map 11 Country Bakers per Parish, 1815–82.[11]

10. Source: Bäckerinnung, Kalender, based on Generalstadtplan 1912 provided by Wien Kulturgut, https://www.wien.gv.at/kulturportal/public/grafik.aspx.
11. Sources: see Map 10.

a total of six official bakers had provided bread to this area around 1815, thirty-four production sites existed by 1858. With deregulation, this number swiftly rose to ninety in 1870 and ninety-five by 1882, thus nearly trebling over the two decades following liberalization. A similar development can be observed in the other areas of drastic population growth in the north-west (Neulerchenfeld, Hernals, Ottakring, Währing). While the combined number of bakeries in the western communities grew from ten to twenty-two between 1815 and 1858, it reached fifty-four and ninety-four in 1870 and 1882, respectively.[12]

However, the accelerated founding of bakeries in the new epicentres of urbanization was not only a reaction to the vast and fast population growth these communities experienced after mid-century. Beyond the *Linienwall*, the number of bakers per capita continued to outpace that of the urban area inside the tax wall. Thus continuing the diversification of the landscape of bread into an urban wheat and a country rye bread circuit of provision, much more country bread bakeries were founded after 1858 per capita compared to the urban wheat workshops. Whereas the landscape of bread inside the urban area appears to have been saturated to a certain degree and its expansion after 1860 did not keep up with the pace of accelerated population growth, beyond the *Linienwall* the number of bakers per resident actually increased until 1870, when it also might have reached a certain level of saturation. Keeping the ratio between bread producers and consumers in the greater area of the capital roughly stable, the expansion of country bread bakers after liberalization secured not only the provision of the urbanizing outskirts but also the ongoing diversification of both supply infrastructures and their specialization on wheat and rye products, respectively, as the *Verzehrungssteuer* registers document. Although fragmentary due to various changes in tax categories and the registration of individual items, the growth of imports of 'bread and baked goods' not only from the communities outside the *Linienwall* into the densely settled urban area is evident. Whereas some 500 tonnes had been imported annually during the first decade of the century, over 2,500 tonnes were sent into the city by the first half of the 1830s; by the late 1880s almost 20,000 tonnes were counted by the custom officials positioned at the *Linienwall*, which by then represented a cumbersome hindrance to traffic that separated a coherent urban area densely developed on both sides of the wall.[13]

Clarifying the contemporary denomination, 'by bread we mean rye bread', baker Ferdinand Boos explained by 1870, underlining that most of those bread products registered by the city toll were actually loaves of country bread baked from rye.[14] 'Masses of untaxed goods are carried inside [the city] in small amounts',

12. Sources: Own calculations based on Bäckerinnung, Kalender, 1815–1884.

13. Source: Friedrich Hauer et al., 'Die Wiener Verzehrungssteuer. Auswertung nach einzelnen Steuerposten (1830–1913)', https://boku.ac.at/wiso/sec/publikationen/social-ecology-working-papers.

14. k. k. Handelsministerium, *Enquête über die Approvisionirung Wiens: II: Theil, Lebensmittel (ausgenommen Fleisch), Brennholz und Mineralkohle*, 2 vols. (Wien: Kaiserlich-königliche Hof- und Staatsdruckerei, 1871), 21.

Enquête expert Quinz had reasoned already by 1870.[15] In order to do so, especially the bakers in the parishes directly bordering on the *Linienwall* employed greater numbers of workers, as Gustav Schimmer elaborated. Bakers located in the parishes closest to the city proper like Simmering, Hernals, Neulerchenfeld, Ottakring, Währing, Fünfhaus, Gaudenzdorf, Rudolfsheim, Sechshaus and Untermeidling hired much more workers than their counterparts in more removed villages of the urban fringe.[16] 'Thanks to the great competition of outside producers, the price of bread, namely rye bread, the production of which Vienna's bakers have neglected for years, is constantly cheap and Vienna is sufficiently supplied at all times, these import opportunities should be encouraged', later *Marktamt* director Karl Kainz observed by 1877.[17]

However, the geographical expansion of the build infrastructure of bread after 1860 was but one of the central developments of the free-market landscape of bread. The mobilization of the ways bread was sold and bought assumed a second crucial role in the changed politico-economic environment.

The hawker's question

'Fellow citizens! The market department has worked wonders. The bread question is solved', satire magazine *Die Bombe* announced on 7 July 1875, underlining the news' value through a liberal use of exclamation marks:

> In the future, grocers will only receive 10% commission instead of 25%!!! Since those 10% will be granted not as tip, like in the past, but as legal, officially permitted commission, grocers will be renamed into Kipfel agents, Baunzerl brokers and Gschradi realtors. The advantages this innovation offers to consumers will be published separately. Anyway, we can ensure openly that the beloved elegance of the famous Viennese vest-pocket-sized rolls is not affected by the new order.[18]

Ridiculing grocers retailing bread as agents, brokers and realtors, the humourous article not only alluded to the grown scepticism about stock markets and stock market-based finance instruments evoked by the crash of the Vienna

---

15. Ibid., 127.

16. Gustav Adolph Schimmer, *Die Bevölkerung von Wien und seiner Umgebung nach dem Berufe und der Beschäftigung: 1. Geschlecht, Civilstand, Wohnverhältnisse, Arbeits- und Dienstverhältnisse* (Wien: Ueberreuter, 1874), 112, 152–5.

17. Wiener Stadt- und Landesarchiv, Marktamt, A2/1: Brot-Markirung, 2258/46, 21.06.1877: Marktamt. Brodmarkirung betffd.

18. *Die Bombe*, 'Kundmachung', 11 July 1875, 27, 110. Kipfel, Baunzerl and Gschradi are names for various kinds of bakery goods.

Stock Exchange two years earlier. Subdividing such actors in various vendors of distinguished kinds of baked goods – *Kipferl, Baunzerl* and *Gschradi* – and pointing to a rather incomprehensible system of commissions with unclear consequences for consumers, the author's satire simultaneously commented on the complexity of bread distribution in Vienna and the residents' ability to negotiate that terrain by the middle of the 1870s. Only a few decades earlier, liberalization had 'set the terms of New Yorkers' food access in the first half of the nineteenth century', where 'residents faced profound changes in the institutional setting and daily practice of household provisioning'.[19] By the last third of the century, written hardly two decades after the *Gewerbefreiheit* had replaced a municipal with a free-market landscape of bread, Vienna's *Die Bombe* magazine took up current struggles over changes of the Austrian capital's landscape of bread brought about by liberalization.

Focussing on the topic of a complex landscape of bread retail dominated by several competing actors, *Die Bombe* took up debates over the consequences of liberalization that were also discussed among high-ranking politicians, economists and academics.

'The Hawker's question ignites the passion of both liberals and anti-liberals in Austria [...] in an antagonism of beliefs behind which lie political, confessional and economic interests', Viennese economist Eugen Schwiedland wrote in 1899. He aimed to deliver a 'clear picture of the conditions' of hawking and peddling to reconcile the debates between economically liberal and less liberal contemporaries that were situated within a broader debate over the consequences of the *Gewerbefreiheit* since 1860.[20] By the late 1800s, German-speaking academics and politicians had adopted the issue and produced extensive inquiries into the consequences of liberalization especially on small businesses. Explaining his interest, none other than Gustav Schmoller had set the agenda for sceptics of free commerce already by 1870:

> In the past I shared [...] the purely positive perspectives of the liberal Nationalökonomie [...] that in the Gewerbefreiheit in itself lies the remedy for all evils. The deeper my studies led me, the more [...] the whitewash optimism changed into the understanding that besides the brilliant, unheard-of progress the great upheavals of our time necessarily carry deep social and economic grievances; to me the nihilism of 'laissez-faire et laissez-passer' transformed into the demands for positive reforms [...].[21]

---

19. Baics, *Feeding Gotham*, 8.

20. Eugen Peter Schwiedland, *Die Hausiererfrage in Österreich* (Leipzig: Duncker & Humblot, 1899), Einleitung zu Band 82 der Schriften des Vereins für Socialpolitik, VII.

21. Gustav Schmoller, *Zur Geschichte der Deutschen Kleingewerbe im 19. Jahrhundert: Statistische und Nationalökonomische Untersuchungen* (Halle: Buchhandlung des Waisenhauses, 1870), VI–VII.

Peddlers and hawkers received special attention by both liberal and more sceptic representatives arguing whether peddling either was a way to make a living for the poor and a means to increase commerce and ensure the distribution of certain goods, or illicit competition for respectable artisans, consumers' fraud and a general hazard to security and sanitation.[22] In Austria, Eugen Schwiedland in particular took up this question by the 1890s, having won his professorship for political economy at Vienna University with an 1894/5 treatise on the consequences of the *Gewerbefreiheit* on small artisans and the putting-out system that closed with a call for 'charges against freedom of trade' and 'reasons for [its] invalidity'.[23]

A heated debate among economists and politicians during the late nineteenth and early twentieth centuries increasingly charged with anti-Semitic notions, a quite similar dispute was carried out on the urban parquet in Vienna between administrators and bakers. While anti-Jewish biases were less present, at least in the official texts consulted for this study, the focal points of criticism were quite the same. Especially the bakers painted gloomy pictures of what a liberalization of intermediate retail channels would bring. 'We have [...] presented the evils produced by the liberalization of the bread retail for the craftsman and the customers that have delivered bakers and consumers alike into the hands of people who [...] press interest rates from poverty', the bakers' guild had reasoned already in 1848, complaining about the permission to sell bakers' bread for Vienna's *Greißler* – grocers – in 1820 and 1832. With such a permit, the guild warned in the spirit of the traditional market laws, 'an independent class of merchants [...] is founded between producers and consumers [...] at the expense of both'.[24] Carving out the main arguments of the following decades, intermediate grocers would diminish the bakers' profits and increase the costs of bread for consumers through the commission granted them for their service, and their 'sheer numbers' made 'official supervision' of the bread market impossible.[25] Allowing bread to be sold

22. For a broad overview about the debate, see e.g. Sigrid Wadauer, 'Ins Un/Recht setzen. Diffamierung und Rehabilitierung des Hausierens', in *Das nennen Sie Arbeit? Der Produktivitätsdiskurs und seine Ausschlüsse*, ed. Nicole Colin and Franziska Schößler (Heidelberg: Synchron Wissenschaftsverlag der Autoren Synchron Publishers, 2013); Sigrid Wadauer, 'Betteln und Hausieren Verboten? Ambulanter Handel im Wien der Zwischenkriegszeit', *Jahrbuch für Wirtschaftsgeschichte / Economic History Yearbook* 48, no. 1 (2007), 181–204; Klemens Kaps, 'Peripherisierung der Ökonomie, Ethnisierung der Gesellschaft: Galizien zwischen äußerem und innerem Konkurrenzdruck (1856–1914)', in *Galizien. Fragmente eines diskursiven Raums*, ed. Doktorratskolleg Galizien (Wien: StudienVerlag, 2009).

23. Eugen Peter Schwiedland, *Kleingewerbe und Hausindustrie in Österreich: Beiträge zur Kenntnis ihrer Entwicklung und ihrer Existenzbedinguen*, 2 vols. (Leipzig: Duncker & Humblot, 1894).

24. Innung der bürgerl. Bäckermeister in der k.k. Haupt- und Residenzstadt Wien, *Darstellung der Gewerblichen Zustände der Wiener Bäcker-Innung* (Wien: Ferd. Jahn, 1848), 17, 11. German Original: '[...] von der Armuth Zinsen zu erpressen'.

25. Ibid., 11.

by others than bakers, the guild concluded, would therefore greatly harm both the bakers' businesses, lead to monopolies by a few rich artisans who could afford to pay a greater number of intermediate retailers, and be detrimental to public concerns of food safety and sanitation. While written within the logics of the disciplinary mechanisms still provided by assize and guild in 1848, these arguments remained at the heart of the debate throughout the second half of the century.

Only three years later, the guild issued a detailed petition to Emperor Franz Josef asking to be 'relieved from the too large number of intermediates' through creation of a 'regulated competition' between bakers 'for the benefit of the consumers'. Harmed by the commission granted to grocers the guild repeated its claims that bakers had to 'diminish the weight of bread' to cover the losses conferred to the capital's residents, of which especially the poor were hit hardest. Bakers depended on the 'expansion of their business' and therefore heavily competed over retailers so that the liberalization of intermediate trade produced 'competition between bakers, yet not in the way bakers attract customers with fine and large bread but in efforts to secure more retailers and thus expand outlets by offering higher provisions'. For these reasons, the guild asked for an 'even limitation of the number of retailers for all bakers in Vienna' to the number of six intermediaries per baker. In doing so, bread would become great and cheap again, bakers would regain financial assets to rid themselves off their dependence on credit with millers, and the bakery trade would become more equal in general.[26]

Intermediate retailers were responsible for the rise of bread prices, city council Steudel agreed in a presentation before the city assembly in early 1865, which had debated over the legalization of hawking for some years.[27] The permission of hawking would produce greater competition among distributors and thus decrease the commissions bakers had to pay to grocers and hawkers altogether, liberal council Frankl and others opposed to eventually approve greater freedoms for intermediaries.[28] Small bakers, a newspaper report argued in April 1870, worked 'only for grocers and innkeepers' and needed to employ two or three helpers for deliveries. This 'hunt for customers at every price', the report calculated, would cause the city bakers to lose 900,000fl. a year, make bread expensive, lead the bakers to 'ruin themselves' and give rise to swindle.[29] 'The fraud of hawking', baker Gaugusch opined in the same year, induced losses through commissions paid to hawkers of up to 30 per cent because 'we only obtain a respectable peddler when we honour him [financially] so high the producer himself earns nothing'. Since 'the producer has to earn this commission in the first place', Gaugusch cautioned,

---

26. Wiener Stadt- und Landesarchiv, Marktamt A2/1: Brotfrage, Nr. 6: Innung der bürgerl. Bäckermeister in der k.k. Haupt- und Residenzstadt Wien. Majestätsgesuch.

27. *Morgen-Post*, 'Die Brodfrage im Gemeinderathe', 22 January 1865, 22.

28. *Die Presse*, 'Wiener Gemeinderath. Sitzung vom 27. Mai', 28 May 1863, 145, 4.; *Fremden-Blatt*, 'Gemeiderath (Sitzung vom 24. Jänner.)', 25 January 1865, 25.

29. *Das Vaterland. Zeitung für die österreichische Monarchie*, 'Zur Brodfrage', 10 April 1870, 99, Beiblatt, 2.

this raised bread prices for consumers – a notion that was largely included into the *Enquête's* final statements.³⁰

A self-declared 'expert' agreed in a newspaper contribution on 'expensive house bread' five years later. Intermediate retail and commissions were to blame, the author argued, as well as bakers who 'went along'. The reason he saw in the 'disproportionate competition' between bakers that forced established artisans to raise commissions for their hawkers every time a new competitor tried to elbow into the trade by undercutting existing businesses. The expert saw the only solution to this downward spiral in the limitation and regulation of bakeries and hawking and the end of the 'hunt for customers'. Therefore, he concluded, 'not the bakers or hawkers are to be blamed for high prices, but our legislation that has extended freedom of trade to the food provision businesses'.³¹ Several years later, a *Das Vaterland* article adopted the same notion arguing how 'highly disadvantageous for the Volkswohl the liberal economic order is' because it created the 'parasite' of hawkers, whose growing numbers squeezed both producers and consumers.³² Rather critical of Vienna's bakers' association, by 1885 another observer offered a slightly deviant remark: 'It is the competition between bakers over hawkers […] that is responsible for the evils presented by hawking, and the bakers are themselves to blame; it is an excess of unhealthy competition which leads only to a struggle for increasing sales […].'³³

Finally, a decade later, director of Vienna's *Marktamt* Karl Kainz summarized the developments somewhat less biased:

> In the past, every baker had been limited to the location of his business and thus built up and secured a customer base. Today this is entirely different. […] Many bakers have their baked goods distributed and hawked by peddlers, whom they grant a high commission in a fashion that is not in line with a reel and rational way to conduct business.³⁴

These extensive debates over grocers and hawkers since the second third of the century highlight the further mobilization and differentialization of the landscape of bread beyond its places of production in bakeries in both the city and its outskirts. Besides having freed the opening of sites of bread production from guild and assize regulations, the *Gewerbefreiheit* and other pieces of legislation drafted

---

30. Handelsministerium, *Enquête*, 74, 445.
31. *Neues Wiener Tagblatt*, 'Das Theure Hausbrod', 30 June 1875, 179, 2.
32. *Das Vaterland. Zeitung für die österreichische Monarchie*, 'Das Brod', 18 January 1878, 18, 1.
33. Matern, *Licht in der Brodfrage*, 28.
34. Wiener Stadt- und Landesarchiv, Marktamt, A2/1: Brotfrage, 02.12.1897: Marktamt. Referat über die Brodfrage für die 9. Sitzung der Approvisionirungs-Conferenz am 21/12 1897.

6. A Free Market Landscape of Bread, 1860–80s   161

in the spirit of the free market had legalized and fostered a significant expansion of the channels of bread distribution through mobile retailers. Having allowed grocers to retail assize bread and other bakery products during the *Vormärz* to secure consumers' access to that basic need, the 1852 imperial *Hausierpatent* had allowed hawking to a certain degree and §60 of the 1860 *Gewerbefreiheit* had largely permitted itinerant trade on the national level. By 1865, the trade ministry expressively legalized 'peddling of bread products from house to house in Vienna'.[35]

By the 1850s, selling bread via contracted grocers had become a usual and important means for master bakers to expand the geographic range of their outlet territories. In their 1851 petition to the emperor, the bakers had claimed to sell only one sixth of their entire production in their own shops while over 2,200 grocers ostensibly sold the rest. Since most people would purchase bread at a grocer's, 'where they buy most of their daily necessities, and do not visit one shop to buy bread, and another to purchase the other victuals', a baker needed to 'apply with retailers to secure his outlet', the guild lamented.[36] Not granted regulation from above, the corporation attempted at self-regulation through mutual agreements since the 1860s. By 1867, a so-called *Revers* was incorporated into the *Bäckerkalender* asking members to sign an agreement not to give credit to retailers who had not paid their debts with other bakers. In 1880, a supplement was added to create a central register of all intermediate retailers indebted to bakers. With that help, when signing up with a new retailer members of the corporation should make sure a grocer, hawker or peddler did not owe money to any other baker; if this was the case, the newly employing baker was to reimburse those debts to the other bread producer. However, highlighting the differences in interests and retail strategies among bakers, only 140 out of 286 city bakers and a mere 18 out of 352 country bakers signed this contract in 1882.[37] As a result, the landscape of baking became much more diverse already by the late 1850s. As an example, Map 12 depicts the bakers located in Vienna's city centre and the listed retailers employed by them according to the 1857 bakers' register. This source lists the roughly 230 bakers across the city as well as several hundreds of retailers, each associated to one baker. Those retailers are divided into 'own' shops, secondary and tertiary shops owned and run by the bakers themselves, and 'intermediates' – grocers retailing a baker's products. For reasons of simplicity, legibility and effort, only the city centre bakers and their retailers are pictured, and no association between bakers and retailers is identified.

As Map 12 highlights, already by 1857 the 26 city centre bakers used over 250 alternate outlets to secure sales and expand their products' ranges. Running 59 own stores other than the bakeries proper and selling bread and rolls through 199

---

35. Wadauer, 'Betteln', 192; Handelsministerium, *Enquête*, XLVI.
36. Bäckerinnung, Majestätsgesuch.
37. Bäckerinnung, Kalender, 1882.

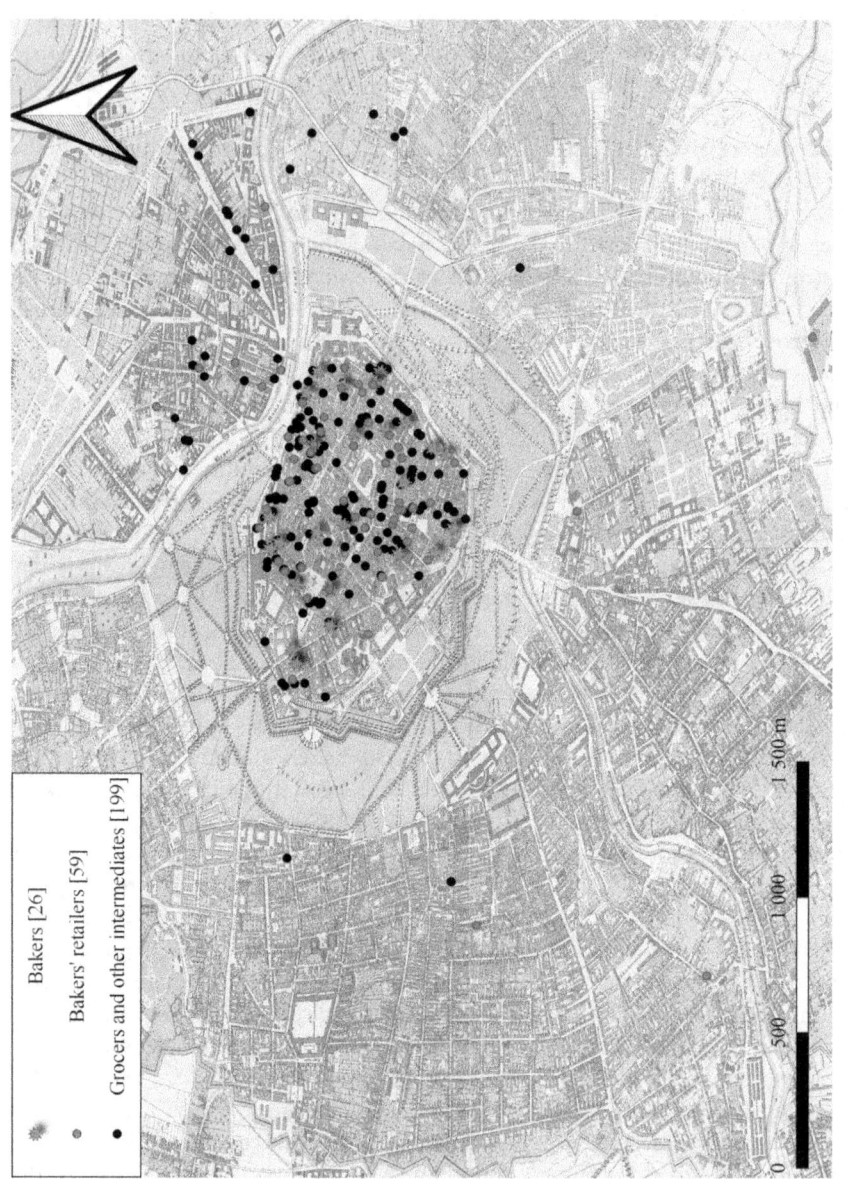

Map 12 City Centre Bakers and Registered Retailers, 1857.[38]

38. Source: Wiener Stadt- und Landesarchiv, Innungen und Handelsgremien 1/B1: Bäcker: Bücher. Bäckerverzeichnis 1.

additional grocers,[39] they attempted to cover most of the old town's surface and even spread out into Vienna's suburbs. In the old town proper, bakeries, shops and grocers could be found in close proximity, often in neighbouring complexes or just across the street, sometimes even in the same building. While most of their outlets could be found in Leopoldstadt area north of the Danube Canal, where they often settled on main thoroughfares and around the suburb's marketplace, the city centre bakers also directly sold their products in other parts of town. These retail infrastructures differed between the twenty-six bakers. Court baker Albert Schachtner, for example, ran six secondary shops, four in the city centre, one on the corner of Gumpendorfer Straße and the church square of western Mariahilf district close to the Wien River and another at Südbahnhof railway station pictured at the very southern fringe of Map 12; no grocers were listed to officially retail the court baker's merchandise at all. Other bakers like Johann Kochem or Ferdinand Holzwart did not have secondary shops on their own but sold their products to a handful of grocers largely located in the city centre. Probably the largest business, Josef Kurz occupied five or six secondary shops and contracted nineteen grocers spread across various suburbs. Most commonly, however, a city centre baker would run one or two shops besides their bakeries and sell through between five and ten additional grocers.

While Map 12 only suggests the complexity of the landscape of bread by the late 1850s, Vienna's bakers not only expanded their customer bases through stationery grocers' shops or itinerant retailers. Large institutional customers also became prime options to increase turnover. 'Every baker,' Karl Kainz summarized in 1897, 'seeks to win as many innkeepers, coffeehouse proprietors and other large buyers, regardless of whether those are located in the same or in remote districts. There is a vivid competition over the acquisition of large restaurants and coffeehouses whereby the overbidding of discounts, more daily deliveries and redeeming unsold goods play the main role.'[40]

Yet, though serving larger customers at what terms whatsoever had become another important means to secure sales, and indeed another object of debate by the very last years of the century, it was itinerant channels of bread distribution that presented the major driver of mobilizing and diversifying the landscape of bread.

Especially after the successive liberalization of street vending around mid-century hawkers increasingly became a crucial means of distributing bread across the growing capital. This does not mean itinerant sales had not existed before, on the contrary. The uncountable number of largely denied applications to hawk and peddle bread and other bakery products as well as the infringements against such prohibitions documented in the guild registers before 1860 speaks for itself.

---

39. Eight out of the 199 grocers could not be identified spatially, the same is true for one shop.

40. Marktamt, Referat über die Brodfrage.

One Elisabeth Schinacker, for example, was caught red-handed illicitly selling so-called 'gusto' pastry in late February 1810. While Schinacker had her merchandise confiscated, baker Rosalia Gerstl, the producer of these goods, received a penalty of 25fl.[41] Cases like that underline the distribution of bread and other bakery products had relied on mobile, hardly authorized networks of supply constantly, and that they had provided a certain income especially, though not exclusively for women. However, the Schinacker-Gerstl case also indicates that, while certainly not impermeable, the existing disciplinary mechanisms regulating the bread market in the forms of both market laws and the guild system had at least provided a certain institutional framework to keep unauthorized intermediate retail at bay.

The gradual legalization of hawking and peddling during the 1850s and 1860s, however, led to a stark increase in the numbers of itinerant retailers during much of the third quarter of the century. While the documented numbers of this often-informal occupation remain somewhat ephemeral,[42] Eugen Schwiedland estimated the numbers of hawkers in the Austrian provinces had risen from around 13,000 to 23,000 individuals between 1862 and 1881. Using official statistics subjected to the same challenges in measuring this elusive trade, Schwiedland reckoned about 2,700 hawking licences were granted in the province of Lower Austria including Vienna by 1890 and that some licensed 3,700 hawkers actually pursued that trade in this territory.[43] The compilation of various official statistics and of contemporary observers like statistician-demographer Gustav Adolph Schimmer equally highlights the rising numbers of both stationary and mobile intermediates since the late 1850s. According to the data collected by Vienna's chamber of commerce and the annual figures drawn up by the municipal statistical bureau, the numbers of licensed grocers grew from under 4,000 around 1855 towards 6,000 by the early 1880s. By that time, debates about hawkers and peddlers had grown more hostile and limiting practices and legislation was re-introduced increasingly.[44] Based on more fragmentary data, the numbers of licensed hawkers in Vienna might have increased from approximately 2,000 to 2,500 individuals between the 1850s and 1890 according to municipal statistics. Including the city's outskirt communities,

---

41. Archiv der Bäckergenossenschaft in Wien, HS 15: Innung der bürgerl. Bäckermeister in der k.k. Haupt- und Residenzstadt Wien. Protocollum uiber merkwürdige Gegenstände, als: Volksaufruhr gegen die Bäcker anno 1805; die den bürgl Bäckermeister geleisteten Vergütungen; mehrere Backproben; Consignation über die Ausgaben eines mitleren Bäckermeisters; dann der vom Jahre 1807 bis 1830 ergangenen Verordnungen und Rathschläge; 22.2.1810.

42. For a detailed discussion of hawkers' statistics, see e.g. Sébastien Rioux, *The Social Cost of Cheap Food: Labour and the Political Economy of Food Distribution in Britain, 1830–1914* (Montreal: McGill-Queen's University Press, 2019), 70–1.

43. Schwiedland, *Hausiererfrage*, XXXIV–XXXV.

44. See e.g. Kaps, 'Peripherisierung'.

the census data registered over 15,000 hawkers including their families and employees. Applying a similarly broadened spatial and categorical definition, Gustav Adolph Schimmer's figures stood above these figures. While counting almost twice as many hawkers, his estimate of over 11,000 grocers including employees in Vienna and outskirts was much more in line with the census survey. Concurring with the rise of intermediate retailers more generally, the numbers of bakery workers in particular rose, too, despite differences in the numbers counted between various statistics. Whereas the *Handelskammer* registered a rise from roughly 2,000 bakery workers in city and outskirts to approximately 3,000 between 1866 and 1875, Schimmer counted over 4,000 bakery labourers in 1874. Fifteen years later, the official census listed 7,525 bakery workers, almost twice as many individuals. Whereas a Viennese baker had employed an average of approximately five labourers by the late 1850s, Schimmer estimated an average of about nine workers per bakery inside the *Linienwall* and of more than seven regarding the bakeries beyond the tax border.[45]

As contemporary observers noted, by the 1870s and 1880s labourers occupied as roundsmen had become a distinct class of employees central to the distribution of bread across the city. 'We find a mass of hawkers in the bread trade, hawking is booming. Intermediate traders sell a lot of bread', the former director of Vienna's first steam mill Quinz told the *Enquête* commissioners. Bread in Vienna, the bakery labourers' representative Mehling reported, was sold

> by way of hawking in enormous amounts. Many masters employ journeymen whose single task it is to go peddle the baked goods, and there are cases a master baker sends a labourer in a different district, there are even cases he [the worker] sells bread in the second and third level of a house in which another bakery is located [at the ground level].[46]

Besides such few and poor, yet tax-paying self-employed licensed hawkers and peddlers who served the interest of consumers, there was 'a second class of hawkers', Dr J. Matern claimed in his fifty-page treatise on the 'bread question' fifteen years later:

> Those are the hawkers with no individual license employed by bakers [...] who serve as intermediates between bakers and consumers. They differ from

---

45. Sources: Bericht der Handels- und Gewerbekammer für das Erzherzogthum Oesterreich unter der Enns an das K.K. Ministerium für Handel und Volkswirthschaft über die Verkehrsverhältnisse des Kammerbezirkes in den Jahren 1852–1885; Schimmer, Bevölkerung; K. K. Statistische Central-Commission, ed., *Berufsstatistik nach den Ergebnissen der Volkszählung vom 31. December 1890 in den im Reichsrathe vertretenen Königreichen und Ländern: Nieder-Österreich*, Österreichische Statistik XXXIII, 2. Heft (Wien: Kaiserlich-Königliche Hof- und Staatsdruckerei/Carl Gerold's Sohn, 1894).

46. Handelsministerium, *Enquête*, 125–7, 81–2.

carriers, who are sent to customers, in the way that they are employed to recruit new customers. They go in another baker's territory, even brazenly into the house in which he has his shop and impose on the residents. A baker pays this service with 20, 25 and 30 per cent commission. [...] Those hawkers are usually apprentices. This way of procedures has the disadvantage that the consumers are now customers of the hawkers. If the hawker leaves one baker and enters a contract with another he brings his customers with him. Therefore, those hawkers are highly sought-for by bakers [...].[47]

'In no other profession is intermediate trade as widespread as in the baker's occupation', a *Marktamt* report declared two decades afterwards:

The needs of the consumer in the metropolis on the one hand and the competitive struggle on the other have led to a situation of the baking trade detrimental to artisans. [...] Based on observations the Marktamt can assert that roundsmen and hawkers represent a firm organization on which most bakers depend because purchases in their shops are dwindling. Vienna's bakers do not know their customers, who are served by roundsmen and hawkers. The customers are the fundus instructus of the roundsman, and he takes good care not to tell the baker [their identities]. It is also usual that a roundsman leaving the occupation for whatever reason sells his customer base to the successor. [...] Roundsmen and hawkers largely recruit themselves from the class of bakery workers.[48]

The report underlines the diversification and mobilization of the landscape of bread not only in terms of the numbers of registered itinerant distributors but also regarding the diversity among this class of labourers across the city – not to mention unregistered actors struggling to make ends meet under the radar of the authorities. While also underlining the close attention the municipality paid to the issue at large, these attempts at surveying the structure of bread distribution highlight the decisive role basically unmappable mobile channels of supply and delivery had assumed by the late nineteenth century. The creation of an intermediate class of distributors came to occupy a double-edged role in Vienna's landscape of bread. 'Contributing further to a highly competitive retail sector', they both secured the expansion of outlet territories as well as sales and represented competitors in the 'hunt for customers' and in the gains of selling bread that affected the 'shopkeepers' economic interests'.[49] Furthermore, the increase in the number of bakery labourers occupied merely as distributors since mid-century represented a 'reorganization of food distribution' and 'the rise of an important class of street sellers, commonly referred to as costermongers, hawkers, hucksters,

47. Matern, *Licht in der Brodfrage*, 27–8.
48. Wiener Stadt- und Landesarchiv, Marktamt A2/1: Brot: Gebäcksausträger, 29.05.1909: Marktamt. Gebäcksausträger.
49. Rioux, *Cheap Food*, 94.

or pedlars' who assumed an increasingly important 'economic function as cheap food distributors' within the landscape of bread.[50]

Bakers had traditionally relied on cheap labour well before industrialization and proletarization immiserated the living conditions of many people over the course of the nineteenth century. Coined by hard work, long working hours, repelling sanitary conditions, bad health and probably untimely death, the lives of bakery workers had been infamously miserable before the 1800s and continued to be that way well into the century. By 1870, for example, a large-scale bakers' 'Strike', as the authorities called it adopting English vocabulary, unsettled masters and municipal administrators in Vienna alike and led to the creation of a 14-page report whose minutes highlight the poor circumstances many bakery labourers suffered. Recapitulating the events, magistrate secretary Wenzl reported that 'thousands left their workplaces' on 19 April 1870 and united to protest their working and living conditions. Their demands were to decrease the actual work hours of between ten and sixteen per day; increase wages that were between three and six Gulden per week; enable uninterrupted resting times in 'clean' places not situated in basements; fresh water and toilets instead of buckets in the bake room, as well as to be served breakfast and dinner. Interviewed about working conditions, master baker Ferdinand Boos conceded most workers were to spend their leisure time with cleaning, chopping wood and doing other chores after shifts as long as twenty-four hours and admitted a labourer did 'not have much free time'. Meanwhile, chairmen Rudolf Plank complained about the labourers' habit 'to go for a walk instead of sleeping' during the short times they were able to escape the heat and dark of the oven rooms. Although masters had apparently agreed to include breakfast and coffee into their labourers' fare, secretary Wenzl still found their demands 'just' after having inspected the city's 282 bakeries, of which he fined 150 for numerous violations.[51]

In the context of these general hardships experienced by many bakery labourers, roundsmen represented the very bottom of those individuals on a baker's payroll. Called *Vice*, they received weekly wages between two and three Gulden around 1870, even less than a baker's boy did.[52] In the words of baker Gaugusch, these men were 'newcomers, apprentices arriving from the provinces who came here [to Vienna] to continue their job training, he earns 2fl. 50Kr because he knows nothing except of getting in the way of the other [workers]. He has nothing to do except to deliver the bakery goods to the customers [...]'.[53] Whereas those workers directly employed by the bakers received room and board – according to Schimmer some 80 per cent of bakery workers lived with their masters by 1874 – and thus remained somewhat better-off comparatively, most of the city's late

50. Ibid., 67–8.
51. Handelsministerium, *Enquête*, Interviews Plank, Boos, Wenzl and Mehling. Quotes from pages 32, 20, 16, 33.
52. Ibid., 82–3.
53. Ibid., 76.

nineteenth-century itinerant petty traders belonged to the impoverished, shunned bottom of the urban society struggling to make a living.[54] While the law foresaw official hawking licences only for those with 'no other option to make a living' and 'offered few perspectives for improvements or social advancement' through limiting the legally permitted profitability of peddling,[55] statements like that of baker Gaugusch further underline both the precariousness and the racialized and ethnicized place in society for those individuals performing an important task within the landscape of bread.

What is more, the mobility, flexibility and spatial comprehensiveness provided by the free-market landscape of bread did come at a price. Although easing and contributing to the solution of some challenges accelerating urbanization and population growth presented to the bread supply of the capital of the Habsburg Empire, free competition failed to deliver the common good in other aspects of the food economy. In some cases, deregulation exacerbated existing issues, in other cases it created new 'bread questions', especially regarding food quality and food security.

54. Schimmer, *Bevölkerung*, 65.
55. Wadauer, 'Betteln', 187.

Chapter 7

THE BREAD QUESTION

The price of bread

As legend has it, Johann Nestroy was sentenced to a night in prison in 1846. Allegedly having replaced his shirt buttons with small wheat rolls during a performance held amid public criticisms over rising bread prices and shrinking loaves, the poet was chastised for derision of a respectable profession, the bakers. Carrying out the dictated public apology after his night in jail, Nestroy was keen to thank the turnkeys for ensuring his accommodation by sticking bread rolls through the prison door's keyhole.[1]

Whether true or not, this legend about Nestroy's satirical performance highlights the close public attention paid to bread weights and prices, and to the merit of the city's bakers not only in times of dearth. Under the moral economy setting of the bread market, consumers and authorities alike were well aware of the state of bread prices and weights. Continuous debates about 'just' and 'fair' price levels prevailed throughout the late eighteenth and the first half of the nineteenth centuries. For example, criticizing high bread prices a lengthy booklet on 'the bakers in Vienna, their character and merits' from the early 1780s satirically described the immoral conduct of a baker's family. In this view, both the life of the lazy son and the lavish household and wardrobe of the baker and his wife were paid by fraudulent as well as expensive products, justified with 'rain in Transylvania, drought in Istria, [and] hoarfrost in Bohemia, which present the bakers in Vienna with reasons to raise prices and fill their pockets at the expense of their fellow people'.[2]

Questions of the moral conduct of bakers on whom large parts of the urban society relied, and issues concerning the price, quality and quantity of bakery products had remained a constant issue under the moral economy of bread, much likely for centuries. Before 1860, the assize had provided a thorough and complex central public institution to judge – and steer – the state of bread weights and

---

1. Gerhard Pfeisinger, *Die Revolution von 1848 in Graz* (Wien: Europaverlag, 1986).
2. Wienbibliothek im Rathaus, A-11304. Die Bäcker in Wien nach ihren Karackter und Verdienst, 21.

prices in comparison to grain and flour prices and qualities. To repeat, rather than keeping prices low, the assize's core function in this system were to provide market transparency, to create an urban welfare system subsidizing the costs of living of the poor and to meet the expectations of fairness and righteousness of several parties – consumers, producers and regulators. The abolition of the disciplinary mechanisms of the assize as official framework providing price, quantity and quality standards in 1849 and 1860 eliminated such a wide-ranging and comprehensive public surveillance and interference in the bread market in Vienna as Josepf Petzl, director of Vienna's *Marktamt*, summarized in mid-September 1861:

> The new Trade Act, which came into effect on 1 May 1860, declared the baker's trade a <u>free trade</u>, so that any assize constraint necessarily ceased in regard to the operation of this free occupation, therefore [...] <u>the determination of the prices of all bakery products is left to free competition</u>.[3]

Instructing the market bureau to investigate the current bread prices, Petzl's contribution was part of a debate about the consequences of liberalization that had commenced even before the assize was terminated on 1 November 1860. 'This week, Vienna's bakers have told the papers that from 1 November [1860] the price of small rolls will be raised by ½ Kreuzer and thus cost 2 Kreuzer instead of 1 ½ Kreuzer', the moderately liberal, rather popular than academic *Morgen-Post* had reported on 24 October 1860, a week before the deregulation act:

> Since in this moment the new associations do not exist yet and the old guilds do not exist anymore it would be of interest to know how this decision to increase prices came about. We do not know if *private agreements*, arranged to raise the price of an item of first necessity, are lawful and we doubt that such should bind Vienna's bakers. This would mean nothing else but to abuse the benefits of free trade and the termination of the assize in an act of terrorism against the consumers. [...] The abolition of the bread assize was welcomed by those institutions concerned with economic issues; certainly, at that time no one would have dreamt that just a couple of weeks later agreements between the bakers would replace the official assize; such a swap is neither in the interest of consumers nor in the spirit of the new trade law.[4]

Though not giving any details, 'much paper and ink are spent in the last time' on the bread question, the labourers' paper *Der Zwischen-Akt* added on 25 November 1860. Proving that something was in the air, by early March 1861 conservative

---

3. Wiener Stadt – und Landesarchiv, Marktamt A2/1: Brot und Gebäcksverkauf nach Gewicht, Z. 68143, 12.09.1861: Marktamt. Äusserung der Direktion des Marktkommissariates Über den bei dem löblichen Gemeinderathe gestellten Antrag, den Gebäcksverkauf in Wien nach dem Gewichte betreffend. Accentuation in original.

4. *Morgen-Post*, 'Wien', 24 October 1860, 295, 2. Accentuation in original.

Das Vaterland was positive that the 'much-discussed bread question will soon be solved by the *Gemeinderat* committee', which had been founded to investigate bread price issues in the meantime.[5]

Like in other Austrian cities, by the summer of that year – merely nine months after deregulation had abolished the disciplinary mechanisms of the assize and left bread prices to market forces – the *Gemeinderat* heavily debated over a perceived misalignment of bread, flour and grain prices.[6] On behalf of a left-wing fraction in the council, Joseph Kleyhonz, a successful carpenter, had suggested reintroducing regulation of bread prices to prevent that 'the poor masses are constantly deceived by the bakers' in mid-August 1861. Publicly denying all accusations made by Kleyhonz, who allegedly 'did not know cordial parliamentary behaviour or even correct German', the Bakers' Association retaliated some ten days later in what grew to become a larger struggle over the price of bread between socialist-minded and rather middle-class representatives among the *Gemeinderat*.[7]

Although Kleyhonz called on the city council in early November to hasten the investigations of the commission, which had allegedly 'done nothing yet to live up to its task', procedures remained sluggish. '19 month ago', *Die Presse* reported by late May 1863, city councils Kraftl and Kleyhonz had urged the assembly to see to 'steering the disproportionate level of bread prices'. In the meantime, this had turned into a 'vivid debate' among the city council, whose members had noticed the price of coarse wheat flour 'had fallen by 42 per cent within one year whereas bread became only 12 ½ per cent cheaper'.[8] A detailed analysis of the reasons for such price movements did not arrive until early 1865, almost two years later, when council Steudel reported over the commission's results how to 'obtain lower bread prices'. Finding an abundance of flour supplies provided not only by hundreds of mills in Vienna's vicinity and the expanding railroad network into Hungary, the commission also proved somewhat bewildered by finding that bread and flour prices had stopped to move unanimously with cereal prices. The council's *Approvisionirungssektion* had, Steudel summarized, reached the conclusion that it was most important to understand 'the reasons of high bread prices vis-à-vis low grain prices'.[9]

Indeed, this realization touched upon the core problem unfolding in the capital since, in the words of *Marktamt* director Petzl, deregulation had left

---

5. *Der Zwischen-Akt*, 'Wiener Plaudereien. Brod', 25 November 1860, 316, 3; *das Vaterland. Zeitung für die österreichische Monarchie*, 'Die Erwählten des III. Wahlkörpers', 5 March 1861, 52, 2.

6. On similar debates in Graz, see Robert Baravalle, 'Preise und Löhne in Graz im 19. Jahrhundert (1820 Bis 1914)', *Zeitschrift des Historischen Vereins für Steiermark* 57 (1966), esp. 108–9.

7. Vorstand der Bäcker-Genossenschaft, 'Zur Abwehr', *Morgen-Post*, 24 August 1861, Nr. 231, 3.

8. *Die Presse*, 'Wiener Gemeinderath. Sitzung vom 27. Mai', 28 May 1863, 145, 4.

9. *Morgen-Post*, 'Die Brodfrage im Gemeinderathe', 22 January 1865, Nr. 22, 3.

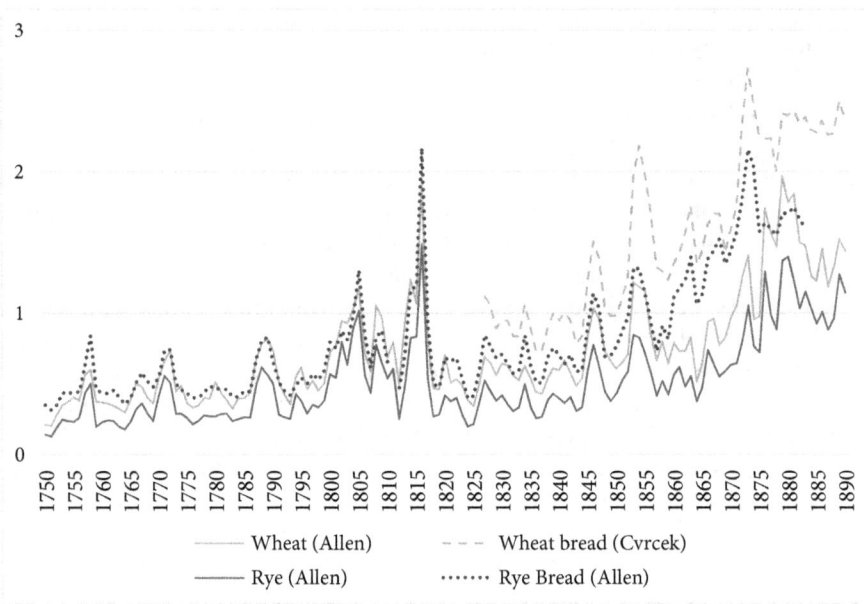

Figure 3 Cereal and Bread prices in Vienna, 1750–1890, in gAg per One Kilogram.

Sources: Robert C. Allen, 'Consumer Price Indices, Nominal / Real Wages and Welfare Ratios of Building Craftsmen and Labourers, 1260–1913. Prices and Wages in Vienna, 1439–1913', International Institute of Social History data files, accessed 5 May 2021, https://iisg.amsterdam/en/blog/research/projects/hpw/datafiles; Tomas Cvrcek, 'Austro-Hungarian Prices and Wages, 1827–1914', International Institute of Social History data files, accessed 5 May 2021, https://iisg.amsterdam/en/blog/research/projects/hpw/datafiles.

the determination of bread prices to free competition. Illustrated in Figure 3, the long-term perspective highlights that bread prices were unusually high in the Austrian capital during the early 1860s, especially compared to grain prices, which remained rather stable before 1865.

Although on a rising trend since the first half of the century, one litre of rye stood at around half a gram of silver between 1857 and 1865, having decreased from notable peaks in 1846/7 and during the Crimean War between 1853 and 1856. Despite an increase compared with the previous century, the price of rye thus remained on a level that was not spectacularly unfamiliar before 1865. This only changed from 1866, when several years of crop failures in Western Europe coincided with the 'miracle harvests' of 1866/7 and 1867/8 in Hungary and huge amounts of cereal exports led to rising prices not only in Vienna.[10] By 1880, one

---

10. See e.g. David F. Good, *The Economic Rise of the Habsburg Empire, 1750–1914* (Berkeley, CA: University of California Press, 1984), 164; Andreas Weigl, *Von der Existenzsicherung zur Wohlstandsgesellschaft: Überlebensbedingungen und Lebenschancen in Wien und Niederösterreich von der Mitte des 19. Jahrhunderts bis zur Gegenwart* (Wien: Böhlau, 2020), 104.

litre of rye stood at almost 1.4 grams of silver, roughly three times higher than it had fifteen years earlier.

The price of wheat developed quite similarly. While it had remained largely stable throughout most of the *Vormärz* period, wheat had been expensive during the years preceding the revolution as well as over the course of the conflict over Crimea, a major wheat exporter by that time. Following the movements of rye, the price of wheat yielded during the late 1850s and first half of the 1860s but rose to spectacular heights in the following decade. Whereas it had hovered between 0.6 and 0.8 grams of silver per litre before 1865, wheat rose to nearly one gram in 1866/1867, 1.4 grams in 1873 and peaked at two grams per litre in 1878 – like rye almost three times as expensive as a decade and a half earlier.

However, whereas the prices of cereals thus remained comparatively stagnant during the early 1860s, bread prices had already entered a path of quick increase. Hovering in the neighbourhood of 0.7 grams of silver per kilogram until the 1840s, rye bread had been expensive around 1848 and during the mid-1850s. After 1857, however, the price of rye bread entered a dramatic growth period, already increasing from approximately 0.8 grams in 1859 to 1.1 grams in 1860 – the year of deregulation. Quick growth continued over the following decades; by 1870 one kilogram of rye bread cost 1.5 grams of silver. It surpassed the threshold of two grams during the 1873 World Exposition – a level only seen once in the century, when the Congress had danced. Although the price of rye bread receded afterwards to a rather stagnant level around 1.7 grams of silver, by the early 1880s it upheld a level more than twice as dear as it had usually been under the assize abolished in 1860.

Wheat bread, on the other hand, became even more expensive after deregulation in 1849. Whereas one kilogram had usually fluctuated between 0.7 and one gram of silver during most of the 1830s and 1840s, the price of wheat shot up to over two grams around 1854. Though declining afterwards, it continued its trajectory of growth throughout the late 1850s and 1860s before also climbing new heights in 1873, when one kilogram of wheat bread was 2.7 grams of silver. Although this price, too, declined in the years to come, compared to the long-run experience it remained on the very high level of around 2.3 grams of silver until 1890.

While the movements of real prices yield more general information on the escalation of the costs of grain and bread after 1850, the relationship between cereal and bread prices presents a more detailed insight into the matter Vienna's city council was arguing about during early 1860s. As Figure 4 highlights, the abolition of regulated prices terminated the synchronized ratio of cereal and bread prices, one of the fundamental functions of the assize.

With regard to rye, before 1860 the silver price of one kilogram of rye bread had usually been between 1.4 and two times the silver price of one litre of rye – indeed comparative to the price structure in the Netherlands – although major deviations upwards and downwards can be observed in periods of crisis.[11] Note, for example,

---

11. On the ratio of bread and cereal prices in the Netherlands see Jan de Vries, *The Price of Bread: Regulating the Market in the Dutch Republic* (Berkeley, CA: University of California Press, 2019), 238–48.

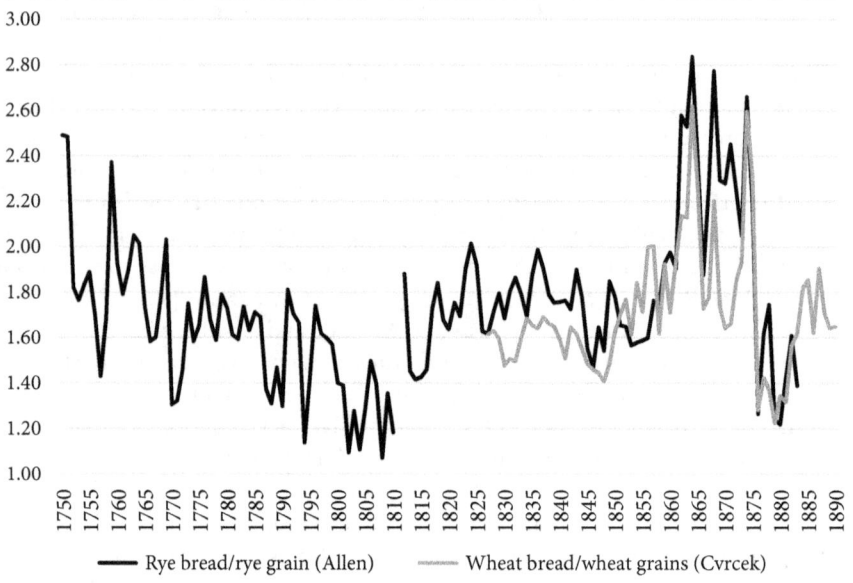

Figure 4 Ratio of Silver Prices for One Litre of Grain and One Kilogram Bread in Vienna, 1750–1890.

Sources: See Figure 3.

the drops of the price ratio in 1757, during the war over Silesia between Austria and Prussia in the context of the Seven-Years War; the more pronounced drop in the course of the intense dearth of 1770/71, during the attempts to deregulation of the very late 1780s; the lasting decrease of the price of rye bread vis-à-vis grain during the Napoleonic Wars of the 1790s and early 1800s; or during the middle of the 'hungry forties'. As those fluctuations underline, under the moral economy mechanisms of embeddedness the assize would keep bread prices at bay and relatively cheap compared to the costs of grain in times of life-threatening episodes by limiting and even preventing profits for merchants, millers and bakers. However, such losses endured by producers could be compensated by allowing higher margins and making bread more expensive relative to grain, for example in 1759, 1791 or 1849.

The termination of the assize on rye ended this institution abruptly. With the dissolution of regulated rye bread prices in 1860, this product became decisively more expensive compared to cereals during the following fifteen years. Reaching a ratio of c. 2.8 in the most expensive years, the ten-year moving average climbed towards 2.4 around 1870, much higher compared to the entire century before. A rather 'regular' ratio in that perspective set in again after 1873, though not because of cheaper bread prices but due to higher grain prices around 1880, as shown in Figure 4 above. Thus, whereas the moral economy prices regulated by disciplinary mechanisms of the assize had kept prices for consumers at bay most importantly in times of life-threatening circumstances, the introduction of free-market prices completely did away with that institution of public welfare. When lifted in 1860, rye bread prices rose quickly both in real and in relative terms because bakers adapted product prices to real raw material market prices and strove to generate higher profits compensating for the losses of the years before.

Simultaneously, the silver price of one kilogram of wheat was equally unhooked from grain prices when the regulation of wheat products was evoked in 1849. Despite data on this scale is only available from 1827, the development is quite similar to that of rye. Whereas one kilogram of wheat bread had cost around 1.6 times more than a litre of wheat during the 1830s and 1840s, the ratio quickly climbed to 1.8 between 1849 and 1852, the years immediately after deregulation. It reached a ratio of two in 1857 and increased to 2.6 in the peak years of the 1860s and 1870s, after which it also fell due to rising grain prices. Like rye and rye bread, the ten-year moving average of 2.0 during late 1860s and early 1870s was notably higher than during the decades before liberalization.

Thus, wheat bread also became more expensive vis-à-vis grain, but its relative price increase was not as high as that of rye. This is due to the cross-subsidization between wheat and rye. To repeat the argument also made by Jan de Vries, via the assize 'bread price commissioners appear to have used their regulatory authority to advance a public purpose: in assigning the constant costs for wheat and rye [differently] they acted to reduce the price of rye bread at the expense of wheat bread', allowing bakers little or no profits of rye and higher profits on wheat products.[12] By doing so:

> [T]he regulatory regime shifted a portion of the joint production cost [of bread] onto the consumers of wheat bread by burdening the price of such bread with a larger portion of the costs of general bakery operation. Correspondingly, they removed some of that burden from the consumers of rye bread. This is what is meant by cross-subsidization: wheat bread consumers paid for a part of the cost of producing rye bread, allowing the latter to be sold at a lower price than would otherwise be the case.[13]

An August 1805 test baking between Vienna's authorities and the baker's guild provides an example for the cross-subsidization between wheat and rye breads in Vienna, showing how the assize authorities actually set rye bread prices so low that bakers suffered losses baking it. These were, however, offset by very generous profit margins on the finest wheat rolls.[14] The abolition of the assize on wheat products in 1849 and on rye bread in 1860 terminated this moral economy welfare

---

12. de Vries, *Price of Bread*, 246.
13. Ibid., 209.
14. Archiv der Bäckergenossenschaft in Wien, HS 15: Innung der bürgerl. Bäckermeister in der k.k. Haupt- und Residenzstadt Wien. Protocollum uiber merkwürdige Gegenstände, als: Volksaufruhr gegen die Bäcker anno 1805; die den bürgl Bäckermeister geleisteten Vergütungen; mehrere Backproben; Consignation über die Ausgaben eines mitleren Bäckermeisters; dann der vom Jahre 1807 bis 1830 ergangenen Verordnungen und Rathschläge.

institution geared towards a certain level of redistribution and the maintenance of the common good.

A massive turnaround of the structure of prices, the abolition of regulated prices and the introduction of free-market prices for bread reversed the subsidization function Vienna's consumers had known and allegedly profited from for decades, probably for centuries. While arguably better-off wheat consumers had subsidized the price of rye bread for poorer urban dwellers under the assize regime, the free-market system turned this upside down. Since the costs added on wheat bread to subsidize rye products were technically eliminated by liberalization in 1849, wheat bread first grew more expensive vis-à-vis rye bread in the years immediately following deregulation because bakers could now profit from free-market revenue margins on the former. When the regulated prices for rye bread were also abandoned, wheat could become relatively cheaper and rye more expensive after 1860. In that way, rye bread eaters subsidized the growing consumption of wheat bakery goods as prices approached to converge especially in the late 1860s. Thus, *wheatification* was paid by rye consumers. One might say that while the free-market system lowered the price of the premium wheat product for some, it raised the price of rye bread for others. Optimistically put, it might have enabled a democratization of wheat bread consumption for many, yet it did so on the back of those still depended on cheaper rye bread. Pessimistically interpreted, deregulation might have lowered the costs of fancy bread and pastry-eating for the privileged few whereas it increased the expenses tied to the basic need of large rye bread loaves for the less-privileged many.

Despite rising living standards, despite declining shares of household budgets needed to be spent on food and housing and despite an improved nutritional situation expressed in decreasing consumption of bread and increasing consumption of other food items like meat after 1850, there are good arguments to follow the latter, rather pessimistic interpretation.[15] Following Jan de Vries's approach, Figure 5 details the ratio of silver prices per pound for the major kinds of bread produced by Vienna's bakers, fine wheat *Rundsemmeln*, second-class wheat *Ordinari Semmeln*, coarse wheat *Pollenes* bread and rye bread loaves.[16] It provides a much more fine-grained picture of the effects of liberalization on cross-subsidization between various sorts of wheat products and rye bread. Most importantly, it underlines that buyers of the finest and most expensive wheat *Rundsemmel* bread roll profited the most relative to rye. Whereas the price of one pound of *Rundsemmeln* had usually cost between 2.5 and 3.5 times as much as one pound of rye bread, the ratio between the premium and the cheapest

---

15. On rising living standards, household budgets and food consumption in Austria see among many others Roman Sandgruber, *Die Anfänge der Konsumgesellschaft: Konsumgüterverbrauch, Lebensstandard und Alltagskultur in Österreich im 18. und 19. Jahrhundert* (Wien: Verlag für Geschichte und Politik, 1982); Tomas Cvrcek, 'Wages, Prices, and Living Standards in the Habsburg Empire, 1827–1910', *The Journal of Economic History* 73, no. 1 (2013), 1–37.

16. See de Vries, *Price of Bread*, 241–8, esp. 242–3.

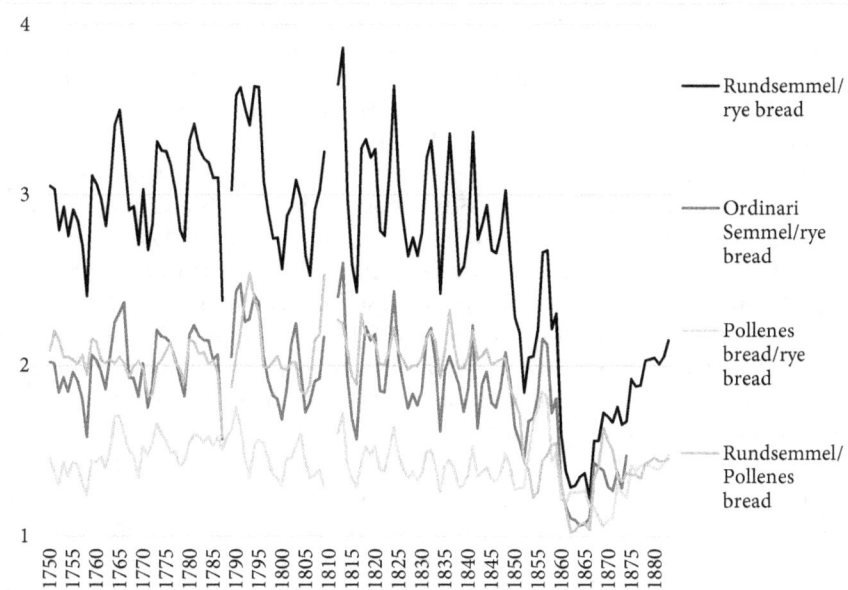

Figure 5 Ratio of Silver Prices of Various Bakery Products, per Pound 1750–1882.

Source: Own compilation based on prices documented in Alfred Francis Pribram, *Materialien zur Geschichte der Preise und Löhne in Österreich*, with the assistance of Rudolf Geyer, and Franz Koran (Wien: Ueberreuter, 1938), 382–4.

product declined quickly after 1849. It reached a first unseen low by 1852 before fine wheat rolls grew more expensive compared to rye bread during the Crimean War as bakers were enabled to balance losses from assize-regulated rye bread. However, when this was also deregulated, the price of *Rundsemmeln* relative to rye loaves plummeted from a ratio of 2.31 in 1859 to 1.31 in 1860, the following year! Maintaining that level for several years, fine wheat rolls started to become more expensive vis-à-vis rye bread since the late 1860. By the early 1880s, they would again cost around twice as much as a pound of dark loaves, a much higher though still very low ratio in the long-term perspective. In that view, in the century after 1750 fine wheat rolls had never been as cheap as they were in the roughly three decades after deregulation, underlining that it was high-end consumers who profited the most from laissez-faire.

This is corroborated by the other ratios depicted in Figure 5. Fine *Rundsemmeln* not only grew cheap relative to rye bread, their price also decreased relative to the price of the coarsest and cheapest kind of wheat bread, *Pollenes* bread. While hovering around a ratio of two before 1849, consumers would find fine rolls and coarse wheat bread at almost the same price in the city's bakeries around 1863. This ratio recovered from the late 1860s but remained on a low level until the 1880s. The same applies for the ratio between *Ordinari Semmeln* and rye loaves. Compared to dark bread, the second-class *Ordinari Semmeln* also grew much cheaper, dropping from between 1.5 and 2.5 times the silver price of rye bread per pound in the century before 1849 to almost the same price by the early 1860s. The ratio was then to climb towards a slightly higher yet still low level in the long-term view. Meanwhile, consumers depending on *Pollenes* bread, the coarsest and cheapest variant of wheat products and arguably the closest substitute to rye loaves for poorer residents, benefitted much less from free-market prices. Whereas *Pollenes* bread had regularly costs around 1.5 times as much as rye bread, the price ratio surpassed 1.8 during 1853–7. A level unseen in the century before compared to fine and second-class rolls bakers increased the price of coarse wheat bread much more to compensate for losses on rye bread still under the assize. Relative to rye bread, in the preceding century coarse wheat bread had never been as expensive. Although coarse wheat would become cheaper in the years to come and follow the general trend, the relative reduction was much less pronounced. Whereas the ratio would approach the level of 1:1 around 1870, between 1861 and 1866 coarse wheat loaves had indeed been more expensive relative to rye than *Ordinari Semmeln*.

In a perspective sympathizing with trickle-down theory, one might argue both well-off and poor consumers benefitted from this development; more affluent consumers had to spend less for basic needs and poorer customers could cheaply substitute putatively higher quality wheat products for rye bread at almost the same costs. However, this conclusion would be misleading given the development of real bread prices. Already pictured in Figure 3 above, the development of more detailed real bread prices highlighted in Figures 6 and 7 below underlines the

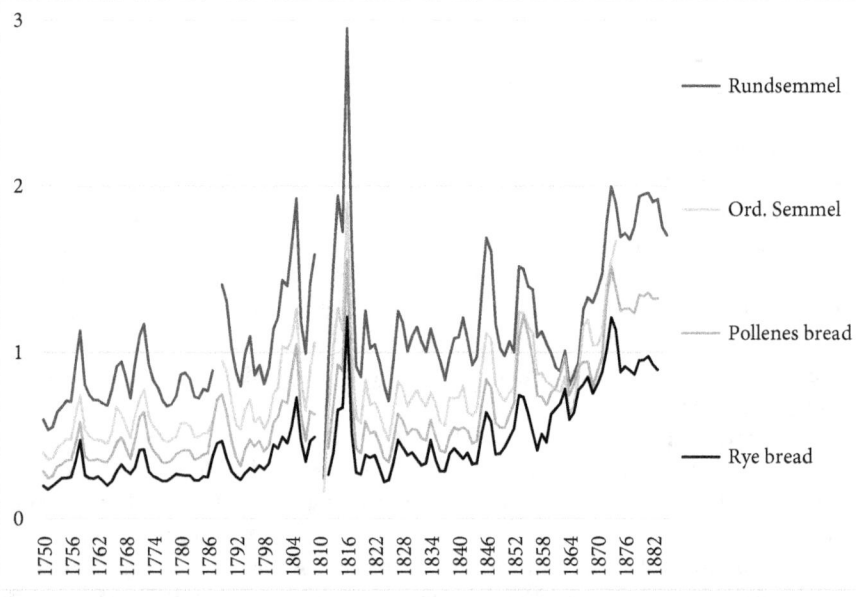

Figure 6 Real Prices for Various Major Bakery Products, in grams of Silver per Pound, 1750–1885.

Sources: See Figure 5.

rather negative impacts of liberalization on the poorest consumers and justifies a rather pessimistic judgement. As Figure 6 shows, the real price of rye bread expressed in grams of silver per pound grew quickly from the late 1850s, when it was already slightly higher compared to much of the 1830s and 1840s. However, the post-deregulation increase was much quicker and sharper. Costing 0.456 grams of silver per pound in 1859, rye bread was 0.779 grams in 1863, 1.7 times more expensive only three years after liberalization. A peculiar situation, wheat products were especially cheap around that point in time theoretically allowing for cheap substitution. However, cheap wheat rolls could only be purchased instead of very expensive rye bread! Although this was certainly a favourable situation for many households, those on the lowest end of the income scale and with the poorest income perspectives were hard pressed by rye prices well above the level of the last decades and indeed the last century – except for 1817, the year without a summer.

Indeed, compared with 1750, rye bread experienced the largest price increase of all major bakery products in Vienna, and this disproportionate increase almost exclusively occurred after 1849/1860 (Figure 7). Whereas the indexed development of the regulated prices for *Rundsemmel* rolls, *Ordinari Semmel* rolls, coarse *Pollen* wheat bread and rye bread was in unison before the abolition of the assize, this ended between 1849 and 1860. Especially the price of the finest wheat rolls stagnated before *c*. 1865; it would then increase from about 1.3 to roughly three times the price of 1750. At the same time, the price of rye bread rose quickly.

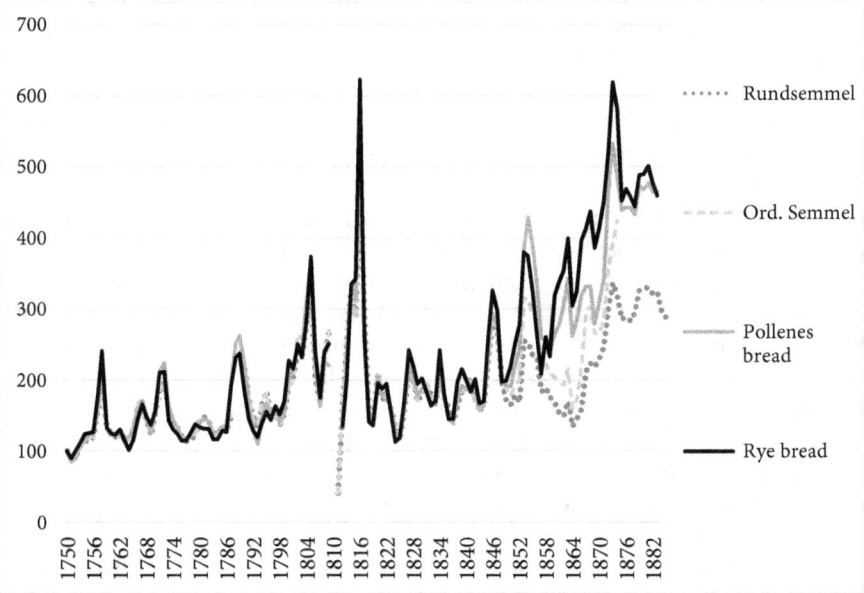

Figure 7 Price Index for Various Major Bakery Products and Cereals, 1750–1890, 1750=100.
Source: See Figure 5.

Halting at about twice the price of 1750 by the late 1850s, it tripled within fifteen years to over six times the 1750-level by 1873 to recede to roughly 450 per cent by the mid-1870s and 1880s. Meanwhile, a similar though less stark development can be observed for coarse wheat bread, the price of which also increased much more compared to both kinds of wheat rolls.

Although liberalization enabled some consumers to change their diets from rye to wheat and lowered the prices of more exquisite diets for those well off, consumers depending on cheap bread made of rye arguably came in last to exploit and enjoy the benefits of free-market bread prices after 1849/60. Whereas the cross-subsidization built into the assize had maintained a certain level of price stability for the poorest – subsidized by more affluent consumers – the abolition of regulated prices terminated this disciplinary mechanism ensuring public welfare and access to basic needs for the poorest. Before 1860, this assize mechanism had maintained a relation between wheat and rye bread that was rather complementary than competitive; the elimination of such an institutional setting reoriented this relationship. Now, 'free competition', as market bureau director Petzl had called it, determined the interplay of the prices of fancy rolls and bulky rye bread loaves. One might say liberalization thus ended a public institution of solidarity, mostly at the benefit of middle class and wealthier strata of the urban society. These were now able to improve their diets and living standards through relatively cheaper wheat prices that were relieved from solidary surcharges levied on premium products before.[17] At the same time, poor consumers lost this implicit institution of societal redistribution ensuring a certain level of subsidies on everyday necessities. Therefore, by and large, the *wheatification* of diets was partly paid for by those reduced to rye. Free-market prices of bread largely benefitted the better-off parts of the urban society and contributed to rising inequality.

Returning to the city council debates of the early 1860s, when rye bread was especially dear and the price of wheat rolls historically low in relative terms, these debates underline that both delegates and *Marktamt* officials took notice that something had changed with deregulation. Yet, there is no evidence in the sources available that either the *Gemeinderat* members or the market bureau clerks recognized and appreciated the gravity and magnitude of change brought about by the liberalization of bread prices. This is partly caused by the limitation of sources and in turn by the limited form of those sources preserved. On the one hand, the protocols of the city council's *Approvisionirungssektion*, the committee centrally involved with all matters concerning food supply, are entirely lost except for a few sessions between 1848 and 1852. On the other hand, the meetings of the *Gemeinderat* itself were only recorded in relatively concise summaries throughout most of the second half of the nineteenth century. Since there are no verbatim protocols most of the debates can only be grasped superficially with no means to capture the debates and arguments in detail, although more comprehensive newspaper coverage of the council sessions permits closer insights in some

---

17. I am hardly pressed not to call it 'Solidaritätszuschlag'.

instances. Furthermore, there are no statements made by the *Marktamt* discussing the issue of the elimination of cross-subsidization. Yet, although the sources do not allow for a conclusive judgement, it does not seem delegates and officials were well aware of the true consequences of terminating the assize.[18]

This does not mean the authorities did not struggle to solve the problem of high prices and find a solution, on the contrary. Whereas apparently ignorant of the issue of prices, very soon after the *Gewerbefreiheit* had introduced deregulation the *Gemeinderat*, the market bureau, the press and partly even the bakers engaged in extensive elaborations, negotiations and investigations of various other issues subsumed under the larger concern of the bread question. Spanning the remaining decades of the century, the core aspects were already discussed in the city council in the early 1860s. Fundamentally, they circled around the erosion of product standards and consumer information, and would incite fierce disputes among lawmakers, the press and between authorities and bakers especially during the 1870s and 1880s.

The bread question

In the autumn of 1861, Josef Petzl, director of Vienna's *Marktamt*, was sceptic about baguettes:

> In Paris, we hear wheat bread is not sold in the form of round rolls but in an elongated shape from which pieces of varying weights are cut according to the customer's demand. The introduction of this practice in Vienna would certainly cause irritation among the population since it is accustomed to the old tradition to buy bread in whole loafs at fixed prices. It also needs to be noted that whole rolls and bread in whole loafs are much more delicious than these cut-up Parisian-style bread pieces which dry out easily and lose much of their appearance.[19]

In this belated response to a motion proposed to the city council to authorize the sale of bread 'according to weight' half a year earlier, Petzl expressed sincere doubts if changes in the way bread was sold in Vienna would be 'in the interest

---

18. Speculatively, the institutional rearrangement of the urban administration since the late 1830s – the centralized *Marktamt* had been created by 1839 and subsequently assumed a wide array of tasks from other administrative bodies, among others from the *Metzenleiheramt* formerly responsible for the assize calculations – might have contributed to a certain loss of knowledge and changes in personnel. However, institutional continuity or break on the lower levels of Vienna's government is hardly researched, except for a broad overview. See Elfriede Sheriff, 'Die Ämter der Stadt Wien von 1783–1848 in verwaltungsgeschichtlicher und personeller Hinsicht' (Diss. University of Vienna, 1977).
19. Marktamt, Äusserung Direktion des Marktkommissariates.

of the customers'. What is more, the superintendent of the city's markets added, any introduction of such a regulation would be in conflict with the abolition of 'all limitations of the production and sale' of bread issued in the previous year.[20] Attempting to solve the problem of high bread prices vis-à-vis declining cereal costs, aforementioned Joseph Kleyhonz had suggested introducing a new regulation requiring the sale of bread at fixed weights and variable prices in the summer of 1861. Kleyhonz had recently visited Paris 'for business purposes' where he might have learned about the French way of selling bread.[21] Instead of the common mode of selling whole rolls and loaves at fixed prices and varying weights, bakers should be compelled to produce standard-weight loaves at moving prices from which poorer consumers could also buy cuts.

Make no mistake, if implemented Kleyhonz's move would have represented a fundamental break with the ways and forms bread had been produced and sold in Vienna for generations. Selling bread at fixed prices and moving weights was as much a function of the moral economy as it was an issue of fiscal policy. Regarding the former, as a 'crude form of rationing, common all over Europe',[22] it secured the consumers' ability to purchase fixed-price loaves at the expense to eat less. Concerning the latter, 'early modern societies resorted to weight-variable bread pricing in order to adjust the price of bread to changing grain prices with an accuracy that exceed the practical limits of the circulating coinage. [...] The loaves varied by weight because weight could be adjusted more readily than price to small fluctuations in the price of grain.'[23]

Before 1860, under the assize the price of bread had been fairly transparent as prices, weights and variations in the cost of bread in periods of price shocks were regulated, officially calculated and publicized. In this system, monetary bread prices had remained fixed at, for example, one Kreuzer per wheat roll. In times of rising prices, the weight of the roll would diminish at officially calculated degrees while the price remained one Kreuzer. Besides cross-subsidization, another core function of the assize had therefore been price transparency.

Hence, criticizing such a central institution of baking, selling and buying bread was far from trivial. On the contrary, simultaneous to discussions in France,[24] the central aim was to remove what Kleyhonz perceived as growing ineptitude of the fixed-price-variable-weight retail system to provide price transparency and cheap bread. More precisely, in the free-market environment without official regulations provided by the assize the socialist city council considered this way

20. Ibid.
21. *Ost-Deutsche Post*, 'Sitzung des Gemeinderathes', 10 July 1861, Nr. 186, 2.
22. de Vries, *Price of Bread*, 31.
23. Ibid., 32.
24. See Marcel Streng, 'Konventionen der Brotqualität in der Bäckereigewerbereform des Zweiten Kaiserreichs in Frankreich (1853–1866)', in *Qualitätspolitiken und Konventionen: Die Qualität der Produkte in Historischer Perspektive*, ed. Robert Salais, Jakob Vogel and Marcel Streng (Wiesbaden: Springer Fachmedien Wiesbaden GmbH; Springer VS, 2019).

of selling bread and rolls as detrimental to market transparency and a driver of increasing information asymmetry between consumers and bakers. Since liberalization and the abolition of the assize in 1860 had removed this important institution of market information, under the liberal free market regime the pricing of bread had become much more opaque. As bakers had been instructed to maintain the production of bread at fixed prices and variable weights in the liberalization act of 1860,[25] the custom to reduce weights in times of high prices remained – only now bakers could legally reduce bread weights freely, by amounts of their own choosing. City council Kleyhonz considered this a quite obscure situation for consumers. In practice, neither would they recognize small weight reductions nor would they be able to make a case against a baker whom they depended on for their daily bread. More generally, even if they would identify weight reductions, consumers also lacked information on raw material prices, production costs, flour-to-bread yields etc., and could not tell if the extent of reduction in bread weights corresponded to increases in production costs. Whereas exactly that information and such price movements had been subject to the assize and thus subject of public, institutional intervention, the elimination of the assize individualized the assessment of the bread price and left consumers to 'look after their interests themselves.'[26]

In Kleyhonz's esteem, this was the true reason for high bread prices. In the liberal environment bakers either obscured reduced bread weights or overcompensated rising cereal costs by inappropriate weight reductions to maximize profits. That way, he claimed, 'the poor masses are constantly deceived by the bakers'.[27] Changing this practice into selling fixed-weight, standardized loaves at varying prices per kilogram would make it impossible for bakers to impose hidden increases by baking smaller loaves. It would make price movements easily detectable and the purchase of bread transparent again.

Supported by other members of the socialist camp in the city council Kleyhonz's quest for transparency, knowledge and equal bargaining power between bakers and consumers was contested from the beginning. On the one hand, the Bakers' Association publicly denied all accusations made by Kleyhonz.[28] Moreover, council Johann Schmidtkunz – a baker – practically denied that bread prices were disproportionally high. Instead, meat was too expensive![29] Next to this rather clumsy red herring the ideological opposition against intervention and in favour of laissez-faire policies was strong during the early 1860s. Addressing the price increases of the weeks immediately following deregulation on 1 November 1860,

---

25. Wiener Stadt- und Landesarchiv, Marktamt A2/1: Brot und Gebäcksverkauf nach Gewicht, 17.09.1860: K.K. nö. Statthalterei.

26. Marcel Streng, *Subsistenzpolitik im Übergang: Die kommunale Ordnung des Brot- und Fleischmarktes in Frankreich 1846–1914* (Göttingen: Vandenhoeck & Ruprecht, 2017), 199.

27. Vorstand der Bäcker-Genossenschaft, 'Vorstand der Bäcker-Genossenschaft zur Abwehr', 3.

28. Ibid.

29. *Fremden-Blatt*, 'Gemeinderath: Sitzung vom 24. Jänner', 25 January 1865, Nr. 25.

the *Morgen-Post* had ensured its readers 'competition is almighty and beneficial, as an encounter in Weinhaus', an outskirt parish, proved:

> There are two bakers there, one of them could not await 1 November to raise bread prices [...]. The other, Hr. Stock, used this to win all the customers by maintaining lower prices. This was fruitful and several days later the other master was forced to sell cheaper rolls. The moral of the story is that total freedom of commerce prevents monopolies.[30]

Three years later, the beliefs of the majority in the city council had barely changed. Still debating Kleyhonz's proposal, several delegates raised stark ideological opposition to the imposition of new regulations. Led by Wilhelm Frankl, a respected philanthropist and elected representative of Vienna's Merchants' League, a liberal fraction argued that only the deregulation of retail restrictions and a general permission of hawking with bread would produce lower prices and an improved market environment for consumers.[31] 'One cannot oblige the baker' to adopt a certain way of selling bread, Frankl would argue in the spirit of free trade – only increasing supply through hawkers could solve the problem.[32] In order to solve the hotly contested issue, the *Approvisionirungs-Sektion* and the *Marktamt* were appointed to investigate facts and solutions.[33]

An extensive report did not arrive before 1865, almost two years later. When speaker Johann Heinrich Steudel delivered the committee's assessment in the sittings of 21 and 24 January, the message was clear. Only the 'absolute liberalization of hawking with bread', Steudel opined, would deliver lower bread prices. Not only would consumers benefit from the 'great convenience' of door-to-door deliveries, peddling was also considered to be much cheaper than other forms of retail and would reduce prices. Any intervention into the practices of bread production and sale as suggested by Kleyhonz, the report's result read, needed to be avoided; 'only competition' would yield lower prices. Further, Steudel's recommendations continued to follow the path of individualization and self-responsibility. Instead of pushing through any institutional regulation so greatly interfering with a free craft to provide systematic information on the prices and standards of bread, he suggested to have bakers put up visible signs informing about prices and weights outside the bakers' shops and stalls so consumers could inform themselves. Underlining the current state of mind, the *Morgen-Post* considered even that 'not worth too much effort'.[34] Following Steudel's advice, magistrate and city council

---

30. *Morgen-Post*, 'Wien', 9 November 1860, 311, 1.
31. *Die Presse*, 'Wiener Gemeinderath: Sitzung vom 27. Mai', 28 May 1863, Nr. 145.
32. *Morgen-Post*, 'Wien. Sitzung des Gemeinderathes vom 27. Mai', 28 May 1863, 145, 2.
33. *Fremden-Blatt*, 'Gemeinderath: Sitzung vom 5. November', 6 November 1861, Nr. 305, 5.
34. *Morgen-Post*, 'Die Brodfrage im Gemeinderathe', 2.

saw 'no reason for complaints against the bakers who cannot be held responsible for these high bread prices'.[35] Under this impression and despite Kleyhonz's furious opposition to pass his motion or to reinstate the assize 'as the only cure, in God's name', the city council voted in favour of the liberalization of hawking, in favour of inducing bakers to provide individual price information, and against any new regulation.[36] Fully in line with free-market policies, there should be 'no intervention by the municipality into the private sector'.[37] A year later, on 28 January 1866, the k.k. Ministry of Trade announced the permission of hawking under the condition that all retailers were to keep written information on weights and prices.[38]

However, neither did bread prices yield nor was the bread question solved. On the contrary, rising bread prices faced by consumers in the form of a continuous decline of roll and loaf volumes remained on the menu throughout the late 1860s and early 1870s. By that period the volume of both premium wheat rolls and rye bread loaves had notably declined compared to the previous decades. Whereas one *Rundsemmel* roll would have reached a weight of around seven Lot – 122.5 grams – before the early 1840s, it had diminished to an average of constantly less than five Lot after 1860 and below four Lot – 70 grams – per piece after 1870. Similarly, after 1860 larger rye bread loaves constantly remained at the bottom end of the assize weight spectrum without any peaks to compensate consumers, as had been the case before deregulation.[39]

Connected to the diminishing size of rolls, by the last years of the 1860s a move by the Bakers' Association to realign the product range available to customers sparked growing public scepticism that free competition and individual consumer responsibility would solve the bread question. In the wake of intensifying disputes between master bakers and workers over wage and labour conditions that would lead to the strike of bakery workers in 1870 centrally addressed by the *Enquête*, chairman of the Bakers' Association Rudolf Plank suggested to introduce a new form of buns. Instead of the traditional *Einkreuzersemmeln*, worth one Kreuzer and corresponding to number 2 in Image 2, bakers should produce *Baunzeln*. Costing two Kreuzer apiece and represented by numbers 4 and 5, these were to be formed in a way they could be sliced in two and thus sold whole or in halves.

The leitmotif for Plank's proposal was economic. Against the background of continuously diminishing weights – Plank claimed the average *Semmel* weight

---

35. *Morgen-Post*, 'Sitzung des Gemeiderathes: vom 27. Mai', 28 May 1863, Nr. 145, 2.

36. *Morgen-Post*, 'Die Brodfrage im Gemeinderathe'; *Fremden-Blatt*, 'Gemeinderath'.

37. *Wiener Zeitung*, 'Aus dem Gemeinderathe. (Plenarversammlung vom 24. Jänner)', 25 January 1865, 20, 267.

38. k. k. Handelsministerium, *Enquête über die Approvisionirung Wiens: II: Theil, Lebensmittel (ausgenommen Fleisch), Brennholz und Mineralkohle*, 2 vols. (Wien: Kaiserlich-königliche Hof- und Staatsdruckerei, 1871), XLVI.

39. Alfred Francis Pribram, *Materialien zur Geschichte der Preise und Löhne in Österreich*, with the assistance of Rudolf Geyer, and Franz Koran (Wien: Ueberreuter, 1938), 381–4. Note: 1 Lot = 17.5 grams.

Image 2 *Baunzeln* and *Kreuzersemmeln*, early twentieth century.

Source: John Kirkland, ed., *The Modern Baker, Confectioner and Caterer: A Practical and Scientific Work for the Baking and Allied Trades. Divisional-Vol. II* (London: The Gresham Publishing Company, 1908), 200–1.

was down to 35 grams by then – the production of these very small rolls had become uneconomic due to high unit labour costs and spoilage. While baking small *Semmel* rolls required trained staff, 'every day-labourer' could make simple-formed *Baunzeln*, the chairman explained. Hiding that replacing small rolls through larger *Baunzeln* could thus be a very useful means for master bakers to tighten the thumbscrews in the struggle with bakery labourers over better work conditions and higher wages, Plank knew to sell the realignment of the product range as beneficial for consumers. 'France or England do not know small forms' of bread, he maintained:

> I believe in economic terms our procedure cannot be endorsed. Larger forms can easily be adopted which allow for substantial savings in labour and are beneficiary to the customers [...]. The taste of the bread would only improve [...]. If it is possible in France to cut a whole loaf of bread and sell it [in pieces], it can be done in Vienna.[40]

However, not only a probable move to gain the high ground in a labour dispute, the Association's plan to eliminate *Einkreuzersemmeln* represented a drastic abandonment of the city's provision tradition. One-Kreuzer rolls had been the backbone of the bread economy for at least a century. Their production and availability had been compulsory under the assize before 1860; after liberalization bakers had originally continued 'our traditional custom to always make bread that costs one Kreuzer'.[41] Indeed, the authorities recognized the scope of the bakers' envisaged reform. The lack of one-Kreuzer rolls 'will be felt dearly by many families', the magistrate publicly announced on 14 May 1870, the day before the bakers would push through the replacement of one-Kreuzer buns through *Baunzeln*. To prevent hardship, the urban government offered lifting all market fees for everyone who would continue to bake and sell small rolls worth one Kreuzer.[42]

'Notwithstanding the customers' protest and the [magistrate's] impulse to continue selling 1x [i.e. one Kreuzer] baked goods, the majority of Vienna's bakers had stopped the production of 1x bakery goods,' Karl Kainz summarized a decade and a half later. 'The opportunity to purchase rolls for 1x has been taken from the poor. The authorities' demands, the reprimands by the press and the consumers' complains were of no use, the bakers had it their way.' Kainz would continue to highlight the bakers' attempts to stop the production of various other kinds of small rolls over the following years, all of which he considered 'of great importance for the provisioning with bread of the poorest classes of the population'.[43]

These proceedings by the bakers to rationalize business procedures to improve both profit margins and their basis for negotiations with employees on whose work they crucially depended in the absence of large-scale mechanization assumed an important role in turning the tide of public opinion against the bakers, and against laissez-faire. This episode and the magistrate's decision in May 1870 to intervene represented a first small break with the authority's rather affirmative position towards free competition and an unregulated bread market held throughout

---

40. Handelsministerium, *Enquête*, 8, 10.

41. Ibid., 10.

42. Wiener Stadt- und Landesarchiv, Marktamt A2/1: Bäckergewerbe: Kundmachungen, 14 May 1870: Magistrat der Stadt Wien.

43. Wiener Stadt- und Landesarchiv, Marktamt, A2/1: Brotfrage, 12.12.1884. Äusserung Marktkommissariat.

most of the previous decade. Partly preceding and partly accelerated by the stock market crash of 1873, various bodies of the urban government – most prominently the market bureau – as well as the public grew ever more sceptical that non-intervention and laissez-passer would solve the bread question in the favour of consumers. Indeed, over the course of the following months, Plank's thrust backfired completely. While the Bakers' Association had tried to lobby for changes in production allegedly facilitating lower bread prices, they had not intended to shed light on or even tackle the fixed-prices-variable-weight system of bread retail city council Kleyhonz had infamously demanded almost a decade earlier. On the contrary, Plank himself was outspokenly against such a change arguing that a variation of '1 or 2 Loth' in the weight of a loaf would 'hardly be felt, however, if one told the customers a loaf of bread is ½ or ¼ Kreuzer more it is quite disastrous for the consumers'.[44]

Yet, a need to reform that retail practice and to reintroduce systematic product information via clear standards became one of the main takeaways the *Enquête* produced and the *Marktamt* came to share as well. 'More important [than qualitative aspects] is the adulteration in weights,' the *Enquête* found. 'Although bakers are obliged to keep voluntary price tables, i.e. to define the weight of bread at a given price, and although the bakers are to inform about this tariff in their shops readable for everybody, [...] it happens that the weight of the loaf is reduced without a change in the price for the customers [...]'.[45]

'In the bakeries of Vienna, [information] is attached that at a price of x Kreuzer, the loaf weights so and so many pounds of bread, but I have never seen a hawker' issuing such information,' former director of Vienna's first steam mill Quinz had told the *Enquête* officials even before such a conclusion.[46] Despite an 1866 lame-duck regulation requiring the hundreds and hundreds of grocers and itinerant hawkers to inform about the prices and weights of their merchandise – hawkers were even obliged to carry scales to weigh out loaves if demanded by customers – 'the sale of bread is free, there is no control of weights', *Enquête* commissioner, popular journalist and later city council Julius Hirsch claimed. 'We have heard of grocers who buy a loaf of bread from the baker for 7 Kreuzer and sell it for 10.'[47] City council Steudel strove to enlighten the commission further: 'I know [...] grocers can offer bread cheaper by asking the baker to provide them with smaller loafs, otherwise the baker could not afford to sell the 10-Kreuzer loaf for 6 Kreuzer to them.'[48] *Enquête* commissioner Ritter von Stahl gave even more details: '[...] bakers produce special loafs for grocers, those are not listed in the official tariff

---

44. Handelsministerium, *Enquête*, 11.
45. Ibid., 445.
46. Ibid., 125.
47. Ibid., 13, 78. The 1866 regulation is reprinted in Handelsministerium, *Enquête* XLVI.
48. Ibid., 21.

lists and one can make no judgement about the weight of these loafs [...]. The chairman of the bakers has stated himself that he sells bread of peculiarly smaller construction [*sic!*] at a higher price to grocers [...]'.[49] Although challenged by the *Marktamt* officers questioned on the matter, Julius Hirsch fervently defended this finding. Given personnel constraints and the market bureau's huge workload, any 'control of the food market seems impossible' and the regulating legislation was merely a lame duck in the face of impossible enforcement.[50]

Therefore, by the beginning of the 1870s the *Enquête* experts, the market bureau and parts of the city council grew ever wearier and more concerned not only about the growing asymmetry of knowledge between consumers and bakers but also about the growing asymmetry and variety of products Vienna's bakers produced and sold in different ways. The authorities sensed a growing variety in products offered between bread shops, and an opacity in the prices, qualities and quantities of bread. Over the following years, the experts' weariness was taken up by the press and grew into a rather prominent public debate on the local level. Especially, though not exclusively conservative newspapers engaged in an accelerating campaign against free-market relations and in favour of new regulations in the case of bread. Already by mid-April 1870 *Das Vaterland* had picked up the issue of the bread question in a namesake contribution in which it argued too much competition among bakers would lead to both their economic demise and adultery of products.[51] Against the background of such accelerating criticism of the state of the bread question and waning public faith in free-market ideologies more generally, from the early 1870s Vienna's market authorities increasingly came to believe that free competition was not suited to provide transparency and cheap bread for consumers.[52] Unlike during the previous ten years, with the new decade the notion that some kind of structural institutional market information was necessary to provide consumers with knowledge enabling them to make informed individual choices came to prevail. Therefore, the last decades of the century were shaped by a fierce struggle between parts of the urban administration, most notably the *Marktamt*, and bakers as well as the liberal and the conservative press over the reintroduction of legislation aimed to reintroduce market information and a system of reference framing the free bread market and enabling consumers to make informed decisions themselves.

---

49. Ibid., 135–6.

50. Ibid., 137.

51. *Das Vaterland. Zeitung für die österreichische Monarchie*, 'Zur Brodfrage', 10 April 1870, Nr. 99, 6.

52. For comparable debates yet rather different solutions to 'shepherd the free market and consumers' in Brussels see Dennis de Vriese, 'Steering the Free Market through a Food Crisis? Fiscal Policy and Meat Consumption in Brussels during the 1840s', *History of Retailing and Consumption* 8, no. 1 (2022). Cite from 13.

Standardizing bread – again

By 1861, the *Marktamt* under director Josef Petzl had still opposed Kleyhonz's request and made the case for a free-market solution. 'With respect to the high directive according to which all limitations of the production and retail of all kinds of baked goods [...] are abolished, [the Marktamt] cannot advise [to introduce] the proposed sale of bakery products according to weight,' Petzl had argued.[53] Not quite a decade later, the mood within the market bureau was changed notably. After the final session in February 1871, the *Enquête* commission suggested lawmakers that 'bread is to be sold according to weight, bakers and hawkers have to visibly inform about weight and prices' in its eleventh proposal.[54] Forwarded by the magistrate in April instructing the *Marktamt* to comment, a statement arrived on the last day of October 1871:

> Today, the individual products greatly differ in both form and composition of flour used, although qualities are usually very good. [...] The current way of selling bread meets the customs of the populace, who would not accept any substantial changes of the prices and qualities of baked goods in the way they accept fluctuations of the weight because they purchase pastry according to form and taste rather than quantity.[55]

Therefore, the market bureau advised, 'the bread retail according to weight should only be introduced in regard of bread proper: Pohlen bread, mixed and rye bread, which are presently sold in loafs of 2, 5, 10, 20 Kreuzer'.[56] Accordingly, the bureau wanted all bakers and retailers to be compelled to weigh out any quantity of bread demanded by customers; all vendors were to publicly display standardized bread prices 'per 1 k[ilogram], ½ k, ¼ k' and one eighth of a kilogram, and even hawkers were to carry price lists at all times:

> The implementation of this measure, which is not at all impeded by technical difficulties, is all the more advisable in the interest of the consumers and to prevent the evil that bakers produce smaller loafs for intermediates', the *Marktamt* advised to conclude, 'the market department considers the introduction of this regulation necessary to protect the customers from cheating by hawkers and roundsmen.[57]

Following these recommendations, in a political climate that had grown less enthusiastic towards laissez-faire the majority opinion within the city council

53. Marktamt, Äusserung Direktion des Marktkommissariates.
54. Handelsministerium, *Enquête*, 528.
55. Wiener Stadt- und Landesarchiv, Marktamt A2/1: Brot und Gebäcksverkauf nach Gewicht, 1106/1871, 31.10.1871: Marktamt. Durchführung des Antrages XI. der Approvsg. Enquete.
56. Ibid.
57. Ibid.

shifted to the detriment of the bakers. Since the abolition of the assize the weight of bread was 'exposed to great fluctuations', the magistrate announced half a year after the *Marktamt* advice had been handed in: 'In order to allow every customer to buy the desired amount of bread and to prevent the evils in the retail of bread produced by intermediates, the city council's resolution of 10 January [1872] mandates the introduction of bread retail according to weight as it exists in other large cities,' Vienna's urban government proclaimed.

The new regulation included six specifications: (1) selling bread according to weight was mandatory from 1 May 1872; (2) the forms of bread remained subject to the baker's free choice but needed to be divisible in standardized weight units; (3) all bakers and retailers needed to clearly inform about prices and weights; (4) standardized tariffs needed to be carried, dated and signed by every retailer; (5) all requirements also applied to hawkers, who were to carry scales, and (6) premium rolls and pastry could be sold in the traditional way at fixed prices and fluctuating weights.[58]

Attaching a model tariff (Image 3) to inform about the new way of price setting and selling bakery products for bakers, retailers and customers alike, the magistrate underlined the effort to introduce standards fostering market transparency. Whereas pastry like *Mund-Gebäck* and other kinds of premium products less considered a staple could still be sold at the fixed prices of one or two Kreuzer with varying weights, white and brown bread were to be retailed at standard weights of 1, ½ and ¼ pounds and at changing monetary costs. 'This presents a direct advantage for consumers who are spared the cutting and weighing', the *Neues Wiener Tagblatt* commented three days later.[59]

As the officials' opinion towards the bakers had shifted for the latter's worse, the 1872 legislation of new retail standards incited a hassle between administrators and bakers comparable to the procedures in Paris over meat.[60] Throughout the early 1870s, the bakers practically resisted to observe and agitated against the new retail law. 'With fixed prices, it is certain, one knows what one's money buys,' baker Ferdinand Boos had argued during his *Enquête* interview in April 1870.

> The labourer knows, if he has a Kreuzer, he will get a roll [...]. It makes a tremendous impression if bread is more expensive and the weight is smaller. However, at what rate can the bread diminish? Probably half a Lot [...]. I believe the child will not notice if it has one bite less; I believe neither child nor adult will notice.[61]

---

58. Wiener Stadt- und Landesarchiv, Marktamt A2/1: Bäckergewerbe: Kundmachungen, 27.03.1872: K.K. nö. Statthalterei.

59. *Neues Wiener Tagblatt,* 'Der Verkauf des Brodes nach Gewicht', 31 March 1872, 88, 3.

60. Anne Lhuissier, 'Cuts and Classification. The Use of Nomenclatures as a Tool for the Reform of the Meat Trade in France, 1850–1880', *Food and Foodways* 10, no. 4 (2002), 183–208.

61. Handelsministerium, *Enquête*, 18.

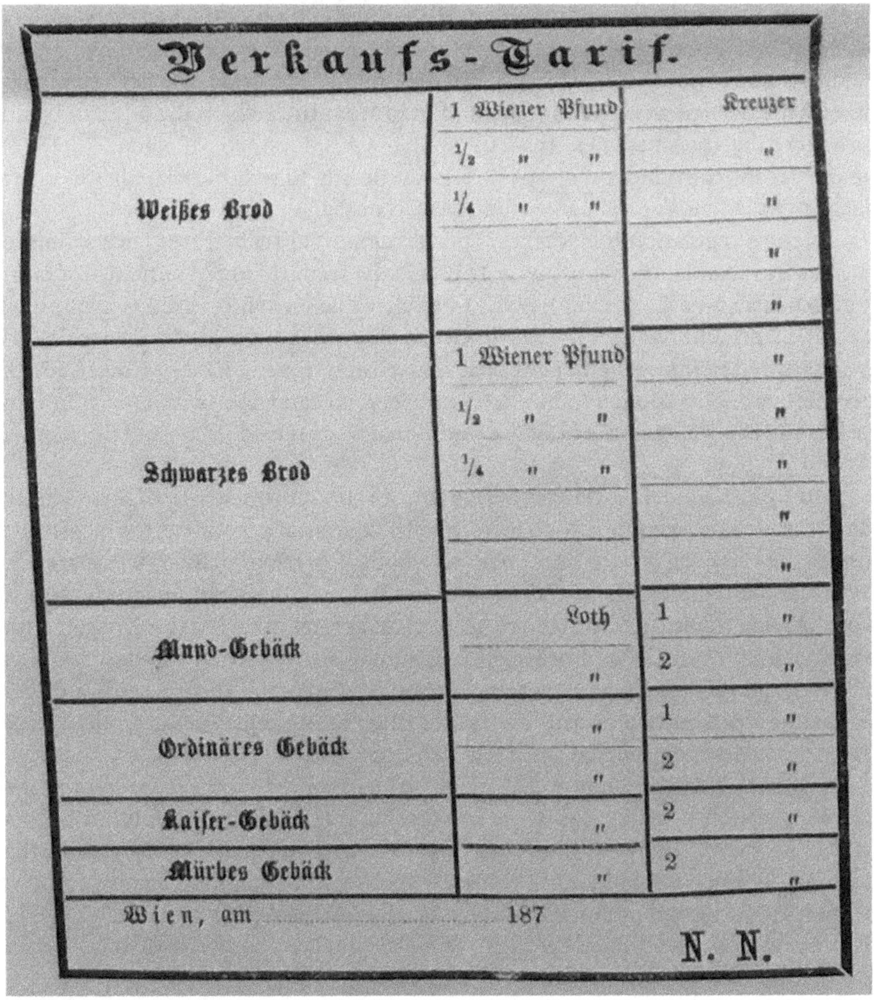

Image 3 Tariff Model for Bread Retail according to Standardized Loaf Weights Provided by Vienna's Magistrate, 27 March 1872.

Source: Wiener Stadt- und Landesarchiv, Marktamt A2/1: Bäckergewerbe: Kundmachungen, 27.03.1872: K.K. nö. Statthalterei.

Technically, the production of standard weights was not at all conceivable, representatives of the trade argued, trying to deny standardization as a feasible option and attempting to protect the 'mysteries' of the bakers' craft'.[62] 'It is impossible to produce standard loafs. Standard amounts of dough are used, but the rush [of baking procedures] makes it impossible to have equal loafs', chairman

---

62. de Vries, *Price of Bread*, 185.

Rudolf Plank told the *Enquête* commissioners while Ferdinand Boos added 'it also depends on the quality of the flour. Dry and strong flour will yield more bread than fresh flour.' Flour quality, however 'is different from one bakery to the other, it depends on the taste of the customers and is not easy to determine'. Finally, Boos claimed, 'not even the producers' could always make sure the final products would be 'in accordance with the quality of the flour used' and therefore be able to produce standardized loaves.[63] By February 1871, when the *Enquête* commission had just finalized its proposals to reintroduce retail legislation, the bakers' chairman Plank sent in a complaint about the retail reform. 'Sticking to the hawkers' fraud,' as *Die Presse* put it, the bakers warned the commissioners of a 'revolution of the "lower classes"' if the reform was implemented.[64]

Despite that magistrate and bakers had seemingly found some common ground in late 1871 and 'reached an agreement on selling bread according to weight',[65] in April 1872, just after the magistrate had announced the new regulation would come into force with 1 May 1872, the Bakers' Association articulated 'a vivid opposition against the new way of retail' and its board decided to file protest with the ministry. To the newspaper, the bakers' reason to oppose the reform was obvious: because the reform was a measure 'beneficial to the consumers'.[66]

'Selling bread according to weight is the rule since 1 May, though only on paper,' *Die Presse* updated readers two weeks after the reform had come into force. 'With regard to business procedures it has not become reality, but the bakers go to great lengths to foil it and to induce consumers to refuse the sale of bread according to weight.' While the new law had been introduced to enable consumers 'only to pay what he really gets, instead of paying a determined sum for an undetermined amount of the commodity completely subject to the discretion of the vendor', bakers attempted to circumvent the regulation with misleading price tariffs and strict refusal to adopt any changes, the report claimed. Since the 'good intent failed because of the bad attitude of one [the baker] and the ignorance of the other [the consumer]', the magistrate needed to strictly control and penalize any violations, the author argued. 'Yet, we are afraid even this will be in vain if the consumers do not stand up for their rights themselves.'[67]

Several days later, the magistrate moved to admonish the bakers to heed the law. Although the changes to the retail of bread were already lawful and had been adopted on the city's marketplaces since,

63. Handelsministerium, *Enquête*, 14, 21, 22.
64. *Die Presse,* 'Theuerungs-Enquete', 9 February 1871, 40.
65. *Neue Freie Presse,* 'Brotverkauf nach Gewicht', 9 November 1871, 2590, 7.
66. *Neues Wiener Tagblatt,* 'Brodverkauf nach dem Gewichte', 9 April 1872, 96, 3.
67. *Die Presse,* 'Der Brodverkauf nach dem Gewicht', 12 May 1872, 130, Beilage, 19.

during the official inspections, the market commissioners have identified many bakers and grocers who do not follow the official order and try to defeat it by selling one and the same loaf more expensive when consumers ask its price to be established according to weight. This way, a one-pound loaf of bread [...] is sold for 12 Kreuzer [...] instead of 10 Kreuzer.[68]

To the magistrate, this represented a reproachful attempt to 'force consumers not to buy bread according to weight' and necessitated the authorities to call on the bakers to adhere to the new rules or face 'severe sanctions'.[69] Whereas other newspapers rather adopted this perspective, in mid-June 1872 the liberal German-nationalist *Deutsche Zeitung* published a prosaic report that took up the bakers' critique of the reform:

When the new regulation came into force on 1 May, the k.k. court baker asked the royal household how to deliver bakery products that would comply with the decree. The court baker received the official notification to deliver all supplies of any kind of bakery goods [...] *as before* because a fixed allowance was assigned to every person of the royal household. [...] The great number of consumers thinks exactly like the court and considers the new regulation [...] very impractical. We doubt that it works as well in practice as in the theoretical approach of the commission; we can only repeat that despite the market bureau's strict intervention the customers are fervently opposed to the sale of bread according to weight.[70]

Adding an expert statement by a baker appearing under the initials 'Ad. J.', the report continued to present the bakers' arguments why the reform would make bread more expensive. Since sales according to weight implicated a switch from round to elongated loaves better suited to be sold in pieces of whole, half, or quarter pounds, the production and retail costs would increase notably, the expert argued. On the one hand, the preparation of the dough would require more and better-trained hands since elongated loaves were 'harder to handle' compared to round ones. 'Whereas a trained journeymen can form two [round] loafs simultaneously with a time requirement of half a minute', elongated forms broke easily when putting the dough to rest or inserting them into the oven, thus demanding two labourers and 'nearly a minute more' per loaf. On the other hand, cutting and weighing out pieces of bread in the shop instead of selling whole loaves would also require more time as 'one consumer takes one pound, the second half a pound, a third and fourth a quarter pound each', demanding 'certainly twice' the time

---

68. *Morgen-Post*, 'Zum Brodverkauf nach dem Gewicht', 15 May 1872, 132, 3.
69. Ibid.
70. *Deutsche Zeitung*, 'Das K.K Hofbrot', 14 June 1872, 162, Morgenblatt, 8. Emphasis in original.

to serve customers compared to the traditional way of selling. Furthermore, the baker added, vending pieces of bread would require the baker to pack the sold cuts into paper to prevent spoilage, but 'who paid the extra amounts of time, labour and paper?' Finally adopting the moral-economy perspective, neither would families notice small fluctuations in whole loaves nor was the currency system with its circulating coins equipped to express price changes of small units of weight. The new system would thus lead to a current under- or overpricing of bread, Ad. J. argued. Concluding, the article opined that the new regulation was 'completely impractical' and bakers would 'win nothing' while 'consumers lost'.[71]

A fortnight later, *Die Presse* retaliated: 'The sale of bread according to weight is fought by the bakers with all their might, and the bakers are able to have a measure introduced only in the best interest of the consumers not accepted by those, therefore it is almost completely doomed to fail,' the author charged. In the meantime, the article reported, the Bakers' Association had filed their complaint with the governor. Though the wording is missing, the governor rejected the bakers' appeal because 'the introduction of selling bread according to weight serves the interest of the consumers, is not in conflict with the trade code, and is based [...] on a lawful decision by the city council'. Since the regulation only applied to 'common bread and pastry' and not to 'luxury' products, bakers were left with a certain leeway anyway whereas the regulation of common baked goods would 'protect consumers, prevent disputes', thwart fraud and foster transparency. Uncovering the association's continued attempts to undermine the reform of bread retail, the governor also rejected the bakers' request to be permitted the traditional way of selling bread with fixed prices and fluctuating weights in addition to the reformed retail mode 'because that way the introduced reform would be repealed indirectly'.[72]

There are few traces of the issue in both the archival sources and the newspaper coverage over the next two years. However, the bakers apparently continued to resist, and the matter of opaque price formation, undue profits and reform continued to simmer. It came to boil occasionally, e.g. in early 1873. Two and a half months before the start of the Vienna World's Fair, the popular liberal *Neues Wiener Tagblatt* published an aggressively worded article on 'the monopolists at the baking trough'. Condemning the bakers' plan to raise roll prices by one Kreuzer apiece in times of already high prices as 'true assassination attempt on the purses of the poorest parts of the population', the contribution warned 'the consumers are alerted and means and ways will be found, if necessary, to deal with the monopolists at the baking trough'.[73]

By 1875, however, the bread question and the matter of a retail reform were not only pending, they were heating again. In the face of stagnating retail prices vis-à-vis declining wholesale prices both the urban and the national administration

71. Ibid.
72. *Die Presse*, 'Der Brodverkauf nach Gewicht', 2 July 1872, 179, Beilage, 15.
73. *Neues Wiener Tagblatt*, 'Die Monopolisten vom Backtrog', 18 February 1873, 48, 3.

doubled down on the policy to implement regulation. Arguably an attempt to undermine the bakers' resistance as well as rising public criticism, the magistrate published an announcement to 'remind consumers of the [1872] regulations in their own interest'. Although the urban government had acted and introduced sales according to weight to 'provide security for consumers', the publication went, this order had never been fully accepted by either bakers or consumers.[74] Around the same time, various papers informed their readers the Minister of the Interior had responded to public indignation and sent an order to the Lower Austrian governor on 17 June. Demanding a solution of the bread question and high prices 'neither caused by the prices of cereals or flour nor by other abnormalities', the minister claimed the 1872 law, passed to allow consumers 'to purchase the desired amount of bread', was 'not heeded'. Ordering the governor to instruct the magistrate to 'reissue the regulation at once and to inform the consumers about its purpose again' as well as to ensure adherence to it to prevent 'unappreciative profits' for producers and retailers at the expense of consumers, the state pushed for stronger intervention.[75] 'We hope', another article on the issue concluded, 'the minister's letter will break the resistance against the sale according to weight, we can only regret the city council has lacked the effort to enforce such an easy measure'.[76]

Despite the relatively explicit legal circumstances, magistrate and bakers met to negotiate over the implementation of the retail reform over the following weeks. Yet, part of the press was quite disappointed over the proceedings. 'The perception of a misalignment between market and wholesale prices of various important food items have induced the magistrate's announcement of 23 June, in which the current market laws are brought to mind again,' the *Neue Freie Presse* informed about these meetings in late July 1875. Reporting about the bakers' general denial of any misalignments of prices and their accusations that the *Marktamt* had collected wrong data and made incorrect calculations, the author grew convinced that 'by way of an amicable settlement the magistrate will achieve nothing'.[77] Offering readers a rather similar impression, according to the *Gemeinde-Zeitung* the bakers' representatives Roman Uhl and Ferdinand Boos 'acted like the fox towards the chicken' in the tale *Reineke Fuchs*. Negating all issues brought up by the authorities, they opposed 'all suggestions made for the benefit of the consumers' because 'their pockets would not fill as fast as hitherto', the author fumed.[78] Instead, Uhl and Boos argued 'strongly against' the sales reform and in favour of maintaining the traditional forms of changing loaf sizes worth 2, 5, 10, 20, and 30 Kreuzer, respectively.[79]

74. *Wiener Zeitung*, 'Lebensmittel', 23 June 1875, 141, Beilage.
75. *Morgen-Post*, 'Der Lebensmittelwucher', 3 July 1875, 182, 2.
76. *Neues Wiener Tagblatt*, 'Die Intervention in der Brodfrage', 3 July 1875, 182.
77. *Neue Freie Presse*, 'Unterhandlungen mit Bäckern und Fleischern', 27 June 1875, 176, Beilage.
78. *Gemeinde-Zeitung. Unabhängiges, politisches Journal*, 'Da muß doch selbst eine Kuh lachen!', 31 July 1875, 89.
79. *Neue Freie Presse*, 'Zur Theuerungsfrage', 30 July 1875, 3925, 5.

'Most of the bakers adhered to the traditional way of retail, which makes possible an arbitrary reduction of the weight without reduction of price,' the Chamber of Commerce would mirror the public sentiment.[80] While there are no further reports on the negotiations, by early August bakers and magistrate apparently reached a compromise agreement about the eventual introduction of bread retail according to weight. To give bakers time to 'train their staff' not only in the baking procedures but also in the compulsory metric weights that were to be adopted, the reform was delayed from 1 August to 1 September 1875.[81]

However, implementation failed again and the public mood about bakers and administrators grew anxious. In late September, *Kikeriki,* a popular satire magazine published an anecdote about how a butcher and a baker met in an exposition on small rabbits – *Kaninchen*. Learning these were eaten roasted or as ragout at Hotel Sacher the butcher decided to raise the price of beef 'as soon as I come home' while the baker agreed: 'And I need to bake smaller rolls; if people can afford roast hare, they can pay more for bread.' 'A propos', the butcher added, 'since we are here already, we can have a treat – I'll buy a rabbit mantilla for my wife – it's 30fl. – but the beef premium will earn it.' On that the baker wouldn't miss out, the story went: 'Right you are; I'll get this 86fl. hare fur coat for my wife – bloody expensive – but the small rolls will buy it ... '. Then, 'both made the purchases, left the exposition satisfied and went to a Prater tavern where they toasted to the exposition and the Approvisionirungs-Kommission over several beefsteaks and many litres of Pilsener'.[82]

On the following day, city council Hirsch regretted the *Gemeinderat* had only republished the 1872 regulation without any strict measures to control and survey.[83] By mid-October 1875, six weeks after the repeated official introduction of the reform, he gave a passionate talk on 'measures against weight fraud' regarding buying and selling bread. Presenting numerous malpractices, Hirsch not only called on the listeners' self-responsibility as consumers, but he also suggested sales according to weight, 'namely the right, [...] clearly standardized weight' would bring a solution when monitored. 'Is it known how much bread 10 Kreuzer will buy today? No! But it will be known when one asks for and buys a pound of bread,' the council asserted.[84]

---

80. *Bericht der Handels- und Gewerbekammer für das Erzherzogthum Oesterreich unter der Enns an das K.K. Ministerium für Handel und Volkswirthschaft über die Verkehrsverhältnisse des Kammerbezirkes während der Jahre 1872–1874* (Wien, 1876), 93.

81. *Gemeinde-Zeitung. Unabhängiges, politisches Journal,* 'Der Brodverkauf nach dem Gewicht aufgeschoben', 27 July 1875, 87, 4.; HKB 1872–1874, 93.

82. *Kikeriki. Humoristisches Volksblatt,* 'In der Kaninchen-Ausstellung', 23 September 1875, 76, 2.

83. *Neues Fremden-Blatt,* 'Die Theuerungsfrage', 25 September 1875, 266, 5.

84. *Die Presse,* 'Gemeinderath Hirsch über die Theuerungsfrage', 13 October 1875, 284, Beilage, 10.

A fortnight later, both the city council and the press continued the heated debate based on a memorandum the Bakers' Association had sent the assembly on 26 October. In a 'passionately worded' appeal against this regulation 'deeply intervening into the nature of the bakers' trade', the Bakers' Association petitioned the city council. Maintaining the population's 'obsession with customs' and 'antipathy towards purchasing cut-up bread loafs', they argued changing the way of bread retail according to fixed weights was not advisable.[85] On this basis, the memorandum held that any far-reaching reforms of producing and selling bread would not solve the matter. Instead, the bakers suggested altering the reform of sales according to weight. Instead of selling loaves per kilogram, they would rather vend whole loaves worth 2, 5, 10, 20, 30 and 40 Kreuzer, respectively. To accommodate the city council, the association suggested issuing receipts containing the producer's name, the price of the loaf and its weight to buyers – a proposal the *Approvisionirungs-Sektion* of the *Gemeinderat* had already made.[86] Council Hirsch fervently opposed any points made by the bakers. If the magistrate did not introduce the reform, he argued, the government would and the people thus 'enjoyed a welfare institution against the will of the city council'. Although the city council largely followed Hirsch's suggestions and decided a week after the memorandum was received to order the bakers again to sell bread according to weight,[87] further examinations from the market department were requested.[88]

The immediate press coverage, however, proved much more sceptical, even scornful about the bakers' proposition. The realization of selling bread according to weight from 1 September had had 'one tangible result', the *Illustrirte Wiener Extrablatt* claimed three weeks after the regulation became law: 'You know how much bread you'll get for your money's worth [...]. However, bread has not become *cheaper* since [...].'[89] It was 'not without good reasons' the bakers were blamed by consumers and authorities alike for expensive and small bread, the *Morgen-Post* reckoned already on the day after the order had been passed.[90] Whereas the association had retorted Minister-President Auersperg's accusations

85. *Morgen-Post*, 'Nochmals die Einrede der Bäcker', 2 November 1875, Nr. 303; *Aussiger Anzeiger*, 'Die Armen Bäcker', 10 November 1875, Nr. 90.

86. *Morgen-Post*, 'Die Einrede der Bäcker', 27 October 1875, 298; Wiener Stadt- und Landesarchiv, Marktamt A2/1: Brot und Gebäcksverkauf nach Gewicht, 2035/1876, 19.06.1876: Marktamt. Eingabe der Bäckergenossenschaft über die Modalitäten des Brodverkaufes nach Gewicht.

87. *Neues Fremden-Blatt*, 'Aus dem Gemeinderathe. (Sitzung vom 4. November.)', 5 November 1875, 306, 4.

88. *Morgen-Post*, 'Sitzung des Gemeinderathes vom 26. Oktober. Spezialdebatte über die Theuerungsfrage', 27 October 1875, 298.

89. *Illustrirtes Wiener Extrablatt*, 'Die Theurung auf der Tagesordnung', 21 September 1875, 262, 4. Emphasis in original.

90. *Morgen-Post*, 'Die Einrede der Bäcker'.

Vienna's bakers were 'selfish and unscrupulous', the journal considered the prime minister a man not against profit yet of the opinion that 'the free play of forces' was not valuable when 'used to exploit the majority of the people'. Moreover, the author claimed – two years after the crash of the stock market – 'we know the gentlemen bakers have not detested [...] to seek their luck in the seductive halls of Schottenring [i.e. the stock exchange]; we also know that many a time these attempts were paid with [the loss of] a lot of hard-earned money and even with a nice apartment building.' Consumers, however, should not pay for any of the bakers' stock market losses, the opinion went.[91]

Equally critical, the bakers' arguments found no sympathy with the *Marktamt* either. 'The present memorandum of the Bakers' Association is in conflict with the introduction of the bread retail according to weight, effective since 1 September 1875 as resolved by the city council and approved by the high Ministry of the Interior [...],' future director Karl Kainz remarked by June 1876:

The market bureau considers any discussion & refutation of the memorandum, aimed at all agencies and bodies supporting the implementation of selling bread according to weight in a passionate tone that is easily explainable because the regulation deeply intervenes into the bakers' business, unnecessary because [...] final resolutions have been passed by all authorities, therefore further deliberations are in no case conducive.[92]

Reviewing the bakers' suggestions to maintain the traditional way of selling bread in whole loaves between two and 40 Kreuzer apiece, Kainz found 'this request precisely contrary to the decisions taken, [it] aims at the reintroduction of the former retail mode of fixed prices and fluctuating weights'. Yet, 'precisely this irrational mode of selling was abolished' by the reform. Any further discussion would only represent a repetition of the numerous reports and opinions already collected, the clerk deflected to elaborate on the bakers' second suggestions, the issuing of receipts. Finding this, too, not at all a 'protection of the customers' because of 'manifold confusions and misunderstandings', the *Marktamt*'s message was clear: 'In the interest of the consumers [...] the market department cannot support the bakers' request.'[93]

Highlighting the scope of the conflict and the vigour of resistance, Kainz needed to push for the realization of the – already lawful – reform several months later: 'The market department has repeatedly indicated that only through the imperative implementation of bread retail according to certain weight units, namely 1 kilo[gram], ½ kilo[gram], 20, 10, 5 decagram, the passiveness of the consumers [...] and the bakers' struggle against the general realization of this sales mode can be broken.' The market bureau again requested that bakers were

91. *Morgen-Post*, 'Nochmals die Einrede der Bäcker', 2.
92. Marktamt, Eingabe der Bäckergenossenschaft.
93. Ibid.

'compelled to bake bread in forms of certain weight units, namely in loafs or rolls of 1K[ilogram], 50D[ecagram], 20D, 10D.'[94]

Kainz's 1876 memo underlines the authorities' continued struggle with bread producers and bread consumers over the day-to-day realization of the bill. Despite having introduced and made lawful the retail reform in 1872 and having reissued the regulation in 1875, the new regulation intervened deeply not only into the bakers' business procedures but also into long-standing consumer habits that had been institutionalized by the assize for generations. Although it might appear a rather small step to the historian-observer, such a reform did represent a significant change to contemporary bakers and consumers adhering to a well-known customary moral-economy organization of buying bread geared to ensure access to bread for everyone.

Marking bread

At the same time as the market bureau and the city council strove to implement the retail reform as a measure to restore price transparency in the free-market setting of buying bread, they also struggled to reintroduce an old means establishing quality information. Whereas the retail reform was geared decisively to abolish an assize institution now considered detrimental to public welfare, the second measure explicitly represented a tested assize-means of public surveillance: marking bread with the producer's sign. Until 1860, assize and market regulations had required bakers to mark bread, that is, larger loaves but not more luxurious small pastry products, with the so-called *Brodstupfer*, an individual number assigned to each bakery. Providing consumers and authorities with valuable information on the origin of loaves, this measure had also been eliminated with the introduction of free trade in 1860. As this made a determination of the original producer in the mobilized bread landscape more or less impossible, by the middle of the 1870s the city council, the magistrate and the market department endeavoured to reintroduce such a means of regulation and market information. Cooperating with provincial and national administrations, the urban authorities proved to be more determined and more successful on this front of the bread question.

Already in October 1875, when the city council had passed the renewed implementation of selling bread according to weight, several delegates had proposed to also reintroduce the 'marking of bread', which the assembly passed.[95] Working on the implementation, busy Karl Kainz handed in a report on possible procedures half a year later, in April 1876. Reviewing the *Brodstupfer*'s history – it

---

94. Wiener Stadt- und Landesarchiv, Marktamt A2/1: Brot und Gebäcksverkauf nach Gewicht, 4381/46, 24.10.1876: Marktamt. Regelung des Brodverkaufes nach Gewicht.

95. *Neue Freie Presse*, 'Wiener Gemeinderath', 27 October 1875, 4014, 6; *Neues Fremden-Blatt*, 'Aus dem Gemeinderathe. (Sitzung vom 4. November.)', 4.

had been reformed from individual signs into numbers in 1758 and limited to bread loaves by 1839 according to Kainz – he considered 'this measure only desirable due to the easier handling of bread retail rules'. However, as under the assize, marking should be applied 'only regarding proper bread [produced] in loafs, which allow imprinting three digits due to their larger forms' whereas smaller rolls could be excluded because they were too small to enable 'clear marking'. Apparently, the market clerk had consulted the Bakers' Association, which suggested to exclude white wheat loaves from the regulation. While rejecting that proposal, Kainz found the bakers' suggested marking scheme quite suited. Accordingly, bakers located in the city's first district were to be assigned numbers from 1 to 50, second-district bakers from 51 to 100 and so forth. The last urban baker's mark should be 500, 'whereas the foreign bakers were to use numbers upwards of 500, if the directive would apply to them at all'. Thinking Vienna's country bakers located in the city's rather immediate environs 'could be included into this measure without particular difficulty', the regulation could not be forced on producers and merchants sending bread from more remote places or provinces because supervision was not feasible for the city's authorities, Kainz argued.[96]

Yet, Kainz's proposal was rejected by magistrate and city council in sittings in May and July; in early September the authorities decided to include only the urban bakers into the new regulation whereas any compulsion of bakers outside the city remained unfeasible.[97] The bakers remonstrated immediately against this configuration, Kainz reported in late September 1876. While rejecting the association's universal claim that marking would harm the bakers in general, the market department clerk actually sided with the bakers' more particular critique, their being discriminated. 'Since a lot of bread is send from the outskirts into Vienna, it would be in the interest of the consumers and favourable for [the] bread marking [regulation] if this measure covered bread send from the outskirt communities,' he argued in favour of a metropolitan realization of the regulation.[98]

In contrast to the retail reform, though the political implementation of bread marks also proved difficult and complicated not only due to matters of geography and political competences, a new directive to regulate this aspect of the bread market was passed with almost surprising speed. Deviating from Kainz's suggestion to include 'all bakers of the Vienna association' in city and environs, the city council ruled in late November 1876 that 'in case a universal marking is not enforceable, it will also be waived for Vienna's bakers', thus making an all-or-nothing decision. Consequently, the magistrate was to examine two measures by February 1877: first, 'only marked bread' was to be sold on all marketplaces and in all shops in Vienna; second, marking was to be implemented in such a way that

---

96. Wiener Stadt- und Landesarchiv, Marktamt, A2/1: Brot-Markirung, 1551/1876, 24.04.1876: Marktamt. Einführung einer Brodmarke.

97. Wiener Stadt- und Landesarchiv, Marktamt, A2/1: Brot-Markirung, 2258/46, 21.06.1877: Marktamt. Brodmarkirung betffd.

98. Marktamt, Eingabe der Bäckergenossenschaft.

'the country, from which bread is delivered to Vienna, is represented by a Roman number, the political district in question by a letter, and the producer by an Arabic number'.

Kainz met these provisions with scepticism. On the one hand, he elaborated in June 1877, foreign vendors of unmarked bread should not be excluded from selling in Vienna because they provided an important service. 'Many producers would thus be discouraged to visit our marketplaces and the disadvantages of this indirect limitation of competition would be felt soon,' he cautioned. On the other hand, the clerk found the modus to mark bread with various kinds of numbers and letters 'due to its complicated combination not practicable' because they gave rise to many 'errors and confusion' and 'the imprint of so many signs (which could be as much as 7 or 8 for one mark)' would have an 'unkind effect on the form of bread'. Further, since retail according to weight had not been implemented comprehensively yet, Kainz wondered whether to 'stand back from the marking of bread altogether, because without the simultaneous introduction of baking bread in definite weight units marking could be very problematic'.[99]

However, despite the market department's somewhat contradictory opinion, the marking of bread was pushed through by urban and provincial authorities over the course of the year. Although not indicating whether the suggested way of marking using Roman and Arabic numbers as well as letters was put into practice, the newspapers reported about the realization of bread-marking from early 1877. It was already implemented in Vienna by early March and the Lower Austrian and Viennese governor had 'recommended' and 'invited' the communities just outside the capital to adopt the practice 'to achieve uniformity in the marking of bread' in the agglomeration. The actual execution was left to the Bakers' Association.[100] In early September, the Ministry of Trade approved the further realization of bread marks because 'nearly 80 per cent of these food items are brought from the neighbouring outskirt communities into Vienna' and ordered the subordinate district administrations to comply.[101] Over the following months, the capital's outskirt communities seemed to heed subsequently. On 8 September, for example, the *Wiener Zeitung* reported Simmering municipality had agreed to implement the provision,[102] two weeks later the local authority of Hernals followed,[103] and by December Floridsdorf and Groß-Jedlersdorf across the Danube joined in.[104]

---

99. Marktamt, Brodmarkirung betffd. Emphases in original.

100. *Neue Freie Presse*, 'Brotmarkirung', 10 March 1877, 4503, 6.

101. *Neues Wiener Tagblatt*, 'Brodmarkirung', 7 September 1877, 246, 4.

102. *Wiener Zeitung*, 'Brotmarkirung', 8 September 1877, 206, 5.

103. *Wiener Vororte-Zeitung. Organ für Communal-, Vereins- und Schulwesen*, 'Communalwesen. Außerordentliche Ausschußsitzung in Hernals Am 17. September 1877', 20 September 1877, 69.

104. *Gemeinde-Zeitung. Unabhängiges, politisches Journal*, 'Brodmarkirung', 15 December 1877, 286, 6.

The way of the exact implementation of the order remains unclear. After 1877, neither Vienna's *Marktamt* nor the newspapers mentioned the issue again. However, the relatively quick reintroduction of a system of marking bread to identify the producer and thus provide certain information regarding issues of quality and market surveillance for authorities and consumers alike apparently represented a success for magistrate, city council and market department in their effort to reinstate measures of market regulation. Whereas struggling especially with the bakers over the retail reform, on this matter the authorities could present relatively straightforward achievements. Unfortunately for Karl Kainz and his superiors, this was much less the case with respect to the third major aspect of the bread question, the search – and struggle over – the right price of bread. Even if marked and standard-weight loaves were to become the rule of selling and buying bread, what would be the fair price of such a loaf? In the absence of the assize, this question represented a last major topic of concern during the 1870s and 1880s.

Rediscovering the right price of bread

At the same time as bakers and officials struggled over the retail reform aimed to reintroduce product standards largely abolished with the assize, they also began to quarrel over what would be a fair and just price for the esteemed standard loaves. In the face of an ongoing sense of a misalignment of cereal, flour and bread prices and especially the *Marktamt's* notion of the bakers' profiteering from free-market prices, the quest for the 'right' price of bread became the centrepiece of the bread question after 1875. On the one hand, the authorities aimed to gain professional insights to constitute the costs of bread production to judge price movements and to find the right policy to solve the bread question. On the other hand, the bakers fiercely tried to 'prove' they did not realize excessive profits and to protect their expert knowledge and exclusive know-how giving them a most valuable advantage on the free market. In principle, these attempts by the market department and other urban bodies, started with vigour by the middle of the 1870s, mirrored the quarrels Vienna's administrations and bakers had cultivated for generations before 1860 to establish the 'typical' baker's business, turnover, profits and the just price of bread in the moral economy. Similarly, the free-market debates after 1870 largely involved the key issues of production costs, profit margins, baking techniques and, crucially, how much bread could be produced from a given volume of flour.

'According to the detailed evidence [given] by a master baker, a small baker only produces for hawkers and innkeepers' eating up the entire profits, a *Das Vaterland* article had raised the issue already in April 1870. Huge competition, large commissions granted to grocers and hawkers as well as the 'hunt for customers at every price' would add vending costs of some 900,000fl. each year, allegedly a third of the urban bakers' entire turnover. 'This way, an unjust increase in the prices of bread is produced and small bakers perish.'[105] Building up their defence publicly, the bakers tried to make that point in a flood of publications throughout the following years. In various newspaper articles and several statements made by the association directly, detailed indications about the costs and profit margins involved in running a bakery were publicized to show the bakers' pressed economic situation.

Tackling the question of 'expensive house bread', in 1875 another 'expert' article in the *Neues Wiener Tagblatt* also came to such a result. As the paper believed they 'had to allow room for the artisans' remarks about the reasons' of high food prices, the contribution aimed to make the bakers' case and shed light on 'the real causes why consumers have to pay bread dearly'. Offering in-depth data of production costs – including flour-bread yields, wages, raw material prices, provision to hawkers and spoilage – the author calculated a profit margin so thin that prices could not decrease: 'Through the general freedom of trade we have a competition that certainly leaves nothing to be desired, however, there was no lack of voices, especially in Vienna's city council, that have foreseen many years ago how too much competition in the case of the provisioning trades will lead to high prices', the contribution continued to find that 'not the hawkers or bakers are to be blamed for high prices but our legislation, which expanded freedom of commerce to the food industry'. Only if the number of bakeries and hawkers would be re-regulated and the 'hunt for customers' stopped could bread become cheap again, the bakers' defendant argued for a return to wide-scale regulation of the entire bread market.[106]

Further denying all allegations of profiteering and presenting evidence for their alleged misery, in their 1875 memorandum the Bakers' Association lamented the whole baking trade was 'barely profitable' and that most bakers were 'poor devils' close to 'total ruin'. Not the bakers' 'lust to enrich' and cheat the costumers but high wages and production costs as well as the 'cancer of hawking' were the cause of all evils.[107] In order to produce a less biased picture of the state of the bakers' business, the factors of bread price determination and a suitable foundation for judging whether prices were indeed high or not, the city council ordered magistrate and market department to investigate. The market department was requested to make fortnightly calculations based on 'the assize prescriptions' and compare the results with the prices actually demanded by bakers.[108]

Meanwhile, the magistrate had already 'proceeded actively and held negotiations with the Bakers' Association [...] over the bread prices [...] and has demanded clarification from them', the *Neues Fremden-Blatt* knew by late June. In several rounds of negotiations during the preceding weeks, the magistrate had presented

---

105. *Das Vaterland. Zeitung für die österreichische Monarchie*, 'Zur Brodfrage', 6.
106. *Neues Wiener Tagblatt*, 'Das theuere Hausbrod', 30 June 1875, 179, 2.
107. *Aussiger Anzeiger*, 'Die armen Bäcker'.
108. *Neues Fremden-Blatt*, 'Aus dem Gemeinderathe. (Sitzung vom 4. November.)'.

market department price collections and calculations according to which, in the light of 'present wheat and rye prices, the average weights' of various pastry products should be higher and the prices of white and dark bread several Kreuzer cheaper per pound than sold by the bakers.

The bakers, however, 'appealed against the price documentation of the market commissioners' and offered their own exposé. Indicating higher production costs and other operational expenses, the association accused the *Marktamt* to have collected wrong price materials and 'made false calculations'. Adding their own price collections and calculations proving bread weights and prices were in the right relation, Vienna's bakers claimed to be only guilty to 'aspire to make the finest and best produce in the world'. As a response, the market bureau recalculated and revised the numbers. Yet, the newspaper reported, 'major differences' between both calculations remained and the bakers eventually conceded the 'correctness' of the market department's figures. Whereas the association withdraw the charges made vis-à-vis the *Marktamt*, they 'did not adapt their exposé according to the calculations of the market authority, probably because the differences' in both assessments were too large. The bakers' representatives only agreed to 'see to diminish the present differences' between should-be prices raised by the authority and the actual prices demanded in bakeries. With the bakers on such a behaviour, 'the magistrate will not reach any conclusion by way of an amicable settlement', the reporter concluded.[109]

Anyhow, the *Marktamt* had grown overwhelmingly doubtful with respect to the bakers' willingness to produce price transparency and to cooperate. A year later, market department director Josef Zecha found the bakers' information on flour-to-bread yields 'not in compliance with empirical results, like those made by experts in the proceedings of the Approvisionirungs-Enquête in 1871'. Whereas the usual, accepted flour-to-bread yield hovered around 'at least 125–135 kilo' – a figure that had also been the foundation of assize prices since the late eighteenth century – the bakers claimed a much lower turnover rate. Furthermore, Zecha considered the association's data on operating costs likely exaggerated because these figures would result in actual losses in most times and only allow for a profit in periods 'when bread prices are very high'. Finally, since the bakers had provided data only on the bakery goods of 'finest quality', these could not be applied as 'general benchmark to calculate the production costs' of all bakery products. The figures presented were not even complete; Zecha found them 'lacking the desired detailed information on […] production costs and other costs of operation'. Therefore, the department director concluded in April 1876, 'we are not spared a <u>baking trial</u> in order to determine the necessary and general information about production costs of the different kinds of rolls and bread'.[110]

---

109. *Neues Fremden-Blatt,* 'Unterhandlungen mit Bäckern und Fleischern', 27 June 1875, Nr. 176.

110. Wiener Stadt- und Landesarchiv, Marktamt A2/1: Brot und Gebäck: Probebackung, 190.306/1876, 03.04.1876: Marktamt. Marktdirektion Äusserung Probebackung. Emphasis in original.

Thus reactivating a key procedure of the moral economy, Zecha suggested the test baking to take place both at the bakery of a member of the association and the k.k. military bakery. However, for reasons unknown such a baking trial – maybe the first in decades – was conducted six weeks later, on 22 May 1876, in the bakery of master baker Franz Buhlheller only. The try-out established the lower production figures claimed by the association; 100 kilograms of wheat flour yielded 110 kilograms of wheat rolls; the same amount of rye flour gave 121 kilograms of rye bread. Consequently, these numbers were accepted to represent baking standards and came to be used for the magistrate's calculations of 'should-be' prices against which market prices were compared for the following years.[111] That way, the bakers had turned the tide in their favour.

Yet, the public remained somewhat doubtful about the state of the bread question and the 'right' relation of cereal, flour and bread prices. 'The most important question of life of the impecunious masses is only superficially treated,' *Das Vaterland* would continue the debate in January 1878 on its front page. The fact that bread prices remained constantly higher vis-à-vis grain prices 'blatantly shows how highly detrimental the liberal economic order is for the Volkswohl' through creating the 'parasitism of hawking and usury' and making bread expensive, the author stated, calling for regulation.[112] A day later, another newspaper contribution joined the choir. 'The consumers have recognized bread prices are increased unjustifiedly, the press has also raised this issue and has proven the disproportionate price level. This has even been constituted by the authorities,' *Die Hausfrau* announced. 'We all know the vivid debates among the city council over the *bread question*,' the report continued. A 'public calamity', while bread prices would rise in times of increasing grain prices, they did not decrease in periods of sinking cereal prices, or 'at least not in the right proportion'. Yet, against the serious efforts by the minister-president, the governor and the urban officials, 'the bread lords countered with their steadfast non possumus. We cannot give the bread cheaper, they say, and they do not give it cheaper.'[113]

'Our latest suggestions regarding the unwarranted increase of bread prices were not without consequences,' the *Neue Freie Presse* continued the bread question later that year. 'To protect consumers from fraud, selling according to weight needs to be implemented imperatively' and intermediate trade through hawkers and grocers needed to be regulated and controlled fervently, the author argued. Rejecting the bakers' long-term counterargument, the paper considered consumers were 'already used to' buy 'all articles, except the liquid ones, lately even wood according to weight.' Realizing the reform represented 'the only control

111. Wiener Stadt- und Landesarchiv, Marktamt, A2/1: Brotfrage, 02.07.1885: Magistrat der Stadt Wien. Magistrats-Referat betreffend: Vorschläge zur Regelung der Brotfrage, 4.

112. *Das Vaterland. Zeitung für die österreichische Monarchie,* 'Das Brod', 18 January 1878, 18, 1.

113. *Die Hausfrau. Blätter für Haus und Wirthschaft.,* 'Eine erfreuliche Erscheinung auf dem Gebiete der Approvisionirung', 19 January 1878, 3. Emphasis in original.

for the buyer, and the only benchmark to judge the prices' of bread and satisfy consumers who would 'finally get cheap bread, again', author Ad. T. concluded.[114]

'Not death, but bread!,' the *Morgen-Post* demanded on its front page by early 1879. As 'just now a new ministry [i.e. a new government] is born by the skin of one's teeth', Austria needed a 'Ministry of Bread, which mitigates the people's economic sorrows, which makes good the social misery of the economic crisis, [...] a Ministry of Bread that endeavours to govern for the tax payers', the paper claimed. 'If the Auersperg ministry [i.e. the previous government] had possessed the spark of divine and folksy genius to tackle the burning bread question' and had not idly wasted years it would still hold power, the author stated to raise the issue of expensive bread to the forefront not only of urban but of national politics.[115] A government should care for the 'mind, heart, and stomach' of its people, the newspaper added in mid-July, shortly before the new Taaffe cabinet was introduced. However, liberalism had cared neither for the mind nor for the heart and 'even less than for mind and heart it has taken care of the stomach of the people', the author constituted. 'May the new representatives remember the sad fate of the previous parliament, which died ingloriously because it failed to act upon the bread question.'[116]

The 'liberal principle of free price determination' was responsible for high prices, *Das Vaterland* exclaimed by the early 1880s, when 'symptoms arose which are capable to create sorrows over the people's "daily bread"', as the *Morgen-Post* would put it.[117] These articles tackled different issues. Whereas the former spoke about the effects of grain tariffs on bread prices, the latter warned about another strike of the bakers' apprentices in Vienna. Both, however, foresaw the consequences of such developments; a disproportionate rise of bread prices as bakers would seize such opportunities to increase profits.

By late 1884, the debate over high bread prices vis-à-vis declining cereal prices grew urgent once again. By mid-October, the *Neue Freie Presse* found cereal prices had fallen by almost 21 per cent since 1876 whereas bread prices only decreased by 3.4 per cent. 'In fact', the author noted, 'bread prices are not in the right relation to cereal prices and the consumers pay this difference'.[118] Simultaneously, the market authority called the magistrate's attention that 'the weight of rolls and the prices of bread are not in the right relation to the prices of flour' and 'the bakers sell rolls too small and bread too dear', as Magistrate Secretary Siegl reported. According to his report, Major Eduard Uhl had also grown aware of the matter and instructed the magistrate to 'investigate these price

114. Ad. T., 'Die Brotfrage', *Neue Freie Presse*, 3 November 1878, 5096, 6.
115. *Morgen-Post*, 'Nicht Tod, sondern Brod!', 9 February 1879, 39, 1.
116. *Morgen-Post*, 'Weniger Reaction und mehr Volkswirthschaft!', 13 July 1879, 191.
117. *Das Vaterland. Zeitung für die österreichische Monarchie*, 'Das Brod des armen Mannes', 4 May 1882; *Morgen-Post*, 'Etwas von der Brodfrage', 15 June 1883, 162, 2.
118. *Neue Freie Presse*, 'Die Brotfrage', 17 October 1884, 7235; *Neues Wiener Tagblatt*, 'Die hohen Brodpreise', 9 October 1884, 279.

differences and find measures enabling the price reduction of the most important daily necessities'. Consequently, director of the magistrate Alois Bittmann put together yet another commission to which both the market department and the representatives of the Bakers' Association were invited. Sitting in October 1884, 'to begin with, using figures presented by the market department a real misalignment of the prices of flour and bakery products was constituted'. Whereas wheat flour prices had decreased by almost 33 per cent compared to 1877, the figures showed the weight of premium wheat *Kaiser* rolls increased only by 7 per cent since and a second-class *Mundsemmel* had not gained any weight at all. Meanwhile, the price of rye had fallen 22 per cent against 1877 while rye bread was only 15 per cent cheaper. Invoking the usual reasons, baker chairman Tobias Ratz quoted 'higher production costs, higher commissions and high quality standards' as causes of the phenomenon that did not allow any downward changes of prices.[119]

To achieve lower prices, the representatives of the association presented the magistrate with a strategy of their own to introduce new standards to the trade, thus somewhat following the authorities' call for uniformity and auditability. Ratz and his deputy planned to reach an internal agreement among all of Vienna's bakers to form a 'cartel' to reduce and standardize commissions paid to hawkers and grocers as well as to introduce the uniform use of flour regarding the amounts and qualities chosen for the various kinds of bakery goods. This was a good call, *Die Presse* commented, since regarding the diverse products, 'one observes in one and the same district many differences'. For example, between bakers the weights of *Kaiser* rolls could vary between 40 and as much as 70 grams apiece and the price of mixed bread fluctuated between twelve and twenty-one Kreuzer per kilogram from one shop to the other. Between the various parts of town, differences were found equally pronounced and equally intransparent. 'The main reason is the different mix [of flour], ingredients', and general overhead costs, the paper noted to declare, 'if all [bakers] agreed to use the same recipe, prices will still be varying but a basis for comparison' could be established and prices would be more transparent. Moreover, since the sale of bread according to standard weights had never been thoroughly realized, the bakers' representatives suggested to introduce standard prices and the obligation to mark the respective minimum weight on the loaves. Having presented those three measures to the authorities, Ratz was sent to collect the opinion of his fellow members of the Bakers' Association.[120]

On the same day, the *Morgen-Post* devoted most of its front page to the issue of high and differing bread prices and noted the quite astonishing price and weight differences within and between the city's districts. *Kaiser* rolls fluctuated between 40 and 75 grams per piece, they were largest in the working-class district 10, *Favoriten* and smallest in the city centre 'due to the quality'. Between September and October, their weight had risen in districts 1, 3, 5, 6 and 8 whereas it had

---

119. Magistrat der Stadt Wien, Regelung der Brotfrage, 1–3.
120. *Die Presse*, 'Die hohen Brodpreise', 16 October 1884, 286.

fallen in districts 4 and 7. Second-grade rolls varied between 60 and 95 grams apiece, their weights also moved differently in various parts of town and the same was true for all kinds of bread. In short, prices were a mess.[121] By early November, the *Wiener Allgemeine Zeitung* took up specifically that matter. 'In what relation should, according to the costs of baking and bread retail, bread weights and flour prices be, and how was the relation of such normal weights to the real bread weights hitherto?,' the paper asked opening a two-parts series investigating a solution. 'Above all, transparency' and information were needed, the general answer was foreclosed. Further, a 'certain continual activity of the police forces and the market department is required to put consumers in the position to defend their interests against the bakers with lasting success'. Accordingly, the plurality of prices represented the key problem of the bread question and market transparency, the article postulated. 'It is obvious that, if one baker makes Kaiser rolls of 70 grams and survives, every other could give the same weight' instead of producing 40-gram rolls and 'earn the fourfold profit with the same effort.'

If the former baker earned a decent income with larger rolls, the latter would 'cheat the ignorant consumers' and turn too high a profit – 'in this large abuse lies the core of our bread question', the author claimed. For the public to judge about the 'right' and 'fair' prices of bread, public knowledge about the costs of baking had to be gained and maintained, his argument continued to offer calculations. Accordingly, a 40-gram baker might earn as much as 200 per cent of his production costs per 100 kilograms of flour in case of Kaiser rolls, 'a truly unjustified profit' in the view of the writer. This was only possible, the article continued, because 'the consumers are ignorant' about the product differences between bakers. To determine such variations, 'they would need to investigate', an unlikely challenge for the individual. 'How would this change if weekly tables were publicized by every newspaper in which the minimum weights of the main kinds of bakery goods were noted?,' the solution to the bread question was announced. Would it not enable consumers to compare and visit the baker with the best offer? The 40-gram bakers then needed to stop 'fishing in murky waters' and accept real competition – to enter the struggle of a 'weight-competition' with their fellow bakers. Accordingly, a standardized loaf was to be introduced and bakers should be held to inform about minimum weights for all baked goods, then to be collected and publicized by the market authorities. This way, consumers had 'an easy task: to occasionally weigh their rolls and check if they comply' with the information provided by the bakers as well as 'consult the baking tables once a week' and take the best offer.[122]

---

121. *Morgen-Post*, 'Die Brodpreise in den einzelnen Bezirken', 16 October 1884, 286, 1; *Morgen-Post*, 'Die Bäckergenossenschaft und die Brodpreise', 16 October 1884, 286, 1.

122. *Wiener Allgemeine Zeitung*, 'Die Brodfrage und deren Lösung', 1 November 1884, 1681; *Wiener Allgemeine Zeitung*, 'Die Brodfrage und deren Lösung', 6 November 1884, 1685.

Meanwhile, Karl Kainz proved perfectly annoyed not only by the bakers' overall proceedings but also by the general diverse and erratic market situation. Although the authorities 'urged the bakers' chairman to reduce bread prices and make suggestions' of continued lower price levels, the association continued to invoke the 'great burdens of the baker's trade' making a reduction of prices 'impossible', Kainz noted ill-humoured by mid-December 1884. Despite the bakers' promise to hold a meeting to attempt to regulate commissions and tackle the problems of intermediate trade internally, the market department clerk had learned 'no official news about any success' of such attempts. 'Alone the few reports in the papers about these negotiations give cause to assume [...] they will lead to no result,' he expected exasperatedly. Anyhow, an internal voluntary commitment, Kainz believed, would clearly advantage bakers vis-à-vis hawkers and grocers: 'If the consumers benefited is questionable because it depends on the will of the bakers to share the gained advantages with the consumers in form of larger loafs and lower prices. According to long-term experience the bakers have repeatedly made bread and rolls smaller and more expensive without the occasion of an increase of flour prices'.

Since 'lately the press has accused [the market department] no decisive measures have been taken regarding the bread question', Karl Kainz went on to present a sweeping blow against the Bakers' Association. According to his most severe critique, the bakers did not heed the 1845 prohibition to allow hawkers and grocers a commission of more than 5 per cent; they had not been able to implement a voluntary limitation of commissions to 10 per cent in 1878; the bakers had raised prices with the currency reform in 1858 despite magistrate orders; they had stopped producing 1 ½ Kreuzer rolls in 1860 and 1-Kreuzer rolls in 1870 despite the 'economic importance of 1x baked goods for family and household'. Thus 'the option to purchase baked good for 1x has been taken from the poor, the manifold demands and warnings of the authority, the criticism of the press and the complaints of the consumers were not fruitvoll' while the bakers had 'had their will'. Further, they had also stopped producing 2-Kreuzer rolls since 1878, a product 'which is consumed namely by day labourers, workers and the poor'; they had shown the 'fiercest resistance to' the 1872 and 1875 retail reform to continue 'hiding weight fluctuations and price increases from consumers'; the association's members neglected producing proper bread of good quality more generally, which was 'usually made from lowest flour qualities, contains too much moisture and is mouldy or too dry, and more often than not, sour'; they aimed to do away the 'pressure of competition' through country bakers by lobbying for a limit of bread deliveries and hawking, which would be 'adverse for consumers'.

Generally, based on the flour prices of last three months, bread could be cheaper and the bakers could pay workers higher wages due to good profits and thus prevent detrimental labour conditions and strikes. 'Given these experiences, there will be no yielding and goodwill from the party of the bakers or a real appreciation of the great importance of a solution of the bread question that satisfies the needs of the consumers, although the bakers have no reason to wail over a decline of their trade,' Karl Kainz summarized. Therefore, he turned to make the same demands he had issued since the early 1870s: to implement the bread retail according to weight 'under all circumstances' and introduce standard loaves of a half, one, one and a half, and two kilograms in weight, respectively, as well as to provide clear price information. Taking the offensive and adopting some demands made in the press, the market director even offered detailed prescriptions of the flour qualities usable for various kinds of standard wheat and rye loaves, thus presenting a comprehensive concept of how regulated and standardized bread products should be produced. According to this plan, white bread, for example, could be made from wheat flour of numbers 5 and 6 produced in Vienna's steam mill; rye bread should be made from 'pure rye flour or an addition of maximum 10% wheat flour', and *Kaiser* rolls were to consist of steam mill wheat flour number 0 or 1. His final, universal request represented an outspoken call for a substantial turn-away from free-market relations in the bread trade and in favour of a return to comprehensive intervention:

> If the bakers do not achieve a common agreement among themselves and do not comply with the demands of the authorities and the rightful urge of the consumers regarding price decreases and weight increases, no other means would remain than a <u>reintroduction of the assize</u>, which would be feasible in the case of the bread trade. Although the system of food assizes has been abhorred by liberal currents for centuries [*sic!*], in that moment when the recognition is asserted that a continuation would create unbearable conditions and the consumers were wrongfully threatened in their most important necessities of life by egoistic producers, the authorities were bound in the interest of the consumers to protect them against arbitrary price increases by employing the right provided by the trade code to determine the retail prices of food items, of which bread is the most important and least dispensable.[123]

The end of the bread question?

'So we have happily returned to the Middle Ages. Vienna's market director and his equal-minded market commissioners found a means to solve the bread question,' the liberal *Neue Freie Presse* announced ironically on New Year's Day 1885, some two weeks after Kainz's statement. Neither based on economic studies nor on a modern mindset but 'through going back several centuries' Karl Kainz found the assize in the 'medieval junk room', the paper sneered. Such a measure had 'rendered completely worthless' since its abolition in 1860 'would only benefit bakers making good profits under the auspices of the authorities' whereas consumers were only harmed.[124]

---

123. Äusserung Marktkommissariat.
124. *Neue Freie Presse*, 'Die Brotsatzung', 1 January 1885, 7307, 6.

While the *Neue Freie Presse* as leading liberal newspaper of the Monarchy strictly condemned the market bureau's move, other opinions proved less determined. The 'long duration' of the negotiations among the bakers about 'measures to lower bread prices' and their 'dubious results' had led the *Marktamt* to suggest 'reactivating' the assize to 'create a regulation with the aim to secure the trade's gains on the one hand, and to protect consumers from cheat on the other', partly publicly owned *Die Presse* captured the proceedings more balanced, though 'hoping' the bakers would achieve a 'free decision' without any 'coercive means' by the authorities.[125] At the same time, the left-liberal *Wiener Allgemeine Zeitung* considered Kainz's proposal 'rather a shot fired in the air' than a serious plan and pushed for increased efforts to implement 'baking tables' suggested already in early November 1884. 'Only this way, competition will lead to lower bread prices,' the paper argued for their own, less drastic interventions.[126]

Between those three poles – no intervention in the market at all, educational interference through price information and drastic public involvement via reactivated assize prices – the peak debate over the bread question unfolded throughout 1885. Captured by the press, the failure of the Bakers' Association to deliver quick solutions and the market department's rather radical propositions once more sparked heated public debates. Only three days after the 1 January article, the *Wiener Allgemeine Zeitung* published another, quite remarkable contribution that connected the bread question to the period's *zeitgeist* issues, anti-Semitism and economic anti-liberalism.

'The value of a good name is proven in the case of the bakers,' the article opened. 'They experience how valuable it is not to carry the names "Jeiteles" or "Kohn". These names, burdened with all evils in these glorious days of Anti-Semitism' could not be found on the bakers' registers, the *WAZ* raised the issue of wide-scale anti-Jewish and anti-Czech xenophobia in late nineteenth-century Vienna. The bakers' trade was 'not yet judaized', the author stated to claim, 'it is good that it is not, but it is only good for the bakers'. If many Jews had had entered the trade, the 'universal remedy of Anti-Semitism' would have solved the bread question already, the author sardonically commented on otherwise widespread discrimination especially of Jewish immigrants. Adopting current slogans of anti-Semitic political debates, Vienna's bakers did not represent 'dirt competition' or the 'might of capital' and did not sell 'Pofelwaren', low-quality goods attributed to Jewish peddlers. Nor was the bakers' trade threatened by factory production. A 'lavish business', there were 'no signs to recognize the ill-fated consequences of the liberal economic order'.

Yet, while the trade was healthy, 'only the bakery products suffered Schwindsucht'. Using the German word for tuberculosis, this phrasing quite elegantly pointed to the diminishing weights and disappearance of small bakery products over the previous years as the related German verb 'schwinden' translates

---

125. *Die Presse*, 'Zur Brodfrage', 1 January 1885, 1, 14.
126. *Wiener Allgemeine Zeitung*, 'Eine Brodtaxe?', 1 January 1885, 1738.

to both 'shrink' and 'disappear', a notion that is lost in translation. Anyhow, after lashing out against both anti-Jewish resentments and Manchesterian laissez-faire politics, the *Allgemeine Wiener Zeitung* went on to equally critique conservative and anti-Semitic anti-globalization. 'We have found only handsome sales girls and gentle masters [of both sexes] in the baking shops, but a vampire we have not met,' the author commented on the notion of 'blood-sucking' capitalists controlling the 'stockyards of world trade'. On the contrary, the global trade especially in grain enabled lower prices for raw materials whereas the bakers as 'nexus between wholesale merchants and consumers' did not fulfil their duty to pass on the benefits of global trade to customers. Finally arriving at the local Vienna level, the author again claimed particularly those bakers producing small loaves realized too high a profit compared to the general economic circumstances. Although the magistrate continuously tried to change that, the authorities only managed to 'threaten the bakers with an official bread tax', the assize. Yet, only the publication of prices would represent a real remedy by enabling consumers to 'take bread from the baker who offers higher weights [and lower prices] and good quality'. This was 'the only practicable means to solve the bread question'.[127]

Three weeks later, the same newspaper ploughed on to comment on the bakers' proposed solution, which had been publicized in the meantime. The author was not at all ecstatic. Lamenting on the Austrian 'habit to light a straw fire and after its fading wait what God and the high authorities will make of it' as well as 'our weakness for the slow falling-asleep' of political debates, Vienna's Bakers' Association knew these habits all too well, the paper alleged. Having collected such a 'rich numbers of proposals, opinions and resolutions' after long-hauled negotiations, these proposals by the bakers would not at all benefit consumers in the form of lower prices. Since the association had agreed to collectively cut commissions, the bakers only harmed 'consumers with such malice' because they would simply pocket the emerging savings. Thus, again the reasoning went, only the publication of prices would protect buyers from cheat and fraud.[128]

At the same time as both the press and the authorities remained sceptical of the bakers' suggestions of self-regulation, in January 1885 a 53-page treatise titled 'Light on the bread question and the safe way to solve it' added fuel to the already simmering fire. Likely, its author was the same person who had written several contributions in the *Wiener Allgemeine Zeitung* previously. Although the newspaper mentioned no name, the arguments of the booklet were quite the same.

'Neither the prices of flour nor any other production and retail costs are the causes' of high bread prices, the brochure's author Dr. J. Matern opened his booklet. 'Therefore, we reduce the bread question to its essence, formulated thus: what are the bakers' profits concerning the major products? Are the low weights [and high prices of bread] and the bakers' respective profits justified? And what is to be done to create the right relation between the bakers' merits, profits, and products?'

---

127. *Wiener Allgemeine Zeitung*, 'Die Brodfrage', 4 January 1885, 1741, 2.
128. *Wiener Allgemeine Zeitung*, 'Wien, 23. Januar', 24 January 1885, 1761.

At the 'core of the bread question', Matern claimed, 100 kilograms of wheat flour would rather yield 135 kilograms wheat rolls and 100 kilograms of rye gave 140 kilograms rye bread, nearly a fourth more than the infamous baking trial of 1876 led by baker Franz Buhlheller had produced. That way, author Dr. J. Matern calculated, bakers making small rolls and loaves continually realized much higher profit margins than previously alleged and maintained by the association. Assuming an average turnover of 350 kilograms per day, Matern presented calculations on profit margins for various goods produced by a baker. Accordingly, a baker who made rather larger loaves and rolls compared to many selling only small pieces would earn an average lower-end annual income of nearly 3,000 Gulden. 'Considering all other classes of the city's population who cannot enjoy such an income', these figures showed 'how much reason we have to shed light on this blatant imbalance of merit and profit concerning most bakers', the author argued. Especially in the sales of such small loaves lay 'the cheating of consumers, which is outrageous in case of the smallest pieces'. Presently, Matern continued, 'in the current situation neither flour prices nor any other costs of production have a substantial impact on the weight of rolls or the price of bread, respectively, rather they are determined by the audacity with which the bakers dare to give small and smaller loafs to the customers'.

That way, each year consumers would pay almost 4.5 million Gulden too much for their daily bread, caused by the bakers' avoidance 'to give objective information on operation costs and bread weights'. Although conceding this was rather a way to put a rough number on the entire issue than a perfectly correct figure, Matern went on to accuse the bakers to have contributed 'obscuration rather than explanation' since 1875. 'There is no precise calculation how much the production and retail' of baked goods was, 'they do not want to provide' such information and try 'to avert this at any cost', he charged. The bakers 'take what customers acquiesce' and thus earned a 'super income', the 'non plus ultra of all usury', to which 'all bread consumers, even the poor, are exposed to on a daily basis'.[129] Therefore, the author presented the key solution to the bread question: 'The first and most necessary measure needed for an actual solution of the bread question is to inform as many consumers as possible about everything that is connected to that question.'[130]

In the words of Magistrate Secretary Siegl, Matern's contribution 'induced the market department [...] to investigate the appropriateness of bread and pasty prices' even more sincerely and provided the voices in favour of intervention with live ammunition.[131] By early February 1885, the *Wiener Allgemeine Zeitung* reported over a planned general assembly of the Bakers' Association that should vote to regulate commissions and intermediate trade and introduce a 'standard rye bread'

---

129. J. Matern, *Licht in der Brodfrage und der sichere Weg zur Lösung derselben* (Wien: Karl Matern, 1885), 4–20, quotes from 4, 5, 6, 9, 11, 16, 17, 18, 19, 20.

130. Matern, *Licht in der Brodfrage*, 1.

131. Magistrat der Stadt Wien, Regelung der Brotfrage, 1–3.

aimed to 'protect consumers from cheat by intermediate retailers'.[132] However, two weeks later the negotiations among the over 600 bakers had 'produced no results' and the increasingly impatient magistrate took to implement 'proceedings on its own'.[133] Apparently, it was high time for the city's government to act. By the end of the month, a front-page article in the Christian-social *Das Vaterland* severely criticized both the bakers and the administration. 'We live in the age of progress and enlightenment [sic!] where the laws of supply and demand reign unrivalled, where everyone may overcharge him who has to endure,' the article stated. This was especially the case regarding the bread question. Thanks to the 'ignorance of consumers and the liberalism of the trade authorities' nowhere else prevailed such a use of the 'fundamental right of the modern economic doctrine, the unlimited right to cheat' like in Vienna's bread retail, the author postulated. Whereas magistrate and city council acted only when the situation grew 'most scandalous' by organizing enquiries about an issue 'every child knows', J. Matern's *Licht in der Brodfrage* had clearly informed consumers how outrageously they were cheated in the case of daily bread, the *Vaterland* picked up the ambitious booklet's arguments. Recounting Matern's points according to which many bakers earned huge profits 'at the expense of consumers', the paper explicitly demanded quick intervention. 'In our opinion, the authorities are obliged to prevent such a horrendous daylight robbery of the people and especially the poor with all rigour,' the report concluded.[134]

Compared to the deliberations about the bread question during the previous decade, this time the authorities seemed to act in a much more straightforward manner. Pressured by the press and the concerned market department, the magistrate called for a new baking try-out to investigate the claims made by Dr. J. Matern, to determine the profit margins of the baking business, and to evaluate the room for manoeuvre. Scheduled on 3 March 1885, the trial was to be carried out in the k.k. Military Bakery without the presence of the bakers. Conducted by 'men of the technical sciences in the most exact manner', this 'neutral' test confirmed the higher results of 135 kilograms wheat rolls per 100 kilograms flour, the magistrate's rapporteur reported to reveal the bakers' systematic counterfeit of business figures and profit margins.[135] Unsurprisingly, the association contested these results, achieved in the absence of their representatives and carried out by a non-representative institution. While this was an argument bakers had made for generations and specifically during assize calculations of bygone times, the magistrate agreed to another test baking verifying the one just conducted – this time with 'intervention of the association's chairmen'.[136] The test of the test was

---

132. *Wiener Allgemeine Zeitung*, 'Zur Brodfrage', 4 February 1885, 1771, 4.

133. *Die Presse*, 'Die Brodfrage', 14 February 1885, 44, 11.

134. *Das Vaterland. Zeitung für die österreichische Monarchie*, 'Das Brod', 27 February 1885, 57, 1.

135. Magistrat der Stadt Wien, Regelung der Brotfrage, 4.

136. *Das Vaterland. Zeitung für die österreichische Monarchie*, 'Die Brodfrage', 25 March 1885, 83, 10.

performed at the bakery of August Riedl in number 6, Maximilianstraße, on 20 April. Enforced by the bakers, it was run without observation by the magistrate.[137] Whereas the previous round had shown a 'surprisingly positive' result, 'the test baking conducted the day before yesterday [...] under technical leadership of the association's representatives [...] took a less positive course', the *Morgen-Post* reported on 22 April. 'By the way, the commissioners did not agree with some steps of the operation,' the paper cautioned rather restrainedly.[138]

Das Vaterland assumed a much more aggressive tone when reporting about the procedures, engaging in an outright campaign against the free bread market and Vienna's bakers. 'One of the most characteristic aspects of our capitalist age is the state of the bread question,' the campaign began. Caused by the 'obsession to become rich at the expense of one's fellows' and by the 'system of credit and usury regarding the most necessary needs, the most abundant harvests and the great streams of foreign cereals do not manage to secure cheap bread'. Through 'great differences in the prices of rye bread, which is more the bread of the poor', the author claimed, consumers were 'cheated like West African negroes'. Without product standards providing systematic market information, most customers knew 'nothing about such differences. They would need to weigh and calculate their purchases and probably visit another baker' or hawker to compare and learn about their being outsmarted by bakers – a rather unlikely measure, the argument went. 'If the lack of knowledge [...] is the main cause, the natural remedy is obvious,' the *Vaterland*'s writer argued: 'clarity for customers' through a regulation of standard loaves and unambiguous price information.[139]

Particularly this, however, the bakers tried to prevent, the newspaper claimed in the following parts of the series on the bread question published in late April and early May. The first baking trial in March 1885 at the military bakery had been conducted 'under strict compliance to all procedures necessary to achieve an absolute reliable result' by a trustworthy and impartial 'technical expert'. Although it 'proved that the 1876 baking try-out was a mistake, or rather: a fake', the present bakers' chairmen had the cheek to 'make eager propaganda for the bakers' sacrificial candour'.[140] Now, in April, during the second attempt in baker Riedl's workshop, 'baking was done not in the way Vienna's bakers usually do, but essentially the way they do not', the author fumed in the third part of the *Vaterland* series. No impartial expert was consulted, and baking was conducted 'against all technical rules, with the open tendency to produce rolls as small as possible; for example, too little water was added and the dough was baked very long in a very

---

137. Magistrat der Stadt Wien, Regelung der Brotfrage, 4.

138. *Morgen-Post*, 'Probebacken', 22 April 1885, 110.

139. *Das Vaterland. Zeitung für die österreichische Monarchie*, 'Die gegenwärtige Lage der Brodfrage I', 29 April 1885, 117, 1.

140. *Das Vaterland. Zeitung für die österreichische Monarchie*, 'Die gegenwärtige Lage der Brodfrage II', 30 April 1885, Nr 118.

sharp heat [...]. During the process, two boys were caught attempting dispose of some quantities of the dough [...]. With this try out, the bakers themselves proved their 1876 result a fraud,[141] and their 1885 procedures fraudulent, too. What was their intention, the author wondered. 'If the commission recommended the magistrate [to reintroduce] the bread assize' and the calculation of such assize prices was based on the results of this second 1885 trial-baking, the falsified results would give the bakers a 'significant advantage' and increase their profits. 'This was the bakers' aim during their forged [...] and incorrect procedures', the author charged. Therefore, any reintroduction of the assize could not be advisable since the authorities would face 'endless problems [...] and a constant fight with the bakers' to establish acceptable assize prices. Instead, *Das Vaterland* joined the other voices demanding the market department to collect and publicize bread and roll prices of all bakeries. This way, 'the magistrate would not impose constraints on the bakers' and deliver a solution of the bread question without 'embarrassing negotiations with the bakers' association'.[142]

However, 'with such a result, the association could not be satisfied, and they are *impertinent* enough to demand a third baking trial', another irritated report followed the developments by late May. Repeating accusations of fraud and profiteering, *Das Vaterland* named chairman Tobias Ratz 'with his 42-grams rolls' in particular to be among those overcharging their customers. Again, no kind of assize regulation but only publicized price tables would 'unleash the weight-competition'. 'This alone is what is missing today [...]. *We do not demand more from the magistrate*', the contribution declared.[143] Indeed, creating a precedent, the newspaper did publish such a price table in early July, '*this time* without the names' of the bakers, although it would be full-fledged only when giving 'the full names and addresses of the different bakers'. Awaiting the magistrate's decision on the bread question, *Das Vaterland* made the case to 'intervene into the bread usury through publicity'. Publicizing the market department's price and weight calculations of May 1885, the *Vaterland* aimed to highlight the striking diversity in bakery products of the same kind across the city. For example, the weights of

---

141. *Das Vaterland. Zeitung für die österreichische Monarchie*, 'Die gegenwärtige Lage der Brodfrage III', 1 May 1885, Nr 119; *Das Vaterland. Zeitung für die österreichische Monarchie*, 'Die gegenwärtige Lage der Brodfrage IV (Schluß)', 2 May 1885, 120. Remember the flour-to-bread yield was a crucial factor for the bakers' income. With lower yields per 100 kilograms, higher loaf prices could be defended. Vice versa, higher flour-to-bread yields would induce lower prices per piece. 'Proving' lower yields in the baking trial gave the bakers a double advantage: defend higher prices per piece and produce more loaves out of 100 kilograms than officially assumed, thus earning a 'shadow income' possibly unnoticed by officials.

142. *Das Vaterland. Zeitung für die österreichische Monarchie*, 'Die gegenwärtige Lage der Brodfrage IV (Schluß)', 120.

143. *Das Vaterland. Zeitung für die österreichische Monarchie*, 'Weiteres zur Brodfrage', 28 May 1885, 145, 1. Emphasis in original.

premium 2-Kreuzer *Kaiser* rolls varied greatly between the 283 bakeries within the *Linienwall*. Especially the bakers located in district I produced comparatively small rolls that apparently did not exceed a weight of 5.2 decagram – 52 grams – per roll while most of Vienna's bakers would make *Kaiser* rolls of up to 60 grams. In almost all other parts of town, consumers were able to visit many bakers who would sell larger rolls than their city-centre competitors. Compared to district I, especially in district X buyers could purchase between three and thirty grams of rolls more for the same amount of money, a fact that was much likely also caused by quality differences. In other words, when shopping for the same product – at least according to price – consumers would find very different roll sizes both across town and between individual bakeries. To the *Vaterland*, such a market overview not only proved that some bakers profited more than others, but that bread roll weights did lie in the hands of the baker and were technically controllable by producers.[144]

Compared to these vivid attacks by the press and especially by *Das Vaterland*, administrators appeared less condemning during the process of baking trials. Diplomatically considering the procedures of the second baking trial of 20 April – which had particularly aroused the press's wrath – as 'inadequacies', the magistrate had agreed to a final test performed at Chairman Tobias Ratz's bakery on 2 June 1885. This time it would be conducted in the presence of a magistrate delegation observing the process. Even though Ratz 'used less water' compared to the military's test run, now the results came close enough to the 'neutral' numbers of between 127 and 141.4 kilograms of produce per 100 kilograms of flour, depending on the kind of product. This confirmed standard yields that were indeed comparable to those applied in Paris and Innsbruck, Magistrate Secretary Siegl noted, and that proved all earlier attempts 'wrong'. However, even in this third round of test bakings aimed to constitute the true costs and profits of bread production, the authorities considered the bakers' statements on production expenses 'hardly truthful'. According to the numbers provided by the association, a baker would generate a loss of 'more than 7,000fl.' per year – a barely credible figure for Siegl. Using their own calculations of average business expenses including a respectable *bürgerlicher* profit for bakers, the magistrate commission went on to calculate expenses, profit margins and possible bread weights and prices.

Most significantly, the *bürgerliche* profit allowed by the clerks structurally resembled those figures that had been constituted under the assize before 1860. While producers were granted a profit of 13 per cent per 100 kilograms of flour for the production of premium *Kaiser* rolls, only 7 per cent were allowed in the cases of second-grade *Mundsemmeln*, wheat bread and rye bread. In so doing, by 1885 the notion of the market department quite resembled that of the assize authorities of bygone decades in assigning higher profits on upper-class items to limit margins on the products bought by those less well-off. Based on these figures, the commission officially took note of the variety of roll and bread prices between

---

144. *Das Vaterland. Zeitung für die österreichische Monarchie*, 'Das tägliche Brod', 4 July 1885, 181, 2. Emphasis in Original.

the city's bakers and came to believe this situation was unjustified. According to the market department's calculations assuming such 'acceptable' profits for producers, the bakers would be able to produce *Kaiser* rolls at 67 grams a piece compared to the current average of 53 grams and *Mund* rolls of 91 grams versus the present 72-gram average. One kilogram of white bread would then be 14.6 Kreuzer instead of the actual average of 19 Kreuzer; mixed wheat and rye bread 12.5 Kreuzer instead of 14.7 Kreuzer per kilo and the price of rye bread could decline from the average of 12.3 Kreuzer per kilogram to 12 Kreuzer and still provide bakers with a decent income.

Given the minimal decrease of rye bread prices and the fact that not all bakers produced too small rolls, the introduction of the assize did not seem a plausible solution to the rapporteur. While 'the regulation of prices can be left to the competition of supply and demand', the referent instead pushed to finally implement the price transparency measures discussed partly for decades. Concluding his expert statement before the magistrate, Siegl presented seven magistrate propositions to be passed by the city council:

1. Bread should only be sold according to fixed-weight loaves of between 0.5 and three kilograms, respectively. Uniform recipes were to be used since otherwise any comparison would be 'not possible' and it was to be defined 'what is understood under white, mixed dark bread'. Both the weight and the baker's mark were to be punched into the loaf. Further, the *Kaiser* roll was to be standardized at 60 grams and the second-grade *Mund* roll at 80 grams apiece. Implementation was to be realized through 'force' to 'eliminate [...] the significant weight differences'.
2. The regulation applied to all bread sold in the city. While producers 'from afar' were spared to mark their products, outskirt bakers as well as grocers and hawkers were particularly included into the measure.
3. Due to these products' 'economic importance [...] for the family' and especially the poor, bakers were to be obliged to reintroduce rolls worth one Kreuzer, which they had terminated during the 1860s and early 1870s.
4. Clear price and weight information including minimal weights and, if applicable, the original producer's name and address was to be displayed in all bakeries and grocer's shops as well as to be carried by itinerant retailers.
5. The market department was to collect flour prices and production costs to calculate norm prices and weights for all products as a means for consumer orientation, and baking trials should be carried out if necessary to command up-to-date information.
6. The *Marktamt* was to publish current market prices and weights as well as official norm figures fortnightly in accumulated form per district, without individual names, and
7. These tables were to be submitted to the newspapers for usage ad libitum.[145]

---

145. Magistrat der Stadt Wien, Regelung der Brotfrage, 6–7.

Secretary Siegl's report before the magistrate was followed by a short debate in which several members wondered whether the re-introduction of the assize would not be an even better solution. Yet, *Marktamt* director Zecha and director-adjunct Kainz fervently opposed this measure.[146] 'The introduction of maximal prices regarding the sale of bread, meat, and coal would be possible and beyond doubt beneficial for consumers,' Kainz would point out several years later retrospectively:

> However, in the currently prevailing economic ideology, according to which the total freedom of trade and commerce is viewed as the most certain remedy against arbitrary price raises and the autonomy of prices is perceived as the sacrosanct right of businessmen, it would be very hard to reach an agreement between authorities and businesspeople with regard to finding a secure basis for the creation of maximal prices (the assize).[147]

Relying on the market department's expertise, the magistrate passed all seven motions by late July 1885.[148] Some ten months later, on 7 May 1886, Vienna's city council approved and passed these motions, too, including the publication of price tables with the bakers' names and addresses.[149] Pushing for wide-scale re-regulation partly relying on former assize mechanisms, Vienna's urban administration decided to turn away from most of the free-market relations in case of bread and finally accomplish the 'end of the bread question', a quarter-century after liberalization had abolished most market laws.[150]

Epilogue: The bread question solved

'At the present way of selling bread the consumers are left in the dark,' *Marktamt* director Karl Kainz stated in late 1897 before the *Ständige Wiener Approvisionirungs-Conferenz*, founded in 1895:

> The present way of selling bread is [...] detrimental for the middle-class household [...]. In the case of every other item of daily necessity, there is a clear price per unit, weight, or piece; one knows exactly how much the product is, where it is cheapest. [...] Only in the case of bread an economic calculus is

---

146. Magistrat der Stadt Wien, Regelung der Brotfrage, Abstimmungsprotokoll.

147. Wiener Stadt- und Landesarchiv, Marktamt, A2/1: Approvisionierung (Lebensmittel-Teuerung), 27.01.1892: Marktamt. Markt-Commissariats-Äußerung.

148. Magistrat der Stadt Wien, Regelung der Brotfrage, Abstimmungsprotokoll.

149. *Das Vaterland. Zeitung für die österreichische Monarchie*, 'Wiener Gemeinderath. (Sitzung vom 7. Mai.)', 8 May 1886, 127, 6.

150. *Das Vaterland. Zeitung für die österreichische Monarchie*, 'Das Ende der Brodfrage', 30 July 1885, 207.

impossible, it is bought per loaf based on visual judgement. […] If this present way to sell bread continues the authorities will not be able to determine the right state of bread prices and the population is exposed to fraud and deception. […] The consumers cannot judge about the coherence of the price of bread.[151]

Despite of the passing of a comprehensive array of regulation by Vienna's administration in 1885, by the last years of the century the market department still felt the need to push for the thorough implementation of and adherence to the directives struggled over for decades. Neither had the bakers adopted sales according to standard weight nor had they accepted to introduce standard bread qualities; bread was too expensive compared to flour prices, great weight and price differences continued to exist, and consumers remained 'used to buy bread in full loafs, in which it looks appetizing and keeps fresh', the market department director summarized the long-standing matter. Indeed, Kainz concluded his presentation before the commission with largely the same applications to the national government Vienna's magistrate and city council had already passed a decade earlier, plus the proposal to build a municipal bread factory so the city could finally intervene directly into the trade.[152]

Kainz's 1897 report highlighted how complex a solution of the bread question proved, how resilient bakers and partly consumers were in opposing a reform, and how astonishingly incapable to push through directives the urban administration remained for almost half a century in this matter. To be sure, the Bakers' Association had viciously protested the renewed attempt at regulation of 1885/1886. Already in late August 1885, just after the magistrate had passed Secretary Siegl's seven proposals, the bakers had petitioned and pressed the city council not to approve.[153] When the council did approve the magistrate's motion in May 1886, the association came together in a full assembly in which fierce opposition and 'most irritated charges' against both the legislation and the legislating bodies were expressed. The assembly unanimously passed a 'resolution' in which the regulation was declared an 'unlawful intervention in the freedom of trade' and the association determined to apply 'all lawful means' against the reform.[154] By 1890, the debate had reached

---

151. Wiener Stadt- und Landesarchiv, Marktamt, A2/1: Brotfrage, 02.12.1897: Marktamt. Referat über die Brodfrage für die 9. Sitzung der Approvisionirungs-Conferenz am 21/12 1897.

152. Ibid.

153. *Das Vaterland. Zeitung für die österreichische Monarchie*, 'Die Vorstellung der Bäcker an das Gemeinderaths-Präsidium', 26 August 1885, 233.

154. *Neues Wiener Tagblatt*, 'Die Bäcker gegen den Gemeinderath', 23 May 1886, 142; *Neue Freie Presse*, 'Zur Brodfrage', 23 May 1886, 7808, 6; *Das Vaterland. Zeitung für die österreichische Monarchie*, 'Die Resolution der Wiener Bäcker', 11 June 1886, 161, 1; *Das Vaterland. Zeitung für die österreichische Monarchie*, 'Die Resolution der Wiener Bäcker (Schluß)', 12 June 1886, 162, 1.

the Imperial Council's House of Deputies, where 'a voice has been raised against the "bakers' cartel"' criticizing the magistrate's ineptitude, the bakers' denial of all regulations and their 'uncontrollable profits'.[155] A year later, the imperial government was urged to push through the reform 'universally and obligatory'.[156] In late November 1891, even the Chamber of Commerce recommended to push through the reforms passed already in 1872, 1875 and 1885/1886 by magistrate and city council.[157] Yet, as Kainz's report shows, no final solution was agreed upon by the last years of the century. Indeed, only the First World War and the shortages induced by warfare would deliver a lasting solution. Issued in late 1914 and early 1915, Vienna's municipality, the Ministry of Trade and the Interior Ministry announced wide-ranging regulations of the bread market including sale of bread 'in pieces', the limitation of commissions paid to intermediaries as well as the standardized use of various kinds of flour and officially fixed prices, weights and forms of bread and rolls.[158] After 1918, a certain kind of weight and price regulation at least of parts of the bread market would remain in place until 1992.[159] However, this is another story.

Conclusion

Part III has examined the effects of liberalization and the abolition of the assize and its disciplinary mechanisms in 1860 on the landscape of bread in Vienna, on the price structure of bread, and on the public debates and market policies unfolding in the quarter century to come.

By the last two decades of the nineteenth century, the free market landscape of bread had tremendously affected the locations where and how the residents of the Austrian capital would buy their daily bread. Liberalization and the abolition of most disciplinary measures embedding the bread market before 1860 intensified and accelerated a mobilization and diversification of Vienna's landscape of bread along three major lines: the expansion of the bread landscape within the city and even more pronounced in the unfolding and urbanizing outskirt districts; the diversification of urban and 'country' bakers into an urban wheat and a 'country' rye bread supply system; and the social differentiation of bread distribution into the three distinct spaces besides marketplaces: the baker's shop, the grocer's store, and the city's streets, doorways and hallways. Some aspects of mobilization

---

155. *Die Presse*, 'Brodverkauf nach Gewicht', 18 May 1890, 136.

156. *Die Presse*, 'Brodverkauf nach Gewicht', 2 July 1891, 200.

157. *Wiener Zeitung*, 'Aus den Verhandlungen der Handels- und gewerbekammer in Wien. Sitzung am 26. November 1891', 12 January 1892, 8, 7.

158. Österreichische Nationalbibliothek, KS 16215321: Handelsministerium; Österreichische Nationalbibliothek, KS 16215134: Magistrat der Stadt Wien.

159. Norbert Wimmer and Thomas Müller, *Wirtschaftsrecht: International – europäisch – national* (Wien: Springer, 2007), 27.

induced by the free-market landscape can be regarded as innovations caused by liberalization. The structural opening of the baker's trade for population groups previously discriminated by the guild system, the large-scale legalization of often impoverished itinerant retailers, or the socialized redefinition of retail spaces into bakery shop, grocer's store and the street – arguably deeply connected to class, income and other factors of social inequality – are cases in point.

Yet, the free market landscape of bread did stand on the shoulders of a giant, its municipal predecessor. Other developments accelerated by the 1859/60 reform were deeply rooted in the socioeconomic environment of bread assize, guild structure and market laws. This was most notably the case regarding the diversification of production into two rather specialized circles of provisioning between urban and 'country' bakers. As the continuity of bakery locations and workshops highlights, the free market was not superimposed on a clean sheet but on a landscape produced, reproduced and embedded in the distinct logics of the moral-economy mechanisms of embeddedness as well as into the urban fabric. Significantly, free-market deregulation did not shuffle the board regarding the existing geography of baking, on the contrary. Most bakeries that had existed before 1860, even before 1815, remained workshops dedicated to the production of bread and rolls throughout the century. In this perspective, the landscape of bread proved highly resilient to deregulation. This was not the case because it was not compatible with the changed politico-economic circumstances of free competition but distinctly because it had operated in accordance with the rules of profit maximization through spatial competition and the occupation of privileged spaces anyway. On both sides of the legislatory gulf of 1860, centrality was key for bakers and retailers generally to 'intercept potential customers and entice them in more or less sophisticated ways to make purchases. Indeed, accessibility was, and still is, the crucial factor in the location of retail activities'.[160]

All in all, by the 1880s and 1890s, consumers would negotiate a thoroughly complex, anthill-like landscape of bread in Vienna. This landscape was produced and reproduced by a diverse group of actors in a dense, citywide network consisting of hundreds of bakeries often run with the hard and even precarious labour of bakery workers. Then, thousands of grocers' shops supplemented by an uncountable number of highly mobile itinerant traders, who would more often than not find themselves at the bottom of the urban society, offered even more access points for the benefit of consumers, at least in spatial terms. Whereas the municipal landscape of bread had thus offered a relatively clear-cut, rather well-regulated range of opportunities to buy bread from a baker, the free-market landscape presented consumers with more, albeit socially and economically

---

160. Clé Lesger and Jan H. Furnée, 'Shopping Streets and Cultures from a Long-Term Perspective: An Introduction', in *The Landscape of Consumption: Shopping Streets and Cultures in Western Europe, 1600–1900*, ed. Jan H. Furnée and Clé Lesger (Basingstoke, Hampshire: Palgrave Macmillan, 2014), 3.

distinct ways to purchase the stuff of life. Thus, the retail of bread had to some degree 'fragmented from a tightly managed world' of the municipal landscape of bread with its privileged master bakers working within the clear-cut frameworks of assize, guild and market laws 'into a free-for-all landscape of private retailers' much less limited by regulatory frameworks.[161]

Consumers likely benefitted from the mobility and spatial flexibility the landscape of bread and the shopping infrastructure certainly won through deregulation, at least in terms of walking distances, reachable access points and maybe even shopping convenience. Yet, the diversification between rye bread 'country' bakers and wheat bread city artisans inaugurated during the first half of the century and intensified after 1860 also rearticulated the meaning of space within Vienna's landscape of bread. Space had largely been an issue of general access and availability of bread, which the municipal regime strove to address fundamentally and successfully by expanding the network of bakeries across town and ensuring exhaustive access points before 1860. Meanwhile, space had been much less an issue of the kinds of products available for consumers since the product range was thoroughly regulated and specified by the assize. Liberalization turned that issue around. Secured especially through the legalization of mobile retailers, space became less important regarding the general access to bread. However, with the abolishment of assize production requirements and, concurrently, the accelerating diversification between rye-bread 'country' and wheat-roll urban bakers, space increasingly defined what kinds of bakery products could be bought in different parts of the city and through which retail channels. While residents of the districts within the *Linienwall* would find mainly wheat products on their bakers' shelves and could also buy rye bread from itinerant peddlers, the inhabitants of the overwhelmingly poorer outskirt parishes beyond the *Linienwall* would much rather find rye-based baked goods in the shops closest to their dwellings and in the sacks of hawkers. While space had largely stopped to affect if residents had geographic access to bread at all, by the late nineteenth century space had come to influence the kinds of products available to different income classes in diverse parts of the city. Liberalization thus, like in New York City, fostered the 'segmentation of food access by income', at least to some degree.[162]

Therefore, the mobility, flexibility and spatial comprehensiveness provided by the free-market landscape of bread did come at a price. Although easing and contributing to the solution of some challenges accelerating urbanization and population growth presented to the bread supply of the capital of the Habsburg Empire, free competition failed to deliver the common good in other aspects of the food economy. In some cases, deregulation exacerbated existing issues; in other cases it created new 'bread questions', especially regarding food quality and food security.

161. Gergely Baics, *Feeding Gotham: The Political Economy and Geography of Food in New York, 1790–1860* (Princeton, Oxford: Princeton University Press, 2016), 9.
162. Ibid., 229.

In this perspective, eliminating the assize with its inbuilt welfare mechanism of cross-subsidization contributed to a relative decrease in the price of wheat products vis-à-vis rye bread. On the one hand, this arguably enabled the unfolding middle class to alter diets from rye and coarser rye-wheat mixed products to more wheat-only baked goods, although probably of lower-quality white bread. On the other hand, however, consumers depending on cheaper kinds of bread made from rye came in last to exploit and enjoy the benefits of free-market bread prices after 1849/1860. Compared to rye bread prices before 1860, when cross-subsidization had maintained a certain level of price stability for the poorest paid for by more affluent consumers, the elimination of officially controlled and calculated prices terminated this disciplinary mechanism ensuring public welfare and access to basic goods for those on the bottom of the income spheres.

Before liberalization, the assize had maintained a relation between wheat and bread that was rather complementary than competitive. The removal of such an institutional setting reoriented this relationship. Now, free-market prices determined the interplay of fancy rolls and bulky rye bread loaves. Laissez-faire after 1860 thus ended a public institution of solidarity, mostly at the benefit of wealthier strata of Vienna's society. These were enabled to improve their diets and living standards through relatively cheaper wheat prices relieved from solidary surcharges levied on premium products before. At the same time, less affluent consumers lost this implicit institution of societal redistribution ensuring a certain level of subsidies on everyday necessities. Judged optimistically, unregulated prices might have enabled a democratization of wheat bread consumption for many, yet it did so on the back of those still depended on cheaper rye bread. Pessimistically interpreted, the free market lowered the costs of fancy bread and pasty eating for the privileged few whereas it increased the expenses tied to the basic need of the less privileged many. Following the latter interpretation, although all consumers were hit by rising food costs during the second half of the nineteenth century, relatively speaking, poorer inhabitants were hit the hardest as the costs of eating cheap bread increased more than the expenses necessary to buy wheat rolls. Therefore, by and large, the *wheatification* of diets was partly paid for by those reduced to rye. Free-market prices of bread largely benefitted the better-off parts of the urban society and contributed to rising inequality in the bakery and on the table.

Although not directly addressing cross-subsidization as an assize mechanism, parts of Vienna's administration recognized the consequences of self-determined prices very early on. Debates about a perceived misalignment as well as a lack of market information and price transparency – the key matters around which the bread question would continue to revolve for the following decades – were already held weeks *before* the assize was eliminated. Discussions accelerated over the following year, just months after liberalization, as officials increasingly came to consider that under the free-market regime the pricing of bread had become much more opaque. Central to that problem was the continuation of the habitual way of selling bread and rolls at fixed prices and moving weights, like the assize had prescribed. Whereas price changes of grain had been translated into weight changes via official calculation before 1860, now bakers could legally reduce bread weights freely, by amounts of their own choosing. Without official guidelines, Vienna's market department and especially Karl Kainz, one of the leading figures of the city's provision administration, came to believe consumers would neither recognize small weight reductions nor be able to make a case against a baker on whom they depended on for their daily bread. Further, even if they identified weight reductions, consumers also lacked information on raw material prices, production costs, flour-to-bread yields etc. to judge whether price and weight movements were 'appropriate'. Whereas exactly that information and such price movements had been subject to the assize and thus subject of public, institutional intervention, the elimination of regulated prices individualized the assessment of the bread price and left consumers to fend for themselves. In turn, a reform geared to change this practice into selling fixed-weight, standardized loaves at varying prices per kilogram would make it impossible for bakers to impose hidden increases by baking smaller loaves. It would make price movements easily detectable and the purchase of bread transparent again.

The bread question thus became a quest for transparency, knowledge and equal bargaining power between authorities, bakers and consumers from the early 1870s, when the ideological opposition against intervention and in favour of laissez-faire policies weakened. By the beginning of the 1870s various experts and administrators grew ever wearier and more concerned not only about the growing asymmetry of knowledge between consumers and bakers, but also about the growing asymmetry and variety of products Vienna's bakers produced and sold in different ways. In these interconnected issues, the authorities sensed a growing variety in products offered between bread shops and an opacity in the prices, qualities and quantities of bread consumers would experience when visiting a baker's. Over the following years, the experts' weariness was taken up by the press and grew into a rather prominent public debate at the local level. Especially, though not exclusively conservative newspapers engaged in an accelerating campaign against free-market relations and in favour of new regulations in the case of bread. Against the background of such accelerating criticism of the state of the bread question in particular and waning public faith in free-market ideologies more generally, Vienna's market authorities increasingly came to believe that free competition was not suited to provide transparency and cheap bread prices for consumers. Between the mid-1870s and mid-1880s, the notion that structural institutional market information was necessary to provide consumers with knowledge enabling them to make informed individual choices came to prevail. Therefore, the last decades of the century were shaped by a fierce struggle between parts of the urban administration, most notably the *Marktamt* and bakers as well as the liberal and the conservative press over the reintroduction of legislation aimed to reintroduce market information and a system of reference framing the free bread market.

Yet, official attempts at reform faced strong resistance by bakers and partly by consumers. Ironically, in the free-market environment of selling bread the bakers had come into the situation to realize higher profits by sticking to the old way of selling bread and rolls at moving weights and fixed prices – a prescription originally intended to ensure price transparency. As deregulation had eliminated the effective control of weight movements, this function was turned into the opposite. Now bakers were enabled to hide price increases in changing bodies of bread that could be reduced largely at will by the producer, Vienna's authorities came to assume. At the same time, consumers seemed reluctant to accept a free-market mode of buying bread instead of the moral-economy way that had ensured access to bread for everyone.

This general pursuit to introduce new regulation exemplified how deeply involved parts of the city's administration remained in notions of fairness and justice when it came to matters of basic necessities. Accordingly, the quest for the 'right' price of bread became the centrepiece of the bread question after 1875. On the one hand, the authorities aimed to gain professional insights to constitute the costs of bread production to judge price movements and to find the right policy to solve the bread question. On the other hand, the bakers fiercely tried to protect their expert knowledge of bread production and exclusive know-how giving them a most valuable advantage on the free market. In principle, these attempts by the market department and other urban bodies mirrored the squabbles Vienna's administrations and bakers had cultivated for generations before 1860 to establish the 'typical' baker's business, turnover, profits and the just price of bread in the moral economy. The peak debate over the bread question unfolded throughout 1885 particularly over these issues, leading the market department, the magistrate and the city council to push for and pass wide-scale re-regulation partly relying on former assize mechanisms. Thus, Vienna's urban administration decided to turn away from most of the free-market relations in case of bread a quarter century after liberalization had abolished most market laws governing the prices and forms of the stuff of life.

However, despite the similarity of the 1885 regulations to those institutionalized by the disciplinary mechanisms of the assize before 1860, the new regulation was of a quite different nature. Contrary to the decisive intervention into the bread market through official price and weight fixation that enabled consumers to negotiate a market moderated and checked beforehand, the regulative measures passed towards the end of the century aimed to provide consumers with the means and capabilities to negotiate a largely unfettered market self-responsibly. In this environment, the target of policies was not the market itself. Rather, it was consumers and bread that needed to be addressed by providing a framework *for* the bread market instead of interfering *into* the market directly. This represented a sea change in the way of governing. The reintroduction of regulation in 1872, 1875 and 1885 was not a mere return to disciplinary mechanisms – it meant attempts to introduce security mechanisms to the bread market in Vienna. This was the gradual birth of biopolitics of bread in the capital of the Habsburg Empire. Now, the authorities aimed less to discipline the market to ensure good and enough bread supplies for all and produce the public good. Instead, the new regulation was geared to provide security mechanisms and technologies of the self to enable self-responsible consumers in the city to make informed and rational choices on their own to distinguish good rolls from bad ones and cheap bread from expensive loaves.

CONCLUSION

BIOPOLITICS OF BREAD

Drawing on the framework provided by Karl Polanyi, E.P. Thompson and Michel Foucault, the preceding chapters have carved out the transformation from moral to market economies of bread in Vienna between 1775 and 1885. Before 1860, producing and selling bread in the Habsburg Capital was deeply embedded into a moral economy of bread access that exceeded the character of a notion of the crowd. Rather, the moral economy as a politico-economic and cultural framework of both a baseline solidarity and a means of the legitimization of government was institutionalized through complex and comprehensive disciplinary mechanisms weaved deep into the fabric of the system of urban bread supply. Embodied by thorough market laws and the guild, these mechanisms fundamentally disciplined the behaviour of the people involved in the production, sales and purchase of this item of first necessity. Personified through the assize of bread, they inherently disciplined the bodies and prices of bread, too. In both cases, market laws, the guild and the assize clearly defined and distinguished between right and wrong, between allowed and forbidden, between good and poor bread, between fair and dear prices. Essentially, by including cross-subsidization between rye and wheat products the assize encompassed one of the most important, though rather hidden mechanism of the moral economy. Nevertheless a messy and chaotic patchwork rug teeming with self-involved individuals, diverging interests, conflicts and infringements, the disciplinary mechanisms also embraced the spatial arrangements of baking and buying bread and created a distinct, regulated and comprehensive landscape of bread in the capital of the Habsburg Empire. Thorough public intervention into the market determined not only what kind of bakery products Vienna's inhabitants could purchase at what price and produced by whom, but also where bread and rolls could be sold and bought. Although agency from below abounded, under the moral economy of bread disciplinary mechanisms profoundly regulated the places, people and products involved in the making of the landscape of the prime non-market good, bread. All these disciplinary mechanisms were created and maintained on the elementary societal conception of bread as a good the access to which everyone shared a basic entitlement and by which nobody should profit unproportionally, at the expense of others.

By the late eighteenth century, both ideational as well as politico-economic and natural-technological changes began to question the moral economy institutionalized by disciplinary mechanisms of market regulation. The ideational notion of bread as a good not to be subjected to the market was contested by physiocrat-inspired market-liberal theorists. These liberal thinkers not only aimed to reconfigure the meaning of bread as a commodity, they aimed at an even larger reconfiguration of the market's place and meaning in society. As the market should be turned from a place where justice needed to be ensured politically based on moral notions into the place of societal veridiction where the free and unhindered convention of self-interest would produce the common good, grain and bread as the heavily regulated off-market goods par excellence became the main targets of attempts at liberalization during the 1780s. Especially Joseph II's government introduced quite radical steps of deregulation to Vienna's bread and grain market. However, by the last years of the decade drastic price increases, war with the Ottoman Empire, a significant bread riot and eventually the French Revolution put a stop to these efforts and liberalization was largely revoked.

At the same time, around the late eighteenth and early nineteenth centuries the practical settings of the assize apparatus were challenged by the expansion of the grain market and the natural-physical implications of different varieties of cereals arriving in the region's mills. State-fostered colonialization of the eastern internal peripheries of the empire had promoted and facilitated the expansion of wheat production since the early 1700s; at the turn of the century, war-induced demand triggered both increased grain production and an expansion and integration of the empire's grain market. Since ever-growing amounts of hard red steppe wheat were shipped up the Danube from the late 1700s, millers and bakers in the capital's vicinity began to adapt and improve the techniques of flour production based on the Hungarian wheat's superior physical conditions. When this fostered the industrialization and capitalization of the milling sector, which was also liberalized from stronger regulation by the 1810s, the flour products coming out of the region's mills diversified and improved in quality. Consequently, by the end of the first third of the century, observers noted that these developments had introduced tangible changes in the day-to-day realities of trading grain, turning cereal into flour and baking meal into bread and rolls. As such changes were recognized to challenge the basic settings of Vienna's assize, proponents of a new economic-liberal order clashed with defendants of the moral economy on both the larger issue of freedom of trade and commerce and on the specific issue of Vienna's bread assize before 1848.

Around 1830, reform proposals from below sketched out far-ranging options for a regulative reform. Rather than eliminate the disciplinary measures of the assize, these local urban attempts at a reform of the regulations would have expanded the assize apparatus regarding space – the marketplaces subjected to price documentation – and concerning the range and standardization of products involved. Deemed unfeasible at least by some experts at that time and apparently in opposition to increasing voices arguing for laissez-faire, in hindsight it seems such a reform could have been a serious alternative to liberalization, which by no means was the only way to proceed by 1848. Within a somewhat different political climate more prone to push through larger reforms, a regulative reform and an expansion of Vienna's local assize mechanism might have been a feasible, though certainly extensive option.

However, while the political circumstances remained rather reform-adverse before 1848, the political alterations in the aftermath of the March Revolution created an environment more fertile for reform. In the new political bodies of the urban government, liberalization was seen as a promising way to introduce a tabula rasa reform regarding the assize, deemed too complex and complicated to correct. Consequently, the elimination of the assize on wheat products in 1849 was pushed through with dramatic speed, moving *Semmel* rolls and other more luxurious baked goods into the sphere of the free market and commodifying this segment of bakery products thoroughly. However, such an abolition of the moral economy institutions was by no means without alternative and unquestioned. Intellectual currents aiming at a broad reconfiguration of market and society at large had grown more dominant over the previous decades. Yet, liberalization in 1849 was first implemented for rather pragmatic reasons of daily food provision in the context of political-economic upheaval, and it was essentially interpreted as having to prove its value by way of trial and error. Moreover, whereas wheat products were declared market commodities by 1849, rye remained under the umbrella of the moral economy as the politicians in charge on Vienna's municipal parquet considered it unsuited for marketization. As a fundamental daily necessity of the poor, rye bread crucially remained outside the free market for another decade. Only by the late 1850s, when Manchesterian freedom of commerce was pushed through on the imperial level, the assize on rye bread in Vienna was lifted because it was deemed incompatible with the general law. Thus, by 1860, most of the crucial parts of disciplinary mechanisms embedding bread into the moral economy were eliminated and bread was given over to a largely unregulated, free market. Having been a non-commodity probably for centuries, after 1780 little more than half a century of intellectual reconfiguration and a mere decade of political implementation forged bread into a commodity fundamentally subjected to the laws of the market as place of veridiction instead of the moral notions of society.

The consequences of liberalization were sincere, yet heterogeneous. On the one hand, deregulation did energize, mobilize and diversify Vienna's landscape of bread in spatial terms. When freedom of trade abolished most limitations to enter the baking trade and open a workshop, the number of bakeries as well as those of itinerant traders soared across town and especially in the growing and urbanizing communities forming the capital's periphery. Although the increase in access points was much faster than during the previous decades, the free-market landscape of bread stood on the shoulders of a giant. Over the course of the *Vormärz* period, the municipal landscape of bread had expanded decisively and seems to have been rather well equipped to meet the quick urban population growth after 1815. In any case, the liberalization of 1860 reinforced a development that rooted in the liberalization of the 1780s; the diversification of the agglomeration's bread landscape into two separate, rather complementary than competitive infrastructures of bread production. While 'country' bakers in the city's more rural environments exercised economic advantages in the production of rye bread and came to dominate Vienna's supply with such products, the urban bakers increasingly specialized on the production of wheaten products. Therefore, on the other hand, another consequence of market deregulation was that space – which had played a minor role in the municipal landscape – became a much more important factor for the resident's accesibility to bread. Whereas the locations of bakeries with their thoroughly regulated product range had been deliberately spread over the urban territory before 1860, deregulation contributed to the creation of a separation of the agglomeration in terms of what kinds of bread consumers would find on their baker's shelves. While residents of the more urbanized and partly better-off parts of town could expect to find primarily wheat products at their neighbourhood bread shops, the rather poorer inhabitants of the more peripheral communities of the agglomeration were much more likely to live close to a bakery producing more rye bread. Certainly, while this separation was far from total, liberalization introduced space as a socio-economic factor for the urbanites' access to different qualities of bread. Whereas the municipal landscape had seen that bakers offered a broad and balanced range of baked goods all across town, the free market landscape at least attenuated this setting and contributed to spatializing inequality.

While rather contributing to spatial inequality in terms of the geographic access to bread, deregulation clearly facilitated inequality among consumers by eliminating cross-subsidization between wheat and rye products. Whereas the former had usually been taxed extra and made more expensive than market prices would have necessitated, the latter's price was thus subsidized by this remarkable institution of solidarity built into the assize. By so doing, wheat and rye products had not competed in terms of prices before 1848/60; rather, the prices of both these goods had been inherently connected and cemented into a complementary relation. In contrast, deregulation made wheat- and rye-baked goods direct competitors on the free market. Essentially, by the abolition of solidary surcharges on wheat, these products could become decisively cheaper compared to rye bread. In relative terms, eating wheat rolls became significantly cheaper after 1860 than eating rye bread. In other words, by losing the subsidies on their daily bread, the poorest strata of consumers reduced to large rye loaves came to subsidize the increasing consumption of those able to purchase fancy wheat rolls. Thus, deregulation might have improved the number and geographical dispersion of access points – bakeries, grocers and peddlers. Yet, it also contributed to rising inequality both between those shops and within the bakery.

Whereas such consequences rather unfolding in relative terms apparently hardly concerned the city's administrators, absolute price increases observed throughout the decades after 1860 became much more of an issue for municipal and market department authorities. Expressed either in real increases of prices, in the diminution of rolls and loaves, in the reshaping of the bodies of bread and rolls or even the disappearance of entire product categories partly deemed essential for poor consumers, the issues of opaque bread prices, intransparent market procedures and diverging positions of power of producers and consumers on the free market became the major concern of municipal regulators. By the early

1870s, some ten years after liberalization, the rather positive attitude towards free-market relations regarding the city's bread supply was replaced by a more sceptic outlook, especially among the clerks of Vienna's market department. Proving they still held certain notions of bread as a specific good from which profits should not exceed an acceptable level, the market department and other members of the public increasingly felt that the free market advantaged producers through their superior knowledge vis-à-vis consumers, especially with regard to the pricing of bread. Believing more and more that the bakers' profits exceeded publicly acceptable levels and that the association continued to resist to help provide market transparency and knowledge, already by the early 1870s Vienna's urban authorities came to regard the free market as detrimental to the common good in this particular case, and that some form of political intervention was necessary. Over the following two decades, market department, city council, the press and the bakers struggled to introduce institutional arrangements to create structural market information available to both producers and consumers. At the heart of these intensive struggles was the public knowledge about the art of baking, the pricing of bread and product standardization. Although the day-to-day realization appears to have been hardly thorough and was met with fierce resistance especially by bakers, over the course of the 1870s, 1880s and even the 1890s Vienna's urban governments repeatedly introduced legislation aimed to provide such legal frameworks intervening into the free bread market. These efforts represented the countermovement.

However, it was no countermovement against the self-regulated market as Karl Polanyi would have it. To describe the efforts to 'tame' the self-regulated market as place of societal veridiction Michel Foucault's concept of biopolitics, involving security measures and technologies of the self, is much more fine-grained and suited. It also contradicts Polanyi's notion of a countermovement against marketization. Essentially, although certainly a thin line partly crossed and often hardly discernible, the legislation introduced to the bread market in Vienna in 1872, 1875 and 1885 was much less dominated by disciplinary measures intervening into the market and regulating it according to public-political-moral notions. Rather, the attempts to gain public knowledge over the baking and pricing of bread, to provide public price information via the press and to generate options for comparison via standard bread loaves and rolls were security measures par excellence. By providing such information and guidelines to administrators and consumers, these efforts represented security measures that should enable technologies of the self. This meant to provide consumers with the knowledge and ability to negotiate the self-regulated veridictive market on their own, without deep regulative intervention for which the government would be responsible. By giving consumers knowledge to judge the prices of bread, by providing product standards and by publicizing all bakers' prices, consumers would be enabled to compare one baker's offer with another's and decide for themselves which offer was best, which bread was good or bad, cheap or expensive. That way, they would be able to make informed, self-determined and self-responsible decisions on a free, chaotic and hardly controllable market. Inherently, these measures tackled people and bread much more than they tackled the market itself.

Therefore, these biopolitics of bread were much more a co-movement than a countermovement; they were not against the self-regulated veridictive market but functioned essentially within the logic of the market as an institution producing its own truth. The biopolitical co-movement did not represent external resistance to bind the market and subject it under processes determining values outside the market. It was an attempt to meet the shortcomings of the free market from within. It is noteworthy that, in contrast to Foucault's assumptions, these security measures as biopolitical co-movement were developed and struggled over *after* administrators had observed a hardly regulated market for several years and concluded a free market was detrimental. These measures were not created in advance but based on such a recognition. Furthermore, especially producers continued to oppose and resist such measures strongly; they tried to protect their information advantage vis-à-vis authorities and consumers.

In any case, rather than binding the market according to public concerns, rather than directly intervening as a Leviathan on behalf of passive subjects, rather than stamping public-moral notions generated *outside* the market onto it, subjects – consumers – should be enabled to roam the free market, to defend and realize their interests as empowered participants on their own, to dispose of the means to be self-responsible, to create public-moral notions and truth *on* the market. While providing such means, no government would then be responsible for the individual fates of subjects or for any results of large-scale intervention. As a fundamental alteration in the concept of market, subject and politics, this represented a sea change in the policy of governing Vienna's bread market.

By way of conclusion, in the small golden wheat rolls and the large brown rye loaves caraway and cobwebs, flour and fleas, salt and sweat, water and worse were blended to form the bread so central and so ordinary to the daily life of everyone. At the same time, these bodies of bread were just as much formed through the blending and kneading together of culture, economy, nature and politics, which would shape the appearances, contents, forms, tastes and prices of bread. Certainly, nature and technology affected the physical conditions of rolls and loaves; culture gave meaning to the forms, locations and habits of bread consumption. Still, economics and politics equally affected how bread looked like, where different kinds of it were produced, bought and eaten by whom, and at what price. Therefore, market regimes directly influenced not only the consumption but the very forms of bread in Vienna. By 1885, the self-regulated market appeared on the shelves of ordinary bakeries, where it had transformed the range of the products available. Consumers might have visited the same bakery location their ancestors would have bought bread when Napoleon had resided in Vienna's Schönnbrun palace almost a century ago. Yet, while some products certainly endured as multifaceted affiliations towards forms, weights and prices equally contributed and retained to carry meaning, many kinds of bread and rolls available would be distinctly different. This was, though certainly not exclusively, a result of the oscillation between moral and market economies of bread in Vienna between 1775 and 1885.

BIBLIOGRAPHY

Archival Sources

Archiv der Bäckergenossenschaft in Wien. HS 2: Innung der bürgerl. Bäckermeister in der k.k. Haupt – und Residenzstadt Wien. Aufding – und Freisprech-Protokoll 1824–1858.
Archiv der Bäckergenossenschaft in Wien. HS 16/2: Innung der bürgerl. Bäckermeister in der k.k. Haupt – und Residenzstadt Wien. Gesetze und Verordnungen von 1853 bis 1868. Exhibiten.
Archiv der Bäckergenossenschaft in Wien. HS 9: Innung der bürgerl. Bäckermeister in der k.k. Haupt – und Residenzstadt Wien. Handwerksprotokolle vom Jahre 1850 bis 1855.
Archiv der Bäckergenossenschaft in Wien: Innung der bürgerl. Bäckermeister in der k.k. Haupt – und Residenzstadt Wien. Kalender für das Gremium der bürgerl. Bäckermeister in der k.k. Haupt – und Residenzstadt Wien.
Archiv der Bäckergenossenschaft in Wien. HS 15: Innung der bürgerl. Bäckermeister in der k.k. Haupt – und Residenzstadt Wien. Protocollum uiber merkwürdige Gegenstände, als: Volksaufruhr gegen die Bäcker anno 1805; die den bürgl Bäckermeister geleisteten Vergütungen; mehrere Backproben; Consignation über die Ausgaben eines mitleren Bäckermeisters; dann der vom Jahre 1807 bis 1830 ergangenen Verordnungen und Rathschläge.
Archiv der Bäckergenossenschaft in Wien. HS 16: Innung der bürgerl. Bäckermeister in der k.k. Haupt – und Residenzstadt Wien. Protokolle über die bei der Bäckerinnung eingelangten Aktenstücke 1834–1868.
Wienbibliothek im Rathaus. A-11304. Die Bäcker in Wien nach ihren Karackter und Verdienst.
Wienbibliothek im Rathaus. A-83171: Rotter, Hans. Die Wiener Bäcker von 1400 bis 1814.
Wiener Stadt – und Landesarchiv: Gemeinderat der Stadt Wien. Protokolle der III. Sektion, 1848–1852.
Wiener Stadt – und Landesarchiv. Vertretungskörper, Gemeinderat B6: Gemeinderat der Stadt Wien. Sitzungsprotokolle: Öffentliche Sitzungen 7.10.1848–8.5.1919.
Wiener Stadt – und Landesarchiv. Zivilgericht, A2, Fasz. 2 – Verlassenschaftsabhandlungen: 1817–432. Verlassenschaftsabhandlung Valentin Sauer.
Wiener Stadt – und Landesarchiv. Innungen und Handelsgremien 1, A1: Akten. Vorschüsse der Stadt an einzelne Meister, 1849–1855.
Wiener Stadt – und Landesarchiv. Alte Registratur A2 – Berichte: 210/1770, 29.07.1769: N.Ö. Regs. Secretär Hägelin. Nota Die von mir Endes gefertigte aufgetragener Massen abgeführte Mahl – und respective Back Probem betreffend.
Wiener Stadt – und Landesarchiv. Marktamt A2/1: Bäckergewerbe: Dekrete, 1793. Verzeichnis der gesamt-hiesigen Bäcker und Ausweiß wie viel jeder derselben an monathlichen Mehlvorrath haben soll.
Wiener Stadt – und Landesarchiv. Marktamt A2/1 – Bäcker: sanitäre Vorschriften, 18.11.1797.

Wiener Stadt – und Landesarchiv. Hauptregistratur A24, Dep. G, 1829, Schachtel 19, 1810/1811: Maria, Johann. Auszug über das von drey Proponenten verfasste ganz neue Vermahlungs und Verbackungs System für die Residenzstadt Wien 808 [Abschrift genommen].

Wiener Stadt – und Landesarchiv. Hauptregistratur A24, Dep. G – Marktsachen, 1812. Schachtel 1.

Wiener Stadt – und Landesarchiv. Serie 1.1.3.2.B1003 (prov.) alt: 301–7 – Erwerbsteuer: Grundbuch 1. Reihe 1828–1861. Erwerbsteuerbücher.

Wiener Stadt – und Landesarchiv. Hauptregistratur A24, Dep. G – Marktsachen, 1829, Schachtel 19, 1828: Maria, Johann. Ideen zu einem, dem Geist der Zeit angemeßenen neuen Mehl und Gebäcks Satzungs Regulativ als Provisorium für die k.k. Residenz Stadt Wien.

Wiener Stadt – und Landesarchiv. Zivilgericht, A2, Fasz. 2 – Verlassenschaftsabhandlungen: 1829–720. Verlassenschaft Johann Gerber.

Wiener Stadt – und Landesarchiv, Hauptregistratur A24, Dep. G – Marktsachen, 1829, Schachtel 19, 04.05.1829: Sittenberger, Wolfgang. Schriftliche Aeusserung des gehorsamsten Metzenleiheramte Uiber den Vorschlag des Bürgers Johann Maria hinsichtlich eines neuen Mehl und Gebäck-Satzungs Regulatives für die kais.könig. Residenzstadt Wien.

Wiener Stadt – und Landesarchiv. Hauptregistratur A24, Dep. G, 1829, Schachtel 19, 1.9.1830: Maria, Johann. Allerunterthänigste Bitte: für den täglich dringender werdenden Fall der Retablierung einer allerhöchsten Hofmommaon in Mahl und Bakgeschäften;; um allergnädigste Verwendung seiner diesfälligen Brauchbarkeit.

Wiener Stadt – und Landesarchiv. Marktamt A2/1 – Bäckergewerbe: Kundmachungen Nr. 18188, 13.02.1850: Magistrat der Stadt Wien.

Wiener Stadt – und Landesarchiv. Marktamt A2/1: Brotfrage, Nr. 6: Innung der bürgerl. Bäckermeister in der k.k. Haupt – und Residenzstadt Wien. Majestätsgesuch.

Wiener Stadt – und Landesarchiv. Marktamt A2/1 – Bäcker: sanitäre Vorschriften Z. 21091, 26.03.1851: Magistrat der Stadt Wien.

Wiener Stadt – und Landesarchiv. Marktamt A2/1 – Bäcker: sanitäre Vorschriften, 08.07.1852: Magistrat der Stadt Wien.

Wiener Stadt – und Landesarchiv. Innungen und Handelsgremien 1/B1: Bäcker: Bücher. Bäckerverzeichnis 1.

Wiener Stadt – und Landesarchiv. Marktamt A2/1: Brot und Gebäcksverkauf nach Gewicht, 17.09.1860: K.K. nö. Statthalterei.

Wiener Stadt – und Landesarchiv. Marktamt A2/1: Brot und Gebäcksverkauf nach Gewicht, Z. 68143, 12.09.1861: Marktamt. Äusserung der Direktion des Marktkommissariates Über den bei dem löblichen Gemeinderathe gestellten Antrag, den Gebäcksverkauf in Wien nach dem Gewichte betreffend.

Wiener Stadt – und Landesarchiv. Marktamt A2/1: Bäckergewerbe: Kundmachungen, 14.05.1870: Magistrat der Stadt Wien.

Wiener Stadt – und Landesarchiv. Marktamt A2/1: Brot und Gebäcksverkauf nach Gewicht, 1106/1871, 31.10.1871: Marktamt. Durchführung des Antrages XI. der Approvsg. Enquete.

Wiener Stadt – und Landesarchiv. Marktamt A2/1: Bäckergewerbe: Kundmachungen, 27.03.1872: K.K. nö. Statthalterei.

Wiener Stadt – und Landesarchiv. Marktamt A2/1: Brot und Gebäck: Probebackung, 190.306/1876, 03.04.1876: Marktamt. Marktdirektion Äusserung Probebackung.

Wiener Stadt – und Landesarchiv. Marktamt, A2/1: Brot-Markirung, 1551/1876, 24.04.1876: Marktamt. Einführung einer Brodmarke.
Wiener Stadt – und Landesarchiv. Marktamt A2/1: Brot und Gebäcksverkauf nach Gewicht, 2035/1876, 19.06.1876: Marktamt. Eingabe der Bäckergenossenschaft über die Modalitäten des Brodverkaufes nach Gewicht.
Wiener Stadt – und Landesarchiv. Marktamt A2/1: Brot und Gebäcksverkauf nach Gewicht, 4381/46, 24.10.1876: Marktamt. Regelung des Brodverkaufes nach Gewicht.
Wiener Stadt – und Landesarchiv. Marktamt, A2/1: Brot-Markirung, 2258/46, 21.06.1877: Marktamt. Brodmarkirung betffd.
Wiener Stadt – und Landesarchiv. Marktamt, A2/1: Brotfrage, 12.12.1884. Äusserung Marktkommissariat.
Wiener Stadt – und Landesarchiv. Marktamt, A2/1: Brotfrage, 02.07.1885: Magistrat der Stadt Wien. Magistrats-Referat betreffend: Vorschläge zur Regelung der Brotfrage.
Wiener Stadt – und Landesarchiv. Marktamt, A2/1: Approvisionierung (Lebensmittel-Teuerung), 27.01.1892: Marktamt. Markt-Commissariats-Äußerung.
Wiener Stadt – und Landesarchiv. Marktamt, A2/1: Brotfrage, 02.12.1897: Marktamt. Referat über die Brodfrage für die 9. Sitzung der Approvisionirungs-Conferenz am 21/12 1897.
Wiener Stadt – und Landesarchiv. Marktamt A2/1: Brot: Gebäcksausträger, 29.05.1909: Marktamt. Gebäcksausträger.

Newspaper Articles

Ad. T. 'Die Brotfrage', *Neue Freie Presse*, 3 November 1878. 5096.
Wiener Zeitung. 'An Herrn Georg Putz', 28 April 1849. 101, Amtsblatt.
Wiener Zeitung. 'Aufforderung an Franz Eder, Bürgerl. Bäckermeister', 11 April 1851. 87, Amtsblatt.
Morgen-Post. 'Aufhebung der Brodsatzung', 20 September 1860. 261.
Morgen-Post. 'Aufhebung der Brodtaxe', 26 February 1860. 57.
Wiener Zeitung. 'Aus dem Gemeinderathe. (Plenarversammlung vom 24. Jänner)', 25 January 1865. 20.
Neues Fremden-Blatt. 'Aus dem Gemeinderathe. (Sitzung vom 4. November.)', 5 November 1875. 306.
Wiener Zeitung. 'Aus den Verhandlungen der Handels- und Gewerbekammer für das Erherzogtum Oesterreich unter der Enns, am 21. September 1859', 13 October 1859. 255.
Wiener Zeitung. 'Aus den Verhandlungen der Handels- und Gewerbekammer in Wien. Sitzung am 26. November 1891', 12 January 1892. 8.
Wiener Zeitung. 'Ausschuß der Bürger, Nationalgarde und Studenten für Sicherheit, Ruhe, Ordnung und Wahrung der Volksrechte. (Vormittags-Sitzung vom 30. Juni)', 2 July 1848. 181, Abendausgabe.
Neues Wiener Tagblatt. 'Brodmarkirung', 7 September 1877. 246.
Gemeinde-Zeitung. Unabhängiges, politisches Journal. 'Brodmarkirung', 15 December 1877. 286.
Neues Wiener Tagblatt. 'Brodverkauf nach dem Gewichte', 9 April 1872. 96.
Die Presse. 'Brodverkauf nach Gewicht', 18 May 1890. 136.
Die Presse. 'Brodverkauf nach Gewicht', 23 July 1891. 200.

Wiener Zeitung. 'Brotmarkirung', 8 September 1877. 206.
Neue Freie Presse. 'Brotmarkirung', 10 March 1877. 4503.
Neue Freie Presse. 'Brotverkauf nach Gewicht', 9 November 1871. 2590.
Wiener Vororte-Zeitung. Organ für Communal-, Vereins – und Schulwesen. 'Communalwesen. Außerordentliche Ausschußsitzung in Hernals am 17. September 1877', 20 September 1877. 69.
Gemeinde-Zeitung. Unabhängiges, politisches Journal. 'Da muß doch selbst eine Kuh lachen!', 31 July 1875. 89.
Das Vaterland. Zeitung für die österreichische Monarchie. 'Das Brod', 18 January 1878. 18.
Das Vaterland. Zeitung für die österreichische Monarchie. 'Das Brod', 27 February 1885. 57.
Das Vaterland. Zeitung für die österreichische Monarchie. 'Das Brod des armen Mannes', 4 May 1882.
Das Vaterland. Zeitung für die österreichische Monarchie. 'Das Ende der Brodfrage', 30 July 1885. 207.
Deutsche Zeitung. 'Das K.K Hofbrot', 14 June 1872. 162, Morgenblatt.
Das Vaterland. Zeitung für die österreichische Monarchie. 'Das tägliche Brod', 4 July, 1885. 181.
Neues Wiener Tagblatt. 'Das theuere Hausbrod', 30 June 1875. 179.
Die Presse. 'Der Brodverkauf nach dem Gewicht', 12 May 1872. 130, Beilage.
Gemeinde-Zeitung. Unabhängiges, politisches Journal. 'Der Brodverkauf nach dem Gewicht aufgeschoben', 27 July 1875. 87.
Die Presse. 'Der Brodverkauf nach Gewicht', 2 July 1872. 179, Beilage.
Morgen-Post. 'Der Lebensmittelwucher', 3 July 1875. 182.
Neues Wiener Tagblatt. 'Der Verkauf des Brodes nach Gewicht', 31 March 1872. 88.
Aussiger Anzeiger. 'Die armen Bäcker', 10 November 1875. Nr. 90.
Morgen-Post. 'Die Aufhebung der Brodsatzung', 3 April 1859. 92.
Neues Wiener Tagblatt. 'Die Bäcker gegen den Gemeinderath', 23 May 1886. 142.
Morgen-Post. 'Die Bäckergenossenschaft und die Brodpreise', 16 October 1884. 286.
Wiener Allgemeine Zeitung. 'Die Brodfrage', 4 January 1885. 1741.
Das Vaterland. Zeitung für die österreichische Monarchie. 'Die Brodfrage', 25 March 1885. 83.
Die Presse. 'Die Brodfrage', 14 February 1885. 44.
Morgen-Post. 'Die Brodfrage im Gemeinderathe', 22 January 1865. Nr. 22.
Wiener Allgemeine Zeitung. 'Die Brodfrage und deren Lösung', 1 November 1884. 1681.
Wiener Allgemeine Zeitung. 'Die Brodfrage und deren Lösung', 6 November 1884. 1685.
Morgen-Post. 'Die Brodpreise in den einzelnen Bezirken', 16 October 1884. 286.
Neue Freie Presse. 'Die Brotfrage', 17 October 1884. 7235.
Neue Freie Presse. 'Die Brotsatzung', 1 January 1885. 7307.
Arbeiter-Zeitung. Zentralorgan der österreichischen Sozialdemokratie. 'Die Brotwucher in Wien', 22 November 1895. 321.
Morgen-Post. 'Die Einrede der Bäcker', 27 October 1875. 298.
Das Vaterland. Zeitung für die österreichische Monarchie. 'Die Erwählten des III. Wahlkörpers', 5 March 1861. 52.
Das Vaterland. Zeitung für die österreichische Monarchie. 'Die gegenwärtige Lage der Brodfrage I', 29 April 1885. 117.
Das Vaterland. Zeitung für die österreichische Monarchie. 'Die gegenwärtige Lage der Brodfrage II', 30 April 1885. Nr. 118.
Das Vaterland. Zeitung für die österreichische Monarchie. 'Die gegenwärtige Lage der Brodfrage III', 1 May 1885. Nr. 119.

Das Vaterland. Zeitung für die österreichische Monarchie. 'Die gegenwärtige Lage der Brodfrage IV (Schluß)', 2 May 1885. 120.
Neues Wiener Tagblatt. 'Die hohen Brodpreise', 9 October 1884. 279.
Die Presse. 'Die hohen Brodpreise', 16 October 1884. 286.
Neues Wiener Tagblatt. 'Die Intervention in der Brodfrage', 3 July 1875. 182.
Neues Wiener Tagblatt. 'Die Monopolisten vom Backtrog', 18 February 1873. 48.
Das Vaterland. Zeitung für die österreichische Monarchie. 'Die Resolution der Wiener Bäcker', 11 June 1886. 161.
Das Vaterland. Zeitung für die österreichische Monarchie. 'Die Resolution der Wiener Bäcker (Schluß)', 12 June 1886. 162.
Neues Fremden-Blatt. 'Die Theuerungsfrage', 25 September 1875. 266.
Illustrirtes Wiener Extrablatt. 'Die Theurung auf der Tagesordnung', 21 September 1875. 262.
Das Vaterland. Zeitung für die österreichische Monarchie. 'Die Vorstellung der Bäcker an das Gemeinderaths-Präsidium', 26 August 1885. 233.
Fremden-Blatt. 'Echtes Kornbrod', 10 January 1857. 7.
Wiener Allgemeine Zeitung. 'Eine Brodtaxe?', 1 January 1885. 1738.
Die Hausfrau. Blätter für Haus und Wirthschaft. 'Eine erfreuliche Erscheinung auf dem Gebiete der Approvisionirung', 19 January 1878. 3.
Morgen-Post. 'Etwas von der Brodfrage', 15 June 1883. 162.
Gemeinde-Zeitung. Unabhängiges, politisches Journal. 'Fruchtbörse', 22 January 1863. 4.
Wiener Zeitung. 'Gemeinde-Ausschuß der Stadt Wien. Sitzung vom 27. Juni', 3 July 1848. 182.
Fremden-Blatt. 'Gemeinderath: Sitzung vom 24. Jänner', 25 January 1865. Nr. 25.
Fremden-Blatt. 'Gemeinderath: Sitzung vom 5. November', 6 November 1861. Nr. 305.
Die Presse. 'Gemeinderath Hirsch über die Theuerungsfrage', 13 October, 1875. 284, Beilage.
Wiener Zeitung. 'Gemeinderaths-Protokoll', 24 November 1848. 315.
Grailich, Andr. 'Die Wieselburger Gespannschaft in Ungern', *Erneuerte Vaterländische Blätter für den Österreichischen Kaiserstaat*, 1 April 1820. 27.
Kikeriki. Humoristisches Volksblatt. 'In der Kaninchen-Ausstellung', 23 September 1875. 76.
Morgen-Post. 'In der letzten Sitzung des hiesigen Gewerbevereins', 7 May 1856. 1252.
Wiener Zeitung. 'Industrie und Gewerbe. Nieder-Oesterreichischer Gewerb-Verein', 31 January 1847. 31.
Klamminger, F. 'Bericht über die von einer Commission der Löbl. Bäckerinnung in Wien an Wochenmayr's Patenofen vorgenommenen Prüfung', *Kremser Wochenblatt*, 21 April 1866. 16.
Wiener Zeitung. 'Kleine Chronik', 24 January 1852. 21.
Wiener Zeitung. 'Kundmachung', 23 February 1849. 46.
Wiener Zeitung. 'Kundmachung', 17 November 1848. 309.
Die Bombe. 'Kundmachung', 11 July 1875. 27.
L.F. 'Die Erste Wiener Dampfbäckerei. Panem et Circenses', *Wiener Zeitung*, 19 January 1848. 19.
Wiener Zeitung. 'Lebensmittel', 23 June 1875. 141, Beilage.
Lochner. 'Bericht über die Probemahlung in der Neuen Leykower Mühle', *Encyklopädische Zeitschrift des Gewerbewesens*, November 1846. 1071–84
Die Presse. 'Müller und Bäcker in Wien', 29 January 1858. 23.
Morgen-Post. 'Nicht Tod, sondern Brod!', 9 February 1879. 39.

Wiener Zeitung. 'Nied. Oesterr. Gewerb-Verein. Ausschreibung eines Preises für die inländische Erzeugung einer vollkommen brauchbaren Kunsthefe (eines Künstliches Gährungsmittels)', 11 June 1847. 159.

Morgen-Post. 'Nochmals die Einrede der Bäcker', 2 November 1875. Nr. 303.

Pappenheim, Gustav. 'Die Müllerei im 19. Jahrhundert', *Oesterreichisch-Ungarische Müller-Zeitung*, 31 December 1899. 53.

Morgen-Post. 'Probebacken', 22 April 1885. 110.

Wiener Zeitung. 'Protokoll der Sitzung des Gemeinderathes vom 13. Dezember 1848', 19 December 1848. 337.

Wiener Zeitung. 'Protokoll der Sitzung des Gemeinderathes vom 7. Februar', 21 February 1849. 44.

Wiener Zeitung. 'Protokoll der Sitzung des Gemeinderaths der Stadt Wien am 2. Mai 1849', 11 May 1849. 112.

Wiener Zeitung. 'Protokoll der Sitzung des Gemeinderaths der Stadt Wien am 20 Juni 1849', 30 June 1849. 154.

Wiener Zeitung. 'Protokoll der Sitzung des Gemeinderaths der Stadt Wien am 20. April 1849', 27 April 1849. 100.

Wiener Zeitung. 'Protokoll der Sitzung des Gemeinderaths der Stadt Wien am 30. Juli 1851', 13 August 1851. 192.

Wiener Zeitung. 'Protokoll der Sitzung des Gemeinderaths der Stadt Wien am 4. November 1851', 20 November 1851. 277.

Wiener Zeitung. 'Protokoll der Sitzung des Gemeinderaths der Stadt Wien vom 21. März 1849', 4 April 1849. 80.

Wiener Zeitung. 'Protokoll der Sitzung des Gemeinderaths der Stadt Wien vom 25. Mai 1849', 8 June 1849. 135.

Wiener Zeitung. 'Protokoll der Sitzung des Gemeinderaths der Stadt Wien vom 26. März 1850', 6 April 1850. 83.

Wiener Zeitung. 'Protokoll der Sitzung des Gemeindrathes vom 1. Februar', 18 February 1849. 42.

Das Vaterland. Zeitung für die österreichische Monarchie. 'Satzung', 1 November 1860. 55.

Morgen-Post. 'Sitzung des Gemeiderathes: vom 27. Mai', 28 May 1863. Nr. 145.

Ost-Deutsche Post. 'Sitzung des Gemeinderathes', 10 July 1861. Nr. 186.

Morgen-Post. 'Sitzung des Gemeinderathes vom 26. Oktober. Spezialdebatte über die Theuerungsfrage', 27 October 1875. 298.

Wiener Zeitung. 'Sitzungsberichte. Protokoll der 209. Sitzung des Gemeinderathes der k.k. Reichshaupt- und Residenzstadt Wien am 27. April 1860', 25 May 1860. 125.

Die Presse. 'Tagesneuigkeiten', 14 April 1850. 90.

Fremden-Blatt. 'Tages-Neuigkeiten', 16 May 1849. 116.

Die Presse. 'Theuerungs-Enquete', 9 February 1871. 40.

Neue Freie Presse. 'Unterhandlungen mit Bäckern und Fleischern', 27 June 1875. 176, Beilage.

Neues Fremden-Blatt. 'Unterhandlungen mit Bäckern und Fleischern', 27 June 1875. Nr. 176.

Vorstand der Bäcker-Genossenschaft. 'Zur Abwehr', *Morgen-Post*, 24 August 1861. Nr. 231.

Das Vaterland. Zeitung für die österreichische Monarchie. 'Weiteres zur Brodfrage', 28 May 1885. 145.

Morgen-Post. 'Weniger Reaction und mehr Volkswirthschaft!', 13 July 1879. 191.

Wiener Zeitung. 'Wien', 19 September 1860. 220.

Morgen-Post. 'Wien', 24 October 1860. 295.

Morgen-Post. 'Wien', 9 November 1860. 311.
Die Presse. 'Wien, 19. Juni', 20 June 1852. 144.
Wiener Allgemeine Zeitung. 'Wien, 23. Januar', 24 January 1885. 1761.
Die Presse. 'Wien, 28. Juni', 29 June 1852. 151.
Die Presse. 'Wien. Brodsatzung', 11 May 1849. 112.
Morgen-Post. 'Wien. Sitzung des Gemeinderathes vom 27. Mai', 28 May 1863. 145.
Neue Freie Presse. 'Wiener Dampfmühlen-Gesellschaft', 25 May 1869. 1701.
Neue Freie Presse. 'Wiener Gemeinderath', 27 October 1875. 4014.
Das Vaterland. Zeitung für die österreichische Monarchie. 'Wiener Gemeinderath. (Sitzung vom 7. Mai.)', 8 May 1886. 127.
Die Presse. 'Wiener Gemeinderath. Sitzung vom 27. Mai', 28 May 1863. 145.
Der Zwischen-Akt. 'Wiener Plaudereien. Brod', 25 November 1860. 316.
Morgen-Post. 'Zum Brodverkauf nach dem Gewicht', 15 May 1872. 132.
Wiener Allgemeine Zeitung. 'Zur Brodfrage', 4 February 1885. 1771.
Neue Freie Presse. 'Zur Brodfrage', 23 May 1886. 7808.
Das Vaterland. Zeitung für die österreichische Monarchie. 'Zur Brodfrage', 10 April 1870. Nr. 99.
Die Presse. 'Zur Brodfrage', 1 January 1885. 1.
Neue Freie Presse. 'Zur Theuerungsfrage', 30 July 1875. 3925.

Publications and Published Sources before 1900

Bericht der Handels- und Gewerbekammer für Das Erzherzogthum Oesterreich unter der Enns an das K.K. Ministerium für Handel und Volkswirthschaft über die Verkehrsverhältnisse des Kammerbezirkes in den Jahren 1852–1885. Wien, 1852–1885.
Bericht der Handels- und Gewerbekammer für das Erzherzogthum Oesterreich unter der Enns an das K.K. Ministerium für Handel und Volkswirthschaft über die Verkehrsverhältnisse des Kammerbezirkes in den Jahren 1857 bis 1860. Wien, 1861.
Bericht der Handels- und Gewerbekammer für das Erzherzogthum Oesterreich unter der Enns an das K.K. Ministerium für Handel und Volkswirthschaft über die Verkehrsverhältnisse des Kammerbezirkes während der Jahre 1872–1874. Wien, 1876.
Blumenbach, Wenzel C. W. *Neueste Landeskunde von Oesterreich unter der Ens, Zweiter Band*. Güns: Reichard, 1835.
Burger, Johann. 'Ueber die Vortheile der Vergrößerung der Cultur des Weizens, und die Anwendung der Schaufelpflüge', *Verhandlungen der k.k. Landwirthschaftsgesellschaft in Wien, und Aufsätze vermischten ökonomischen Inhalts*. Neue Folge, Zweyter Band, no. 1 (1833): 57–79.
Exner, Wilhelm F., ed. *Beiträge zur Geschichte der Gewerbe und Erfindungen Oesterreichs von der Mitte des XVIII. Jahrhunderts bis zur Gegenwart*. Wien: Wilhelm Braumüller, 1873.
Gigl, Alexander. *Geschichte der Wiener Marktordnungen: Vom Sechzehnten Jahrhundert bis zum Ende des Achtzehnten aus Urkunden entwickelt*. Wien: Kais. Kön. Hof- und Staatsdruckerei/Karl Gerold's Sohn, 1865.
Horsford, Eben N. *Report on Vienna Bread*. Washington: Government Printing Office, 1875.

Innung der bürgerl. Bäckermeister in der k.k. Haupt – und Residenzstadt Wien. *Darstellung der Gewerblichen Zustände der Wiener Bäcker-Innung*. Wien: Ferd. Jahn, 1848.

Jackson, Charles L. 'Eben Norton Horsford', *Proceedings of the American Academy of Arts and Sciences* 28, no. 28 (1892): 340–46.

k.k. Handelsministerium. *Enquête über die Approvisionirung Wiens: II: Theil, Lebensmittel (ausgenommen Fleisch), Brennholz und Mineralkohle*. 2 vols. Wien: Kaiserlich-königliche Hof – und Staatsdruckerei, 1871.

k.k. Österreichisches Central-Comité, ed. *Officieller Ausstellungs-Bericht, 7. Lieferung: Nahrungsmittel und Getränke auf der Welt-Ausstellung zu Paris im Jahre 1867*. Wien: Braumüller, 1868.

K.K. Statistische Central-Commission, ed. *Schifffahrt und Verkehr auf der Donau und ihren Nebenflüssen im Jahre 1865*. With the assistance of Johann Winkler. Mittheilungen aus dem Gebiete der Statistik 13, IV. Heft. Wien, 1867.

K.K. Statistische Central-Commission, ed. *Berufsstatistik nach den Ergebnissen der Volkszählung vom 31. December 1890 in den im Reichsrathe vertretenen Königreichen und Ländern: Nieder-Österreich*. Österreichische Statistik XXXIII, 2. Heft. Wien, 1894.

Kick, Friedrich. *Die Mehlfabrikation: Ein Lehrbuch des Mühlenbetriebes*. 2nd ed. Leipzig: Arthur Felix, 1878.

Kohl, Johann G. *Hundert Tage Reisen in den Oesterreichischen Staaten: 4. Teil, Reise in Ungarn, Zweite Abtheilung*. Dresden: Arnoldische Buchhandlung, 1842.

Leuchs, Johann C. *Vollständige Brod-Bak-Kunde oder der Europäische Bäkermeister. Wissenschaftlich-Praktische Darstellung der Bäkerkunst in ihrer größten Vollkommenheit und nach ihrem Zustande in allen Ländern der Welt*. Nürnberg: C. Leuchs und Comp., 1832.

Luca, Ignaz de. *Wiens gegenwärtiger Zustand unter Josephs Regierung*. Wien: Georg Philipp Wucherer, 1787.

Matern, J. *Licht in der Brodfrage und der sichere Weg zur Lösung derselben*. Wien: Karl Matern, 1885.

Niederösterreichische Handels – und Gewerbekammer. *Statistische Übersicht der wichtigsten Productionszweige in Oestereich unter der Ens*. Wien: L. Sommer, 1855.

Paton, Andrew A. *Researches on the Danube and the Adriatic: Or, Contributions to the Modern History of Hungary and Transylvania, Dalmatia and Croatia, Servia and Bulgaria*. II. Leipzig: F.A. Brockhaus, 1861.

Payen, Anselme. *Manuel du Cours de Chimie organique appliquée aux Arts industriels et agricoles*. Paris: N. Béchet Fils, 1842.

Schimmer, Gustav A. *Die Bevölkerung von Wien und seiner Umgebung nach dem Berufe und der Beschäftigung: 1. Geschlecht, Civilstand, Wohnverhältnisse, Arbeits – und Dienstverhältnisse*. Wien: Ueberreuter, 1874.

Schmoller, Gustav. *Zur Geschichte der Deutschen Kleingewerbe im 19. Jahrhundert: Statistische und nationalökonomische Untersuchungen*. Halle: Buchhandlung des Waisenhauses, 1870.

Schwiedland, Eugen P. *Kleingewerbe und Hausindustrie in Österreich: Beiträge zur Kenntnis ihrer Entwicklung und ihrer Existenzbedinguen*. 2 vols. Leipzig: Duncker & Humblot, 1894.

Schwiedland, Eugen P. *Die Hausiererfrage in Österreich*. Leipzig: Duncker & Humblot, 1899. Einleitung zu Band 82 der Schriften des Vereins für Socialpolitik.

Uhl, Roman. 'Producte der Brot – und Kuchen-Bäckerei', In k.k. Österreichisches Central-Comité, *Officieller Ausstellungs-Bericht, 7. Lieferung* (1868): 29–34.

Uhl, Roman. 'Brodbereitung', In Exner, *Beiträge zur Geschichte der Gewerbe und Erfindungen Oesterreichs von der Mitte des XVIII. Jahrhunderts bis zur Gegenwart* (1873): 179–83.
Uhl, Roman. 'Mühlen-Industrie', In Exner, *Beiträge zur Geschichte der Gewerbe und Erfindungen Oesterreichs von der Mitte des XVIII. Jahrhunderts bis zur Gegenwart* (1873): 173–78.
Weiß, Karl. *Rückblicke auf die Gemeineverwaltung der Stadt Wien in den Jahren 1838-1848*. Wien: Manz, 1875.
Winkler, Johann. 'Wien und die Entwicklung des Donauhandels', *Mittheilungen der k.k. geographischen Gesellschaft in Wien* 15 (1872): 73–92.
'Wochenmayr's Backofen. Mit einer Abbildung', *Polytechnisches Journal* 185, LVI (1867): 190–94.
Zichy, H. 'Cerealien und Mehl', In k.k. Österreichisches Central-Comité, *Officieller Ausstellungs-Bericht, 7. Lieferung*, 3–21.

Bibliography

Ahrens, Ralf, Marcus Böick and Marcel vom Lehn. 'Vermarktlichung. Zeithistorische Perspektiven auf ein umkämpftes Feld', *Zeithistorische Forschungen/Studies in Contemporary History* 12, no. 3 (2015): 393–402.
Albrecht, Jonas M. '"Das Ringen des Freihandels mit dem Prohibitivsystem". Politische Ökonomie und Infrastruktur der Brotversorgung Wiens, 1815–1847', *Österreichische Zeitschrift für Geschichtswissenschaften* 30, no. 2 (2019): 67–99.
Albrecht, Jonas M. 'The Need for Wheat. The Pre-Industrial Expansion of Vienna's Grain Supply, 1800–1840', in *Stocks, Seasons and Sales: Food Supply, Storage and Markets in Europe and the New World, C. 1600–2000*. Vol. 17. Edited by Wouter Ronsijn, Niccolò Mignemi and Laurent Herment, 103–27. Turnhout: Brepols Publishers, 2019.
Albrecht, Jonas M. 'The Struggle for Bread. The Emperor, the City and the Bakers between Moral and Market Economies of Food in Vienna, 1775–1791', *History of Retail and Consumption* 5, no. 3 (2019): 276–94.
Albrecht, Jonas M. 'Brot für die Hauptstadt. Niederösterreich und die Nahrungsversorgung Wiens', in *Geschichte Niederösterreichs: Band 2. Gesellschaft und Gemeinschaft. Eine Regionalgeschichte der Moderne*. Edited by Oliver Kühschelm, Elisabeth Loinig and Willibald Rosner, 449–75. St. Pölten: Verlag NÖ Institut für Landeskunde, 2021.
Albrecht, Jonas M. 'Surprising Similarities? Food Market Deregulation and the Consequences of Laissez-Faire in Vienna, Paris and New York City, C. 1840–1880', *Geschichte und Region/Storia e regione* 30, no. 1 (2021): 19–54.
Alexander, David. *Retailing in England during the Industrial Revolution*. London: Athlone Pr, 1970.
Alix-Garcia, Jennifer, Sarah Walker, Volker Radeloff and Jacek Kozak. 'Tariffs and Trees. The Effects of the Austro-Hungarian Customs Union on Specialization and Land-Use Change', *The Journal of Economic History* 78, no. 4 (2018): 1142–78.
Appleby, Joyce. *Economic Thought and Ideology in Seventeenth-Century England*. Los Angeles: Figueroa Press, 2004.
Atkins, P. J., Peter Lummel and Derek J. Oddy, eds. *Food and the City in Europe Since 1800*. London, New York: Routledge, 2016.

Aulenbacher, Brigitte, Richard Bärnthaler and Andreas Novy, eds. 'Karl Polanyi, "The Great Transformation" and Contemporary Capitalism', Special issue, *Österreichische Zeitschrift für Soziologie* 44, no. 2 (2019): 105–260.
Baics, Gergely. *Feeding Gotham: The Political Economy and Geography of Food in New York, 1790–1860*. Princeton, Oxford: Princeton University Press, 2016.
Baltzarek, Franz, Alfred Hoffmann, Hannes Stekl and W. Mayer. *Wirtschaft und Gesellschaft der Wiener Stadterweiterung*. Wiesbaden: Steiner, 1975.
Banik-Schweitzer, Renate, ed. *Wien im Vormärz*. Forschungen und Beiträge zur Wiener Stadtgeschichte 8. Wien: Jugend und Volk, 1980.
Baravalle, Robert. 'Preise und Löhne in Graz im 19. Jahrhundert (1820 bis 1914)', *Zeitschrift des Historischen Vereins für Steiermark* 57 (1966): 89–125.
Barles, Sabine. 'Feeding the City: Food Consumption and Flow of Nitrogen, Paris, 1801–1914', *Science of The Total Environment* 375, no. 1 (2007): 48–58.
Baryli, Andreas.'Gewerbepolitik und gewerbliche Verhältnisse im vormärzlichen Wien', In Banik-Schweitzer, *Wien im Vormärz* (1980): 9–31.
Baryli, Andreas. *Konzessionssystem contra Gewerbefreiheit*. Frankfurt am Main: Lang, 1984.
Batzell, Rudi, Sven Beckert, Andrew Gordon and Gabriel Winant. 'E. P. Thompson, Politics and History. Writing Social History Fifty Years after the Making of the English Working Class', *Journal of Social History* 48, no. 4 (2015): 753–58.
Beckert, Jens. 'The Great Transformation of Embeddedness: Karl Polanyi and the New Economic Sociology', in *Market and Society: The Great Transformation Today*. Edited by C. M. Hann and Keith Hart, 38–55. Cambridge: Cambridge University Press, 2009.
Belderok, B., J. Mesdag and D. A. Donner. *Bread-Making Quality of Wheat: A Century of Breeding in Europe*. Dordrecht: Springer Netherlands, 2000.
Berghoff, Hartmut, and Jakob Vogel, eds. *Wirtschaftsgeschichte als Kulturgeschichte: Dimensionen eines Perspektivenwechsels*. Frankfurt/Main: Campus Verlag GmbH, 2004.
Berghoff, Hartmut, and Jakob Vogel, eds. 'Wirtschaftsgeschichte als Kulturgeschichte. Ansätze zur Bergung transdisziplinärer Synergiepotentiale', in *Wirtschaftsgeschichte als Kulturgeschichte: Dimensionen eines Perspektivenwechsels*. Edited by Hartmut Berghoff and Jakob Vogel, 9–42. Frankfurt/Main: Campus Verlag GmbH, 2004.
Berthold, Werner. 'Brotsatzungen – Weizenpreis und Brotgewicht in Wien und Niederösterreich vom Spätmittelalter bis um 1600', *Jahrbuch für Landeskunde von Niederösterreich* NF 72/74 (2006–2008): 23–46.
Biebricher, Thomas. *Neoliberalismus zur Einführung*. Hamburg: Junius, 2018.
Billen, G., S. Barles, P. Chatzimpiros, and J. Garnier. 'Grain, Meat and Vegetables to Feed Paris: Where Did and Do They Come From? Localising Paris Food Supply Areas from the Eighteenth to the Twenty-First Century', *Regional Environmental Change* 12, no. 2 (2012): 325–35.
Blackbourn, David. *The Conquest of Nature: Water, Landscape, and the Making of Modern Germany*. New York, NY: Norton, 2007.
Blum, Jerome. *Noble Landowners and Agriculture in Austria, 1815–1848: A Study in the Origins of the Peasant Emancipation of 1848*. Baltimore: Johns Hopkins University Press, 1948.
Bobrow-Strain, Aaron. 'White Bread Bio-Politics: Purity, Health, and the Triumph of Industrial Baking', *cultural geographies* 15, no. 1 (2008): 19–40.
Bohstedt, John. 'The Moral Economy and the Discipline of Historical Context', *Journal of Social History* 26, no. 2 (1992): 265–84.

Bohstedt, John. *The Politics of Provisions: Food Riots, Moral Economy, and Market Transition in England, C. 1550-1850*. London: Taylor and Francis, 2016.

Borodajkewycz, Taras von. 'Gewerbefreiheit und konservativer Geist', In *Festschrift Walter Heinrich: ein Beitrag zur Ganzheitsforschung*. 371-87. Graz: Akad. Druck – u. Verl.-Anst, 1963.

Bouton, Cynthia A. *The Flour War: Gender, Class, and Community in Late Ancien Régime French Society*. Pennsylvania: Pennsylvania State University Press, 1993.

Brantz, Dorothee. *Slaughter in the City: The Establishment of Public Abattoirs in Paris and Berlin, 1780-1914.*, 2003. (University of Chicago PhD Thesis).

Braudel, Fernand. *Civilization and Capitalism, 15th – 18th Century, Vol. 1: The Structures of Everyday Life*. New York: Harper & Row, 1981.

Bruckmüller, Ernst. *Sozialgeschichte Österreichs*. Wien. München: Verl. für Geschichte und Politik; Oldenbourg, 2001.

Bruckmüller, Ernst 'Eine "grüne Revolution" (18.-19. Jahrhundert)', in *Agrarrevolutionen: Verhältnisse in der Landwirtschaft vom Neolithikum zur Globalisierung*. Edited by Markus Cerman, Ilja Steffelbauer and Sven Tost, 206-26. Innsbruck: Studien-Verl., 2008.

Brugger, Eva, Alexander Engel, Christof Jeggle, and Tim Neu. *Marktgeschehen: Fragmente einer Geschichte frühneuzeitlichen Wirtschaftens*. Frankfurt: Campus, 2023.

Brunt, Liam, and Edmund Cannon. 'Variations in the Price and Quality of English Grain, 1750-1914: Quantitative Evidence and Empirical Implications', *Explorations in Economic History* 58 (2015): 74-92.

Brusatti, Alois. *Österreichische Wirtschaftspolitik vom Josephinismus zum Ständestaat*. Wien: Jupiter-Verl., 1965.

Buchmann, Betrand M. 'Dynamik des Städtebaus', In Csendes; Opll, *Wien. Geschichte einer Stadt* (2006): 47-84.

Buchmann, Betrand M. 'Politik und Verwaltung', In Csendes; Opll, *Wien. Geschichte einer Stadt* (2006): 85-128.

Burnett, John. 'The Baking Industry in the Nineteenth Century', *Business History* 5, no. 2 (1963): 98-108.

Chaloupek, Günther, Michael Wagner, and Andreas Weigl. 'Handel im vorindustriellen Zeitalter: der kanalisierte Güterstrom', in *Wien Wirtschaftsgeschichte 1740-1938*. Edited by Günther Chaloupek, Peter Eigner and Michael Wagner. 2 vols., 1001-38. Wien: Jugend und Volk, 1991.

Chevallier, Jim. *August Zang and the French Croissant: How Vienneroiserie Came to France*. North Hollywood, CA: Chez Jim Books, 2009.

Cobbold, Carolyn A. 'The Rise of Alternative Bread Leavening Technologies in the Nineteenth Century', *Annals of science* 75, no. 1 (2018): 21-39.

Collins, E. J. T. 'Dietary Change and Cereal Consumption in Britain in the Nineteenth Century', *The Agricultural History Review* 23, no. 2 (1975): 97-115.

Collins, E. J. T. 'Why Wheat? Choice of Food Grains in Europe in the Nineteenth and Twentieth Centuries', *Journal of European Economic History* 22, no. 1 (1993): 7-38.

Csendes, Peter, and Ferdinand Opll, eds. *Wien. Geschichte einer Stadt: Band 3. Von 1790 bis zur Gegenwart*. Wien/Kön/Weimar: Böhlau, 2006.

Cvrcek, Tomas. 'Wages, Prices, and Living Standards in the Habsburg Empire, 1827-1910', *The Journal of Economic History* 73, no. 1 (2013): 1-37.

Dale, Gareth. *Karl Polanyi: The Limits of the Market*. Oxford: Polity Press, 2010.

Dányi, Deszö. *"Az Élet Ára": Gabona És Élelmiszerárak Magyarországon, 1750-1850*. Budapest: Központi Statisztikai Hivatal Könyvtár és Levéltár, 2007.

Davis, James. 'Baking for the Common Good: A Reassessment of the Assize of Bread in Medieval England', *The Economic History Review* 57, no. 3 (2004): 465–502.

de Vries, Jan. *The Price of Bread: Regulating the Market in the Dutch Republic*. Berkeley, CA: University of California Press, 2019.

Dewilde, Brecht, and Johann Poukens. 'Bread Provisioning and Retail Dynamics in the Southern Low Countries. The Bakers of Leuven, 1600–1800', *Continuity and Change* 26, no. 3 (2011): 405–38.

Ebner, Alexander. 'Karl Polanyi: The Great Transformation', in *Schlüsselwerke der Wirtschaftssoziologie*. Edited by Klaus Kraemer and Florian Brugger, 169–75. Wiesbaden: Springer VS, 2017.

Eddie, Scott M. 'The Terms and Patterns of Hungarian Foreign Trade, 1882–1913', *The Journal of Economic History* 37, no. 2 (1977): 329–58.

Ehmer, Josef. 'Produktion und Reproduktion in der Wiener Manufakturperiode', In Banik-Schweitzer, *Wien im Vormärz* (1980): 107–32.

Ehmer, Josef 'Zünfte in Österreich in der frühen Neuzeit', In *Das Ende der Zünfte: Ein europäischer Vergleich*. Edited by Heinz-Gerhard Haupt, 87–126. Göttingen: Vandenhoeck & Ruprecht, 2011.

Fata, Márta. *Migration im kameralistischen Staat Josephs II: Theorie und Praxis der Ansiedlungspolitik in Ungarn, Siebenbürgen, Galizien und der Bukowina von 1768 bis 1790*. Münster: Aschendorff, 2014.

Feigl, Helmuth, ed. *Die Auswirkungen der Theresianisch-Josephinischen Reformen auf die Landwirtschaft und die ländliche Sozialstruktur Niederösterreichs: Vorträge und Diskussionen des ersten Symposiums des Niederösterreichischen Institutes für Landeskunde, Geras, 9. – 11. Oktober 1980*. Wien Selbstverl. d. NÖ Inst. für Landeskunde, 1982, 1982.

Foucault, Michel. *Sicherheit, Territorium, Bevölkerung: Geschichte der Gouvernementalität I. Vorlesungen am Collège de France 1977/1978*. 5. Auflage. Frankfurt am Main: Suhrkamp, 2017.

Foucault, Michel. *Die Geburt der Biopolitik: Geschichte der Gouvernementalität II. Vorlesungen am Collège de France 1978/1979*. 6. Auflage. Frankfurt am Main: Suhrkamp, 2018.

Fraser, Nancy, and Rahel Jaeggi. *Kapitalismus: Ein Gespräch über Kritische Theorie*. Berlin: Suhrkamp, 2020.

Frevert, Ute. 'Introduction', in *Moral Economies*. Edited by Ute Frevert, 7–12. Göttingen: Vandenhoeck & Ruprecht, 2019.

Fullilove, Courtney. 'The Price of Bread. The New York City Flour Riot and the Paradox of Capitalist Food Systems', *Radical History Review* 2014, no. 118 (2014): 15–41.

Fullilove, Courtney. *The Profit of the Earth: The Global Seeds of American Agriculture*. Chicago: University of Chicago Press, 2017.

Gates-Coon, Rebecca. *The Landed Estates of the Esterházy Princes: Hungary during the Reforms of Maria Theresia and Joseph II*. Baltimore: Johns Hopkins University Press, 1994.

Gingrich, Simone, Gertrud Haidvogl, and Fridolin Krausmann. 'The Danube and Vienna: Urban Resource Use, Transport and Land Use 1800–1910', *Regional Environmental Change* 12, no. 2 (2012): 283–94.

Glassl, Horst. 'Der Ausbau der ungarischen Wasserstraßen in den letzten Regierungsjahren Maria Theresias', *Ungarn-Jahrbuch – Zeitschrift für die Kunde Ungarns und verwandte Gebiete* II, no. 2 (1970): 34–66.

Good, David F. *The Economic Rise of the Habsburg Empire, 1750–1914*. Berkeley, CA: University of California Press, 1984.
Götz, Norbert. '"Moral Economy": Its Conceptual History and Analytical Prospects', *Journal of Global Ethics* 11, no. 2 (2015): 147–62.
Gräser, Marcus. 'Historicizing Karl Polanyi', *Österreichische Zeitschrift für Soziologie* 44, no. 2 (2019): 129–41.
Guizzo, Danielle, and Iara Vigo de Lima. 'Polanyi and Foucault on the Issue of Market in Classical Political Economy', *Review of Radical Political Economics* 49, no. 1 (2017): 100–13.
Güldner, Dino, and Fridolin Krausmann. 'Nutrient Recycling and Soil Fertility Management in the Course of the Industrial Transition of Traditional, Organic Agriculture: The Case of Bruck Estate, 1787–1906', *Agriculture, Ecosystems & Environment* 249 (2017): 80–90.
Gutkas, Karl. *Geschichte Niederösterreichs*. Wien: Verl. für Geschichte u. Politik, 1984.
Hackl, Bernhard. 'Die staatliche Wirtschaftspolitik zwischen 1740 und 1792. Reform versus Stagnation', in *Josephinismus als Aufgeklärter Absolutismus*. Edited by Helmut Reinalter, 191–272. Wien, Köln, Weimar: Böhlau, 2008.
Hanak, Peter. 'Jews and the Modernization of Commerce in Hungary, 1760–1848', in *Jews in the Hungarian Economy 1760–1945: Studies Dedicated to Moshe Carmilly-Weinberger on His Eightieth Birthday*. Edited by Michael K. Silber, 23–39. Jerusalem: Magnes Press, Hebrew University, 1992.
Hansen, Hendrik. 'Adam Smith, Der Wohlstand der Nationen (1776)', in *Geschichte des politischen Denkens: Ein Handbuch*. Edited by Manfred Brocker, 318–48. Frankfurt am Main: Suhrkamp, 2007.
Hart, Emma. *Trading Spaces: The Colonial Marketplace and the Foundations of American Capitalism*. Chicago: The University of Chicago Press, 2019.
Harvey, David. *A Brief History of Neoliberalism*. Oxford: Oxford University Press, 2010.
Haselsteiner, Horst. 'Cooperation and Confrontation between Rulers and the Noble Estates, 1711–1790', in *A History of Hungary*. Edited by Peter F. Sugar, 138–73. Bloomington: Indiana University Press, 1990.
Hassinger, Herbert. 'Der Aussenhandel der Habsburgermonarchie in der zweiten Hälfte des 18. Jahrhunderts', in *Die Wirtschaftliche Situation in Deutschland und Österreich um die Wende vom 18. zum 19. Jahrhundert: Bericht über die erste Arbeitstagung der Gesellschaft für Sozial – und Wirtschaftsgeschichte in Mainz 4. – 6. März 1963*. Edited by Friedrich Lütge, 61–98. Stuttgart: Fischer, 1964.
Hauer, Friedrich. *Die Verzehrungssteuer 1829–1913 als Grundlage einer umwelthistorischen untersuchung des Metabolismus der Stadt Wien*, 2010. Social Ecology Working Paper 129.
Hauer, Friedrich, ed. *Die Versorgung Wiens 1829–1913: Neue Forschungsergebnisse auf Grundlage der Wiener Verzehrungssteuer*. Innsbruck/Wien: StudienVerl, 2014.
Hauer, Friedrich, Severin Hohensinner and Christina Spitzbart-Glasl. 'How Water and Its Use Shaped the Spatial Development of Vienna', *Water History* 8, no. 3 (2016): 301–28.
Heller, Victor. *Der Getreidehandel und seine Technik in Wien*. Tübingen: Mohr, 1901.
Hoffmann, R. C. 'Frontier Foods for Late Medieval Consumers: Culture, Economy, Ecology', *Environment and History* 7, no. 2 (2001): 131–67.
Hohensinner, Severin, Christoph Sonnlechner, Martin Schmid and Verena Winiwarter. 'Two Steps Back, One Step Forward: Reconstructing the Dynamic Danube Riverscape Under Human Influence in Vienna', *Water History* 5 (2013): 121–43.

Horowitz, Roger, Jeffrey M. Pilcher and Sydney Watts. 'Meat for the Multitudes. Market Culture in Paris, New York City, and Mexico City over the Long Nineteenth Century', *The American Historical Review* 109, no. 4 (2004): 1055–83.

Horvarth, Gergely K. 'Rendi Autonómia És Fiziokratizmus. Kísérlet a Hanság Lecsapolására Az 1820–30-as Években (2. Rész)', *Soproni szemle* 62, no. 4 (2008): 170–87.

Horvárth, Gergely K. 'Rahmen des bäuerlichen Handelns im Wieselburger Komitat (Ungarn) in der ersten Hälfte des 19. Jahrhunderts. Modell der Kommerzialisierung einer west-ungarischen Region', in *Bauern als Händler: Ökonomische Diversifizierung und Soziale Differenzierung Bäuerlicher Agrarproduzenten (15. – 19. Jahrhundert)*. Edited by Frank Konersmann and Klaus-Joachim Lorenzen-Schmidt, 163–84. Berlin: Walter de Gruyter GmbH, 2016.

Joyce, Patrick. *The Rule of Freedom: Liberalism and the Modern City*. London: Verso, 2003.

Judson, Pieter M. *The Habsburg Empire: A New History*. Cambridge, MA; London, England: The Belknap Press of Harvard University Press, 2016.

Kállay, István. *Management of Big Estates in Hungary between 1711 and 1848*. Budapest: Akad. Kiadó, 1980.

Kaplan, Steven L. *Provisioning Paris: Merchants and Millers in the Grain and Flour Trade during the Eighteenth Century*. Ithaca: Cornell University Press, 1984.

Kaplan, Steven L. *The Bakers of Paris and the Bread Question, 1700–1775*. Durham: Duke University Press, 1996.

Kaplan, Steven L. *Bread, Politics and Political Economy in the Reign of Louis XV*. Second edition. London, New York: Anthem Press, 2015.

Kaps, Klemens. 'Peripherisierung der Ökonomie, Ethnisierung der Gesellschaft: Galizien zwischen äußerem und innerem Konkurrenzdruck (1856–1914)', in *Galizien. Fragmente eines diskursiven Raums*. Edited by Doktorratskolleg Galizien, 37–62. Wien: StudienVerlag, 2009.

Kirkland, John, ed. *The Modern Baker, Confectioner and Caterer: A Practical and Scientific Work for the Baking and Allied Trades. Divisional-Vol. II*. London: The Gresham Publishing Company, 1908.

Kocka, Jürgen. *Geschichte des Kapitalismus*. 3., überarbeitete Auflage. München: Verlag C.H. Beck, 2017.

Komlos, John. *The Habsburg Monarchy as a Customs Union: Economic Development in Austria-Hungary in the Nineteenth Century*. Princeton, NJ: Princeton University Press, 1983.

Komlos, John. *Nutrition and Economic Development in the Eighteenth-Century Habsburg Monarchy: An Anthropometric History*. Princeton, NJ: Princeton University Press, 1989.

Komlosy, Andrea. 'Innere Peripherien als Ersatz für Kolonien? Zentrenbildung und Peripherisierung in der Habsburgermonarchie', in *Zentren, Peripherien und kollektive Identitäten in Österreich-Ungarn: Kultur-Herrschaft-Differenz*. Edited by Endre Hárs et al., 55–78. Tübingen, Basel: Francke, 2006.

Kratochwill, Max. 'Ein Bäckerschupfen in der Roßau (1728)', *Jahrbuch des Vereins für Geschichte der Stadt Wien* 21, no. 22 (1965/1966): 250–54.

Kretschmer, Sigrid. *Wiener Handwerksfrauen: Wirtschaft und Leben im 18. Jahrhundert*. Wien: Milena, 2000.

Landesinnung der Wiener Bäcker, ed. *700 Jahre Wiener Bäcker-Innung*. Wien: Verlag der Wiener Bäcker-Innung, 1927.

Langthaler, Ernst. 'Vom transnationalen zum regionalen Hinterland – und retour. Wiens Nahrungsmittelversorgung vor, im und nach dem Ersten Weltkrieg', in *Erster Weltkrieg*

Globaler Konflikt – Lokale Folgen: Neue Perspektiven. Edited by Stefan Karner and Philipp Lesiak, 307–18. Innsbruck/Wien: Studien-Verl., 2014.
Langthaler, Ernst, and Fridolin Krausmann. 'Nahrungsregime und Umwelt in der Globalisierung (1870–2010)', in *Rohstoffe und Entwicklung: Aktuelle Auseinandersetzungen im historischen Kontext.* Edited by Karin Fischer, Johannes Jäger and Lukas Schmidt, 85–103. Wien: New Academic Press, 2016.
Langthaler, Ernst, and Elke Schüßler. 'Commodity Studies with Polanyi. Disembedding and Re-Embedding Labour and Land in Contemporary Capitalism', *Österreichische Zeitschrift für Soziologie* 44, no. 2 (2019): 209–23.
Lemke, Thomas. '"The Birth of Bio-Politics": Michel Foucault's Lecture at the Collège de France on Neo-Liberal Governmentality', *Economy and Society* 30, no. 2 (2001): 190–207.
Lemke, Thomas 'From State Biology to the Government of Life: Historical Dimensions and Contemporary Perspectives of "Biopolitics"', *Journal of Classical Sociology* 10, no. 4 (2010): 421–38.
Lesger, Clé. 'Patterns of Retail Location and Urban Form in Amsterdam in the Mid-Eighteenth Century', *Urban History* 38, no. 1 (2011): 24–47.
Lesger, Clé, and Jan H. Furnée. 'Shopping Streets and Cultures from a Long-Term Perspective: An Introduction', in *The Landscape of Consumption: Shopping Streets and Cultures in Western Europe, 1600–1900.* Edited by Jan H. Furnée and Clé Lesger, 1–15. Basingstoke, Hampshire: Palgrave Macmillan, 2014.
Lhuissier, Anne. 'Cuts and Classification. The Use of Nomenclatures as a Tool for the Reform of the Meat Trade in France, 1850–1880', *Food and Foodways* 10, no. 4 (2002): 183–208.
Li, Lillian M., and Alison Dray-Novey. 'Guarding Beijing's Food Security in the Qing Dynasty. State, Market, and Police', *The Journal of Asian Studies* 58, no. 4 (1999): 992–1032.
Maderthaner, Wolfgang, and Lutz Musner. *Die Anarchie der Vorstadt: Das andere Wien um 1900.* Frankfurt/Main: Campus-Verl., 2000.
Matis, Herbert. 'Leitlinien der Österreichischen Wirtschaftspolitik', in *Die Habsburgermonarchie 1848–1918.* Vol. 1. Edited by Alois Brusatti, Adam Wandruszka and Helmut Rumpler, 29–67. Wien: Verl. der Österr. Akad. der Wiss, 1973.
Mautner-Markhof, Georg J. *Von Irgendwo in alle Welt – Geschichte der Familie Mautner Markhof.* Wien: Guardaval Verlag, 1998.
Metcalfe, Robyn S. *Meat, Commerce and the City: The London Food Market, 1800–1855.* London: Routledge, 2016.
Miller, Judith A. 'Politics and Urban Provisioning Crises. Bakers, Police, and Parlements in France, 1750–1793', *The Journal of Modern History* 64, no. 2 (1992): 227–62.
Miller, Judith A. *Mastering the Market: The State and the Grain Trade in Northern France, 1700–1860.* Cambridge: Cambridge University Press, 1999.
Mirowski, Philip. 'Postface: Defining Neoliberalism', in Mirowski; Plehwe, *The Road from Mont Pèlerin,* 417–56.
Mirowski, Philip, and Dieter Plehwe. 'Preface', in Mirowski; Plehwe, *The Road from Mont Pèlerin* (2009): ix–xxiii.
Mirowski, Philip, and Dieter Plehwe eds. *The Road from Mont Pèlerin: The Making of the Neoliberal Thought Collective.* Cambridge, MA: Harvard University Press, 2009.
Mitchell, Ian. *Tradition and Innovation in English Retailing, 1700 to 1850: Narratives of Consumption.* London: Taylor and Francis, 2016.

Moon, David. 'In the Russians' Steppes: The Introduction of Russian Wheat on the Great Plains of the United States of America', *Journal of Global History* 3, no. 2 (2008): 203–25.

Moon, David. *The Plough That Broke the Steppes: Agriculture and Environment on Russia's Grasslands; 1700-1914.* Oxford: Oxford University Press, 2013.

Moore, Jason W. 'Sugar and the Expansion of the Early Modern World-Economy: Commodity Frontiers, Ecological Transformation, and Industrialization', *Review (Fernand Braudel Center)* 23, no. 3 (2000): 409–33.

Murphey, Rhoads. 'Provisioning Istanbul. The State and Subsistence in the Early Modern Middle East', *Food and Foodways* 2, no. 1 (1987): 217–63.

Nagy, Mariann. 'The Regional Structure of the Hungarian Agriculture in the Beginning of the 20th Century', *Zgodovinski časopis (Historical Review)* 67, no. 3–4 (2013): 406–27.

Nally, David. 'The Biopolitics of Food Provisioning', *Transactions of the Institute of British Geographers* 36, no. 1 (2011): 37–53.

Neweklowsky, Ernst. *Die Schiffahrt und Flößerei im Raume der oberen Donau.* Linz: Linz [Donau] Oberösterr. Landesverl., 1952.

Nieradzik, Lukasz. *Der Wiener Schlachthof St. Marx: Transformation einer Arbeitswelt zwischen 1851 und 1914.* Wien: Böhlau, 2017.

Nolte, Paul. 'Der Markt und seine Kultur – ein neues Paradigma der amerikanischen Geschichte?', *Historische Zeitschrift* 264, no. 1 (1997): 329–60.

Olmstead, Alan L., and Paul W. Rhode. 'The Red Queen and the Hard Reds: Productivity Growth in American Wheat, 1800-1940', *The Journal of Economic History* 62, no. 4 (2002): 929–66.

Opll, Ferdinand. 'Markt im alten Wien', *Wiener Geschichtsblätter* 34, no. 2 (1979): 49–73.

Opll, Ferdinand. 'Studien zur Versorgung Wiens mit Gütern des täglichen Bedarfs in der ersten Hälfte des 19. Jahrhunderts', *Jahrbuch für Geschichte der Stadt Wien* 37 (1981): 50–87.

Pappenheim, Gustav. 'Geschichte der Österreichischen Müllerei 1848 bis 1898', in *Geschichte der Österreichischen Land – und Forstwirtschaft und ihrer Industrien: 1848-1898: Festschrift zur Feier der am 2. December 1898 erfolgten Fünfzigjährigen Wiederkehr der Thronbesteigung Sr. Majestät des Kaisers Franz Joseph I. Supplementband I.* 236–85. Wien: Moritz Perles, 1901.

Pauly, Anneleen, Bram Pareyt, Ellen Fierens and Jan A. Delcour. 'Wheat (Triticum Aestivum L. And T. Turgidum L. Ssp. Durum) Kernel Hardness: I. Current View on the Role of Puroindolines and Polar Lipids', *Comprehensive Reviews in Food Science and Food Safety* 12, no. 4 (2013): 413–26.

Perren, R. 'Structural Change and Market Growth in the Food Industry: Flour Milling in Britain, Europe, and America, 1850-1914', *The Economic History Review* 43, no. 3 (1990): 420–37.

Persson, Karl G. *Grain Markets in Europe, 1500-1900: Integration and Deregulation.* Cambridge: Cambridge University Press, 2005.

Petersen, Christian. *Bread and the British Economy, C1770-1870.* Aldershot: Scolar Press, 1995.

Petrović, Nikola. *Die Schiffahrt und Wirtschaft im mittleren Donauraum in der Zeit des Merkantilismus: Der Bau des Donau-Theiß-, des Franzens-Kanals und die Bestrebungen gegen Ende des XVIII. Jahrhunderts, den mittleren Donauraum mit dem Adriatischen Meer zu verbinden.* Novi Sad: Akademie der Wissenschaften und Künste der Wojwodina, 1982.

Pfeisinger, Gerhard. *Die Revolution von 1848 in Graz.* Wien: Europaverlag, 1986.

Piketty, Thomas. *Kapital und Ideologie*. München: C.H. Beck, 2020.
Pinke, Zsolt. 'Modernization and Decline: An Eco-Historical Perspective on Regulation of the Tisza Valley, Hungary', *Journal of Historical Geography* 45 (2014): 92–105.
Plumpe, Werner. *Das kalte Herz: Kapitalismus: die Geschichte einer andauernden Revolution*. Berlin: Rowohlt Berlin, 2019.
Polanyi, Karl. *The Great Transformation: The Political and Economic Origins of Our Time*. 2. Beacon Paperback. Boston: Beacon Press, 2001.
Pribram, Alfred F. *Materialien zur Geschichte der Preise und Löhne in Österreich*. With the assistance of Rudolf Geyer and Franz Koran. Wien: Ueberreuter, 1938.
Přibram, Karl. *Geschichte der Österreichischen Gewerbepolitik von 1740–1860; auf Grund der Akten*. Leipzig: Duncker & Humblot, 1907.
Rácz, Lajos. *The Steppe to Europe: An Environmental History of Hungary in the Traditional Age*. Cambridge: White Horse Press, 2013.
Reinert, Sophus A., and Steven L. Kaplan, eds. *The Economic Turn: Recasting Political Economy in Enlightenment Europe*. London: Anthem Press, 2019.
Ressel, Gustav A. *Das Archiv der Bäckergenossenschaft in Wien: Ein Beitrag zur Geschichte des Wiener Handwerkes*. Wien: Gerlach & Wiedling, 1913.
Rezneck, Samuel. 'The European Education of an American Chemist and Its Influence in 19th-Century America: Eben Norton Horsford', *Technology and Culture* 11, no. 3 (1970): 366–88.
Richards, John F. *The Unending Frontier: An Environmental History of the Early Modern World*. Berkeley, Los Angeles, London: University of California Press, 2005.
Ringrose, David R. *Madrid and the Spanish Economy 1560–1850*. Berkeley, CA: University of California Press, 1983.
Rioux, Sébastien. *The Social Cost of Cheap Food: Labour and the Political Economy of Food Distribution in Britain, 1830–1914*. Montreal: McGill-Queen's University Press, 2019.
Rodgers, Daniel T. *Age of Fracture*. Cambridge, MA: Harvard University Press, 2012.
Rogan, Tim. *The Moral Economists: R. H. Tawney, Karl Polanyi, E. P. Thompson, and the Critique of Capitalism*. Princeton: Princeton University Press, 2017.
Rosenblatt, Helena. *The Lost History of Liberalism: From Ancient Rome to the Twenty-First Century*. Princeton: Princeton University Press, 2020.
Rossbacher, Karlheinz. *Literatur und Liberalismus: Zur Kultur der Ringstrassenzeit in Wien*. Wien: J&V, 1992.
Sandgruber, Roman. 'Die Agrarrevolution in Österreich', in *Österreich-Ungarn als Agrarstaat: Wirtschaftliches Wachstum und Agrarverhältnisse in Österreich im 19. Jahrhundert*. Edited by Alfred Hoffmann and Roman Sandgruber, 198–271. Wien: Verl. für Geschichte und Politik, 1978.
Sandgruber, Roman. *Die Anfänge der Konsumgesellschaft: Konsumgüterverbrauch, Lebensstandard und Alltagskultur in Österreich im 18. und 19. Jahrhundert*. Wien: Verlag für Geschichte und Politik, 1982.
Schorske, Carl E. *Fin-de-Siècle Vienna: Politics and Culture*. New York, NY: Vintage Books, 1981.
Scola, Roger. *Feeding the Victorian City: The Food Supply of Manchester, 1770–1870*. Manchester: Manchester University Press, 1992.
Segers, Yves. 'Oysters and Rye Bread: Polarising Living Standards in Flanders, 1800–1860', *European Review of Economic History* 5, no. 3 (2001): 301–36.
Seliger, Maren, and Karl Ucakar. *Wien, Politische Geschichte 1740–1934: Entwicklung und Bestimmungskräfte großstädtischer Politik*. Wien: Jugend & Volk Verl.-Ges, 1985.

Sheriff, Elfriede. 'Die Ämter der Stadt Wien von 1783–1848 in verwaltungsgeschichtlicher und personeller Hinsicht', Diss. Univ. Wien, 1977.

Short, Nicola. 'Market/Society: Mapping Conceptions of Power, Ideology and Subjectivity in Polanyi, Hayek, Foucault, Lukács', *Globalizations* 15, no. 7 (2018): 941–55.

Slezak, Friedrich. 'Zur Geschichte der Donauschiffahrt (1765–1829)', *Der Donauraum* 19, no. 1–2 (1974): 77–81.

Slobodian, Quinn. *Globalisten: Das Ende der Imperien und die Geburt des Neoliberalismus*. Bonn: bpb: Bundeszentrale für politische Bildung, 2020.

Spitzbart-Glasl, Christina. 'Feste Wassermühlen und Schiffsmühlen als Bestandteil der Wiener Gewässerlandschaft', in *Donau-Stadt-Landschaften. Danube-City-Landscapes*. Edited by Máté Tamáska, 263–78. Berlin: LIT, 2016.

Stadler, Gerhard A. '"Es Hat Fürchterlich Gestunken, Grauenhaft!" Bürgerprotest gegen Umweltbelastungen aus der Hefefabrik', in *Technik, Arbeit und Umwelt in der Geschichte*. Edited by Torsten Meyer and Marcus Popplow, 395–404. Münster: Waxmann Verlag, 2006.

Steidl, Annemarie. 'Silk Weaver and Purse Maker Apprentices in Eighteenth- and Nineteenth-Century Vienna', in *Learning on the Shop Floor: Historical Perspectives on Apprenticeship*. Edited by Bert de Munck, Steven L. Kaplan and Solym Hugo, 133–57. New York, NY: Berghahn Books, 2007.

Steinberg, Marc W. *England's Great Transformation: Law, Labor, and the Industrial Revolution*. Chicago, London: The University of Chicago Press, 2016.

Stobart, Jon, and Lucy Bailey. 'Retail Revolution and the Village Shop, C. 1660–1860', *The Economic History Review* 71, no. 2 (2018): 393–417.

Stobart, Jon, and Ilja van Damme. 'Introduction: Markets in Modernization. Transformations in Urban Market Space and Practice, c. 1800–c. 1970', *Urban History* 43, no. 3 (2016): 358–71.

Streng, Marcel. *Subsistenzpolitik im Übergang: Die kommunale Ordnung des Brot - und Fleischmarktes in Frankreich 1846–1914*. Göttingen: Vandenhoeck & Ruprecht, 2017.

Streng, Marcel. 'Konventionen der Brotqualität in der Bäckereigewerbereform des Zweiten Kaiserreichs in Frankreich (1853–1866)', in *Qualitätspolitiken und Konventionen: Die Qualität der Produkte in historischer Perspektive*. Edited by Robert Salais, Jakob Vogel and Marcel Streng, 153–82. Wiesbaden: Springer Fachmedien Wiesbaden GmbH; Springer VS, 2019.

Tangires, Helen. *Public Markets and Civic Culture in Nineteenth-Century America*. Baltimore: Johns Hopkins University Press, 2003.

Taverner, Charlie. 'Moral Marketplaces: Regulating the Food Markets of Late Elizabethan and Early Stuart London', *Urban History*, 2020, 1–17.

Thiel, Viktor. 'Geschichte der Donauregulierungsarbeiten bei Wien II. Vom Anfange des XVIII. bis zur Mitte des XIX. Jahrhunderts. Von der Mitte des XIX. Jahrhunderts bis zur Gegenwart', *Jahrbuch d. Vereins f. Landeskunde von Niederösterreich* 4–5 (1905/1906): 1–102.

Thompson, E.P. 'The Moral Economy of the English Crowd in the Eighteenth Century', *Past and Present* 50, no. 1 (February 1971): 76–136.

Thompson, E.P. *The Making of the English Working Class*. Harmondsworth: Penguin Books, 1981.

Thompson, E.P. *Customs in Common: Studies in Traditional Popular Culture*. New York: The New Press, 1994.

Till, Rudolf. *Geschichte des Wiener Marktwesens*. Wien: Geitner, 1939.

van Bavel, Bas. *The Invisible Hand? How Market Economies Have Emerged and Declined Since AD 500*. Oxford, UK: Oxford University Press, 2016.

van Cruyningen, Piet, and Erik Thoen, eds. *Food Supply, Demand and Trade: Aspects of the Economic Relationship between Town and Countryside (Middle Ages – 19th Century)*. Turnhout: Brepols, 2012.

Vári, András. *Herren und Landwirte: Ungarische Aristokraten und Agrarier auf dem Weg in die Moderne (1821–1910)*. Wiesbaden: Harrassowitz, 2008.

Veichtlbauer, Ortrun. 'Zwischen Kolonie und Provinz. Herrschaft und Planung in der Kameralprovinz Temeswarer Banat im 18. Jahrhundert', Institute of Social Ecology Vienna (SEC), 2016.

Velkar, Aashish. *Markets and Measurements in Nineteenth-Century Britain*. Cambridge: Cambridge University Press, 2012.

Vries, Jan de, and A. M. van der Woude. *The First Modern Economy: Success, Failure, and Perseverance of the Dutch Economy, 1500–1815*. Cambridge: Cambridge University Press, 2008.

Vriese, Dennis de. 'Steering the Free Market through a Food Crisis? Fiscal Policy and Meat Consumption in Brussels during the 1840s', *History of Retailing and Consumption* 8, no. 1 (2022): 31–48.

Wadauer, Sigrid. 'Betteln und Hausieren verboten? Ambulanter Handel im Wien der Zwischenkriegszeit', *Jahrbuch für Wirtschaftsgeschichte/Economic History Yearbook* 48, no. 1 (2007): 181–203.

Wadauer, Sigrid. 'Ins Un/Recht setzen. Diffamierung und Rehabilitierung des Hausierens', in *Das nennen Sie Arbeit? Der Produktivitätsdiskurs und seine Ausschlüsse*. Edited by Nicole Colin and Franziska Schößler, 103–24. Heidelberg: Synchron Wissenschaftsverlag der Autoren Synchron Publishers, 2013.

Watts, Sydney. *Meat Matters: Butchers, Politics, and Market Culture in Eighteenth-Century Paris*. Rochester: University of Rochester Press, 2006.

Weigl, Andreas. *Demographischer Wandel und Modernisierung in Wien*. Wien: Pichler, 2000.

Weigl, Andreas. 'Gewerbepolitik', in *Wien. Geschichte einer Stadt: Band 2. Die Frühneuzeitliche Residenz (16. bis 18. Jahrhundert)*. Vol. 2. Edited by Peter Csendes and Ferdinand Oppl, 176–82. Wien/Kön/Weimar: Böhlau, 2003.

Weigl, Andreas. *Von der Existenzsicherung zur Wohlstandsgesellschaft: Überlebensbedingungen und Lebenschancen in Wien und Niederösterreich von der Mitte des 19. Jahrhunderts bis zur Gegenwart*. Wien: Böhlau, 2020.

Wimmer, Norbert, and Thomas Müller. *Wirtschaftsrecht: International – europäisch – national*. Wien: Springer, 2007.

Ziak, Karl. *Des Heiligen Römischen Reiches grösstes Wirtshaus: Der Wiener Vorort Neulerchenfeld*. Wien: Jugend und Volk, 1979.

Digital Sources

Allen, Robert C. 'Consumer Price Indices, Nominal/Real Wages and Welfare Ratios of Building Craftsmen and Labourers, 1260–1913. Prices and Wages in Vienna, 1439–1913', International Institute of Social History data files. Accessed 5 May 2021. https://iisg.amsterdam/en/blog/research/projects/hpw/datafiles.

Cvrcek, Tomas. 'Austro-Hungarian Prices and Wages, 1827–1914', International Institute of Social History data files. Accessed 5 May 2021. https://iisg.amsterdam/en/blog/research/projects/hpw/datafiles.

Gatzke, Marcus, Marlies Uken, and Klaus Schwab. '"Der Neoliberalismus hat ausgedient"', *Zeit Online*, 21 September 2020. Accessed 4 May 2021. https://www.zeit.de/wirtschaft/2020-09/corona-kapitalismus-rezession-wef-neoliberalismus-klaus-schwab.

Govrin, Jule. 'Der Markt regelt das nicht', *Zeit Online*, 9 April 2020. Accessed 4 May 2021. https://www.zeit.de/kultur/2020-04/pandemie-coronavirus-kapitalismus-wirtschaft-wachstum-deutschland.

Hauer, Friedrich, Sylvia Gierlinger, Jonas M. Albrecht, Maximilian Martsch, Clara Nagele and Till Uschmann. 'Die Wiener Verzehrungssteuer. Auswertung nach einzelnen Steuerposten (1830–1913)'. Accessed 14 March 2024. https://boku.ac.at/wiso/sec/publikationen/social-ecology-working-papers.

Herrmann, Ulrike. 'Corona-Dämmerung für Neoliberalismus', *taz*, 21 March 2020. Accessed 4 May 2021. https://taz.de/Corona-Daemmerung-fuer-Neoliberalismus/!5669238/.

Hutton, Will. 'Lost in Space and a Broken Energy Market: Blame It on the Obsession with a Small State', *The Guardian*, 31 July 2022. Accessed 10 July 2023. https://www.theguardian.com/commentisfree/2022/jul/31/lost-in-space-and-broken-energy-market-blame-it-on-tories-small-state-stupidity.

Junginger, Bernhard, and Christian Grimm. 'Wildweststimmung auf dem Energiemarkt sorgt für Verzweiflung bei Verbrauchern', *Augsburger Allgemeine*, 24 August 2022. Accessed 10 July 2023. https://www.augsburger-allgemeine.de/politik/verbraucherschutz-wildweststimmung-auf-dem-energiemarkt-sorgt-fuer-verzweiflung-bei-verbrauchern-id63718086.html.

Kainrath, Verena, Jan M. Marchart and Aloysius Widman. 'Maskenkrise. Hygiene Austria: Wie aus einem Zufallsfund ein Maskenskandal wurde', *Der Standard*, 13 March 2021. Accessed 4 May 2021. https://www.derstandard.at/story/2000125011151/hygiene-austria-wie-aus-einem-zufallsfund-ein-maskenskandal-wurde.

Kaiser, Thomas. 'Die EU plant einen Strompreisdeckel, Der nicht so heißen darf', *Welt*, 3 September 2022. Accessed 10 July 2023. https://www.welt.de/wirtschaft/article240837405/Energiepreise-EU-Kommission.html.

Lewis, Paul. 'The Energy Market Is Broken – but Only One Thing Needs to Change to Fix It: Our Regulator Has Made a Catalogue of Errors and It Has Cost Consumers Billions', *The Telegraph*. Accessed 10 July 2023. https://www.telegraph.co.uk/money/consumer-affairs/energy-market-broken-one-thing-needs-change-fix/.

Liboreiro, Jorge. 'Energy Crisis: Ursula Von Der Leyen Calls for "Emergency Intervention" in Electricity Market', *Euronews*. Accessed 10 July 2023. https://www.euronews.com/my-europe/2022/08/29/energy-crisis-ursula-von-der-leyen-calls-for-emergency-intervention-in-electricity-market.

Der Spiegel. 'Maskenaffäre. Alle Unionsabgeordneten unterzeichnen Ehrenerklärung', 12 March 2021. Accessed 4 May 2021. https://www.spiegel.de/politik/deutschland/cdu-csu-nach-masken-skandal-alle-unionsabgeordneten-unterzeichnen-ehrenerklaerung-a-f6d1943b-76a6-430c-a690-8f50cfdddf12.

Österreichische Nationalbibliothek. KS 16215321: Handelsministerium.

Österreichische Nationalbibliothek. KS 16215134: Magistrat der Stadt Wien.

Pope Francis. 'Encyclical Letter Fratelli Tutti of the Holy Father Francis on Fraternity and Social Friendship', Accessed 4 May 2021. http://www.vatican.va/content/francesco/en/encyclicals/documents/papa-francesco_20201003_enciclica-fratelli-tutti.html.

Deutsche Welle. 'Pope Says Capitalism Failed Humanity during Coronavirus Pandemic', 4 October 2020. Accessed 4 May 2021. https://p.dw.com/p/3jPoa.

Ramonet, Ignacio. 'Die Märkte entschärfen', *Le Monde diplomatique*, 1997. 12, reprinted in 5/2020, Jubiläumsausgabe.

Tharoor, Ishaan. 'World Leaders Pledge a "Great Reset" after the Pandemic', *The Washington Post*, 29 January 2021. Accessed 4 May 2021. https://www.washingtonpost.com/world/2021/01/29/davos-merkel-macron-coronavirus/.

Tharoor, Ishaan 'Biden and the Waning of the "Neoliberal" Era', *The Washington Post*, 5 April 2021. Accessed 4 May 2021. https://www.washingtonpost.com/world/2021/04/05/biden-infrastructure-plan-neoliberalism/.

Thier, Hadas. 'The Pandemic Has Exposed the Free Market's Fundamental Flaws. We Need a Democratically Planned Economy', *Jacobin*, 1 November 2020. Accessed 4 May 2021. https://www.jacobinmag.com/2020/11/planned-economy-coronavirus-hospitals-ppe-masks.

World Economic Forum. 'The World Must Move on from Neoliberalism after the Pandemic', Accessed 4 May 2021. https://www.weforum.org/videos/20462-the-world-must-move-on-from-neoliberalism-after-the-pandemic-davos-agenda.

INDEX

abstract market mechanism 7, 25
agricultural products 118
Allgemeine Wiener Zeitung 213
Annona, Roman 54
anti-food-shortage-system 28
Approvisionirungssektion 133, 137–9, 142, 171, 180, 184, 198
assize 11–13, 28, 50–6, 59, 62–4, 77–8, 100, 116, 121, 123, 169–70, 211, 220
  abolition of 138–9, 143, 173, 175, 179, 183, 191, 222, 224
  of bread 121, 123, 128, 131–2, 136–8, 140–2, 145–7, 223, 229–31
  calculations 123–8, 133–5, 145, 181 n.18, 204, 215, 217
  deregulation 170–1
  free competition 131–9, 143
  prescriptions 204
  prices 98, 127, 130, 182, 205, 212
  reform 123, 135
  regulations 95, 135, 142, 160, 200, 217, 227
  re-regulation 220
  total liberalization 138–43
Austrian urban modernity 147
Auszugsmehl 118, 120

Bäckerkalender 161
Bäckerschupfen 51
Bäckerverzeichnis 82
bakeries 44, 46, 50, 52, 58–9, 68, 76, 97, 124, 126–7, 151–2, 167, 177, 218, 223, 231–2
  baking (*see* baking)
  cost calculations 60
  landscape 48, 73, 144
  large-scale industrial 140
  operations 144
  small- and medium-sized 61, 75–6, 86
  urbanization 154–5
  in Vienna (1775–1847) 68–9, 72, 76, 188

workers 81, 166, 167, 185, 223
work in 46–7
bakers 46–7, 49–51, 53–4, 56–7, 62–3, 65, 126, 226
Auszug 118
authorities and 58–9, 61, 94, 121, 175, 181, 187, 210, 218
bürgerliche profits 44, 48, 136, 218
compulsory flour stocks 77, 80–1, 84–5, 90
consumers and 183, 189
critique of reform 194
dispersion of 87
fees 60
flour stocks, composition of 78–9, 92–3
guild/association 13, 43–4, 66–7, 73, 75, 80–2, 86, 95, 97, 111, 123, 130, 133–4, 151, 175
profits 58, 146, 158, 183, 203–4, 211, 213, 219, 227, 233
quality and quantity standards 51
regulated competition 159
self-regulation 213
social responsibilities 53
standard prices and obligation 208
trade 49, 67, 133, 137, 142, 198, 210, 212, 223
trade taxes 74–5
Bakers' Association 171, 185, 188, 193, 195, 198–9, 201, 204, 208, 213–14, 221
bakery products 49–51, 60, 75, 80, 138, 161, 163–4, 212, 224, 229, 231
  misalignment of prices 208
  price index for various 179
  price setting and selling 191
  production costs 205
  ratio of silver prices of 177
  real prices for 178
baking 12, 24, 46–7, 56, 58, 60–1, 81–2, 118, 123, 139, 151, 175, 202, 229

art of 233
economic aspects of 60
municipal landscape of 49–50, 68
rules of 52
rural landscape of 95, 97
tables 209, 212
technological improvements 82
test millings and 124
trade 49, 58, 79, 83–4, 166, 204, 231
trials 58, 60, 62, 124, 205–6, 214, 216–18, 217 n.141
on urban marketplaces 52
Banat 101, 103, 107
markets 110
wheat 101, 111, 113–14, 117–18, 123
Baunzeln 185–7
biopolitics 12, 15, 25–35, 227, 233–4
biopolitical co-movement 234
defining 34
regulative mechanisms and 37
birth of the market economy 17, 23, 37
bread 11–13
black 98
consumption 80, 88, 91, 112, 144, 176, 225, 234
distribution 40, 147, 157, 161, 163–6, 222
free market economy 13
magistrate propositions 219
marking 200–3
moral economy of 40, 50, 138, 169, 195, 229
moral to market economies 11–12, 35–8, 229
provisioning 12, 40, 97, 142, 144, 187
quality of 47–8, 58, 88, 123–4
rolls and types 50–1, 94, 138, 205, 234 (*see also* rye bread; wheat bread)
selling according to weight 181, 190–1, 193–200, 206
selling and buying 40, 44, 49, 64, 182, 193, 203
setting weights 62–3
standard bread qualities 221
standardizing 190–200
trade 12, 56, 127, 134, 147, 151–2, 165, 211
bread assize 11, 50–61, 142, 146, 217, 229–30

abolition of 142–3, 147
socioeconomic environment of 223
system 125, 133
bread landscape 13, 40, 43, 46, 50, 66, 144, 153, 223–4
business structures 72–87
competing circuits of bread provision 94–100
decisive mobilization 151
deregulation 148
free-market 148
geographies 68–72
liberalization 157
mobility and spatial flexibility 224
mobilization and differentialization 160, 163, 166
mobilization and diversification 155, 163, 166, 222, 224
wheatification 87–94, 100
bread market 12–13, 52, 64, 112, 126, 146, 170, 189, 222, 227, 234
free 189, 216, 226, 233
legislation 233
liberalization 13, 148
regulation 112, 125, 164, 201, 204, 222
security mechanisms to 227
bread prices 12, 28, 40, 46, 53–6, 58, 60–1, 134, 169–81, 206, 227, 232–3
calculations 62, 205
cereal and 171–3
effects of grain tariffs on 207
free-market 180, 225
intermediate retailers 159–61, 165
just price 61–4, 203, 227
materials 13
monetary 182
and product standardization 233
public calamity 206
ratio of silver prices 174, 176
rediscovering right price 203–11
regulation 123, 171, 195
regulation, specifications 191
standardized 190
bread production 12–13, 58–9, 77–8, 87–8, 98, 135, 139, 143–4, 147, 160, 184, 227, 231
costs of 60, 203, 218, 227
and distribution 147
geography of 68–73

and retail 40
rural landscape of 144
bread question 148–9, 156, 165, 168, 181–9, 195, 206, 210, 215, 224, 226
  hawker's question 156–68
  and high prices 196
  and market transparency 209
  solution 213–14, 220–2, 227
bread retail 127, 188, 190–1, 199, 211, 215
  reform 196, 201, 210
  regulation 193–4
  tariff model for 192
British Industrial Revolution 20
Brodbeschauer 49
broodzetting system 55, 63
Brotstupfer 51, 200
Bürgerausschuss 133
business location 72–3, 72 n.13, 160, 223, 232, 234

Caisse de Poissy 140
central place theory 70–2
cereals 57, 106, 109–10, 124, 230
  price index for various 179
  prices 59, 171–4, 183, 196, 203, 206–7
  production 102, 104, 111
  quality/quantity of 124
  supplies 98–9
  transports 107, 117
city centre bakers 161–3
city councils 13, 55, 59, 129, 137, 159, 171, 173, 180–5, 188–91, 195–201, 203–4, 206, 215, 219–22, 227, 233
climate change 1, 4
commercial liberty 44, 129
common weal 24
consumers 1, 13, 31–3, 43, 47–8, 51, 53–4, 56, 61, 73, 79, 91, 118, 137, 142, 155, 160, 178, 180, 183–4, 199–201, 213, 216, 218, 224, 227, 232–4
  bakers and 53, 56, 91, 128, 158, 165, 183, 200, 226
  to negotiate the self-regulated market 13
  of rye bread 63, 175–6
  of wheat bread 63, 175–6
cornucopia 101
  fruits of 112–18, 120–1, 145
  grain trade by ship 112

countermovement 13, 15, 23, 25, 37, 233–4
country bakers 94–5, 97, 99–100, 144, 152, 161, 201, 210, 222–4, 231–2
  lower wages and trade tax 98
  per parish 96, 154
Covid-19 pandemic 1–4
Crimean War 139, 172, 177
cross-subsidization 62–3, 148–9, 175–6, 180–2, 225, 229, 232
culture of the market 9

Dampfmühle 120
Danube 86, 99, 103, 107, 230
  Győr/Raab 111
  waterway/water transportation 107–8, 110, 145
Danube-Tisza-Maros water system 111
deregulation 2, 11–13, 21, 126, 128, 130, 139, 141–2, 146–8, 153, 155, 168, 170–1, 173–7, 180–1, 183–5, 223–4, 226, 230
disciplinary mechanism(s) 12, 25–35, 37, 40, 44, 63, 95, 136, 139, 143, 146, 159, 164, 170–1, 174, 180, 222, 225, 227, 229, 231
  comprehensive system of surveillance 28
  disciplinary normalization 30
  freedom of trade and grain circulation 29, 33
  governmental policies 30
  juridical-disciplinary 27
  of market regulation 230
  medieval handling of leprosy 27
  physiocratic doctrine 29
  security mechanisms 27–8, 30, 33, 38
  self-limited government 32
disembedded market 15, 25, 31, 37, 148
  countermovement 15
  and fictitious commodities 17–23
Dorotheermühle 76
double movement 23–4

ecological crisis (1817) 145
economic exchange 18, 22
economic liberalism 20–2
economic uncertainty 1
economization 8

Index

economy. *See also* moral economy
    food 53, 168, 224
    of interests 44
    reforms 131
    and society 17, 19, 21
    urban 11, 48, 147–8
Einkreuzersemmeln 185, 187
electricity market 1–2
Elisabethviertel 70
energy market 1
    energy crisis 4
    prices/price caps 2, 10
Enquête 83, 94, 99–100, 156, 160, 185, 188–91, 193
European guild system 43
Exposition Universelle (Paris) 84, 112–13

financial crisis (2008) 2, 8
fixed-price-variable-weight retail system 182–3, 188
Fleischkassa 140
flour 46–7, 51, 57, 98, 105, 108, 113–14, 117, 124, 127, 206, 230
    assize 116, 127, 136, 140
    composition of stocks 79, 87
    compulsory stocks 75–6, 78, 81, 84–6, 90, 92–3
    exchange 138
    Mund 91
    prices 59, 118–19, 130–1, 134, 139, 170–1, 203, 207–10, 214, 219, 221–2
    production (Austrian Empire) 12, 114, 116–17, 145, 230
    quality of 57–8, 60, 118, 120, 123, 145, 170, 193, 211
    stocks, dispersion of bakers across size categories 87
    trade 127–8, 141, 143
food economy 53, 168, 224
food market 37, 147–8, 189
    free 140
    regulation/deregulation 10, 26, 148
food supply system 11, 83, 99, 116, 180
    Habsburg capital 40
    market-politics of 10
Foucault, Michel 11, 15, 31, 229, 233
    biopolitics 12, 15, 25–35, 37, 233
    Birth of Biopolitics 26, 31, 33

    disciplinary and security mechanisms 25–35
    governmental reason of self-limitation 32
    Security, Territory, and Population 26, 28
Franzenscanal 108–9
free competition 95, 126, 131–9, 141, 143, 147, 168, 170, 172, 180, 185, 187, 189, 223–4, 226
freedom of commerce. *See Gewerbefreiheit* (freedom of commerce)
freedom of trade 29, 33, 147, 158, 160, 204, 220–1, 230–1
free market(s) 2–3, 6, 6 n.21, 24, 139, 146, 161, 183, 226–7, 231–4
    bread prices 225
    disruptive effects 23
    free-market prices 31–2, 130, 134, 174, 176, 180, 200, 203, 225
    for labour 22
    liberated 26
    supply and demand 25
free-market landscape of bread 148, 157, 168, 222–3, 231
    mobility and spatial flexibility 224
    mobilization and continued diversification 151–6
French Revolution 105, 230
frontier 103–5, 107–9, 111

Gemeindeausschuß 133–4
Gemeinderat 133, 135–40, 142, 146, 171, 180–1, 197–8
Gemeinschaft und Gesellschaft (Tönnies) 17, 19
geographic information system (GIS) mapping technology 12–13, 40, 148
Gesellschaft 22
Gewerbefreiheit (freedom of commerce) 40, 125, 130, 132, 141–3, 145–8, 153, 157–8, 160–1, 181, 184, 204, 230–1
Gewerbe-Ordnung 143
Glacis 76, 152
grain 55, 60, 88, 105, 111–12, 117
    exchange 135–6, 138
    hinterland 41, 102
    history of 29

milieu of 29–30, 55–6
prevent circulation 28–9
prices 28–9, 52–4, 56, 59, 61–3, 107–8, 124, 131, 135, 139, 171–5, 182, 206, 213
quality/quantity of 57–8, 115, 124
reality of 29
trade and flour production 12, 29, 54, 100, 104, 108–10, 112, 116, 124, 141–2, 145–6, 230
grain market 28, 30, 52, 54, 59–60, 127, 230
Großenzersdorf 59
transactions in Hungarian markets 106
Great Transformation theory 9, 15, 35–8
greedflation (Übergewinne) 2, 10
Greißler 158
Grundbücher 1. Reihe 74, 74 n.19
guild baker/bakeries 43, 46, 48, 66–7, 66 n.4, 70, 72–3, 75, 80–1, 86, 94–5, 97, 111, 118, 128, 130, 134, 144
hired and discharged apprentices 82
urban and rural 144, 151
guild masters 44, 51, 79, 151

Habsburg capital 63, 66, 79, 91, 107, 146–7, 168, 229
bread supply of 168, 224
economic policies 11
food supply system 40
guild system 43
Handelskammer 165
hawkers 159–60, 163–4, 166, 184, 188, 190–1, 203–4, 206, 208, 210, 224
intermediate trade 206
and peddlers 158, 164–5, 168
high milling 113, 115–18, 145
Hobbesian, nature of man 21
Holy Roman Empire 11, 68
householding 18–19
Hungary 101, 105, 107, 114, 134, 146
agricultural sector 110
cereal exports 172
grain transactions in 106, 110
steppes and pusztas 114
wheat 101, 106, 113, 116, 230

industrialization 117, 167
of baking trade 83

and concentration 116, 117, 120, 145
milling sector 117, 230
inequality 7–8, 13, 180, 223, 225, 232
institutional bread market regulation 41
institutions of embeddedness 40–1, 121, 125, 143–4, 147
assize 50–7
just price of bread 61–4
nature and the market 57–61
people and places, regulating 43–50

Josephinian free-competition-position 126
juridical-disciplinary set of mechanisms 27
just price 31, 53, 53 n.46, 61–4, 203, 227

Kaiserauszug 118
Kaiser-Auszugsmehl 120
Kaiser rolls 208–9, 211, 218–19
Keynesian 'embedded liberal' economies 5
Klassenerwerbssteuer 74
knowledge 34, 47, 55–6, 58, 61, 114–15, 134, 148, 183, 189, 209, 226–7, 233
Kunstöfen 83

labor power 23
laissez-faire 21, 125, 145, 177, 187, 190, 213, 225, 230
and free-market 132, 146
policies 183, 226
Landbrot 98
land, labour and money 9, 22–3
modernity of markets 36
landscape of bread. *See* bread landscape
liberalization 2, 10, 13, 40, 65–6, 98, 125, 128, 131, 137–8, 148, 151, 155, 157, 163, 170, 176, 179–80, 222–5, 230–3
act (1860) 183
of bread retail 158
flour trade 128
of grain trade 124
hard reds and economic 116
of hawking 184–5
laissez-faire 145
liberal market policies 26
of markets 10, 13, 35
of milling 116
on price movements and cross-subsidization 148–9

on small businesses 157
socio-economic factor 232
tabula rasa reform 231
of white bread and wheat products 139, 146
liberal principle of free price determination 207
Linienwall 67–8, 70–1, 76, 80, 91, 95, 97–8, 144, 152, 156, 165, 218, 224
urban bakers 154–5
Lower Austria 102
abolition of bread assize 147
agricultural land use 102
average wheat harvests 106
barley cultivation 105
Board of Trade 111
cereal production 102, 104
Chamber of Commerce 98, 140
Gewerbeverein 140, 146
hawking licences 164
mills 114, 117
rye and wheat 104–5
Theresienfeld/Oeynhausen 103
low milling 115

Malthus, Thomas 21
March Revolution (1848) 13, 67, 131, 146, 231
market 7, 230. *See also* bread market; grain market
capitalism 3
deregulation 232
economy 20–3, 37, 54
exchange 6, 23
interventions 2, 4
as loco of veridiction 32
nature and 55–61
paradigm 9
pattern 18, 20
re-regulation 4, 134
revolution 9–10, 12, 15, 147
and society 9, 10, 12–13, 15, 17, 231
transformation 10
marketization 7–8, 23, 231, 233
countermovements 23, 37
development and impacts of 9
historic formation of 9
market revolution and commodification 9

marketplaces 52, 66 n.4, 95, 116, 124, 127, 135, 201, 222, 230
market prices 22–3, 54–5, 59, 206, 232
free 31–2, 130, 134, 174, 176, 180, 200, 203, 225
of grain 54, 59, 62
self-regulated 32, 233
Marktamt 13, 156, 160, 166, 170, 180–1, 181 n.18, 184, 188–91, 196, 199, 203, 212, 219, 226
baguettes 181
wrong price materials 205
Marx, Karl 17
Das Kapital 81
mask scandals 3
master baker 44–6, 48, 51, 55, 58, 60, 66–7, 71–3, 81, 83, 94–5, 134, 144, 161, 185, 203, 224
Mehlgrube 110
Mehlkassa 131
Metzenleihamt 57, 57 n.69, 59, 62
Metzenleiher 62, 65, 128–9
Metzenleiheramt 181 n.18
mill/milling 57, 76, 87, 115–16, 123–4, 134, 145
Dominicaner and Dorotheer 58
and flour regulations 126
high milling 113, 115–18, 145
industrialization and capitalization 230
low milling 115
and miller 57–9
steam 120–1, 211
trade 116
mitigation of the markets 3
moral economy 15, 24–5, 31, 35–7, 39, 46, 49, 53, 55, 62, 126, 139, 146, 174, 182, 195, 229
of bread 12, 40, 50, 138, 169, 203, 206, 227, 231
dualism of 25
institutions of embeddedness 40–1, 174, 223
trade and consumption 25
Mühlenordnung 116
Mund flour/rolls 91, 219
Mund-Gebäck 191
Mundsemmel/Rundsemmel 50, 124, 176, 179

municipal landscape of food access 48, 64. *See also* bread landscape
Muth flour stocks 76–7, 81, 85

Nahrungsprinzip 53, 53 n.46
Napoleonic Wars 46, 66, 95, 106, 108, 174
nascent market economy 20
Navigationsdirektion 107–8
neoliberalism (neoliberal) 4–7
    diversity of neoliberal arrangements 5
    on equality 8
    globalization 3
    occidental societies 26
    politics 2, 4
    reforms 15
New York City 10, 66, 151, 224

Occupy Wall Street 2
oeconomia 18
organization of exchange 18

Paris 10, 66, 88, 120, 131, 140, 151, 181–2, 191, 218
pastries 50–1, 84, 94, 164, 191, 195, 205
paternalistic regulationism 20
physiocratic doctrine/thinking 29, 32
Pistorey 124, 127
Pohlenbrot 50, 137
Pohlmehl 78, 118
Polanyi, Karl 6 n.21, 9–12, 15, 24 n.50, 26, 31, 36–7, 37 n.114, 229, 233
    disembedded market and fictitious commodities 17–23
    enlightened intellectuals 21
    The Great Transformation 17, 37
    mercantilist capitalism 20
    Speenhamland, abolition of 22
poor hygiene 47
Poor Laws 21
power 26–8
    labor 23
    practices of 26
pre-industrial urban economy 48
price regulations 55–6, 123, 138, 222
principle of free grain circulation 29
privatization 2
product standards 13, 124, 148, 181, 203, 216, 233

Quatember 81

radizierte baking licences 45, 70
Realgewerbe 45
reciprocity 17–19
    equitability and 24
    and redistribution 17–19, 23, 26
rediscovery of the market 7
redistribution 17–19, 23, 26, 176, 225
regulation 10–13, 19–20, 23, 29, 31, 38, 40–1, 49, 52, 56, 145, 182, 200, 212, 227, 230
    assize 95, 135, 142, 160, 200, 217, 227
    bread market 112, 125, 164, 201, 204, 222
    bread prices 123, 171, 191, 195
    bread retail 193–4
Reichsrat 142, 146
retail 10, 12, 24, 30, 39–40, 50, 59, 64, 68, 127–8, 134–5, 145, 147, 157–61, 163–4, 184, 188, 190–4, 197–9, 202, 211, 213–15, 223–4
Revers 161
Ricardo, David 21
Ringstraße 147–8, 152
Roman Empire 19
Russian war of Ukraine 1–3
rye bread 50–1, 57, 62–3, 99–100, 138, 140, 142, 144, 155–6, 173, 180, 206, 208, 211, 214, 224–5, 231–2
    assize on 137–8, 140, 142
    flour 94
    prices 139, 146, 173–5, 178, 216, 219
    real price of 177–9
    standard 73, 214
    wheat and, cross-subsidization 175–6, 229, 232

Sattelzeit (Koselleck) 9
Satzungen 59
Schottenfeld 68, 70
Schwarzbäcker 98, 99
security mechanism(s) 12, 25–35, 37–8, 56, 227
self-regulated markets 12–13, 15, 17, 20–2, 31–3, 233–4
    commodification and marketization 37
    double movement 23
Seven Years' War 65, 106

Smith, Adam, man's moral sentiments 18, 21, 35
socio-economic transformation 9
spatial analysis 13, 73, 148
stagflation 5
state-administered capitalism 7
state guild organization 43
Statthalterei 142–3
steam bakery 52, 74, 82, 86, 90, 140
steam mill 117–18, 120–1, 211
steppe 87, 89, 110, 114–15, 145, 230
stock market crash (1873) 156–7, 188, 199
sweet fermentation 88
system of lawfulness (*Legalitätssystem*) 27
system of ordinance (*Verordnungssystem*) 27

technological improvements 21, 84, 107
Thompson, E.P. 9–12, 15, 26, 28, 31, 229
   moral economy 24–5, 35–7
trade 2, 18, 28, 44, 46, 54, 56–7, 116, 147, 152, 164, 192, 212, 221
   bakers 49, 67, 133, 137, 142, 198, 210, 212, 223
   baking 49, 58, 79, 83–4, 166, 204, 231
   bread 12, 56, 127, 134, 147, 151–2, 165, 211
   and consumption 25
   free 147, 170, 184, 200
   freedom of 29, 33, 147, 158, 160, 204, 220–1, 230–1
   ports 109, 111
   regulation and monitoring 13
   trading mills 116
Trade Act (1860) 170
trickle-down theory 178

urban bakers 50, 94–5, 97–8, 152, 154, 201, 203, 224, 232
urban centres 10, 39

Vienna 13, 65, 90, 106, 138, 173, 233
   apprenticeship 45, 82
   assize system 95, 100, 127, 145, 231
   average wheat supply 106
   bakeries in 68–9, 72, 76, 188
   exchange wheat flour prices 119

geography of bread production 68–73
Habsburg Empire 63, 79, 100, 147, 168, 224, 227, 229 (*see also* Habsburg capital)
market economies of bread 11–12, 229, 234
population growth 11, 66, 73, 94, 114, 231
stock exchange, crash 11
urban economy 11, 148
vicinity, mills 113–14, 121, 171
Vormärz period 13, 66, 73, 88, 110, 114, 125, 129–30, 145, 173, 231
bakers 89
immigration and urbanization 97

Wallerstein, Immanuel 24 n.50
Washington Consensus 5
water-driven mills 117
Weber, Max 17, 53, 53 n.46. *See also Nahrungsprinzip*
wheat bread 50, 57, 62–3, 73, 88, 94, 112, 143, 173
   democratization 176, 225
   Ordinari Semmeln 176–8
   Pohl flour 91
   Pollenes bread 177–8
   production 102, 230
   products, abolition of assize 143, 175
   revolution 88
   Rundsemmel 176–7
   rye and, cross-subsidization 175–6, 229, 232
wheatification 87–91, 94, 100, 144, 176, 180
   of diets 225
wheat price 137, 173, 175–6, 180, 225
   silver price of 175
white bread 88, 98, 106, 139, 146, 211, 219, 225
Wochenmayr's steam oven 90–1
women, role of 44–5, 49–50, 152–3
World Economic Forum (Davos) 4
World Exposition (1873) 173
World Fair (1873) 114

Zollverein 132